YIDDISH AND THE CREATION OF SOVIET JEWISH CULTURE

1918–1930

Yiddish and the Creation of Soviet Jewish Culture changes our perception of Jewish cultural history by giving voice to those pioneering activists who created a vibrant Yiddish culture in the Soviet Union in the 1920s. Empowered by the Soviet state and the Communist Party to create a secular culture for the "new" Soviet Jew, these activists sparked a cultural flowering in the official national language of Soviet Jews: Yiddish. The writers, artists, and intellectuals chronicled here founded Yiddish-language schools, wrote for Yiddish newspapers, published scholarly works, and dedicated themselves to an unprecedented burst of secular Jewish artistic and cultural expression.

David Shneer explores the role these Jewish activists played within both Soviet and Jewish history. These activists deeply engaged widespread Jewish cultural trends of the era while simultaneously building the Soviet state and spreading its ideology. They were not passive objects of Soviet policies toward Jews, but rather they actively participated in the creation of these policies. Shneer shows how these activists were an integral part of twentieth-century Jewish history, and at the same time he addresses some of the painful truths about their involvement in the propagation of the Soviet system.

Dr. David Shneer is Director of the Center for Judaic Studies and assistant professor of history at the University of Denver. He is the editor of *Queer Jews* and author of the forthcoming book, *Jews Dismantling Diaspora*. Professor Shneer has appeared on television and radio as an expert on issues of contemporary Jewish culture. He has lectured in Russia, Germany, Canada, and across the United States on modern Jewish culture and Soviet Jewish history, and he has served as scholar-in-residence at the Hebrew Union College and as the Pearl Resnick postdoctoral Fellow at the United States Holocaust Memorial Museum. His academic articles have appeared in journals in the United States, Britain, Israel, and Russia.

Yiddish and the Creation of Soviet Jewish Culture

1918–1930

DAVID SHNEER

University of Denver

CAMBRIDGE
UNIVERSITY PRESS

PUBLISHED BY THE PRESS SYNDICATE OF THE UNIVERSITY OF CAMBRIDGE
The Pitt Building, Trumpington Street, Cambridge, United Kingdom

CAMBRIDGE UNIVERSITY PRESS
The Edinburgh Building, Cambridge CB2 2RU, UK
40 West 20th Street, New York, NY 10011-4211, USA
477 Williamstown Road, Port Melbourne, VIC 3207, Australia
Ruiz de Alarcón 13, 28014 Madrid, Spain
Dock House, The Waterfront, Cape Town 8001, South Africa

http://www.cambridge.org

© David Shneer 2004

First published 2004

Printed in the United States of America

Typeface Bembo 10.5/12.5 pt.   *System* LATEX 2$_\varepsilon$ [TB]

A catalog record for this book is available from the British Library.

Library of Congress Cataloging in Publication Data

Shneer, David, 1972–
Yiddish and the creation of Soviet-Jewish culture: 1918–1930 / David Shneer.
    p.   cm.
Includes bibliographical references and index.
ISBN 0-521-82630-6
1. Jews – Soviet Union – Intellectual life.   2. Yiddish language – Social aspects – Soviet Union.
3. Yiddish literature – Soviet Union – History and criticism.   4. Jews – Soviet Union – Identity.
5. Jews – Cultural assimilation – Soviet Union.   6. Jewish socialists – Soviet Union – History.
I. Title.
DS135.R92S523   2004
306.44'089'924047–dc21   2003055185

ISBN 0 521 82630 6 hardback

Production of this book was made possible, in part, by subventions from the Koret Foundation
and from the Lucius N. Littauer Foundation.

Contents

Acknowledgments

I want to thank all of my teachers, especially my Russian, Yiddish, and Hebrew language instructors without whom I could never have accessed the material I have fallen in love with; and my advisors, who mentored the dissertation on which this book is based: Yuri Slezkine, Reggie Zelnik, Chana Kronfeld, and David Biale. I have also been fortunate to interact with scholars around the world (thanks to the conference network and the Internet) who have helped me sharpen my ideas, including: Mordechai Altshuler, Yael Chaver, Gennady Estraikh, Max Friedman, Matthew Hoffman, Alan Karras, Brian Kassof, John Klier, Mikhail Krutikov, Kenneth Moss, Ben Nathans, Jan Plamper, David Roskies, Naomi Seidman, Anna Shternshis, Jeffrey Veidlinger, Mark von Hagen, Robert Weinberg, Seth Wolitz, and Steven Zipperstein, among others. At the University of California, Berkeley, I want to thank the faculty, students, and staff of the history department, the Russian History Working Group, the Joint Doctoral Program in Jewish Studies, and the informal Yiddish Studies reading group. At the University of Denver, I owe thanks to the faculty and staff of the history department and the Center for Judaic Studies, especially Leah Garrett, Ingrid Tague, Ari Kelman, and Nancy Reichman.

In Moscow, Rashid Kaplanov and Victoria Motchalova made sure that I was well taken care of and kept me connected to their amazing group of Moscow-based Jewish Studies scholars. The archivists and librarians at all the Moscow, Kiev, and New York archives and libraries in which I worked made sure that I had access to the materials I needed. In Kiev, Irina Sergeyeva was my guardian angel, who connected me with the archives and libraries that gave this study the pan-Soviet approach it needed. In New York, the knowledgeable staff at the YIVO archives helped dig up vital material that related to Soviet Yiddish culture.

I owe my biggest thanks to the University of California, Berkeley, where I earned my degrees, and the University of Denver, which has supported my scholarly endeavors. Numerous campus administrators, faculty, and staff at Berkeley helped me through the years, especially those at Doe Library and the Institute of Slavic, East European, and Eurasian Studies. At the University of Denver, I owe special thanks to the staff of Penrose Library, especially the Interlibrary Loan division, and the Office of Sponsored Programs. I also want to thank the International Research and Exchange Council (IREX), the Mellon Foundation, the Koret Foundation, the Lucius Littauer Foundation, the University of California, and the University of Denver for their financial support during the research, writing, and publication of this book. Thank you to Cambridge University Press and Andrew Beck for supporting the project, and the production and editing staff, including Michael Kofman, who turned the manuscript into the beautiful book you now hold in your hands.

Thank you to my family: James, Diane, and Rob for being friends; and my grandparents, Lottie, Charles, Kate, and Harry, for inspiring me to study the past. Finally, thank you to Gregg Drinkwater, my husband, friend, and *bashert*.

A Note on Translation and Transliteration

This book uses primary source material in Yiddish, Russian, Ukrainian, and a small number of sources in Hebrew and German. Since it is my goal to make this text as accessible as possible to all readers, I have rendered all titles of organizations, bureaucracies, and other institutions in English, although the original will also be provided on its first use. The endnotes will provide all original names and sources. For this reason, the same institution may be referred to in Yiddish, Russian, or at times, Ukrainian, depending on the source. For short poems, I have included both the original and the translation in the text; the original of longer poems can be found in the appendixes.

For Yiddish I have used the YIVO transliteration system. For Hebrew I have used a simplified, standard transliteration system. And for Russian I have used the Library of Congress transliteration system. For common personal names in the text, I have used spellings more familiar to readers of English (Alexander, rather than Aleksandr). Many of the people mentioned in the book used different names in different languages. For consistency, I have used the name by which I believe they are most widely known. Unless otherwise indicated, all translations are my own.

Introduction

In no other country and in no other period of the history of the Yiddish language have such important foundations for a permanent life for Yiddish been laid as now in the Soviet Union.

– Baruch Glazman, 1924[1]

How does one reconcile the pull of one's membership in a particular people's existence with one's pull to partake in the whole wide world? . . . Jews have always been keenly alive to the exquisite agonies of being pulled apart by loves pointed, like vectors, in opposite directions.

– Rebecca Goldstein, 2001[2]

Nathan Englander opens his 1999 collection of stories, *For the Relief of Unbearable Urges*, with "The Twenty-seventh Man," about the 1952 execution of a group of Soviet Yiddish writers in Stalinist Russia. As four prisoners sit in one of Stalin's prisons, Vasily Korinsky, a Communist Party functionary and Yiddish writer, imagines that if only Stalin knew he was sitting in prison, he would rescue him because of his Party loyalty. "He doesn't know. He wouldn't let them do this to me." To which Y. Zunser, the old man of Yiddish literature, the one who rode out the ebbs and flows of Soviet policies without ever politically affiliating, says, "Maybe not to you, but to the Jew that has your name and lives in your house and lies next to your wife, yes." And then the two return to the only thing they have in common, the thing that landed them in prison, Yiddish:

"It's not my life. It's my culture, my language. Nothing more."

"Only your language?" Zunser waved him away. "Who are we without Yiddish?"[3]

NARRATIVES OF SOVIET JEWISH HISTORY

In the 1920s, the Soviet Union was the only country in the world to have state-sponsored Yiddish-language publishing houses, writers' groups, courts, city councils, and schools. The Soviet Union also supported the creation of a group of socialist Jewish activists – a Soviet Yiddish intelligentsia – dedicated to creating a new kind of Jewish culture for a new kind of Jew. This book examines what this cultural experiment looked like, why it was produced, and what it meant. Why would the Soviet Jewish writers in Englander's story, his fictionalized Soviet Yiddish intelligentsia, have asked "Who are we without Yiddish?"

Most histories of the Soviet Jewish experience echo Englander's tragic story, asking why so many important Yiddish writers, activists, publishers, critics, teachers, and others died at the hands of the very state that had given them the power to carry out their cultural visions. Nearly all of the major figures in this book were dead by 1952. They, like others who lived the tragic narrative of Soviet history, died in the Russian Civil War, during the Great Purges in 1936–9, during World War II and the Holocaust, and then in the anti-Semitic purges of 1948–52 that wiped out the final remnants of the Soviet Yiddish intelligentsia. The last Soviet Yiddish school closed in the late 1930s, the Moscow State Yiddish Theater had its final performance in 1949, and Yiddish books and newspapers were not published between 1949 and 1958. The exploration of how and why this was so is an important historical endeavor, one in which many people have been and are currently engaged.

But that is not the only story to tell. Zunser poses another one: "Who are we without Yiddish?" Or put another way, why were these people who worked for and with the Soviet state so interested in creating Soviet Yiddish culture? Who were they, what did they do, and why did they have the state's support?

The focus on tragedy has led most scholars to deem the project of building Soviet Yiddish culture a failure, by which they mean that this group of people failed to achieve its goal of creating a lasting Yiddish-language Soviet Jewish culture. But as scholars of other times and places in Jewish history have demonstrated, tragedy is a narrative option, and just one of many a writer can choose. As Amos Funkenstein has noted, "Historical accounts do indeed choose a certain mode of narrative – romance, tragedy, comedy, satire. . . . Form and content, imposed categories and received facts, cannot easily be separated – or rather, they cannot be separated at all. . . . [O]ur choice of a 'form of narrative' dictates the facts we select to fit into it."[4] Tragic history is a narrative strategy, whose crafters select particular historical moments for the telling; it puts the end of the story before the story itself, and in its most extreme case, puts death before life.

Most scholars fall back on tragedy, because, for one, death and oppression are compelling. That is why Englander chose the prison cell as the setting for his story. But it is also because scholars often impose outcomes on the events they study, a practice sometimes referred to as hindsight. But this practice also entails significant consequences, as Michael Bernstein has shown with his concept of "backshadowing." Backshadowing affects all historical writing, but in the twentieth century – especially in the writing of Jewish history after the Holocaust – it has come to overshadow other modes of history telling. According to Bernstein, "backshadowing is a kind of retroactive foreshadowing in which the shared knowledge of the outcome of a series of events by narrator and listener is used to judge the participants in those events *as though they too should have known what was to come.*"[5] Soviet Jewish culture, in what little has been written about it, has been viewed almost exclusively through the lens of the Purges. Those who were killed emerge as Jewish martyrs (except perhaps for the fictional Korinsky, the Communist writer in Englander's story, whose tale is the most tragic because he cannot see how he is "being used" by the Soviet state to betray his own people).

I try to avoid backshadowing the deaths of these people and their cultural project by focusing on the contingencies they encountered and the complex choices they were making in their time, the social and cultural context of the 1920s. By doing so, I hope to put secular, socialist Jewish culture back into the narratives of Jewish and Soviet history.

Until very recently, the production of such a Jewish culture in the Soviet Union has not been at the forefront of the research agenda within Jewish or Soviet history. Gennady Estraikh's work on the linguistic and cultural role Yiddish played in Soviet Jewish culture has shown the central role language played in Soviet Jewish cultural politics.[6] And in his recent monograph on the Soviet Jewish theater, Jeffrey Veidlinger countered the long-held argument that Soviet Yiddish culture was merely an outgrowth of the Soviet state's propaganda campaign by showing that it in fact had a "distinct Jewish identity." Jewish actors, directors, and producers used the stage to bring Jewish themes into Soviet cultural contexts, and could do so, in Veidlinger's view, due to the ignorance of its cultural supervisors. "Bolshevik propagandists failed to realize that national forms – languages, myths, archetypes, and symbols – were semiotic systems that aroused pre-existing emotions and expectations among audiences familiar with the codes." In other words, no matter how seemingly empty of Jewish content Soviet Yiddish culture might have appeared to some, there was no such thing as a "denationalized" Soviet Jewish culture.

Veidlinger is right to emphasize that Soviet Jewish cultural activists were actively, not passively, fostering Jewish identity. However, there remains a division in Veidlinger's work between culture producer and "Bolshevik propagandist," the former being "Jewish," the latter being somehow opposed to authentic Jewishness. In fact, within the Soviet Yiddish intelligentsia, it is very hard to tell the difference between the Bolshevik propagandist and the Jewish cultural activist. All of them were part of the national construction of Soviet Jewish culture that simultaneously helped build support for the Soviet state and the Communist Party.[7]

The turn to culture allows scholars to see Soviet Jewish history as a history of production rather than as a history of destruction, and gives agency back to Soviet Jewish intellectuals. Western Jews have tended to see Soviet Jews either as tragic subjects or repressed, silenced objects.[8] Subjectivity appeared with "collaborators" like Korinsky, who participated in the state's propaganda project for their own self-interest, or "resisters," who opposed it in underground Hebrew classes and secret prayer groups or in the dissident and refusenik movements of the 1970s and 1980s.[9] Soviet Jews have, therefore, been portrayed either as tragic failures, silent bystanders, or rebellious heroes. The Soviet Yiddish intelligentsia, which was involved in the state and the Party and was part of the power structure, however, complicates these categories.

I center this history on cultural production, rather than cultural repression, in order to move away from the tragic narrative. Perhaps this move runs the risk of simply telling a different narrative, a romantic one. A book focusing on the expression, production, and flowering of Yiddish culture in the Soviet Union without telling how the story ends risks sentimentality and romanticization, just as much as focusing solely on repression risks backshadowing. But the emphasis on cultural production also shows how Soviet Jews were part of, not apart from, the Soviet system and part of, not apart from, Jewish history. The historiographic focus on the oppression of Jews makes it easier to sidestep their own imbrication and implication in the Soviet system. But this focus also prevents us from talking about the ideological excitement and emotion the Soviet Yiddish intelligentsia invested in this unique cultural, political, and aesthetic project – the creation of a particularly Jewish *Soviet* culture and a particularly Soviet *Jewish* culture.

YIDDISH AND THE IDEOLOGY DRIVING SOVIET JEWISH CULTURE BUILDING

Most of this book focuses on a small group of Jewish writers, activists, Communist Party bosses, censors, publishers, cultural critics, scholars, and intellectuals who made up the Soviet Yiddish intelligentsia. They were drawing on a tradition of leftist, populist, and socialist Jewish culture and politics, which made Yiddish – the vernacular language of Eastern European Jewry – the defining feature of their cultural project. For this group, which worked with and for the Soviet state, Yiddish marked Jews as a distinct ethnic group – or, in the language of the Soviet Union, a distinct nationality. Yiddish defined the new Soviet Jewish culture that this intelligentsia created.

These activists were not alone in believing that language defined modern nationhood. For many intellectuals in the age of nationalism, language was not just a means of communication; it was the embodiment of a people. In this case, Yiddish reflected the soul of the Jewish *folk*. By the turn of the twentieth century, some intellectuals thought that Yiddish was fundamental to the preservation of Jewish culture in the modern world. "In Yiddish the Jewish spirit is reflected and its value for the survival of our nation is beginning to be comprehended," read the invitation to the Czernowitz Language Conference in 1908 – the first major gathering of people interested in raising the status of the Jews' lowly "jargon," their kitchen language and mother tongue.[10] In 1923, fifteen years after Czernowitz and six years after the Bolshevik Revolution, Esther Frumkina, one of the chief socialists at Czernowitz and one of the most important Yiddish cultural activists in the Soviet Union, wrote:

How much long-held pain and joy, how many profound experiences, how many gray secrets, how many eternal longings are embodied in the language. And how much intrinsic beauty and harmony lies within it. Whether it is beaming or laughing, serious and harsh or soft and dreamy, dry or damp – [Yiddish] is always a divine work of art, always a picture of the people that created it.[11]

Yiddish was much more than a language before, during, and even after the 1917 Bolshevik Revolution that brought to power a political party seemingly opposed to nationalism in all of its forms. Why then would Yiddish, that marker of Jewish nationhood and Jewish difference, still be important in a class-based, socialist world?

Throughout the 1920s and 1930s, the Soviet Union invested greatly in developing social, political, and cultural institutions in the native languages of its many ethnic minorities so that each Soviet ethnic group could be inculcated with enlightened Soviet values in its own language. Within Soviet policy, it was language, more than any other single characteristic, that defined a nation. Ukrainians were Ukrainian because they spoke Ukrainian, Jews were Jews because they spoke Yiddish. Had all Jews already assimilated into Russian-language culture, presumably the state would not have considered them a separate nation. Because Soviet Jews were still overwhelmingly Yiddish-speaking, Soviet policies supported the formation of Soviet Jewish schools, clubs, newspapers, and other cultural institutions conducted in the Jews' native language: Yiddish. Jewish populist intellectuals and Soviet theoreticians working on policy toward ethnic minorities agreed that language would define the modern Soviet Jewish nation.[12]

Mikhail Levitan, an editor and important member of the Soviet Yiddish intelligentsia in Ukraine, joined the Communist Party shortly after the Bolshevik Revolution and was charged with ensuring that the goals of the state and the Party were at the core of Soviet Jewish culture building in Yiddish.[13] He wrote a series of articles in 1926 explaining what he thought Soviet Jewish culture was, and was not, about.

Yiddish is, for us Communists, not a goal in and of itself, but is only a means for Communist education and re-education of the Jewish masses. But does that mean that the culture building that we've done in Yiddish is just a tactical maneuver for us? . . . Do we approach Yiddish from the standpoint that it is a lesser evil than Hebrew? . . . Is it just meant to elicit sympathy from the worldwide Jewish masses to our work in the Soviet Union? And finally, does it mean that after we completely liquidate Zionist influence from the Soviet Union, and if the Communist International finds the key to the hearts and minds of the Jewish workers of bourgeois lands, will we suddenly throw out, as unnecessary baggage, all of Yiddish-language culture building?[14]

For Levitan, these rhetorical questions all had the same answer: no. In this litany of questions, Levitan summed up the utilitarian arguments why the Soviet state was supporting and helping build a Yiddish culture of its own. Some Soviet activists thought that it was a convenient way to spread Soviet propaganda to the Yiddish-speaking Jewish masses, both within the Soviet Union and abroad. Until Soviet Jews all spoke Russian, the state would have to bring them Communism in Yiddish. Other critics thought that the Soviets' use of Yiddish was tactical – to encourage Jews from around the world to support the fledgling and desperately poor country both politically and financially. Others thought that the Soviet state's support of Yiddish was simply a front masking its persecution of Judaism, Hebrew culture, Zionism, and other forms of Jewish culture and politics. Finally, Levitan posed the ultimate question: once all Jews became Communists, would Yiddish still be necessary?

There was a degree of truth to all of these notions. The Soviet state and the Soviet Yiddish intelligentsia wanted the support of Jews for the new socialist experiment, and Yiddish – whose speakers now spanned the globe after the great migration of Jews from Eastern Europe – was a great way of helping build that support. The intelligentsia's creation of an alternative Jewish culture in Yiddish would certainly serve as a substitute for the forms of Jewish culture it was suppressing, such as "bourgeois, nationalist" Zionism and "benighted, backward" traditional Jewish religion. And there were some among the intelligentsia who considered Yiddish simply a means to a larger end of turning Jews into non-Jewish (Russian-speaking) Soviets.

The utilitarian arguments Levitan raised were not just about Communist internationalism and Soviet politics, but were also about the many approaches Jewish intellectuals had taken to modernizing Eastern European Jewry. Many nineteenth-century Jewish modernizers, known as *maskilim*, thought that to be modern, Jews needed to speak the languages of the high cultures that surrounded them – Russian and German – and needed to resurrect the Jews' classical language, Hebrew. For most *maskilim*, Yiddish was a relic of a time past, when Jews had their own vernacular language because they lived in a world apart. In the modern world, Jews were part of, not apart from, society, and therefore the continued use of Yiddish worked against their modernizing and integrating project. Those *maskilim* who chose to work in Yiddish saw its use in literature, newspapers, and other forms of print culture as a temporary means of bringing new ideas to the Jewish population in its native tongue. Yiddish was seen neither as a language of high culture, nor as a language of the future. It was a language of convenience. Most *maskilim* would have approved of abandoning Yiddish once their modernizing goals had been accomplished – in this case, once Soviet Jewry was speaking Russian and quoting Lenin.

But Levitan and the members of the Soviet Yiddish intelligentsia were not *maskilim*.

The place of Yiddish in Jewish culture began to change when Eastern European Jewish intellectuals encountered nineteenth-century nationalism. Benedict Anderson, one of the foremost scholars of nationalism, has shown that secularization, imperialism, the rise of vernacular languages, and the dissemination of print were four of the processes that led to an era when national identification came to supersede local, religious, and other kinds of identities.[15] In the Russian empire, these processes came to Yiddish-speaking Jews in the nineteenth century. Secularization came as traditional forms of communal and religious organization began breaking down, and modern European philosophies changed the way Jews understood the world. The nineteenth century was also the heyday of Russian empire building, as Russia was struggling to define itself as both an expanding empire and an ethnic nation. This tension fostered nationalist politics among the elite of many of the Russian empire's ethnic minorities. For Jews, the question was in what language should they develop a new post-religious Jewish communal – or Jewish national – identity. In the second half of the nineteenth century, Jewish cultural activists in the Russian empire began developing a literature, a periodical press, school systems, and other institutions that laid the groundwork for new forms of collective Jewish identity, in both Yiddish, the Jews' vernacular, and Hebrew, the Jews' classical language, as well as in Russian and Polish.[16]

The most important political movement for the development of Yiddish culture in Eastern Europe was the socialist General Jewish Workers' Union, known as the Bund, which in 1897 held its first conference. It soon began publishing its Yiddish-language newspaper, *The Worker's Voice (Di Arbeter Shtime)*, and in 1901, officially adopted a platform calling for "national and cultural autonomy," and made its official language "that of the Jewish working classes – Yiddish."[17] Zionists, who also convened their first world congress in 1897, eventually placed Hebrew at the center of their national platform, and, over time, did for Hebrew what socialists did for Yiddish – created a Jewish culture in the one and only language that each believed embodied the Jewish people. Both Zionists and Jewish socialists were envisioning "an alternative construct of Jewish identity grounded in a secular definition of Jewish peoplehood and reinforced by secularized narratives of the Jewish past."[18] Levitan and the Soviet Yiddish intelligentsia were a product of all of these movements – the Jewish enlightenment, Jewish socialism, and Jewish nationalism. As enlighteners, they believed Jews needed to become part of Soviet society. As socialists, they believed in elevating the (Jewish) working classes to positions of power and in working toward the creation of a classless society. And as nationalists, they believed that the use of Yiddish and the development of Yiddish culture made Jews a nation different from all other nations. If Jews were no longer defined by religious practice and separate communities, then language could serve as a substitute.[19] Despite the linguistic assimilation of many Soviet Jews into Russian culture, there was a concerted effort on the part of the intelligentsia to make Yiddish the defining feature of Soviet Jewishness. After all, without language what would define Jews in a socialist, atheist, modern world?[20]

The first step in building Soviet Jewish culture was the creation of an elite group of Jewish intellectuals to serve as the Soviet Yiddish intelligentsia. Chapter One describes how Soviet state policy and Jewish socialist ideology meshed to create such a group. The intelligentsia then needed to establish Yiddish as the one and only language that defined Soviet Jewry, the subject of Chapter Two. The next step in creating Soviet Yiddish culture, examined in Chapter Three, was the modernization of Yiddish so that it would be worthy of its new, proud status as the language of modern Soviet Jewish culture.[21] Chapters Four, Five, and Six examine the institutions and people who built Soviet Jewish culture, from the publishing houses where Yiddish was printed, to the books and newspapers they produced, to the poets who created a new kind of Soviet Yiddish literature. These people and institutions propagated Yiddish and built a culture that they hoped would develop a new secular Soviet Jew.

If the Jewish intelligentsia worked for a Soviet Jewish culture to create a modern Jewish nation, why did non-Jewish Soviet and Party leaders of the new state listen to and support these activists? In October 1917, the Bolsheviks suddenly found themselves in charge of, rather than trying to overthrow, a multinational empire. If they had clearcut ideas about the class struggle and economics, they were less prepared to deal with the legacies of tsarist imperialism. With the fall of the tsar, in an era of anticolonial nationalism and self-determination, some of the empire's ethnic minorities were calling for cultural and political autonomy, if not complete independence. The Bolsheviks needed to incorporate socialist internationalism and the ethnic minorities' anti-colonial nationalism into state policy.

Studying the Soviet Union as a multiethnic empire became popular after the collapse of the Soviet Union in 1989–91 and the rise of ethnic nationalism in Communism's place. The most pressing question for those studying this movement has been how Russia and the Soviet Union managed, and in some cases created, ethnic difference. Many scholars took theories of imperialism and post-colonialism as their point of departure for studying how the tsarist and Soviet empires imagined their ethnic minorities.[22] Because of this, there has been a focus on state policy toward ethnic minorities. Terry Martin's work on Soviet nationalities policy, for example, showed how the Soviet Union's interest in developing national minorities was an integral part of Soviet imperial policy. He coined the term "affirmative action empire" to describe the way Soviet policy fostered ethnic minorities by supporting and creating intelligentsias for them, and then giving them conditional access to power to remake the ethnic group in the state's own image.[23]

One might call this a state-building model of imperialism.[24] Other empires created a native intelligentsia and systems of imperial power in the language of the metropole, which makes sense if part of the empire's civilizing mission was to teach the "natives" how to be Western. All roads led to London and Paris, to English and French culture. The only other empire that vaguely resembled Russia was the Austro-Hungarian Empire, but even there, the state administration encouraged the use of German and Hungarian to maintain the empire's cohesion. In the Soviet case, why was the natives' own language important – central in fact – to Soviet imperial policy?[25] Lenin himself suggested that the tsarist Russian empire was different from Western empires in that it was both the oppressor of other national groups within its borders and the victim of oppression by the capitalist West.[26] It was, Lenin argued, a prime candidate for both a proletarian socialist revolution and anti-imperial national liberation. Once the revolution happened, the Bolsheviks found themselves in the position of being state-building modernizers of a multinational empire, revolutionaries dedicated to inaugurating socialism, and decolonizers combating the pernicious effects of tsarist Russian imperialism on its constituent nationalities. As Francine Hirsch has argued, "for Soviet policymakers, colonization and 'making nations' went hand in hand."[27]

Soviet state building and Jewish nation building in Yiddish were not mutually exclusive. One could create Yiddish culture and help foster the Soviet state. One could call for class struggle and insist that Jewish children go to Yiddish schools. Soviet socialism and secular Jewish nationalism were not opposite ends of a spectrum in which the Soviet Yiddish intelligentsia operated. In the 1920s, these ideologies and cultural and political projects developed together, each simultaneously informing and circumscribing the other.

A UNIQUE SOVIET NATIONAL MINORITY

Within Soviet nationalities policy, Jews were generally treated just like – and in many cases, better than – any other national minority until World War II, but they were still in a category unto itself. In the Soviet categorization of its national minorities, Jews were often compared to Poles and Germans, due to their common "Westernness," their high level of education, their high rate of literacy, and their history of socialist culture. This perceived level of cultural development allowed Jews more autonomy to develop their own Soviet culture. At the same time, Jews were compared to the Roma, more commonly known as "Gypsies," because of their common landlessness. This lack of a defined and bounded place put Jews in an anomalous position within Soviet nationalities policies, which used territory as well as language to define national groups. In fact, Jews' lack of a defined territory was a source of definitional challenge for many Soviet theoreticians, who thought that nations were defined by territory. The Yiddish intelligentsia (not to mention Zionists and other Jewish nationalists) also found Jews' landlessness an impediment to the full creation of a Soviet Jewish nation. Like Zionists, who needed territory in which to incubate a Hebrew nation in Palestine, Soviet Jewish activists fought to establish Jewish agricultural colonies, Jewish city councils, and eventually an entire Jewish region, in which the official languages were Yiddish and Russian, in order to create the territorial foundations of their Soviet nation.[28]

The aspect of Jewish collective identity that has made Jews perennially unique is that they have been and still are both a religious and an ethnic group. Even Hitler, whose anti-Semitism was firmly based in theories of race, mixed the two up when the Nuremberg Laws of 1935 denied citizenship to converts to Judaism, who had no connection to "Jewish blood."[29] Until 1917, many Russian state leaders and members of the Russian intelligentsia saw Jews as both a religious and an ethnic entity living within its borders. Jewish marriages were handled by Jewish religious courts, most Jewish children went to Jewish schools overseen by official Jewish councils headed by rabbis, and enmity toward Jews still often came from Christian-based anti-Jewish polemics despite the appearance of a racial anti-Semitism after the 1905 revolution. At the same time, since the mid-nineteenth century, Jews and Russians began to see Jews in overlapping categories – sometimes as a nation and other times as a "religious faith." The officially atheistic Soviet Union inherited this problem. Did fighting against religion, Marx's opiate of the masses, mean fighting against Jews as Jews? Would Jews be treated like Christians in the Soviet Union or would they be treated like Ukrainians or Russians? Would they have religious representation that maintained official relations with the Soviet state like the Orthodox Church had?

As an atheist state, official Soviet policy marked Jews as an ethnic minority, like Russians and Ukrainians. To achieve their purely ethnic identity in practice, the intelligentsia's and the Soviet state's goal was to eliminate a religious identity and support a secular one, whose culture would be in Yiddish. To this end, one of the first actions of the Soviet Yiddish intelligentsia was to close down traditional Jewish religious communities (*kehilot*) that had served as independent political and religious authorities in the Jewish world. Members of the Soviet Yiddish intelligentsia also closed down synagogues and traditional Jewish schools, and arrested rabbis, Hebrew teachers, and others who were continuing to serve as leaders of traditional Jewish communities. Although some non-Soviet Jews accused the intelligentsia of self-hatred because they suppressed traditional expressions of Jewish identity, their actions are better viewed as an attempt to wrestle with the question of Jewish identity. In place of these institutions, the intelligentsia established new Yiddish ones that would inculcate a new secular Jewish identity.

Jews were also different because they were overrepresented in the Soviet professions, in Soviet cities, in the Soviet bureaucracy, in the Russian-language intelligentsia, and in the Communist Party until and even after World War II.[30] The Soviet Union treated the Jews well by giving them social, economic, and political opportunities that the conservative tsarist government, and even neighboring countries in Eastern Europe, denied them.[31] Jews were also not like any other minority, because the fight against anti-Semitism was a defining policy of the Soviet regime in the 1920s. The Communist Party interpreted anti-Semitism as a backward relic of capitalist economic relationships, and stridently fought populist anti-Semitism. Hatred against other ethnic groups was not marked as a separate category in the same way.

The other obvious difference is that, between 1941 and 1945, in the German campaign against the Soviet Union, all Soviet citizens were killed as Soviets, but the Nazis and their allies murdered Communists as Communists and Jews as Jews.

✧   ✧   ✧

Since both the intelligentsia and the state defined Soviet Jewish culture by its use of Yiddish, this book focuses on Yiddish cultural production rather than the widespread cultural production of Soviet Jews in Russian, by such well-known culture-producers as Isaac Babel, Eduard Bagritsky, or even Osip Mandelshtam. Their cultural project was different from that of the Soviet Yiddish intelligentsia, because they created culture within the rubric of Russian-language culture and the Russian intelligentsia, even if these intelligentsias overlapped. I am also limiting my examination to these activists' Yiddish-language cultural products, though all of them produced culture in other languages. From David Hofshteyn's Hebrew feuilletons to Izi Kharik's occasional article in Russian, this intelligentsia worked in a multilingual world. I am focusing on Yiddish culture because it is in Yiddish where the intelligentsia's visions of a new Jewish culture and the larger ideological goals of state and nation building intersect. I am also not examining the suppressed print culture produced in Hebrew, which fell outside the bounds of officially sponsored Soviet Jewish culture. Finally, I limit my discussion to Yiddish and not to the other "native languages" of Jews in the Soviet Union, such as Judeo-Tat (the language of the Dagestani Jews) or Judeo-Tadzhik (the language of Bukharan Jews), because these groups fell outside of the boundaries of the community on whose behalf this intelligentsia worked.[32]

One final explanatory note. Aside from this introduction, when discussing the relationships between the Soviet state and the intelligentsia, I try to use the more specific designation of a particular state or Party bureaucracy involved in a given issue. I do this because, in relation to Jewish culture building in the 1920s, there was no such thing as a monolithic state that spoke with one voice and that dictated policy from the top down or from the center to the periphery. Most of these Jewish cultural activists were "the state" by virtue of their holding positions in the state and Party bureaucracies and making decisions in the name of state and Party organizations. Therefore, while it may seem overwhelming to the reader, the overlapping agencies and names do mean something. I use these names, although I am aware I might confuse the reader, in the hope that it will demonstrate how complex the negotiation of power was in trying to create culture in the Soviet 1920s.

Finally, I refer to Jews in the Soviet Union sometimes as a nation and other times as an "ethnic minority," although Soviet Jews in the 1920s would have been referred to and would have referred to themselves as a nationality, a nation, a national minority, or a religious group. The intricacies of the Soviet labeling system have been well covered elsewhere, and I prefer to use accessible language that suggests how the government saw these groups of "ethnically" different people, and how these people formed a collective identity around these labels.[33]

The power of the Soviet Yiddish intelligentsia was at its peak in the 1920s, even if quantitatively, the number of institutions dedicated to Soviet Yiddish culture reached a high point in the early 1930s. The number of students in Soviet Jewish schools operating in Yiddish peaked in 1931;[34] the number of teachers in Jewish training colleges reached its high in 1933–4;[35] and the quantity of Yiddish publications increased through the mid-1930s. But the rise of Stalinism and the first Five-Year Plan in the late 1920s and early 1930s meant a dramatic restructuring of the Soviet Yiddish cultural project. The Jewish sections of the Communist Party, the *Evsektsiia*, along with all ethnic minority sections of the Party, was eliminated in 1929–30. The School and Book (*Shul un Bukh*) Publishing House, a primary site of Soviet Yiddish print culture, was closed down in 1928, and nearly all Soviet Jewish bureaucratic institutions were incorporated into general Soviet ones. By the late 1930s, all Yiddish schools closed, fewer publications appeared, the theater system shrank, and many of the leaders of this cultural movement were killed in the Great Purges.

In the 1920s, the Soviet Yiddish intelligentsia had the ideological and institutional space to determine what Soviet Jewish culture would look like. It was a time when the intelligentsia saw Jewish national building as part of the Soviet socialist revolution. Levitan, the enlightening, nationalist Communist Party leader, summed up the complicated relationship this group of people and the Soviet state had toward Yiddish culture. In response to the question, "Is Yiddish just a means to an end of assimilating Jews into Soviet society?" he responded:

The first problem is the concept of means and ends. Such a division is rather artificial. Culture-building . . . is one of the most secure means to building our international socialist culture in the transition period from capitalism to communism. . . . If we say that Yiddish is not an end, but a means, then can we come to the conclusion that we Communists are not interested in the Yiddish language, in its purity, its blossoming, and its refinement? Does it mean that we are nihilists toward the Yiddish language? . . . Of course not. . . . We don't talk about making the language eternal. Historical materialists don't talk about things being eternal. . . . We have established a tremendous network of institutions to serve the Yiddish speaking masses. We are not building just any Jewish culture; we are building a Soviet Jewish culture, a socialist Jewish culture, and a part of international socialist culture.[36]

I

Soviet Nationalities Policies and the Making of the Soviet Yiddish Intelligentsia

The Bund was made up of Zionists who were afraid of seasickness.
— Georgy Plekhanov, founding Russian Marxist theoretician

The February Revolution, like the French Revolution, granted Jews rights as citizens. But the Bolshevik Revolution had to go one step further to relate to the Jews, as to all other ethnic groups in the Russian empire, as a *nation*.
— Hersh Smolar, member of the Soviet Yiddish intelligentsia

In the Soviet Union, socialist Jewish writers, ideologists, poets, political activists, and teachers who had been active in organizing the Jewish working classes of the Russian Empire became the Soviet Yiddish intelligentsia. Before the Bolshevik Revolution, this group had deep ideological and political divisions, often fighting more intensely with each other than with the perceived capitalist or tsarist enemy. Bundists, socialist Zionists, socialist autonomists, and others created new political movements as new ideas about how to lead Jews into the future arose. This diversity of political expression continued in Poland, Lithuania, and in other parts of Europe in the interwar period, but political diversity was not tolerated in the Soviet Union as the Bolsheviks quickly turned the Soviet Union into a one-party state. With the formation of the *Evsektsiia*, and with the closing down and consolidation of all remaining political parties, Jewish political and cultural activists across the political, ideological, and aesthetic spectrum were forced to come together. Some of them chose to join the Communist Party; many did not. But party affiliation did not determine whether a cultural or political activist was a member of the Soviet Yiddish intelligentsia. Working in Yiddish did. Communists and those who became politically unaffiliated, literary realists and modernists, former Zionists and radical socialists all came together to form the Soviet Yiddish intelligentsia.

This group was Soviet, because it was engaged in the state building process that the Communist Party and the Soviet state made its highest priority. This

intelligentsia, like other non-Russian, ethnic intelligentsias in the Soviet empire, was created "in the image" of the Party to bring enlightenment and Soviet
ideology to the multiethnic Soviet empire. It was "Yiddish," because Yiddish
marked the Jews as a Soviet nation, as opposed to a religion, and in Yiddish,
Soviet Jewry would foster a new kind of collective identity – secular and socialist,
but marked as Jewish. It was Yiddish, because Yiddish is what brought this group
of people together. This group was an intelligentsia, because, for one, it was a
very small and highly educated group of people who had taken it upon themselves to lead "their people" into the socialist future. They were an intelligentsia
engaged in a project of cultural translation – bringing Soviet ideology and cultural trends to Soviet Jews and lobbying for Jewish issues before the non-Jewish,
and usually more authoritative, members of the Party and the state.

In some ways, the role of the Soviet Yiddish intelligentsia was like that of
a traditional Jewish intermediary between Jews and outside sources of power,
known as *shtadlanim*.[1] Before the nineteenth century, Jewish communities used
shtadlanim to negotiate with secular authorities on behalf of the Jewish community. In nineteenth-century Russia, *maskilim* embodied this traditional form of
negotiating power between the state and the Jews. *Maskilim*, however, worked
in two directions: on the one hand, they wanted to use state power to break the
hegemony of the traditional rabbinic élite and encourage the modernization of
Eastern European Jewry. On the other hand, the fact that they were Europeaniz-
ers and that some of them moved within élite, non-Jewish circles made them
perfect apologists for Jews and Judaism.[2] Unlike the *shtadlan* of pre-modern
Jewish society, who represented a particular Jewish community, *maskilim* were
not representatives of the community on whose behalf they claimed to speak.
They claimed the mantle of "representative" themselves, and used state power
to further their own enlightening agenda.[3] By the late nineteenth century, with
Jewish socialism and nationalism and radical politics becoming more popular
than enlightenment and integration, and with the tsarist state wracked by social
strife, the idea that Jews needed to petition the tsar for help and protection lost
favor. With Jewish intellectuals calling for Jews to emancipate themselves, the
shtadlan seemed to lose its role.

In the Soviet Union, the relationship of Jews to the Soviet state called for
the emergence of a new kind of cultural and political mediator. The state tried,
once again, to make itself the guarantor of the community's structural integrity,
and it did this for all Soviet ethnic minorities. The Soviet Yiddish intelligentsia
served as intermediaries, envisioning the future of Jewish culture and society
for the state and for Jews, and using state power to realize those visions.

Like their nineteenth-century *maskilic* predecessors, most Soviet Jews did
not ask the intelligentsia to take on this role. But unlike their predecessors, for
whom the distance between themselves and the state defined their role, in the

Soviet Union these new intercessors *were* the state when it came to articulating a vision of Soviet Jewish culture. Their role happened within the state and Party apparatus. For example, Moshe Litvakov, the editor of the central Party Yiddish newspaper, *Der Emes*, and the de facto cultural commissar of Soviet Jewry, was frequently called in by non-Jewish Party and state organizations to serve as a "Jewish expert" to inform an uneducated audience about Jewish issues.[4] In terms of language, Litvakov could speak both Yiddish and Russian, and in terms of culture and discourse, he spoke both "traditional Jewish" and "Bolshevik" (and it is important to remember that both of these cultures were operating in Yiddish). Litvakov taught Bolsheviks to speak Jewish and within Soviet Jewish cultural institutions, he taught Jews to speak Bolshevik.

This intelligentsia, however, was also engaged in a project of Jewish nation building, seeing the Soviet state and its policies as incubators of a modern, secular Jewish identity and culture. They were an intelligentsia located in between the people for whom they claimed to speak and the political power that they represented to the people. It was an awkward place to be. But how often does a group of secular, socialist Yiddish-writing Jewish intellectuals receive this kind of offer?

The offer was of course not one-sided. Communist theoreticians from Stalin to Lenin wrestled with the idea of fostering native leadership among the Soviet Union's many ethnic minorities. Stalin and Lenin had each written on the subject in the early 1910s, and much of what drove these two socialist internationalists to theorize the question of national identity and Marxism were Jewish socialists, especially the Bund, who wanted to be both national and socialist. In his response to the Bund's national version of socialism, Stalin wrote the often quoted *Marxism and the National Question*, which lays out what a nation is, and questions whether Jews fit into the category: "A nation is a historically evolved, stable community of language, territory, economic life, and psychological make-up manifested in a community of culture." Stalin asks: "What national cohesion can there be . . . between the Georgian, Dagestanian, Russian, and American Jews?" Jews, he believed, were headed for assimilation, because once religion was removed, Jews had little in common, and they lacked a single, compact territory.[5] Those Marxists who advocated for the preservation of Jewish culture and for separate organizing among Jewish workers, such as the Bund, were in Stalin's and Lenin's opinion, fostering nationalism and working against the larger aims of the international workers' movement. Although he threw into question Jews' claims to nationhood, Stalin did not deny that national identity was significant in helping create an international workers' movement.[6]

Lenin's *Critical Remarks on the National Question* focused on the idea of national privilege, and argued that no national group or nation's culture and language should have privileges that others don't. His first object of criticism was the privilege Russian culture experienced under the tsars, one that stunted the growth of other national cultures. But Lenin also went on the offensive against the Bund, which had argued since the turn of the century that Jewish workers had issues particular to them *as Jews*. Because of this, the Bund needed to remain an autonomous socialist organization to serve the Jewish working class as Jews and as workers. Lenin saw this as bourgeois nationalism and separatism, reminding the Bund that "the same [principle of privilege] applies to the most oppressed and persecuted nation – the Jews. Jewish national culture is the slogan of the rabbis and the bourgeoisie, the slogan of our enemies. But there are other elements in Jewish culture and in Jewish history as a whole. . . . Whoever . . . puts forward the slogan of Jewish 'national culture' is . . . an enemy of the proletariat, a supporter of all that is outmoded and connected with caste among the Jewish people. . . . On the other hand, those Jewish Marxists who mingle with the Russian, Lithuanian, Ukrainian and other workers in international Marxist organizations make their contribution toward creating the international culture of the working-class movement."[7] Lenin supported the Jews' claim to national identity, something that Stalin did not. However, Lenin denied that such national difference should lead to organizational separatism. He also distinguished between the "complete equality of nations and languages," the opposite of national privilege, and "cultural-national autonomy," which "divides the nations and in fact draws the workers and the bourgeoisie of any one nation closer together."[8] The question of whether "complete equality" meant equality of opportunity – meaning no language would be restricted in any way – or equality of condition – which would necessitate government support for cultures that had previously been suppressed – was left unstated. Soviet nationalities policies, which were based on these ideas, showed that in practice, the state deemed non-discrimination insufficient. This "affirmative action empire" built institutions to support the growth of ethnic minorities' cultures, including Yiddish ones.

Although Stalin and Lenin disagreed on the Jews' claim to nationhood, they both agreed that a Marxist state would have to allow and support the diversity of workers' cultures. After the revolution, with Ukrainians declaring independence, Jews organizing their own political and cultural institutions, and Poles leaving the empire, the Soviet leadership would have to balance ideological desire and political pragmatism to keep the country together. Seen through the lens of political pragmatism, supporting the leadership of ethnic minorities might sway them to join the Soviet state rather than fight against it. Supporting the creation of ethnic intelligentsias and ethnic minorities' cultures was a means of creating a single Soviet socialist state out of diverse ethnic groups.

These ethnic intelligentsias also served as the cultural translators bringing Communist ideology to all ethnic groups, and in the Soviet case, cultural translation was taken literally. In 1932, the quantitative peak of Soviet Yiddish book publishing, 62 percent of all Soviet Yiddish books were translations, primarily from Russian.[9] Statistics like these demonstrated how Soviet nationalities' policies translated into the pithy phrase, "national in form, socialist in content" – in other words, that all Soviet ethnic cultures had the same "content," but each was produced in its native language. It might seem that Soviet Yiddish culture was similar to all other Soviet ethnic minorities' cultures. It was Yiddish in form, universal socialist in content.

But it wasn't. Most Soviet Jews, although they spoke Yiddish, preferred that their children learn Russian, and many Jews, from Lev Trotsky to Jewish mothers in tiny hamlets in Belorussia, thought of Yiddish as a relic of small town Jewish life. By the late-1930s Russian had caught up to Yiddish as the day-to-day language of Soviet Jews, and there were plenty of Soviet Jews who were producing culture in Russian. The migration to and modernization of Eastern European Jews in places like Kiev, St. Petersburg, Warsaw, and also New York, London, and Berlin had been taking place since the mid-nineteenth century.[10] These social, cultural, and economic processes only increased after the Russian Revolution and the removal of Jewish residency restrictions that defined the Pale of Settlement, the region of the Russian Empire in which Jews were permitted to live most freely during the tsarist period. The Jewish population of Kharkov, Ukraine, for example, increased 900 percent between the 1897 and 1926 censuses, and the Jewish population of Moscow went from 28,000 in 1920 to 131,000 in 1926.[11] As Jews moved to large Russian-speaking cities, they began to speak Russian (and as they moved to New York and London, they spoke English). The 1926 Soviet census showed that 72.6 percent of Soviet Jews listed Yiddish as their native language, down from 97 percent in 1899, and the numbers in the larger cities showed a dramatic turn toward Russian. (According to the 1989 Soviet census, 93.7 percent of Moscow's Jews named Russian as their native language.[12]) Linguistic and cultural modernization and assimilation were happening "from the bottom up" without any outside interference from Jewish intellectuals or the Soviet state.

One seemingly comic, but very real, illustration of this problem: Volodymyr Zatonskyi, a Soviet Ukrainian activist, sarcastically recounted how Yiddish-speaking children in Russian-language schools in Ukraine were "caught" and sent to Yiddish schools. "We have received information from Nikolaev, from Kiev, and from a series of other places, that during preenrollment examinations children 'suspected of belonging to the Jewish nation,' if it becomes clear that these malefactors know Yiddish, are automatically sent to a Yiddish school 'for, you see, we give every nationality full possibilities in this respect, so off you go to a Yiddish school.' The children don't want this, and their parents instruct them not to admit that they know Yiddish. And so, comrades, an exam is conducted in order to trick these children – they speak with the child in Russian or Ukrainian, and then, when the child has calmed down (they speak nicely with them), suddenly the examiner tells them in Yiddish to go home. The child Jewishly [sic] turns around and leaves. 'That means you know Yiddish. We'll send you to a Yiddish school.'"[13] Although the Soviet Yiddish intelligentsia supported the idea of a Soviet Jewish culture in Yiddish, many others did not. These activists were creating a culture that at least according to the political rhetoric, was being created to reach the "Jewish masses," but Jews were happy, and in some cases preferred, to read Russian. Soviet Jews then were reading Lenin in the original, so cultural translation could not have been the primary motivation for the creation of Soviet Yiddish culture. Why then would the Soviet Yiddish intelligentsia and non-Jewish Communist Party leaders be interested in bringing socialism to Jews in Yiddish?

As much as it was a project of cultural translation and ideological propaganda, the building of Soviet Yiddish culture was driven by a newly empowered socialist national intelligentsia that wanted to create a secular Soviet Jew through the framework of Yiddish rather than through linguistic and cultural assimilation that many Jews seemed to embrace. At times, it had to convince Soviet Jewry that Yiddish and the culture this intelligentsia was producing were worthy of their time and effort. One headline in a 1923 edition of *Der Emes* (*Pravda* or *The Truth*) read "Jewish Kids Can Also Earn a Good Living From Yiddish," suggesting that the intelligentsia had to prove to Jews that Yiddish was a language of social mobility in the modern world.[14]

Because this intelligentsia had very clear ideas about culture that meshed well with other Communist Party and Soviet state goals, it had relative autonomy to produce state-sponsored Soviet Jewish culture. In fact, it wasn't until the 1930s that translations became the foundation of Soviet Jewish culture, and even then, never to the extent of other ethnic minorities' cultures. Until 1928, Soviet Yiddish culture was produced primarily in establishments dedicated exclusively to Jewish culture. In the 1920s, the production of Soviet Jewish culture was primarily a Jewish affair.

It was this very autonomy, this sense of empowerment of ethnic intelligentsias, that at times raised the fear of nationalism among some members of the Communist Party, fears that went back to turn-of-the-century battles between Lenin and the Bund. Although Lenin and Stalin may have been in favor of developing the Soviet Union's ethnic minorities, many Party leaders thought such active participation in nation building contained the seeds of nationalism that undermined the goal of working class internationalism. Equality of condition for Soviet cultures rather than equality of opportunity was working against the historical processes on which Marxism was based, historical processes that were in fact leading to cultural assimilation. The Communist leadership, including many Jews among them, felt conflicted about the dual tasks of fostering proletarian collective identity and universal socialism while encouraging the creation of Soviet national identities.

Mordechai Altshuler has framed the particular problem of the relationship between Yiddish and Russian in the 1920s as a balancing act among members of the Soviet Yiddish intelligentsia: the historic desire of many Jewish socialists to become part of Russian culture, and the romantic desire for Yiddish populist nationalism and a new national culture. He situates this group of people "between nationalism and socialism," associating the first with Yiddish and the second with Russian.[15] Avrom Merezhin, one of the leading Jewish Communists and members of the intelligentsia, put it best in saying that the *"Evsektsiia* has fought against both deviations of Russification and of Yiddishism," of cultural imperialism on the one hand, and Jewish nationalism on the other.[16] The intelligentsia was charged with defining what that in-between space would look like.

IF YOU BUILD IT: HOW THE SOVIET STATE AND
THE ETHNIC INTELLIGENTSIAS CREATED CULTURE

When the Soviets began creating a government, one of the first departments they established was the Commissariat of Nationalities, headed by the Bolsheviks' leading expert on nationalities, Stalin. The Commissariat's function was to encourage national groups that had been oppressed by the tsarist state to support the Soviet state in its battle for life and death. Within the bureaucracy of Russia's Commissariat of Nationalities, each national minority had its own division that was staffed by a member of the minority's intelligentsia.[17] As new republics were brought into the Soviet sphere, each one had its own network of institutions for its own national minorities. Ukrainian Communists, for example, were given some sense of cultural autonomy in the hopes that they would help keep Ukraine in the Soviet Union. With Jews, the people without any particular territory, this policy proved to be quite successful. During the Russian Civil War (1918–21), most Jews in the embattled empire supported the Soviet's Red Army over any of its adversaries, both because of positive gestures the Soviets made and also because the wave of violent pogroms during the War was attributed to the White Army and to roving bands of Ukrainian militias. (With other ethnic groups, like some in Central Asia, Soviet rule proved a much harder sell.) A Jewish commissariat was formed in January 1918, although it only existed for one year before its responsibilities were divided into numerous bureaucracies. There were Jewish subdivisions, divisions, or units in most commissariats in the new state, with the hope that within each division, someone would make sure both that Jewish issues were being addressed and that the policies implemented by a given division were properly brought to the Jewish population. In many cases, this dual role meant that the Jewish representative in a given commissariat was the one setting policies directed at Jews.

As for the Communist Party, as opposed to the Soviet state, each Soviet republic established nation-specific sections (*sektsii*) to better coordinate Bolshevik policy with more regional and language-specific Party work. The national sections, such as the *Evsektsiia*, were included in the Agitation and Propaganda Division (*Agitprop*). As these new nation-specific forms of power were established, members of national intelligentsias were expected to fill the new positions.

The Soviet and Party bureaucracies were divided into a seemingly tight hierarchy of central, republic, regional, city, and local committees that all reported up the chain of command and took orders down the chain. In addition to the geographic hierarchies, each nationality had its own chain of command. Hersh Smolar describes, in almost comic detail, the many committees, subcommittees, and sub-sub committees that he belonged to when he was a young member of the Soviet Yiddish intelligentsia in Kiev in 1921–2. He also reminds the reader that there were not only separate hierarchies based on ethnicity and geographic reach, but also based on constituency. Smolar, who was in his teens when he moved from Poland to the Soviet Union in 1921, worked primarily for the Jewish sections of Communist Youth Leagues (*Komsomol*), a kind of Communist Party training wheels before a Soviet citizen became a full (adult) Communist Party member. There were other organizations for women, peasants, and other social groups.[18] These overlapping hierarchies often created conflicts over policy and authority. For example, did the *Evsektsiia* of the Ukrainian Communist Party report to the Ukrainian Central Committee of the Communist Party – giving the Ukrainian Jewish activists quite a bit of control over Jewish culture in Ukraine – or to the Central Bureau of the *Evsektsiia* in Moscow, which would imply responding to Jewish activists in Moscow? In the Jews' case, there was no central geographic area, which made this tension, among members of the Soviet Yiddish intelligentsia in Moscow, Kiev, Kharkov, and Minsk, more visible.

Georgians, Jews, and Ukrainians already had well-developed socialist or socialist-leaning political and cultural leaders that could be brought into state and Party institutions. For some ethnic groups, however, the Soviet government actually had to create an intelligentsia to serve the dual role of state functionary and national leader when one did not exist. Some ethnic groups in Siberia in fact had to have whole bodies of literature, newspapers, publishing houses, and even languages created for them.[19] In this way, through the 1920s and into the 1930s, the Soviet state took its charge to create Soviet ethnic cultures to its logical conclusion.

The Commissariat of Nationalities was closed down in 1924 at the height of the period in Soviet history known as the New Economic Policy (NEP). Inaugurated in 1921, NEP involved dismantling the state-monopolized economy established during the war, known as War Communism, in favor of a mixed capitalist system meant to spur production, personal consumption, and small-scale private trade. Politically, it was a period of debate that led to the ousting and exile of Trotsky, the head of the Red Army and member of the Politburo, and the rise of Stalin to total power. Stalin's decision to inaugurate the first Five-Year Plan in late 1928, and the subsequent crash industrialization and collectivization of agriculture, usually mark the end of NEP and the period of cultural, and sometimes political, debate.

Culturally, the 1920s were the heyday of the avant-garde among the intellectual classes, and of much imported, especially American, popular culture for mass entertainment.[20] In the early NEP period, the state began to take shape, with the establishment of the Union of Soviet Socialist Republics in 1922, the first Soviet constitution, and the drafting of the Soviets' first international treaty with Germany in 1923. In 1925, Stalin and the Central Committee inaugurated the "socialism-in-one-country" policy, which made state building and not international proletarian revolution the ideological foundation of the Soviet Union. As politically stable as the Soviet Union started to seem, the fact remained that it was an ethnically diverse empire.

Just as the Commissariat of Nationalities was being phased out, the Communist Party made nationalities a higher priority with the policy of "nativization" (*korenizatsiia*). The Twelfth Party Congress in 1923 made fostering national cultures a priority by instituting this policy, which called for, among other things, the expansion or creation of social and cultural institutions that operated in a given ethnic group's language as a way of accelerating the process of bringing new ideas to Soviet ethnic groups. For Soviet Jews, this meant the creation of Jewish courts, Jewish town councils (*soviets*), and Jewish cultural organizations, which operated in Yiddish.

Many people anxious about fostering national identities were concerned that the Party's nativization policy would foster political autonomy and territorial borders based on national identities. Was this a way of stabilizing the new country or was it causing further divisions? The ethnic groups that made the internationalists the most nervous were the Ukrainians and Belorussians, who were the largest and among the most politically developed ethnic groups in the Soviet Union. By the late 1920s, many of those involved in Ukrainian and Belorussian nativization were being accused of "national deviations" as the fears of nationalism became more palpable. These fears led to bureaucratic and institutional restructuring that eliminated the separate sections of the Party designated to each ethnic minority. The *Evsektsiia*, for example, was closed down in 1930.

In the case of Jews and Yiddish, nativization and the Soviet Yiddish intelligentsia were generally less threatening to internationalists, because in 1924, there was no single territory that held a majority of Yiddish-speaking Jews, no place for Jews to develop political autonomy. They shared other Soviet nationalities' land. But many thought that this lack of territorial integrity prevented Jews from being a real nation. Jews began to settle on the land shortly after the revolution when a small number of Jews moved from economically dying small trading towns (*shtetls*) to Jewish agricultural colonies that served two functions. They gave poverty-striken Jews a source of productive labor, and they also created Jewish space that could preserve Yiddish culture in the face of mass urbanization and Russian acculturation. In the mid-1920s, some members of the Soviet Yiddish intelligentsia backed a movement to establish a single, large Jewish agricultural settlement in Crimea with the hopes of creating a territorial basis for their claims to national autonomy. But given the rising fears of nationalism and competing claims over the territory, in 1926, the Crimea project was scuttled, and in its place in 1928, the Central Executive Committee of the Soviet state designated Birobidzhan, a territory in the Far East on the Chinese border, a future Jewish territory. In 1934, the region's status was elevated and it became the official Jewish Autonomous Region, with Yiddish and Russian as its official languages.[21] Even with Birobidzhan, the development of Yiddish-language institutions would have to happen where Jews actually were, within republics whose own majority nationalities were establishing their own cultural and political institutions.[22] Over time, the increased fears of national "deviations" from the path toward international socialism led to the abandonment of some institutions designed for ethnic minorities. Smolar said that the 1930 closure of the *Evsektsiia* was the end of an era of autonomy, when the Soviet Yiddish intelligentsia used the structures established by the government to create a Soviet Jewish culture.[23]

WHO WAS THE SOVIET YIDDISH INTELLIGENTSIA?

Jews were well represented in the Russian Social Democratic Workers' Party (RSDWP), both in its Menshevik branch and, to a lesser extent, in the Bolshevik leadership, with Lev Bronshtein (Trotsky), Grigory Apfelbaum (Zinoviev), and Lev Rosenfeld (Kamenev) among the top leaders of the Communist Party. Despite Jews' presence in Bolshevik leadership positions, the Bolsheviks faced several problems in trying to organize Soviet Jewry. First, even though many leaders were Jewish, numerically, there were not many Jews in the

Bolshevik Party. Most socialist Jews opted for Menshevism, Bundism, or any
of the other varieties of Jewish socialism. The second problem was that in the
words of the Yiddish writer Daniel Charny, in 1918, "there still was no sign
of a *Jewish* Bolshevism."[24] While most Jewish socialists organized the Jewish
population in Yiddish, Bolshevik Jews like Trotsky, Zinoviev, and Kamenev,
were more Russified, and like Stalin, believed that the path to political emancipation was through the assimilation of Jews into broader Russian culture.
They did not speak to a specifically Jewish audience. These Jews were not
interested in fostering a particularly Jewish socialist culture and would never
have formed the backbone of a Soviet Yiddish intelligentsia, because they had
no desire to do so.[25] As the Soviet state consolidated its power and took an
intolerant attitude to competing forms of political power, Jewish socialist organizations like the Bund were shut down and incorporated into the Communist
Party. This new infusion of Jewish socialist talent brought Bundist cultural
politics to Soviet Jewish policy and formed the basis of the Soviet Yiddish
intelligentsia.

This new expansion of the Party lists also brought with it suspicions that former Bundists and even some socialist Zionists entered the Party out of political
opportunism. Such suspicions lingered throughout the Jewish culture-building
period; by the 1930s, a person's pre-revolutionary membership in a Jewish political party could be harmful to a continued career as a Communist activist. Jews,
like other members of Soviet ethnic intelligentsias with a pre-revolutionary
political past, had to live with the suspicion of a tainted political biography.

Many different kinds of people became involved in building Soviet Jewish
culture, and yet, quantitatively, there were never very many people involved
in the Soviet Yiddish intelligentsia. There were so few that most members
of the intelligentsia served many roles simultaneously – members of commissariat sub-committees, editors of Party newspapers, and teachers in schools.
In the early years of Soviet rule, many of the important figures of Eastern
European Yiddish culture were involved in building the Soviet state's Yiddish
cultural apparatus. The literary critic, Shmuel Niger, wrote and edited Soviet journals, and his brother Daniel Charny founded the Moscow Circle of
Yiddish Writers and Artists, one of the most important Yiddish literary groups
in the world in the early 1920s. For one year Charny even edited the central
Communist Party newspaper. David Hofshteyn, Perets Markish, Leyb Kvitko,
and other well-known Yiddish writers wrote, edited, and translated for Soviet
Yiddish publications until many of them temporarily left the country in 1921.
The most significant group of Soviet Jewish activists, the group that served as
the basis of the Soviet Yiddish intelligentsia, came from Jewish socialist parties,
most importantly the Bund and the United Ones *(Fareynikte)*, a union of several
socialist parties in Ukraine.[26]

There were many motivations for taking part in culture building, but all were somehow motivated by the desire to create a secular Yiddish culture and, through it, a new kind of Jewish identity. At the same time, given the historic divisions among these Jews (Bundists and socialist Zionists rarely agreed on anything), it is no surprise that there was little consensus on what the Jewish future would or should look like. Would Jews just resurrect Bundist ideology under the mask of the *Evsektsiia*? Would Yiddish be used solely as a means to the end of making Jews into good Soviet citizens? And who would have power over the Soviet Yiddish intelligentsia, activists in Moscow who were far removed from most Yiddish-speaking Jews, or those in Kiev, Minsk, and other more "Jewish" cities who were on the frontlines?

It is difficult to draw a composite sketch of such a diverse group of people, but Soviet activists were obsessed with the practice of drawing composite sketches of their own collective identity. At major conferences, organizers circulated petitions asking the delegates to answer a series of questions – name, age, sex, current and former Party affiliation, level of education, languages spoken, parents' occupations, place of birth, and so forth. The categories on these surveys changed across disciplines and over time, so to provide a composite of these composites is not an especially useful exercise. The one statistic I will provide, from one particular conference, deals with the question of language. At the Fourth All-Russian conference of *Evsektsiia* in fall 1922, more than 80 percent of the delegates attending had been members of either the Bund (60 percent) or the *Fareynikte* (21 percent), and currently, most were politically "unaffiliated," meaning they were not card-carrying members of the Communist Party. When responding to the question, "What languages do you know?" more than half of the delegates said they knew two languages, which generally meant Russian and Yiddish. Those who said they only knew one language listed Yiddish. The report provided the following statistics:

> Delegates who know only one language: 5.6% (8 delegates)
> Delegates who know only two languages: 54.5% (43 delegates)
> Delegates who know three or more languages: 23.6% (34 delegates)
> Delegates who did not respond: 6.4% (9 delegates)[27]

Most members were multilingual and operated in a multilingual universe, perhaps speaking Yiddish with parents and at Soviet Jewish cultural conferences like these, Russian with non-Jews, and a combination of the two with other members of the Soviet Yiddish intelligentsia. By the late 1920s, after nativization had begun to take effect, the Ukrainian Soviet Yiddish intelligentsia increasingly learned and spoke Ukrainian in official contexts and the Belorussian Yiddish intelligentsia, Belorussian. The Soviet Yiddish intelligentsia came primarily from more traditional Jewish, and therefore Yiddish-speaking, backgrounds, unlike many Jews active in Russian-language Soviet culture who were already a generation removed from traditional Jewish culture.

Politically and culturally, there was little consensus on what the role of the Soviet Yiddish intelligentsia was. Smolar broke the intelligentsia down into two political camps – the "autonomists" who saw the intelligentsia's mission as developing an independent Soviet Yiddish culture, and the "assimilationists" who saw the use of Yiddish as a means to the end of assimilating Jews into Soviet Russian culture. What the two groups agreed upon was the need and the desire for Yiddish culture in the Soviet Union.[28]

A SOVIET YIDDISH TRIUMVIRATE

Esther (1880–1943), the pseudonym and socialist persona of Malka Frumkina, was one of the key figures in pre-revolutionary socialist Yiddish activism and in the Soviet Yiddish intelligentsia.[29] Esther, born Malka Lifshitz, grew up in a wealthy merchant family in Minsk. Her grandfather was a rabbi, her father though received both a secular and a traditional Jewish education. Esther was fluent in Russian, Yiddish, and Hebrew, and knew three other languages. Her first husband, Boris Frumkin, died just a few years after their marriage, and during World War I, she was briefly married to a rabbi.[30]

Esther was a woman in a man's world. Although Bundism had many women in its local leadership, in the Soviet Yiddish intelligentsia there were very few women. The absence of women in Soviet Yiddish culture is ironic, since historically, while Hebrew had been the domain of educated Jewish men, Yiddish, the Jews' jargon, had been seen as the language of women and the lower classes. Esther got her socialist start as a women's "circle activist" in the early days when Jewish men and women were organized separately in order to maintain the sexual modesty rules of traditional Judaism.[31] She had been one of the most active and high profile members of the Bund, and had also been one of the most vocal Yiddishists calling for Yiddish, as opposed to Hebrew, Russian, or any combination thereof, to be the Jews' national language. Her vision of the relationship between Yiddish and Jewish national development was complicated by her mutual political support of socialism and Yiddish-language Jewish nationalism. Her nationalist self saw Yiddish as the embodiment of the Jewish people, while her socialist self did not believe in the concept of a *klal yisrael* (the Jewish people), but rather worked in and for Yiddish on behalf of the Jewish working classes. "The Jewish worker created national values, and a national culture, without making it a special objective, and the education that he will provide for his children will also be national, although that will not be the primary objective. The reason is that the Jewish worker is deeply national."[32] Frumkina desperately tried to balance the national with the socialist by emphasizing the "Jewish folk masses" and the worker's relationship to the national. She was trying to fuse two discourses: the dominant discourse of nationalism and its argument to elevate Yiddish; and the dominant discourse of socialism to break down national barriers and heighten class consciousness. This tension between the Romantic nationalist relationship to language and a more utilitarian and class-based one was endemic to Soviet ethnic intelligentsias. They had to be nationalists and socialists, Romantics and utilitarians, at the same time.

At the time of the Bund's consolidation with the Communist Party in 1921, Frumkina became one of the most powerful members of the Soviet Yiddish intelligentsia in her many roles – member of the Central Bureau of the *Evsektsiia* in Moscow, rector of the Communist University for National Minorities, and the leading translator of Lenin into Yiddish. Among former Bundists, she was more involved in Party and state politics than other members of the Soviet Yiddish intelligentsia, who often focused on culture building over political activism. She was the leading expert on establishing "Leninist" answers to Jewish questions, and according to some, even the head of the Central Bureau and former Bundist, Alexander Chemerinsky, came to her with ideological problems.[33] She translated Jewish issues and problems into socialist idiom.

If Frumkina was the ideological visionary of Soviet Yiddishism, the literary critic and newspaper editor, Moshe Litvakov (1875?–1937), served as the de facto commissar of Soviet Yiddish culture.[34] Litvakov was born to a self-described "poor family" in either 1875 or 1879, making him the same generation as Frumkina, the older generation of the Soviet Yiddish intelligentsia. His father was a *melamed*, a teacher in a traditional Jewish elementary school, from Lithuania. Moshe Litvakov received a traditional male Jewish education and then became an extern, an affiliated but not enrolled student, at a Kiev high school (*gimnazium*). He then lived in Paris from 1902 to 1905 studying at the Sorbonne. Before he left for Paris, Litvakov was active in the Zionist Ahad Ha'am's cultural nationalist group, and later, in labor Zionist groups. Litvakov helped found the Zionist Socialist party, and came back to Russia in 1905 during the Russian Revolution. He edited socialist Zionist journals, and wrote for the influential Russian-language daily newspaper *Kiev Idea (Kievskaia mysl')*. After the February Revolution of 1917, Litvakov helped found the United Ones party and edited its daily newspaper, *New Times (Di Naye Tsayt)*. He was also a co-founder of The Culture League (*Kultur Lige*), an organization in Ukraine that established an infrastructure for secular Jewish cultural development.[35] In 1918, he published his first book of literary criticism, *In a State of Discontent (In Umru)*, which examined the modernist literary and cultural trends that had begun to sweep Eastern European Jewish culture in the second decade of the twentieth century.

Litvakov joined the Communist Party in early 1921, shortly after moving from Kiev to Moscow, where he remained until his arrest and murder during the Great Purges. He is first mentioned in official state records in Moscow as the representative of the Jewish Section of the Commissariat of Enlightenment (*Narkompros*), when he gave a lecture to the commissariat's staff on the Jewish Chamber Theater of Moscow. His entry into the Soviet bureaucracy was, therefore, a direct result of his role as a literary and theater critic.[36] His experience as a newspaper editor, and his new Party card made him the perfect person to become the editor of *Der Emes*, a role that helped vault him into the position of Soviet Yiddish cultural commissar.[37] He also served as editor-in-chief of the School and Book Publishing House, the primary site of Yiddish cultural production in Moscow during NEP. Litvakov was also the military censor of Yiddish-language materials and, in 1923, was named the Jewish censor for the Main Administration for Literature (*Glavlit*), the newly established state censorship agency.[38] His titles continued to multiply: instructor at the Pedagogy Institute in Moscow, member of the Institute for Jewish Culture at the Ukrainian Academy of Sciences, and so on.[39]

He and Frumkina exemplify the first generation of the Soviet Yiddish intelligentsia. Reared in traditional Jewish, usually Yiddish-speaking, environments, they became socialist, sometimes Zionist, activists in the pre-revolutionary period, and were then offered positions of power as the Soviet state demanded the creation of a Soviet Yiddish intelligentsia.[40]

The writers who made up the backbone of the Soviet Yiddish intelligentsia were a diverse and complicated group, and Chapters Five and Six are devoted to them. But one other political activist must be mentioned as a linchpin in the intelligentsia. Semen Dimanshteyn (1888–1937), the rabbi-turned-Communist, was the only longtime Bolshevik who was also active in the Soviet Yiddish intelligentsia. He was born in a Belorussian shtetl and received a traditional Jewish education in Belz, Slobodke, and Lubavitch, and went on to be ordained as a rabbi. In 1904, he joined the Bolshevik faction of the Russian Social Democratic Workers' Party and was forced to flee to Paris for his political activities. He skipped the Bundist labor Zionist stage of Jewish socialism that forged the cultural and political ideology that came to define the Soviet Yiddish intelligentsia. Instead, he began working for the Russian Social Democratic Party, translating its materials into Hebrew and Yiddish. He was arrested, sent to Siberia, fled to Europe during World War I, and returned to Russia in May 1917, just in time for the October Revolution. Lenin named him Jewish Commissar in January 1918, when Dimanshteyn was just thirty. He became the first editor of *Der Emes*, the job that Litvakov took over in 1921.

Bolshevism had taken such little interest in particularly Jewish affairs, that Dimanshteyn complained that he had to bring on people to do "Jewish work" who didn't speak any Yiddish, because there wasn't anyone else who could do it. He trained writers in proper Yiddish and worked tirelessly to get non-Communists to support his project of Yiddish cultural and political development *within* the Soviet and Communist state. His work laid the ground for the Soviet Yiddish intelligentsia. He once wrote: "Several eminent comrades accused me of wanting to create a new Bund in the Party, when I first outlined the form of the [Jewish] sections."[41] His political biography shows that such a comment couldn't have been further from the truth.

Dimanshteyn was an outsider among the Soviet Yiddish intelligentsia because of his past entirely within Russian socialism. If the intelligentsia's role was to serve as cultural translator between the new state and Soviet Jewry, Dimanshteyn's role was as intermediary between the intelligentsia and the Communist Party. As soon as former Bundists moved into positions of power, Dimanshteyn moved up the hierarchy within the Party's nationalities and cultural bureaucracies and phased out his career in specifically Yiddish cultural work. In the 1930s, he brought all of his roles together when he served as the head of the Society for Settling Jews on the Land (*Gezerd*) while also serving as a member of the Communist Academy, director of the Nationalities Institute of the Central Executive Committee, and editor of the Russian publication, *Revolution and Nationalities (Revolutsiia i natsional'nost')*. One might say that he worked with, rather than was a member of, the Soviet Yiddish intelligentsia, once such an intelligentsia came into existence in the 1920s.

These representatives of the intelligentsia – former rabbis, Zionists, and socialist nationalists – were the Soviet Union's version of the Jewish native elite, the ones invested by an imperial power to remake Jews and Jewish culture. And as some postcolonial historians have shown, although they got their power from the imperial state, they brought their own cultural, political, and ideological agenda with them, with Yiddish as the centerpiece of their modern Jewish revolution.

Ideology and Jewish Language Politics

How Yiddish Became the National Language of Soviet Jewry

Since we [Jews] speak a distinct language, we are obligated to ensure that the Jewish masses have an opportunity to satisfy all their spiritual needs in that language. We are not fanatics of the Yiddish language. For us, it is not a holy Yiddish [*yidish ha-kodesh*] as it is for our Jewish nationalists. No, the language for its own sake is not important to us. Our task is to bring together the workers of all nationalities and to unite them in one international family.

– Semen Dimanshteyn, 1919[1]

God speaks Yiddish during the week and Hebrew on the Sabbath.

– Yiddish Proverb

HISTORY OF INTERNAL JEWISH BILINGUALISM

Eastern European Jewish culture has been defined, among other things, by its bilingualism. Since the birth of Ashkenaz as a cultural entity in the Middle Ages, Ashkenazic Jews, those Jews who migrated from Germany to Eastern Europe, have created their culture in at least two Jewish languages – Yiddish and what was called *the holy language (loshn koydesh)*, which incorporated Hebrew and Aramaic. The holy language was the language of the Jewish textual canon; from the Bible to rabbinic literature, it was the language that bound international Jewish communities together and defined the corpus of texts that lay at the heart of Jewish culture. Yiddish was one of many vernacular Jewish languages. Like Aramaic, a Jewish vernacular from the ancient Babylonian exile, and like Ladino within Sephardic Jewish communities, Yiddish was formed out of various component languages: the holy language and, more dominant, the vernacular language of the surrounding people, in this case Middle High German. As Jews moved from the Mediterranean into the Rhine Valley, they began speaking a particular Judeo-German, known at various times as *Taytsh* (German) or *loshn ashkenaz* (the language of Germany), reflecting the early cultural assumption that Jews were not speaking a language distinct from the German spoken around them. It combined aspects of the holy tongue, the Latin root languages spoken earlier, and German. Jews in different parts of Europe began to speak different dialects of this new language influenced by other neighboring languages. Eventually, once Jews lived in a territory where German was not the co-territorial language, the name *yidish*, meaning Jewish or a separate language spoken by Jews, came to be used.[2] As Jews moved into Eastern Europe, a Slavic component was added to the language, further complicating its linguistic structure.

For centuries, the vernacular Yiddish and the non-vernacular holy tongue worked in tandem, each occupying specific social fields and different positions in a cultural hierarchy. Max Weinreich refers to this phenomenon of Jewish culture as "internal Jewish bilingualism," to distinguish it from the near ubiquitous bilingualisms of other cultures that had one language peculiar to a defined ethnic group and one other language used for communication with a larger religious or political community.[3] Jews had two languages that only Jews used, not to mention the other languages of larger co-territorial people or other political powers.

Yiddish and the holy tongue interacted with one another in a hierarchical way – holy tongue as the language with high status, Yiddish as the lowly vernacular. One traditional explanation for the difference between the two languages is that Yiddish was the oral language of Ashkenazic Jews while the holy tongue was the literary language of written culture. This was, in fact, how the Jews who experienced this linguistic hierarchy thought of each language's role.[4] But this overly simplified hierarchy does not reflect the complex reality of the existence of Yiddish literature going back to the sixteenth century, or the use of spoken holy tongue in Jewish liturgy. Others have attempted to see the hierarchical polarization between Yiddish and the holy tongue as one between secular and religious uses. Yiddish was the language of mundane interactions, while the holy tongue was reserved for communing with God. (That's where the Yiddish proverb about the languages God speaks comes from.) Like the vernacular/written dichotomy, the obvious division between the holy language and Yiddish was part of the ideology of languages in which Ashkenazic culture operated. Seventeenth-century Jews did see the holy tongue as a holy language (perhaps this restates the obvious) and Yiddish as a day-to-day language. But this ideological hierarchy is broken down by examining the actual uses of Yiddish in women's religious liturgy and as a language of translation for a wide variety of religious texts, and the holy tongue's role in many forms of day-to-day contractual relations.[5] As more research on the role of language in Jewish culture has shown, the reality of the language hierarchy was more complex than Ashkenazic culture presumed it to be.

What holds for all of these dichotomies is that the holy tongue was reserved for high status language uses: men's prayer, rabbinic correspondence, poetry,

legalistic contracts; Yiddish was assigned low status uses: women's personal petitions, popular fiction, and day-to-day conversation. Weinreich shows that even
religious works written in Yiddish were constantly disparaged.[6] Joshua Fishman
explains the complex hierarchy by pointing out that "Yiddish did enter perva-
sively into the sacred, but it never existed in that domain as a fully free agent,
never as the sole medium of that domain in its most hallowed and most textual
realizations."[7] One common metaphor for this diglossia is that of a handmaiden
to her queen, denoting the two languages' hierarchical relationship. The image
of the handmaiden and the queen also suggests a class division – Yiddish as
handmaiden is serving the exalted queen, the holy tongue.

It is true that early Yiddish literature was reserved for particularly low-status
literary genres within Jewish textual culture: popular literature and liturgical
texts intended for use by Jewish women. In much sixteenth-century Yiddish
literature, authors prefaced their texts by defining the intended audience as
"women or men who are like women," in their mutual ignorance of the proper
literary language, the holy tongue.[8] Early Yiddish versions of canonical Jewish
texts such as the classic *Tsenah u-re'enah*, a series of Biblical *midrashim* (interpretive stories) written in Yiddish that were intended as a women's substitute for
the men's Hebrew-language Torah, were intended to edify Jewish women and,
of course, "men who were like women."[9] There was also a belief that those
who wrote Yiddish literature were somehow feminized by the act, which is
why many Yiddish texts were written under pseudonyms, often using female
names.[10] Until the early nineteenth century, the association of Yiddish with the
feminine, with popular culture, and with the uneducated (and therefore low
class) was a defining feature of Ashkenazic Jewish culture. The normative use
of written Yiddish was, in Fishman's words, for *traditional utilitarian* purposes,
in which Yiddish was only to be utilized in print for various moralistic and
Jewish legal (*halachic*) educational purposes,[11] particularly directed at women,
the uneducated, and children. Until the nineteenth century, Yiddish authors
never pressed for a place of honor within the Jewish cultural hierarchy, nor did
they challenge the idea that Yiddish was used in text for utilitarian purposes.

YIDDISH AS MORE THAN A MEANS TO AN END: MAKING YIDDISH A NATIONAL LANGUAGE

Two movements changed the linguistic history of Ashkenazic Jewish culture –
the Jewish enlightenment movement known as the *Haskalah* and nationalism,
which influenced Jewish ideologies of the nineteenth century. The enlightenment and secularization of European society brought external pressures on Jews
to modernize and become part of the dominant society and culture. For many
Jewish enlighteners, this meant becoming part of the new nations forming in

the late eighteenth and nineteenth centuries and speaking the language of these new nations. The rise of the nation-state and the concept of citizenship and citizens' rights in France and later in Germany encouraged Jews toward the co-territorial language and away from Yiddish.[12] The pressures that pushed Jews away from Yiddish and toward German, French, and later, Polish and Russian were both internal to Jews' own modernization and external from civil society, which asked Jews to shed some of their differences if they wanted to become part of the nation. In the words of Osip Rabinowitch, who published in the first Russian Jewish weekly, *Dawn* (Rassvet), "The Russian language must serve as the primary force animating the masses, because, apart from divine providence, language is the constitutive factor of humanity."[13]

For centuries, the traditional hierarchy between the holy tongue and Yiddish remained unchallenged. But by the mid-nineteenth century, Eastern European Jewish enlighteners began directing their linguistic efforts "not at ending the diglossia, but at replacing the two component languages: the state language or a European language for Yiddish, and biblical Hebrew for *loshn koydesh*."[14] Indeed, this had been the goal for some German Jewish enlighteners who invested much time and energy into creating a German-language Jewish culture and in preserving and elevating Hebrew as a language of Jewish history and religion. The movement for creating a modern Hebrew culture took off once the *Haskalah* moved to Eastern Europe, where, unlike the more modernized enlighteners in Germany, most male Jews in Eastern Europe still used the holy tongue in daily prayer and study. As Hebrew, Russian, German, and Polish gained prestige, Yiddish lost it.

What's more, as the space in Jewish culture for Yiddish began to disappear, those who chose to write in it became even more self-conscious about using it. One of the earliest enlightenment practitioners of Yiddish, Mendel Lefin of Satanov, began translating the Bible into Yiddish as part of his project of bringing the German *Haskalah* and modern Jewish culture to Eastern European Jews. A.B. Gottlober, a disciple of Lefin, said: "Finding no other way to be useful to his brethren in his country except to speak to them in their language [Yiddish]...he girded up his loins to translate the books into the people's language."[15] In other words, enlighteners used Yiddish for utility's sake – to reach the relatively uneducated masses.

It was also a useful medium for transmitting new ideas, because other new Jewish ideologies, especially Hasidism, were using Yiddish precisely because of its populist connections. Hasids, and among them most famously Nachman of Bratslav, saw the use of Yiddish as a populist move to "reach the Jewish masses," and used Yiddish's low status to create a charismatic Jewish culture in opposition to traditional holy-tongue-based rabbinic culture. Despite the need to transmit modern ideas in Yiddish – if only to stave off the mass movement of

Hasidism – those *maskilim* who chose to write in Yiddish were raised on the anti-Yiddish ideology of the *Haskalah*, and believed that Yiddish was not equal to the task of disseminating modern ideologies; but, they saw no choice if they were to combat the populist influences of the Hasidim, who seemed to use Yiddish quite effectively.[16]

Most scholars agree that the beginning of the changing relationship between the Jewish intellectual élite and the Yiddish language occurred with the Yiddish writer S.Y. Abramovich, more widely known by one of his literary characters, *Mendele*. Later Yiddish writers named him the "grandfather of modern Yiddish literature," in a retrospective attempt to create a Yiddish literary tradition. Like other *maskilim* working in Yiddish, Abramovich began his career by writing in Hebrew. (He returned to Hebrew again, later in life, and is also considered the founder of modern Hebrew literature.[17]) For most *maskilim*, according to Weinreich, "it seemed that the belletristic form was merely a means of better conveying their ideas to the simple readers."[18] Abramovich too was angst-ridden about his decision to write in Yiddish. Although he wrote numerous stories and novellas in Yiddish, he believed that using Yiddish was a temporary concession to the Eastern European Jewish cultural reality. In theory, he wrote quality literature to engage and educate the masses. In fact, he was the seminal author who made writing in Yiddish socially and culturally acceptable.

Throughout his career, Abramovich felt compelled to justify to his colleagues his choice to write in Yiddish. Not only did his missives to other writers deal with the language politics in which he was embroiled, but also the literary strategies within his fictional work developed as a way to navigate more effectively the distance between his position as an élite Jewish intellectual and his intention of "talking" with the Jewish masses. To accomplish this, he invented the interlocutor *Mendele*, neither a pseudonym nor merely a character of his stories. Rather, *Mendele* was a fictionalized mediator who bridged the political distance between Abramovich's *maskilic* self and the Jewish everyman whom he hoped to engage.[19]

Modern Yiddish literature developed alongside other forms of Yiddish print culture that emerged out of earlier *maskilic* forms. In the late eighteenth and early nineteenth century, *maskilim* published in Hebrew throughout central and Eastern Europe. Hebrew became the textual lingua franca for enlightened Jews living throughout the Hapsburg and Russian empires, and the Hebrew journal became a meeting place for the exchange of ideas. For those *maskilic* practitioners of Yiddish in the Russian Empire, like Mendel Lefin and his followers – Shloyme Etinger (1801–56), Avrom Gottlober (1811–99), Yisroel Aksenfeld (1787–1866), or Yitzhak Ber Levinson (1788–1860) – publishing in Yiddish was nearly impossible. Under Tsar Nicholas I, who reigned from 1825 to 1855, only two Jewish printers, in Vilna and in Zhitomir, were allowed to operate, and neither published many *maskilic* Yiddish texts.[20] Aksenfeld had to wait until 1862 to publish his Yiddish works, and even then, he did so in Germany. Etinger's play *Serkele* was not published in his lifetime.[21] It was not until after the tsar's death in 1855 – when Russian social and political reforms opened up the publishing industry and loosened state rules regulating Jewish life – that a Jewish intelligentsia society emerged around developing modern Jewish print cultures in Russian, Polish, Hebrew, and Yiddish. It is at this time that the first Jewish newspapers appeared within the Russian Empire.[22]

The first Eastern European Yiddish newspaper, *The Herald (Kol Mevaser)*, came out in 1862 in Odessa. Not coincidentally, it was in this paper that Abramovich first published his Yiddish stories in serial form. The newspaper was a supplement to the first Russian Empire Hebrew-language newspaper, *The Advocate (Ha-melits)*, published by Alexander Tsederbaum, who intended to broaden his readership and raise necessary funds by publishing a Yiddish supplement. He initially published the newspaper for purely *maskilic* reasons: "We know quite well that the enlightened men of the present day cry that the people should be weaned away from speaking Yiddish and be accustomed to speak the language of the country. Perhaps they also are not completely unjustified, for in the country where one lives one ought to understand the language. But in what language should one speak to the common people so that they may learn what is necessary for every man, if they still understand nothing other than Yiddish?"[23] But Tsederbaum also stated, "Here you have a newspaper printed in such a simple language that every Jew – even women – can actually read it! From then on this thought would sneak up: Can the Hebrew language with its fine figurative style give sustenance to anybody except those selected few who have mastered it? That's one point. And the other: even when you write Hebrew, you think in Yiddish – wouldn't it be better for you to write the way you think?"[24] Although Yiddish still played a subordinate role to Hebrew, Tsederbaum's words show that the publication of *Kol Mevaser* marked a transition from a *maskilic*, utilitarian to a proto-national use of Yiddish. By adding the second point, "Wouldn't it be better to write the way you think," Tsederbaum charted a future for Yiddish print culture. He pulled Yiddish away from its focus on the needs of the audience and turned it back to the desires and needs of the author. One could write in Yiddish for one's self, and not for the Jewish masses. With this idea, Tsederbaum suggested that Yiddish could be both a vernacular and a print language, and that Yiddish literature could meet the needs of both the audience and the writer. Yiddish was both a means and an end.

After newspapers and modern literature, the next step in the development of the national use of Yiddish was the birth of Yiddish philology as a field of study. Jewish scholars had been studying Hebrew syntax, grammar, and morphology since the Spanish Middle Ages; *maskilim* had also been interested in

Hebrew linguistics. There was no such interest in Yiddish, because until the late nineteenth century, it was not seen as a language in need of such study.

This was the case for many languages of the Russian empire that did not develop national identities until the nineteenth century. Nationalist interest in the Ukrainian language began, for example, in the first half of the nineteenth century as is evidenced by the grammars, lexicons, and other texts about Ukrainian that began appearing. In the 1840s, Taras Shevchenko, the bard of modern Ukrainian culture, began publishing poetry that served as a nascent canon of modern Ukrainian literature in the face of cultural Russification on the part of the tsars.[25] And the sense of Ukrainian as an oppressed language, culture, and nationality only increased after the tsarist government banned printing in the Ukrainian language in 1863, just as Yiddish was developing a print culture in the Russian empire.[26] Other national groups have similar histories. According to Soviet historian Sh. Chkhetiia, "In Georgia up to the 1860s,...not more than 160 to 180 books had been printed in the Georgian language; not one permanent Georgian theater existed...[and] only three Georgian printing presses had existed."[27] Nineteenth-century nationalism, especially its populist and Romantic forms, helped change the status of many of these languages and cultures.

For Yiddish, the national turn occurred with *Kol Mevaser* and Yehoshua Lifshits, whom many term the first "Yiddishist," the man credited with encouraging Abramovich to write in Yiddish.[28] At the same time that Abramovich wrote his first fictional works and *Kol Mevaser* created a Yiddish periodical culture, Lifshits began work on a Russian-Yiddish dictionary.[29] Like earlier Yiddish *maskilim*, he wanted to bring European culture to the Jewish public, and Yiddish, he thought, was the perfect medium. Unlike other *maskilim*, however, he saw no inherent flaw in the language itself, but thought that with time and work, it would become a language of European culture.[30] By compiling a dictionary with a finite number of words Lifshits set Yiddish on the path to becoming a standardized, modern language, and, like Tsederbaum, charted a future for Yiddish.

The 1890s were a turning point in the history of Jewish-language politics for many reasons. In literature, Sholem Aleichem, the well-known Yiddish writer who had given Abramovich the title "grandfather of Yiddish literature," had already published his *Popular Jewish Library* (*Yidishe Folksbibliotek*), which began to lay the groundwork of a Yiddish literary canon. In Warsaw, the young upstart Y.L. Perets began writing in Yiddish out of a Romantic urge to express the writer's inner creativity. Yiddish was becoming a language of self-expression rather than a language of didacticism, a literary end rather than a medium of ideology. More Yiddish periodicals were published, and the first secular Yiddish school opened in 1898 near Minsk.[31]

Underlying all of these cultural changes was the breakdown of the political and cultural strategy of the *Haskalah,* which called for Jewish integration into surrounding societies, and the rise of radical political ideologies throughout Eastern Europe. Marxist socialism, anarchism, populism, and other ideological movements changed the face of Eastern European politics since the 1870s. Jews were among the most involved in propelling these new ideas. Of the many movements, the Bund was central to the elevation of Yiddish's status. Initially, like other socialist groups, the Bund was made up of Russian-speaking intellectuals who worked with a small segment of the Jewish working classes. In many ways, the Bund's initial relationship to language resembled that of the original *maskilim* – both groups were going to bridge the cultural and political gaps between Jews and others by educating Jews about modern ideologies in the coterritorial language, Russian. By the turn of the century, like early Yiddish *maskilim*, leading Bundists recognized that their theoretical constituency, the Jewish working classes, spoke (and if literate, read) Yiddish, not Russian. The Bund began to carry out political and cultural work in Yiddish in order to make its rather élite movement into a popular one.[32] The 1901 adoption of a platform calling for national and cultural autonomy and the general turn to a more nationally oriented political movement caused the Bund to break with the umbrella Russian Social Democratic Workers' Party in 1903.[33] Once the break with the Russian socialists took place, the Bund had more freedom to tailor its platform to its Jewish audience and to compete with other Jewish socialist and nationalist groups that were working in Yiddish.

The turn toward Jewish nationalism had been happening since the breakdown of the *Haskalah* in the 1870s and 1880s. Bundist and other Jewish socialist movements were informed by Eastern European populism, the turn "to the people" and to the vernacular languages of "the people." At the same time, the turn toward nationalism also spawned Zionism, a Jewish national rejection of the *Haskalah's* enlightened integration into Russian culture, a turn away from Russia toward "the historic Jewish homeland" in Palestine, and eventually, a turn away from the Jews' "language of exile," the mixed jargon known as Yiddish, toward the pure, ancient Jewish tongue, Hebrew.

Despite these pressures, until the first decade of the twentieth century, Eastern European Jewish culture as a whole was still bilingual. Modern language politics had done much to erode the symbiotic relationship between Hebrew and Yiddish, but had not undermined it totally. At the turn of the century, there were still Zionists who wrote in Yiddish and socialists who worked in Hebrew; most Eastern European Jewish writers wrote in both languages. One decade later, politics and language choice would be completely enmeshed. In the atmosphere of rising political polarization in the Russian empire, and the outbreak of the Revolution of 1905, Jewish politics too became more polarized, and with it

Jewish language politics. Zionist print culture became predominantly Hebraic; Jewish socialist print culture, Yiddishist, and the two only moved further and further apart.

Yiddishism, the movement to make Yiddish the central definer of modern Jewish culture and identity, crystallized as an ideology in 1908, at the Czernowitz Language Conference. Czernowitz in Bukovina, Austria-Hungary, was a turning point in internal Jewish bilingualism, because for the first time, an organized group of Jewish intellectuals declared that Yiddish needed to become a high-status language. The invitation to this momentous language conference sheds light on the sense of history these intellectuals felt.

In the past several decades the Yiddish language has made great progress. Its literature has achieved a level of which no one had imagined it capable. Yiddish newspapers are distributed in hundreds of thousands of copies daily and weekly. Yiddish poets write songs, which are sung by the people; stories, which are read by the people; plays, which the people eagerly flock to see. Every day the language itself becomes more refined and richer.[34]

Its authors then suggested why there was a need for a Yiddish conference:

[Yiddish] continues to lack one thing that older tongues possess. The latter are not permitted to roam about freely and wildly in the linguistic world to attract all sorts of diseases, defects, and perhaps even death. They are guarded as a precious child is guarded. No one, however, pays heed to the Yiddish language. Thousands of Yiddish words are replaced by German, Russian, and English words, which are completely unnecessary. The live rules of the language, which are born and develop with it in the mouth of the people, go unrecorded, and it appears not to possess any such rules. Each person writes it in another way with his own spelling because no standard authoritative Yiddish orthography has thus far been established.[35]

The desire to codify and standardize Yiddish was needed for both ideological and practical reasons. As Joshua Fishman has shown, unless a language has regular and universally agreed upon rules of spelling and grammar, it becomes difficult to use that language in modern contexts.[36] The Czernowitz organizers recognized the weaknesses of a multi-dialect, multi-orthographic Yiddish and wanted to remedy the situation.

These intellectuals wanted to bring status to Yiddish, which they did, and to create an authoritative institution for the development of Yiddish, which they did not. That would not occur until the 1920s. In addition, the conference discussed the types of institutions that would be needed if Yiddish were to compete as a modern language of a modern nation. Yiddish needed newspapers, literature, publishing houses, and schools that would create a linguistic and cultural framework in which to maintain a collective identity in the face of modern, secularizing, linguistically assimilatory pressures.

The biggest battle that took place at the conference was over a resolution to define the relationship between Yiddish and the Jewish people: was Yiddish *a* national language of the Jewish people or *the* national language of the Jewish people? This semantic subtlety summarized the political stakes of the conference. If the conference declared Yiddish *a* national language (one of a number), then the organizers were preserving Jewish bilingualism, albeit on new, national terms. But if Yiddish was *the* national language, that implied no role for Hebrew in the Jewish future, and an end to Jewish bilingualism. Most participants recognized that the original goal of the conference had not been the elimination of Jewish bilingualism, but rather the reevaluation of the hierarchy within that bilingualism. Thus, a majority of the conference voted for the following wording: "Yiddish is a national language of the Jewish people, and we demand complete political and social equality for it in the lands of compact mass settlement by Jews."[37] The author of the more radical proposal to make Yiddish *the* national language of the Jewish people was Esther Frumkina, one of the highest ranking members of the Soviet Yiddish intelligentsia.

The visions of the Czernowitz conference were grand, and invited a response from Hebraists, who held their own "Czernowitzs" in 1909 and 1913. Both Yiddishists and Hebraists rushed to open up schools in their chosen language to create the human resources of the future Jewish nation. In Eastern Europe, the language wars were put on hold during World War I, when Hebrew and Yiddish language publishing was banned in the Russian Empire, and communication across large distances became much more difficult. But the tensions between the two groups and the modern and nationalist pressures toward a single Jewish language exploded once tsarist power imploded.

JEWISH LANGUAGE POLITICS AND THE RUSSIAN REVOLUTIONS

The year 1917 was a long one for Russia. The country overthrew its tsar, experienced two revolutions, and, in 1918, pulled out of a world war. During the February Revolution, the tsarist regime collapsed and in its place the liberalizing provisional government filled the power vacuum. In its relations with Russia's national minorities, such as the Poles, Ukrainians, Armenians, or Jews, the provisional government attempted to dismantle the Russo-centric state cultural apparatus that the tsarist regime had created to help unify the empire.[38] For Jews, this meant dismantling the residency restrictions that had forced Jews to concentrate in the Pale of Settlement and abolishing other special laws relating to Jews. In September 1917, the provisional government also passed the following code: "in their places of permanent residence, laws shall guarantee to national minorities the free use of their native tongues in schools, courts, and organs of self-government, and in their relations with the local organ of the central government."[39] The government was responding to a breakdown in central authority, and hoped that if it appeased ethnic minorities by meeting some of their demands for cultural autonomy, they would in turn support the new state.

Jewish organizations were quick to respond to the new political and cultural opportunities following the February Revolution. In the political arena, Zionists, socialists, and liberals all clamored to be heard among the new chorus of voices calling for the political mobilization of Russia's Jews. Zionists tended to support Hebrew-language culture through the *Tarbut* (culture) organization, Hebrew-language writers groups, and Hebrew publications. In May 1917, Zionists from across Russia called a conference, one of the primary issues of which was the language of instruction in secular Jewish schools throughout the new state. Would it be Hebrew or Yiddish? Invoking the new language of Zionism, which envisioned Jews as a biblically derived "Hebrew nation," rather than a group of diasporic wandering Jews, the conference passed the following resolution: "The language of instruction in all schools of the communities should be Hebrew. This rule does not apply to the instruction of the government language and other languages. The Hebrew language is the official language of all public institutions of the Hebrew nation (*ha-am ha-ivrî*)."[40] Hebrew-language schools, overseen by *Tarbut*, flourished in the rapidly decentralizing former Pale of Settlement.

Jewish socialists had several cultural options. Some socialist political parties, such as the Bund, chose to foster a particularly Jewish workers' culture in the "native language of the Jewish working classes" – Yiddish. Like the Hebrew culture that developed in 1917, socialist Yiddish newspapers, schools, cultural organizations, and writers' groups expanded as wartime state restrictions on culture in Jewish languages were lifted and as socialism emerged from the underground as a legal political movement. Other more Russified Jewish liberals and socialists did not want separate schools for Jews and thought that Jewish children should be taught in Russian.

The basis for the Jewish language wars under the Soviet state had emerged prior to the Bolsheviks' takeover of power in October. Hebraists and Yiddishists were already envisioning secular and monolingual Jewish cultural autonomy, and the provisional government had given its support to "native languages," which in the bilingual Jewish case was still undefined. Given the socialist politics of the new regime, the Yiddishists, who came from primarily socialist political parties dominated by the Bund, should have had state support.[41]

By 1921, the nascent Soviet Yiddish intelligentsia had won the language wars against Hebrew and had elevated Yiddish to the status of *the* language of the Soviet Jewish people. The hard-line activists at Czernowitz saw at least in theory, the realization of their vision — the creation of a modern Jewish culture in Yiddish. Hebrew-language culture continued, almost entirely underground, throughout the Soviet period. In addition, there was an explosion in the number of Jews active in the creation of Russian-language Soviet culture. But Soviet Yiddish culture was marked as *the* Soviet Jewish culture because Yiddish became the native language and national language of Soviet Jewry. In the Soviet Union, Yiddish moved from its supporting role as Hebrew's handmaiden to queen in her own right.[42]

THE LANGUAGE DEBATE IN SOVIET JEWISH SCHOOLS

The initial site of contested Jewish language politics was the nascent Soviet Jewish school system that was established almost immediately after the founding of the Jewish Commissariat (*Evkom*) in 1918. Schools were the central site of these battles since they were the places for inculcating values in the future Jewish nation; all ideological movements focused on schools and youth movements to build a future constituency. Soviet ideology also placed schools at the center of the propagandizing and modernizing project of the new state. For modern nation states, government-run schools were a primary site for inculcating national values and forging a national identity from disparate ethnic and religious groups.[43] In the Soviet case, the state tried to accommodate both missions. To garner support from peripheral ethnic groups, the Soviet state offered conditional cultural autonomy to national minorities through the Commissariat of Nationalities (*Narkomnats*) and officially demoted Russian from the status of an imperial language to one of many national languages and cultures of the new country. Cultural de-Russification was brought to children's education; in the future, children would be taught in their native language. Both Jewish national politics and Soviet educational philosophy made the native language of instruction one of the bases of the new education for ethnic minorities.[44]

The Jewish Commissariat, headed by Semen Dimanshteyn, immediately got to work turning the many competing networks of schools into a Soviet Jewish school system. But lots of questions came up for local teachers, school administrators, and other activists. For example, local Jewish cultural activists in Nizhnii Novgorod requested further information from the Commissariat of Enlightenment about the necessary requirements for a Jewish school to receive state funding. "1. Is the teaching of Hebrew permitted in schools and, if it is, is it a required course for students? 2. Is the teaching of Bible permitted in schools if the goals are not religious, but are for moral upbringing? 3. Are Jewish schools acceptable for children of other nationalities on a general basis, or do they only serve children of the Jewish nationality?"[45] These questions show that creating a school system was a process of reenvisioning Jewish identity. Were

Jews a religious or a national group? Was the Bible a religious text or a moral text? Were Jewish schools only for Jews? Although the Jewish Commissariat left some of these questions unanswered, it sent out an announcement throughout Soviet Russia about the conditions needed to be met to receive state funding for Jewish schools: "1) the language of instruction had to be the native tongue (Yiddish); 2) In the first school year Hebrew was not to be taught; 3) In the second year Hebrew was not to be taught for more than six hours a week; 4) In the schools that are being opened now, Hebrew was to begin with the fourth grade; 5) Religion was completely banned from the Jewish folk schools."[46]

While the Jewish Commissariat's activists were wrestling with the role of language in the new Jewish schools, the Jewish representatives for the Commissariat for People's Education (*Kommisariat narodnogo obrazovaniia*) went on the offensive to prove the case of Yiddish over Hebrew. This Commissariat claimed that Zionists were "clouding the minds of the working masses by romanticizing the former greatness associated with Hebrew. [. . .] In their schools they teach in the foreign, ancient Jewish language [*drevne-evreiskii iazyk*] . . . and this entire educational system conducted in the foreign, ancient Jewish language serves as a great weapon for the petty bourgeoisie against democracy. The ancient language calls up chauvinistic feelings."[47] The Education Commissariat moved the field of the Soviet Jewish language battle from purely pedagogical concerns to politics equating Yiddish with socialism and Hebrew with nationalism and religion. By shifting the debate in this way, it imported the socialist Jewish rhetoric – associating Hebrew with Zionism, clericalism, and the Jewish bourgeoisie, and Yiddish with internationalism and the lower classes – into Soviet discussions about native language education. It also demonstrated how the Soviet Yiddish intelligentsia intended to shape state policies as members of state bureaucracies.

The final blow to Hebrew's chances of being the language of instruction in Soviet Jewish schools came when Dimanshteyn petitioned the general Commissariat of Nationalities to issue a blanket decree "prohibiting the teaching of general subjects in a national school in a non-mother tongue." In this generalized and not-specifically-Jewish way, Dimanshteyn intended to ban Hebrew in general education.[48] But for Dimanshteyn's plan to work, Yiddish would have to be declared the official "native language" of Soviet Jews.

During the first half of 1919, the tenor of the debate escalated as Hebraists petitioned non-Jewish state authorities, such as the heads of the Commissariat of Enlightenment and the Commissariat for People's Education, to guarantee the existence of Hebrew language schools, and possibly, to subsidize them under a different state decree guaranteeing the "equality of national languages."[49] Some Jewish Communists associated with socialist Zionist movements were swayed by these arguments and supported maintaining a role for Hebrew in children's education in order to keep children connected to traditional Jewish culture and to teach children the Hebrew aspects of Yiddish.[50]

By petitioning higher, non-Jewish authorities, the political battles between Hebraists and Yiddishists resembled the traditional ways competing Jewish groups petitioned non-Jewish secular authorities to weigh in on an internal Jewish debate. For example, in the late eighteenth and early nineteenth centuries, the battle between Hasids (*Hasidim*) and the Opponents (*Mitnagdim*) for the power to control Jewish communal affairs was eventually brought before Tsars Catherine and Alexander.[51] In the case of Soviet Jewish language debates, Hebraists knew that the Jews in control of Jewish cultural issues were Yiddishists, and most of them anti-Hebraists, so they petitioned a higher, non-Jewish power. This method of political lobbying shaped the Jewish language debates throughout the 1920s. The one very important difference between nineteenth century petitioning and early Soviet petitioning was that, in the Soviet case, the Yiddishists had the distinct advantage of being granted state power.

The most decisive act against Hebrew came in the latter part of 1919, when the Jewish Subdivision of Commissariat of Enlightenment (with many of the same faces from the Jewish Commissariat) passed a resolution to 1. close down the Hebraist *Tarbut* school system; 2. transform those schools into Yiddish-language schools; and 3. ban the teaching of "ancient Jewish" in Soviet Jewish primary schools.[52] The Jewish sub-division claimed that the more than fifty delegates at its most recent meeting accepted this resolution unanimously. To add further support to these calls to ban Hebrew-language education, the Collegium of the Division for National Minority Enlightenment, under influence from the Jewish Subdivision, petitioned to have Yiddish declared the official native language of the Jewish masses.[53]

Not to be outflanked, Hebrew-language advocates petitioned the executive board of the Commissariat of Enlightenment to permit Hebrew-language schools. One petition from a Hebrew club raised two concerns about the dominance of Yiddish-language education. First, the petitioners were worried about the assimilationist politics of many Yiddishists, who, they claimed, only saw Jewish schools as a temporary means to achieve the complete linguistic assimilation of Soviet Jewry into Russian. In their opinion, this smacked of Russian language imperialism, which was politically problematic in 1919. In addition, they continued, many of the Jewish children, especially in the Russian Republic, "do not speak Yiddish, and thus Yiddish-language education is just as foreign to them as Hebrew-language education."[54] He was referring to both completely assimilated Russian Jews and to the non-Ashkenazic Jews who lived in Central Asia and the Caucasus, areas that were quickly becoming incorporated into the Soviet Union. If there was, in fact, no single native language of Soviet Jewry, then, these petitioners argued, the state could support a Hebrew-language school system.

In July 1919, the executive board of the Commissariat of Enlightenment published a decree that in theory resolved the debate over language in Jewish schools.

We (a) recognize that "Hebrew [*ivrit*] is not the vernacular [*razgovornyi*] language of the Jewish folk masses, and therefore it cannot be selected as the language of a national minority. As for pedagogical concerns, it [Hebrew] must be placed in the same status as other foreign languages that are not vernacular languages of peoples living on Russian territory. (b) We recognize that Hebrew language instruction in primary education must be eliminated gradually by the beginning of the next school year. (c) Those students in secondary education who began to study in Hebrew are permitted to complete their studies in that language; but for those entering secondary school, instruction must be carried out in Yiddish or in another language recognized as a vernacular of the folk masses of the RSFSR. (d) All efforts at requisitioning and confiscating, and the forced closing of Hebrew-language schools are to be cancelled.[55]

With this resolution in hand, the Jewish Subdivision of the Commissariat of Enlightenment could officially implement its vision of a single Soviet Jewish school system in Yiddish. At the same time, point D suggested that the non-Jewish state authorities wanted a more measured and regulated process for bringing about a state Jewish school system in Yiddish in place of the abrupt closures the Jewish activists advocated.

This decree laid the foundation for future language battles between Yiddishists and Hebraists in several arenas: schools, publishing, theater, and other areas of Jewish culture that had previously been bilingual. Some of these members of the Soviet Yiddish intelligentsia did not think the resolution went far enough. The Jewish Section of the Commissariat for National Minority Enlightenment claimed that by equating Hebrew with other foreign languages, they were leaving loopholes for Hebrew-language education to continue. More important, the group claimed, this decision contradicted the decisions of Jewish state organizations in charge of Jewish cultural enlightenment and education. The resolution challenged the right of Jews to regulate their own culture. The Commissariat of Enlightenment resolution "allowed the possibility for reactionary-clerical elements of the Jewish teaching establishment who have influence over many school committees to use this influence to work against the leadership of the Jewish proletariat. What may end up happening is the appearance of nationalistic schools for Jewish children who speak Yiddish, but whose education might be in any language."[56] The Jewish Subdivision was even angrier at point D, which they claimed, "made it possible for schools that used Hebrew as the language of education to exist, and this clearly contradicts points A and B." The authors angrily concluded:

In view of the above, the Jewish Section of the National Minorities Commission demands the repeal of the Enlightenment Commissariat resolution and expresses its belief that in the future, the Jewish Organ for People's Enlightenment, as representative of the Jewish proletariat, will be given the total ability to decide questions of the Jewish people's enlightenment, as it corresponds to the wishes of the Jewish Proletariat.

The Jewish Commissariat decided that it would not play by the political rules of engagement from the nineteenth century. As the state representative of Jewish affairs, it wanted to decide matters of Jewish cultural concern. In all areas of Jewish cultural policy, the Soviet Yiddish intelligentsia wanted to maintain control, if not autonomy, in shaping secular, Soviet Jewish culture.

Despite the state's official endorsement of Yiddish as the native tongue of Soviet Jewry, and its clear statement against Hebrew, petitions for subsidized Hebrew-language education continued throughout most of the 1920s. In one example from 1921, the Crimean Division of the People's Education Organization (ONO) unilaterally changed the language of instruction in one Jewish school from Yiddish to Hebrew. The decision was quickly undone after it was brought to the attention of central Jewish authorities.[57] But the example shows that in outlying areas there was a concerted effort by some to continue Hebrew-language education.

To some extent, the language issue for teaching Hebrew to children had been resolved; but the same was not true for adults. There was no official ban on Hebrew education for adults, as long as it was privately funded. In 1922, the Jewish Bureau of the Commissariat of Enlightenment passed a resolution permitting private Hebrew classes for adults under the following conditions:

a) Students in the classes cannot be under age 18; b) teachers of these classes must be approved by the People's Education Organization through the Jewish Bureau; c) these classes cannot teach other subjects such as the history of Jewish culture, Hebrew literature, etc.; d) they need to . . . show which textbooks and which material they need, and these must be free of clerical and nationalistic elements; e) understanding that the proposal to establish such classes comes from nationalist and clerical elements attempting to establish a political base through these classes, the Jewish Bureau of the People's Education Organization must maintain strict control over all details, otherwise they will be closed.[58]

In theory, then, there was the possibility for adult Hebrew-language education. In fact, the tight restrictions and the assumption that Hebrew by nature was nationalistic made such classes rare, and eventually, they disappeared entirely.

In late 1925, a final round in the language battle between Hebrew and Yiddish in the schools took place after a petition from a quasi-legal socialist-Zionist youth movement, *The Young Guard (Ha-shomer ha-tsair)*, was circulated to all of its constituents. The nationalistic petition called on *Young Guard* members to start a movement against the power of the Soviet Yiddish intelligentsia that had effectively eliminated Hebrew from Soviet Jewish culture. In nineteenth-century petitioning style, the organization called on children to write letters to the Central Executive Committee (*TsIK*) of the Soviet Union to overturn the power of the Jewish state cultural organizations.[59] In one petition, thirty-two Jewish children of the town of Koriukovka requested that the Central Executive Committee publish a decree about the free study of the Jewish language "Hebrew" and of Hebrew literature, since "at the moment, in our town, the Jewish population needs to study its native (*rodnoi*) Jewish language 'Hebrew' and its native Hebrew literature, but the Jewish Section of the Communist Party (*Evsektsiia*) prevents this and even subjects us to persecution."[60] Another group of children wanted the government to "give Hebrew the right to be a language in school, and as it regards Jewish history, let it be studied in school in Yiddish."[61] Numerous other petitions with similar requests poured in from the provinces, and each one relied on Soviet language politics (native language education and anti-Russian imperialism) to make its claim for Hebrew-language education in Soviet Jewish schools.[62]

The Central Executive Committee had no idea what to do with these petitions from Jewish youth in Khvantsy, Chechelnik, Dunaevtsy, Yarmolintsy, Kutsnevtsy, Kupin, Zinkov, Kupel, Satanov, and Letichev, so it relied on the Soviet Yiddish intelligentsia for its answer. On February 2, 1926, the Main Bureau of the Ukrainian Jewish Section of the Party resolved the situation as follows:

1. We are aware that given the character and content of these petitions, they came from an organized Zionist group, whose very existence must be seen as an attempt to undermine Soviet Jewish schools and turn them into nationalistic Hebrew schools.
2. We therefore must note the weakness and shortcomings of the Jewish school system in the shtetls, and also the weakness of our general work among children that allowed Zionists to cause such delusions among the given groups of Jewish children under the banner of fighting for Jewish schools.
3. We believe it is necessary to debrief the workers in those areas from which these petitions came to inform them of the situation.
4. We want this issue to be publicized in the press.[63]

The Central Executive Committee concurred, and the Soviet Yiddish intelligentsia used the issue to call for more attention (and financial resources) to be paid to the Soviet Jewish school system.

This well-coordinated campaign to put Hebrew-language study on the agenda did not succeed. Hebrew was not put back in the Soviet school curriculum; in fact, a renewed round of attacks on Zionists, Hebrew language schools, and traditional Jewish schools (*heders* and *yeshivas*) began in 1926–7, after a lull during the early NEP period. The same arguments in favor of Yiddish and against Hebrew ruled the day. Both pedagogically and politically, the Soviet state supported the Soviet Yiddish intelligentsia in its drive to make Yiddish the language of Soviet Jewish schools.

THE END OF BILINGUALISM IN THE PRINTED WORD

The suppression of Hebrew in schools, theaters, and literature was not only directed at Zionist, nationalistic, religious, or other politically problematic uses of the language, but at the language itself. Content only mattered if the texts were deemed religious in nature. Thus *all* religious books, from Hebrew-language prayer books to Yiddish-language penitential prayers, were suppressed. But the content of secular Hebrew-language culture was irrelevant. The form itself, the Hebrew language, was targeted in this cultural battle. Many members of the Soviet Yiddish intelligentsia viewed the language, and not what was written in it, as Zionist and nationalistic by nature. Like the battle over language in the schools, the official elimination of the printed Hebrew language was swift and decisive.

In 1917, Hebrew-language publishing boomed due to the cultural and political freedoms after the liberalizing February Revolution, but by 1918–19, the quantity of Hebrew publications dropped off precipitously, as it did for the Soviet publishing industry in general. Unlike the rest of the industry, however, Hebrew publishing never rebounded. Hebrew as a cultural medium and a marker of Jewish identity was suppressed, and Hebrew publishing eventually went underground, although a few collections of Hebrew-language literature were published in the 1920s in the Soviet Union. If the new Soviet Jewish culture needed published material, it was going to be in Yiddish, not in Hebrew, especially after the 1919 resolution declaring Yiddish the native language of Soviet Jewry.[64]

One of the most visible debates about Hebrew-language publishing occurred in 1920 over the publication of a Hebrew-language calendar for the Jewish New Year, 5681 (1920–1). In fall 1920, a Zionist organization petitioned the State Publishing House of the Russian Republic (*Gosizdat*) to publish a Hebrew calendar for the new Jewish year. In September, the publisher produced 30,000 of these calendars, and it did so at a time when paper and printing presses were a scarce resource. The appearance of these calendars generated a storm of protest from the Jewish Division of the Nationalities Commissariat and from the Central Bureau of *Evsektsiia*. They were outraged, not only that Hebrew language calendars advertising the "particularistic" Jewish New Year were published, and that these calendars had a "Zionist character," but also that the State Publishing House produced them at a time when paper was scarce.[65] *Evsektsiia* also reminded the publisher that it was not supposed to publish any Jewish material "without the prior approval of the Jewish Division of the Nationalities Commissariat."[66]

At the same time that *Evsektsiia* petitioned the State Publishing House, the Jewish Division of the Nationalities Commissariat petitioned the Moscow Soviet's Division of Print (*Mossovet, otdel pechati*), the state body overseeing publishing in Moscow. The Jewish Division elaborated on the dangerous nature of the calendar, and proposed strengthening its own oversight of any publication in Jewish languages.[67] As in the battle over the schools when Hebrew-language advocates went to non-Jewish sources of power, Hebrew publishing advocates gave their material directly to the publisher, and circumvented their Yiddishist adversaries in positions of power. As a result of this incident, the Jewish Division was granted supervisory power over publishing material that used the Hebrew alphabet, giving the Soviet Yiddish intelligentsia autonomy to shape printed culture that was visibly marked as Jewish. It is important to note that the definition of Jewish publishing was based, once again, not on content, but on the form of the publication. The visual appearance of the publication – that is to say Jewish letters – determined who had oversight. In theory, Russian-language publications by or about Jews were regulated by central, non-Jewish organizations rather than by Jewish ones.[68]

Arlen Blium, a scholar of Russian censorship, has shown that the drive to extirpate Hebrew from Jewish publishing originated with Soviet Yiddish activists, although he tends to locate these people solely within the *Evsektsiia* party apparatus. "The most sinister role in the fate of Hebrew was played by the Communist *Evsektsiia*, which was under the control of orthodox Communists who supported Yiddish. [...] They approached the ancient language with loathing often moving 'ahead of progress.' The leaders of the Central Bureau of *Evsektsiia* banned individual publications even in cases when the official censors had given approval."[69] In phrasing the problem this way, he follows the same line of argument of Jeffrey Veidlinger, who writes about the state Jewish theater. Both suggest that it was Party members who tried to de-Judaize Soviet Jewish culture, even if such a task, according to Veidlinger, was impossible.

It is true that *Evsektsiia* banned publications, like the calendar, that had already received some kind of official approval, but Blium's emphasis on the

Communist Party connections and Communist ideology is misplaced. Structurally, the oversight of Jewish language publishing was primarily in the hands
of the Jewish Division of the Nationalities Commissariat, a state organization
that employed many non-Party members. More important, the suppression of
Hebrew was part of the internal Jewish battle for more than a decade to create
a monolingual, modern Jewish culture, a battle taken on by – not created by –
the Communist Party and Soviet state. These activists utilized state power to
accomplish long-held desires, rather than to impose a foreign ideology onto
Jewish culture.

Even possession of state power did not initially guarantee the Soviet Yiddish
intelligentsia complete control over Soviet Jewish culture. That power had to be
negotiated with other sources of state power. In a 1921 report on its activities,
the Jewish Division reflected on the crisis over the Hebrew calendar and how
it inspired them to seek more direct oversight over Jewish language publishing.
The Jewish Division "proposed to the Enlightenment Commissariat, the Land
Commissariat [*Narkomzem*], the Internal Affairs Commissariat [*NKVD*], and
the State Publishing House 1) not to register Jewish organizations, institutions,
circles, and others, and 2) not to provide paper and not to print anything of
any existing organizations *without the prior approval of the Jewish Division*."[70] Even
with Jewish Division oversight, unapproved publications continued to appear,
much to the chagrin of state Jewish activists. In late 1926, the modernist and
pro-Soviet Hebrew literary publication, *In the Beginning (Bereshit)*, appeared in
Moscow and Leningrad with the official permission of the Leningrad Regional
censor, *Gublit*.[71] In one report after its publication, the Jewish Division complained that the print house was to blame for printing unapproved publications.
If the publishers let material slip through Jewish Division control, then, this
report suggested, the print house should have been the last means of preventing
Hebrew publications from seeing the light of day.[72]

The "state" had no singular opinion, and at times the Jewish Division found
itself reprimanding high-ranking non-Jewish Soviet state officials for making
gestures supporting the "wrong side" in the Jewish language battles. In April
1921, Hebrew-language activists organized a celebration in honor of the poet,
Chaim Nachman Bialik, whose exodus from the Soviet state for the nascent
Hebrew settlement in Palestine was filled with symbolic import. Although
Bialik also wrote in Yiddish, he is best known as the national Hebrew poet,
and was canonized as the father of modern Hebrew poetry by ideologically
driven writers in Palestine and later, Israel. By 1921, Bialik and other Hebrew-
language writers from the Jewish cultural center of Odessa had petitioned for
exit visas to go to Palestine; and, with the support of popular socialist writer
Maxim Gorky, were granted visas.[73] To show due respect to the great poet, the
People's Commissar of Enlightenment, A.V. Lunacharsky, agreed to appear at

the celebration. Word got out beforehand, and some members of the Soviet Yiddish intelligentsia were angry. The Central Jewish Bureau for Enlightenment (CJEB), the Ukrainian version of the Jewish Division of the Enlightenment Commissariat, wrote directly to Lunacharsky:

We are not going to challenge the importance of Bialik as a great poet. But Bialik is, at the same time, the bard of Zionism, representing the Jewish Middle Ages with his reactionary ideology. During the tragic years of the Civil War in Ukraine he was on the side of the Jewish bourgeoisie. [. . .] And you, Comrade Lunacharsky – the People's Commissar for Enlightenment of the RSFSR – one of the most visible members of the Russian Communist Party, and one of the most prominent of its ideologues – are preparing a speech on Bialik. All the while the Jewish sub-division is carrying out a pitched battle with all of those ideological movements and poetic ideas that Bialik serves. We, of course, are not opening a discussion of your literary and artistic sympathies and antipathies, but as for Bialik, this is a question of cultural politics. Therefore, we hope that you, despite the aesthetic value of Bialik, will similarly judge his politics that are reflected in all of his work.[74]

The Jewish Division was not about to let Lunacharsky unwittingly support Jewish nationalism and Hebraism at the expense of Jewish socialism and Yiddishism. In the end Lunacharsky rescinded his promise, and the reception was cancelled.[75]

   The suppression of Hebrew-language publishing was in fact relatively easy. Publishing involved the allocation of very scarce material resources: paper, printing press time, and Jewish language typeface. As time went on, publishing was concentrated in fewer places and always left traces, making it easier to regulate publishing than to oversee schools, which could open in any basement at any time. As with Hebrew in the schools, however, the elimination of Hebrew-language publishing in the Soviet Union had one more dramatic confrontation.

   In early 1924, seven well-known cultural figures wrote a petition to the Commissariat of Nationalities calling for the re-legalization of Hebrew-language publishing:

The [Hebrew] language and the books published in it, regardless of their content, have for all practical purposes been banned in the Soviet Union. It has been removed from the curriculum of Jewish schools, and even as a subject of instruction; . . . Hebrew language books have been removed from libraries and will not be given to readers; there are even cases of the destruction of these books; getting Hebrew books from abroad is increasingly difficult, and printing them in the Soviet Union is practically impossible.[76]

The authors then provided a defense of Hebrew's role in modern secular Jewish culture, and showed that the politicized association of Hebrew with Zionism and clericalism was both misapplied and harmful to cultural development.

To a great extent the spiritual development of the Jewish people in the last three-fourths of a century has taken place in [Hebrew]. Especially important is the fact that Hebrew and its literature have served and continue to serve as a great and indispensible weapon for the secularization of Jewish culture. [. . .] Under these conditions, nothing is more mistaken than calling this language 'dead'. Ancient Egyptian, for example, is dead and no one writes or thinks in it. *Hebrew is a literary language of modern Jews, and exists alongside Yiddish as a literary and spoken language.* Both languages make up inseparable parts of Jewish culture. . . . Based on all of these considerations, the undersigned propose that local Soviet state organizations be instructed not to put up obstacles for Hebrew.[77]

The seven authors of the petition came from diverse backgrounds, but none of them was known as a Hebrew-language writer. Two were involved in music: D. Shor was a professor at the Moscow Conservatory, and Mikhail Gnessin was a composer.[78] M. Tubiansky, S. Ginzburg, and Nikolai Marr were academics not particularly involved with Soviet Jewish culture; Marr became famous as founder of the school of Soviet linguistics known as Japhetism.[79] And Mikhail Gershenzon was a well-known Russian Jewish liberal intellectual, but was not directly involved in the building of Soviet Yiddish culture. By far, the most controversial name to appear on the petition was David Hofshteyn, a member of the Soviet Yiddish intelligentsia, an editor of the most important Soviet Yiddish literary journal, *Stream (Shtrom)*, and member of the board of *Culture League*, one of the biggest Yiddish-language cultural societies and publishing houses.

His signature caused an outcry among other Soviet Yiddish activists – one of their own was defending the linguistic enemy. The response to the petition from the Central Jewish Bureau of the Council for National Minorities (*Sovnatsmen*), part of the Enlightenment Commissariat, addressed all of the main points raised in the pro-Hebrew petition:

Ancient Jewish (Hebrew) is not a spoken language, not among any strata of the Jewish people. For almost 2000 years it has played a role in Jewish culture similar to that of medieval Latin, in that it had a role among materially privileged segments of the Jewish population [. . .] These segments [of Jewish society] had a contemptuous attitude toward Yiddish, the language spoken by the Jewish poor, and thought of it as a language of the 'servants' and the 'simple folk.' Hebrew culture had a religious character, but was connected with all aspects of Jewish life.

With the rise of the Jewish toiling masses and especially the workers' movement, Jewish culture began to be created in Yiddish. Unlike Hebrew culture, Yiddish culture was completely infused with and reflected the needs of the exploited classes;

therefore culture in Yiddish reflects the demands of those downtrodden laboring masses.[80]

The Jewish Bureau commented on the credentials and reliability of the original authors. The Bureau pointed out that Shor was a member of the Moscow Jewish Religious Council, making him a religious supporter of Hebrew and thus an unreliable critic of the policy; Tubiansky and Gershenzon "do not know anything and are completely unknown in Jewish culture." The only person they devoted time to was Hofshteyn. "The association of his name with this petition . . . is a further step in his ideological development, and shows that he is a complete failure as a poet for Jewish workers and their culture."[81] Others were angry that Hofshteyn had used his positions within the Soviet Yiddish intelligentsia to speak for the whole group. The Presidium of *Culture League* and the Moscow-based writers' group that put out *Stream* issued their own comments on the Hebrew petition that echoed the sentiments of the Jewish Bureau's response, by calling Hebrew a "dead language" and comparing it to Latin. They further developed the arguments associating Hebrew with the bourgeoisie and Zionism, and declared it an impediment to the development of a Jewish laborers' culture. They reserved the concluding words for their former colleague: "Every activist of Jewish literature and art who attached his name to the given pronouncement, like the poet David Hofshteyn, has excluded himself from the laborers and from the family of cultural-artistic activists."[82] Hofshteyn lost both of his positions, and he left the country a few months after the flurry of condemnations.[83] This was the final blow in the resistance against Yiddish becoming the language that defined Soviet Jewry. Although there were last gasps of Hebrew literature in the Soviet Union, by 1926, it went underground.[84]

NON-ASHKENAZIC SOVIET JEWS AND JEWISH LANGUAGE POLITICS

One argument Hebrew activists had made against Yiddish was that there were many non-Ashkenazic Jews in the Soviet Union for whom Yiddish was neither their native nor their national language. Dagestani (commonly known as Mountain) Jews, Bukharan Jews, and other groups of Soviet Jews had no relationship to Yiddish.[85] In the 1926 census, there were officially six categories of Jewish ethnicity – Jews, Crimean Jews, Dagestani Jews, Georgian Jews, Central Asian Jews, and Karaite Jews – from which people could select, suggesting that Yiddish-speaking Jews were the "default" Jewish category.[86] In the minds of the Soviet Yiddish intelligentsia and the Soviet state, were non-Ashkenazic Jews considered "Soviet Jews" if they did not speak Yiddish? Did they fall under the purview of the Jewish cultural authorities, whose work was entirely in Yiddish, or did they fall under the authority of the surrounding culture with which they had more in common linguistically? In what language would their schools and cultural institutions be?[87]

In October 1920, representatives from state Jewish organizations met to discuss how to deal with the Dagestani Jews who had recently been brought into the Soviet fold.[88] The discussion hinged on whether or not state Jewish organizations could legitimately carry out work among this group of Jews that was so culturally and linguistically distinct. In other words, the Soviet Yiddish intelligentsia struggled with the question of its own cultural imperialism with Ashkenazic Yiddish-speaking Jews bringing their cultural mission to non-Ashkenazic Jews. If, in theory, the Jewish sub-divisions of the Enlightenment and Nationalities Commissariats and the *Evsektsiia* were dedicated to fostering a Soviet Jewish culture in Yiddish, then how could they relate to these Jews, who knew no Yiddish? One speaker at the conference pointed out that some Dagestani Jews considered Hebrew to be "their" language. Was Hebrew in fact a "native language" for some Soviet Jews, as Hebrew advocates had been claiming? And if so, would this force these state Jewish organizations to rethink their political position toward Hebrew? Given the ferocious battles that these groups had been waging against Hebrew language culture, these activists could not have sanctioned the use of Hebrew in the fostering of Soviet culture among Dagestani Jews. A very small minority advocated bringing these Jews into the larger "Soviet Jewish nation" by doing cultural work in Yiddish, but most agreed that Yiddishizing the Dagestani Jews was both imperialistic and against the whole concept of working in one's native language. State and Party Jewish institutions did not suppress Hebrew culture in non-Ashkenazic areas with the same determination as they pursued it in Yiddish-speaking areas, precisely because these places and cultures did not have the same political history. But the most common response of those activists who favored bringing Dagestani Jews under the scope of the state Jewish organizations was to turn to the discourse of Soviet nationalities policies and emphasize these groups' native languages.

Alexander Chemerinsky, the head of *Evsektsiia*, was the lone voice against making the Jewish organizations responsible for the Dagestani Jews: "To include them formally in the Jewish Division of the Enlightenment Commissariat is impossible, since it only carries out its work in Yiddish. They can have their own representatives in local organizations. . . . We need to carry out work in a specific language."[89] He was quickly overruled by Avrom Merezhin, head of the Jewish Division of the Nationalities Commissariat, who feared that if left to their own devices or if left under the control of local bureaucrats, the Dagestani Jews could become the target of Zionist propagandizers. Since Yiddish was not their native language, Merezhin called on the state Jewish organizations to work in their native languages. One other speaker supported Merezhin, saying, "We need to teach them in Judeo-Tat [the vernacular of Dagestani Jews], and then we can have some kind of political influence on them." Since language was at the heart of the matter, this committee resolved to work with the Dagestani Jews, despite Chemerinsky's objections.[90]

To carry out native-language work for Dagestani Jews, these groups were going to have to begin publishing in Judeo-Tat (*gorsko-evreiskii*). To this end, they set up a printing house. The two crowning moments of early work in Judeo-Tat were the publication of a single-sheet, wall-mounted newspaper called *Kavkaz Rosta*, and shortly after, the first Judeo-Tat language primer.[91]

Although the plans for cultural work in Judeo-Tat seemed grand, Dagestani Jews lived far away, and the activists organizing this work had little experience with this cultural group. In addition, Judeo-Tat was not a well-developed written language, so much philological work needed to be done before it would be a language of cultural activity. Like many of the smaller towns throughout the former Pale of Settlement, many Dagestani Jews wanted Hebrew-language education for their children and Hebrew-language cultural activity for adults. In 1923, the Central Bureau of *Evsektsiia* was asked to rule on the question of Hebrew-language instruction in Dagestani Jews' schools. Similar to the earlier debates about Hebrew schools for Yiddish-speaking children, the *Evsektsiia* came down against Hebrew. They decided that no Hebrew education was permitted in primary schools, and in secondary schools it was permitted only if parents paid for it. To combat the desires for Hebrew, *Evsektsiia* increased the production of textbooks in Judeo-Tat.[92] Over the course of the 1920s, Dagestani Jews' Soviet culture was shifted toward local production and away from the Soviet Yiddish intelligentsia in Moscow. By 1929–30, one state Jewish organization officially declared Dagestani Jews' cultural work part of the work of other people of the Caucasus.[93]

Because of the emphasis on native languages, the Soviet Yiddish intelligentsia had nothing culturally to offer non-Ashkenazic Jews. It didn't speak these Jews' languages and did not know the history of their cultural development. Soviet Jewish culture for Bukharan Jews in Uzbekistan was produced in Hebrew through the 1922–3 school year when Tadzhik replaced Hebrew, in the hopes of increasing the distance between different Jewish ethnic groups and of bringing Jews and Tadzhiks closer together. Bukharan Jews' native language, however, was not Tadzhik, but was a Judaized version of Tadzhik called Judeo-Tadzhik. The switch from Hebrew to Tadzhik was still not providing Bukharan Jews native-language culture. With the inauguration of nativization in the mid-1920s, cultural production for Bukharan Jews was switched from Tadzhik to Judeo-Tadzhik, a cultural project that lasted until World War II. Most Soviet Judeo-Tadzhik culture was didactic in nature including grammar books, literary anthologies for use in schools, textbooks, and histories of the Uzbek Communist Party.[94] Books in Judeo-Tadzhik reflected the overall Soviet nationalities project of bringing a particular set of ideas and ideologies to the Soviet people, and it also reflected another aspect of nativization, which called for a rapprochement among minority cultures in a given republic and that republic's dominant culture. If Jews in Ukraine had to study Shevchenko and learn Ukrainian, which they did, then Bukharan Jews needed to know Uzbek Party history.

The distance between Ashkenazic and Bukharan Jews increased to the point that the Judeo-Tadzhik alphabet, which, like all Jewish languages, used Hebrew letters, was replaced with Latin letters in 1929–30.[95] The one remnant of a pan-Soviet Jewish culture was the publication of three translations of Sholem Aleichem that appeared in Judeo-Tadzhik in 1931, 1934, and 1937.[96] Despite this thin thread, the official creation of Soviet Jewish print culture excluded non-Ashkenazic Jews, because they did not speak or read Yiddish.

SOVIET JEWISH CULTURE AND THE RUSSIAN LANGUAGE

Yiddish triumphed over its internal linguistic challenger – Hebrew – a few years after the Bolshevik Revolution gave Yiddishists power to shape Jewish culture. But what about Russian – the language that many Russian Jews had associated with high culture, education, and social mobility in the tsarist empire? How did this positive association Jews had with Russian interact with the Leninist association of Russian with cultural imperialism? How did the Soviet Yiddish intelligentsia deal with these competing pressures – assimilating into Russian culture and resisting "cultural assimilation" by advocating Yiddish? In the Soviet understanding of tsarist treatment of its national minorities, these Russifying policies were intertwined with the colonialism that often brought these new nationalities into the Russian empire, which for Ashkenazic Jews, happened in the late eighteenth century. Local cultures were, according to Soviet ideology, at best neglected, at worst crushed, and Russian language culture reigned supreme as the empire's language.[97] Soviet nationalities policy in the 1920s, based on the ideas of Lenin and Stalin, was very clear in its desire to address these past wrongs and worked against any perceived recurrence of Russian cultural imperialism.[98] Russian was not seen as the lingua franca of the new Soviet state, or as the language into which the many ethnic groups of the Soviet Union would assimilate.

That said, when it came to Jews, there were competing feelings about how Jews fit into Russian culture. On the one hand, some who did not see Jews as a distinct national group called for the eventual assimilation of Jews into Russian.

Others sought new forms of Jewish identity to develop in order to maintain Jewish national distinction. For this group, Jews' attraction to Russian was a by-product of this Russian cultural imperialism.

The irony that underlay much of the discussion about language and Jewish cultural policy was the ubiquity of Russian within the Soviet Yiddish intelligentsia, the group of people most vehemently advocating a linguistically defined collective Jewish identity. Jews had traditionally seen Russian as the language of cosmopolitan high culture, Yiddish the language of insular Jewish culture. Even the pre-Revolutionary Jewish intelligentsia had a conflicted relationship with Russian. Sholem Aleichem, for example, spoke Russian and did not teach his children Yiddish. Many Zionist Hebrew activists continued to speak Yiddish and Russian while strolling on the beaches of Tel Aviv. Soviet Yiddish activists, in fact, worried that many of the Jewish activists recruited for Yiddish-language cultural work knew Russian, but not Yiddish.

The Soviet Yiddish intelligentsia had to cultivate an appreciation of Yiddish to those very activists bringing the new Soviet Jewish culture to the masses. At the first *Evsektsiia* conference in October 1918, the delegates debated whether the language of the conference would be Yiddish or Russian, since most of the delegates were more comfortable in Russian. Yiddish won, because the activists felt that they needed to use the language of the "Jewish masses."[99] Even though Russian had more status among Jews, even though Jews were urbanizing and speaking Russian in greater numbers, and even though there were calls for Jewish assimilation into Russian culture, the Soviet Yiddish intelligentsia wanted to foster a new secular Jewish culture and identity with language as its marker. They had their ideological work cut out for them.

The intelligentsia struggled with the role of Russian in their socialist-national project. Should the network designed to create a Soviet Jewish culture in Yiddish include cultural material in Russian? Who would be the intended audience for the intelligentsia's Russian-language material? In 1919, along with the Yiddish-language journal *Culture and Enlightenment* [*Kultur un Bildung*], the Commissariat of Enlightenment began publishing a Russian-language journal, *Jewish Tribune* (*Evreiskaia Tribuna*), which in the words of its creators was "intended for Russian comrades and for Jews who don't know Yiddish," ironically echoing the early modern preamble to Yiddish texts, which were written "for women and for men who are like women in that they don't know Hebrew."[100] Also in 1919, the Nationalities Commissariat began publishing the *Journal of the Jewish Division of the Nationalities Commissariat* (*Vestnik evreiskogo otdela narkomnatsa*), with Merezhin as editor. In its first edition, he felt compelled to explain the journal's choice of language: "The current *Journal* is intended for those who do not know Yiddish and for those who need to get in touch with the Jewish masses and their issues."[101]

From the outset, state Jewish organizations worked in Yiddish and would only make special considerations for Jews who did not know Yiddish. The phrasing of the audience of the *Tribuna*, "Jews who don't know Yiddish," rather than something like "our Jewish comrades who speak Russian," shows the emphasis on Yiddish as the defining feature of the new Soviet Jewish culture. But these journals were primarily targeting progressive Russian comrades interested in the development of Jewish culture and society, and only tangentially for Russianized Jews, who were reading *Pravda*. The publication was to introduce a non-Jewish audience to Jewish issues and to sensitize it to the fight against anti-Semitism, which had become one of the centerpieces of Soviet policy toward Jews after the Revolution. Neither of these journals lasted very long, but a number of the Commissariat's activists began publishing in *The Life of Nationalities* [*Zhizn' natsional'nostei*] in order to address "Jewish life for a non-Jewish audience." Even though the journal was supposed to cover all ethnic groups, articles about Jews were almost always on the front page.[102]

Some members of the Soviet Yiddish intelligentsia, such as Esther Frumkina, recognized that they would reach a larger audience in Russian, so they published their works in both Yiddish and Russian. Shmuel Agursky published *The Revolutionary Movement in Belorussia* [*Di revolutsionerishe bavegung in Vaysrusland*] in Russian before it came out in Yiddish. "I wanted it to be read by non-Jews. This is because my work is the first about the history of the revolutionary movement in Belorussia, so it was important for the book to come out first in the language that non-Jews can read too."[103] Such sentiments reveal the competing pressures on these activists to work and write in Yiddish (Agursky wrote the book in Yiddish and then translated it into Russian for publication), and at the same time, to make a name for themselves among a larger intellectual audience.

In the negotiations over the shape of the Soviet Jewish school system, the choice of which Jewish language was fundamental. But some parents of these school children wanted to send their children to Russian schools in order to facilitate assimilation and social advancement in general Soviet culture. The story about Ukrainian educational officials trying to trick Jewish children into speaking Yiddish attests to the desire of Jewish parents to get their kids into Russian and Ukrainian schools. The Commissariat was firmly against sending Yiddish-speaking kids to Russian schools, arguing that those Jews who thought Russian was the only path to future social achievement had been brainwashed by tsarist Russificatory policies; there was a future in Yiddish. Even some state institutions were slow in shedding the traditional association of Russian with social mobility and high culture, and Yiddish with Jewish insularity. One commissariat report states: "Several Soviet organs are working against having schools in the Jews' native language, and have not included these schools in the [state educational] network, believing that these schools were a nationalistic danger and in opposition to the idea of internationalism. This kind of 'Great Russian internationalism' has been dangerous not only in the political arena, by pushing away Jews from the Soviet state, but also for purely cultural reasons, by exposing Jewish children to the crippling influence of education in a non-native language."[104]

What about Jewish children whose native language was Russian? Most activists agreed that they should go to a Russian school, and these children did not fall under the purview of the state Jewish organizations. These children would attend Russian school, and over time, would lose any distinction as Jews.[105] The most interesting cases that tested the boundaries of the intelligentsia's Yiddish-centric conception of Jewish culture occurred in areas that were not traditionally Yiddish speaking. In 1921, it came to the attention of the Baku division of *Evsektsiia* that a school in Baku with an entirely Jewish population was being conducted in Russian. The Azerbaijani *Evsektsiia* asked the local education authorities to close the school because, they argued, if these children all spoke Russian, then the only thing uniting them was a sense of national unity. It also claimed that the head of the school was a known Zionist, and the school only observed Jewish holidays, not any Soviet holidays. Therefore, the Azerbaijani *Evsektsiia* said, "Children who know Yiddish should be transferred to a normal Jewish school, and the rest to a normal Russian school. If it turns out that not a single child knows Yiddish, then we will mix this school by sending away 50 percent of its Jewish children to study in local schools and bring in a new 50 percent of various nationalities."[106] The "Jewishness" of this Russian school, a Jewishness not defined by language, had to be broken, and they would bus in children of different ethnicities to achieve ethnic balance. A Jewish school was to be defined by its language alone.[107]

In the same year, Jewish cultural activists met in Voronezh, deep in the heart of the Russian Republic and far removed from the culture of the Pale, to discuss the progress of Jewish cultural activities. Comrade Klein made a vibrant speech (in Yiddish) about Yiddish: "The Yiddish language is the primary source of the ridicule [heaped on] Jewish culture. . . . Our task at the moment is for the Russian-speaking Jewish intelligentsia not to Russify the Jewish street, but rather to carry out broad enlightenment work in Yiddish."[108] Comrade Farber framed the language question a bit differently. "The language question is not a political, but a pedagogical question. It is no surprise that for some, Russian is a sign of intelligence. That is a legacy of the old days. The children who were born and raised in Voronezh, and who don't have Yiddish do not belong to the Jewish school or to Jewish culture. Among those children newly arrived in Voronezh, although they speak Russian, for them Yiddish is their language. . . . There needs to be respect for Yiddish among the teachers of these schools."[109]

The fact that Russian was associated with education, and Yiddish with ignorance, only furthered the activists' resolve to establish Yiddish language schools.
Most interesting is his statement that Russian-speaking Jewish children do not
belong to "*yidish*" culture. In Yiddish, the word "Yiddish" means both Jewish
in general and Yiddish-language in particular, in the same way that the adjective French refers to both the language and the broader culture. When speaking
in Yiddish, then, activists could blur the boundaries between a cultural community and a linguistic one. Even in Russian, for the most part at the time, the
cultural and linguistic words were blurred, and Hebrew was referred to as "ancient Jewish." In English, with the distinction between the *Yiddish* language and
the *Jewish* people, no such blurring can take place. Farber's statement summed
up the dilemma of Yiddish-language culture building and its relationship to
Russian: were Russian-speaking Jews part of Soviet "Jewish" culture at all?

By the late 1920s the role of Russian in Yiddish institutions had changed,
reflecting the growing recognition that Russian was becoming the lingua franca
of the Soviet state, and that Jewish families wanted their children to be equipped
to excel in Soviet society. This was especially true after the 1926 census showed
that, although 75 percent of Belorussian Jews still listed Yiddish as their native
language, only one third of Moscow's Jews did the same. Certainly Jews in the
Russian Republic were more urbanized, and therefore spoke more Russian.
But another reason Jews in Belorussia and Ukraine spoke Yiddish at higher
rates than those in Russia was because the 1923 Party resolution on nativization
gave each republic new powers to create institutions in the republic's dominant
language. In Belorussia and Ukraine, this resulted in fostering Belorussian and
Ukrainian institutions along with the cultures of its national minorities (mostly
Jews and Poles). Jews in Belorussia were encouraged to participate in Yiddish
or Belorussian culture, not in Russian culture. Within the Russian Republic,
this resulted in a new interest in increasing the presence of the Russian language
within other national minorities' institutions.

The Soviet Yiddish intelligentsia successfully convinced all those in power
that Yiddish, and not Hebrew, was the language that marked Jews as a separate
community by turning its ideological beliefs into state policy. But as Gennady
Estraikh has convincingly shown, the battle against Russian language assimilation was not winnable. With each passing year, there were fewer native Yiddish
speakers. From the beginning, the impetus to create Yiddish-language culture
came from the Soviet Yiddish intelligentsia, not from the "Jewish masses," who
were not, in fact, clamoring for material in "their language."[110] The intelligentsia had an uphill battle; but, like other activists working on behalf of ethnic
minorities, the Soviet Yiddish intelligentsia believed that with a network of
institutions, a driving ideology, and millions of Yiddish speakers, it could foster
a secular Jewish culture in Yiddish.

3

Modernizing Yiddish

Because [Yiddish] is such an important tool, we in the Soviet Union should make sure that anarchy and wildness don't reign in the language . . .[1]
 —Mikhail Levitan, Chairman of the Jewish Enlightenment Bureau of the Ukrainian Commissariat for Enlightenment (*Narkompros*), 1926

Oh, let me through to the joy of the Yiddish word.

 — Jacob Glatshteyn

In their protracted debates with advocates of Hebrew, proponents of Yiddish admitted that Yiddish was a chaotic, undisciplined language that lacked standardization and rules. These activists argued that for Yiddish to be the language of the Jewish future, it had to be modernized, just like the Jews who spoke it. In the Soviet context, language reform was fundamental to turning the ethnic groups of the former tsarist empire into modern nationalities. One key component of language reform was alphabet reform, the visual representation of languages. According to Terry Martin, "Alphabet reform assumed such significance because the written script proved an extraordinarily multivalent symbol, capable of communicating a variety of different messages about the national constitution of the Soviet Union as a whole, as well as about the cultural and political orientation of its component nations and groups of nations."[2]

There were many motivations for modernizing languages. The Communist Party wanted each national group of the Soviet Union to receive Communist ideology in its native language. For some ethnic groups without a written culture, those in charge of propaganda actually created one for them. The large investment of state resources to give people languages, establish language academies, and create usable forms of script was motivated by didactic goals of bringing new ideas to people through propaganda. But this investment was also prompted by the desire to build support for the new Union by elevating national élites and investing in ethnic minorities' cultures to right past wrongs of Russian cultural imperialism.[3]

From the minorities' perspectives, and specifically for the Soviet Yiddish intelligentsia, language reform was part of the nation-building process. The spread of a standard modern language through print – and later radio, television, and other forms of mass media – was one of the building blocks of modern nationalism.[4] The Soviet Yiddish intelligentsia had both advantages and disadvantages in modernizing Yiddish. First, these activists did not have to create Yiddish "from scratch," a cultural process that some ethnic minorities without well-developed literate cultures had to do.[5] Yiddish had been the object of much ideological attention and practical reform since the late nineteenth century. Second, like Ukrainian and Belorussian, proponents had seen Yiddish as a downtrodden language, suppressed by the desire of the tsarist regime to Russify the former empire and by Jewish cultural elites and rabbis who thought of it as a lowly "jargon." Third, socialist Yiddish activists had successfully linked the Jewish vernacular to the Jewish toiling masses (and Hebrew to "bourgeois Jewish nationalism"), and associated Yiddish with socialism, adding to its political caché after the revolution.

The adversarial relationship between Hebraists and Yiddishists shaped the process of Yiddish modernization in the Soviet Union. Soviet Yiddish language reformers attempted to decouple Yiddish from its historic relationship with Hebrew. But the drive to separate the two languages was only one of several ideological motivations. More important was the hope that, through the intelligentsia's efforts, Yiddish would become a modern language that embodied the modern Jewish people.

To achieve modernity, a language needed a group of trained professionals who tended to its changing needs. If Russian had a language academy, French had the Académie Française, and more importantly, Hebrew had the Hebrew Language Committee, then Yiddish needed its own protective institution. Because of this need, the Soviet Yiddish intelligentsia created institutions devoted to language research and publishing that were seen as an integral part of the cultural development of Soviet Jewry. They also created an infrastructure to employ Yiddish linguists and literary scholars, hardly the most employable people at that time.

Until the late 1920s, when the Soviet Yiddish intelligentsia parted ways more generally with the international Yiddish intelligentsia, Soviet language reformers saw themselves as part of an international community of scholars and activists working to modernize Yiddish. In some cases, these reformers were more radical than those outside the Soviet borders; in other cases, they were less so. Some scholars have attributed the more radical nature of Soviet Yiddish language reform to the fact that it was "dictated by the state," suggesting that Yiddish linguists were taking orders from some state body to implement changes in their language. Joshua Fishman, in his discussion of the Soviet Yiddish journal *The Yiddish Language (Di Yidishe Shprakh)*, says that the state ordered the journal to abide by new Yiddish spelling reforms established in 1928 that eliminated all final letters from Yiddish.[6] Fishman quotes that "by order of the State Commissariat of Education and Culture, the new orthography must be implemented."[7] However this quote does not emphasize that the commissariat was merely enacting, or putting into law, spelling reforms that a conference of Soviet Jewish linguists had decided upon one year earlier. When it came to Yiddish language reform in the 1920s, there was no state body dictating reforms to linguists; the reverse was true. If Soviet language reform was more radical in the 1920s, it was because Yiddish linguists were working in an environment that was exploding all cultural norms. Yiddish linguists who were part of the Soviet Yiddish intelligentsia worked in earlier Yiddish nationalist traditions of modernizing Yiddish as well as the radical Soviet context of reinventing the future. As Gennady Estraikh has shown, "the Soviet reforms of Yiddish spelling may be regarded as a logical development of pre-revolutionary philological and political ideas of non-Bolshevik socialists and liberal champions of Yiddish expansion."[8]

The lack of interference from non-Jewish state and Party officials in Yiddish language reform was unique in the Soviet context in which all languages, including Russian, were being modernized. For example, in 1926, the Central Committee of the Belorussian Communist Party, rather than Belorussian linguists, convened a conference for Belorussian language reform. However, Yiddish linguists themselves and the corresponding state apparatus organized their main language conference. Despite the difference in political oversight, the goals set for the Belorussian conference were similar to those of Yiddish reform. According to one organizer, "The conference is very important in the cultural construction of the BSSR. This is the first time in the history of Belorussian culture that we have had a conference, in which broad theoretical work on preparing the simplification and clarification of Belorussian orthography and spelling was discussed; in addition, we have the participation of well known philologists from the Soviet Union and abroad."[9]

This sentiment was expressed by V. Ignatovsky, a member of the Central Committee and chairman of the Institute for Belorussian Culture, who wrote this letter to the secretariat of the Communist Party in Moscow in response to a flurry of angry correspondence about "political mistakes" that had taken place at the language conference.[10] The Secretariat was so disappointed by the political mistakes because the Central Committee of the BCP had established a special five-person bureau to avoid such errors in the first place. Underlying the secretariat's statement about political mistakes were grave fears from

Moscow that Belorussian language reform – and this international conference in particular – smacked of Belorussian nationalism. Similar accusations against certain Yiddish language reformers came in 1929–30, but were made by other Yiddish linguists. There was never a blanket suspicion of Yiddish language reform itself.

Yiddish linguists may have had more autonomy to modernize than Belorussian reformers, but Yiddish linguists were not alone in having the added problem of dealing with internal bilingualism. In 1926, modern Greek underwent a major reform in the Soviet Union, with motivations closely resembling the ones about Jewish languages.[11] Like the reformers of Yiddish, Soviet Greeks faced a historic internal bilingualism. Alexis, a leading reformer, summed up the issues: "In Greek there are two written languages: Katarevusa, the official language of the [Greek] state, and Demotika, the language in which the population of Greece speaks, and in which literature is written. Katarevusa is a language that no one speaks [in fact, it was a nineteenth-century construction], but state documents are written in it, and newspapers and scientific literature are often published in it. Demotika is only used in fiction."[12] Soviet Greek reformers, like their Yiddish counterparts, aimed to eliminate the internal bilingualism of Greek culture and make Greek overall a more modern "living" language. They, however, had an additional complication – most Soviet Greeks spoke an independent dialect called Pontic that had little relationship to either Katarevusa or Demotika.[13] Neither Greek language was the "native language" of Soviet Greeks. Nonetheless, the 1926 reform made Demotika – the downtrodden vernacular of the Greek nation – the standard language of Soviet Greek education. It was not until the late 1920s and early 1930s that the Soviet Greek cultural apparatus shifted from Demotika to the language of the Soviet Greek diaspora, Pontic.[14] The elevation of Demotika and Yiddish in the late nineteenth and early twentieth centuries was the linguistic centerpiece of the populist re-imagination of the nation, while the elevation of Pontic – similar to the elevation of Judeo-Tadzhik for Bukharan Jews – was part of the Soviet project of elevating the status of all native languages. As evident in the Belorussian case, when language reformers were accused of fostering nationalism, the deep connections between language reform and nation-building were a source of tension in the Soviet context.

THE UGLY LANGUAGE: A BRIEF HISTORY OF YIDDISH LANGUAGE REFORM

Yiddish, which emerged as a spoken language around the year 1000, had been a written language using the Hebrew alphabet since the Middle Ages.[15] Modern Jewish languages – whether they be Yiddish, whose dominant root language is German; Ladino, the Sephardic Jewish vernacular whose root language is

Spanish; or Judeo-Tadzhik – have used the Hebrew alphabet, making them visually similar to one another and, at the same time, obviously different from the base languages from which they emerged. Since the migration of Jews to Eastern Europe from the thirteenth to sixteenth centuries, Yiddish has had four primary root languages: German, which serves as the base language; the *holy tongue (loshn koydesh)* referred to here as Hebrew; Latin/Romance (called La'az); and Slavic (Polish/Ukrainian). Of these, Hebrew was given a special status in Yiddish spelling. Yiddish words that came from Hebrew, such as *shabbes* (Sabbath), *ganef* (thief), or *emes* (truth) preserved their original Hebrew spelling.

When Yiddish became a written language, Hebrew and Yiddish formed a bilingual Jewish language system, and each language was dependent on the other. Yiddish readers could recognize those words that came from Hebrew even though they were not written the way words from all other root languages were written. More importantly, Yiddish readers accepted the special status of Hebrew root words as a given. This special status, which caused no concerns for Yiddish writers at the time, would become an issue in the modern Yiddish language movement.

The founding of modern Yiddish literature and the birth of the Yiddish language movement are usually dated around the mid- to late nineteenth century. At that time Eastern European Jewish intellectuals became interested in European Romanticism and the linguistic nationalism associated with it. In the words of Benedict Anderson, "the nineteenth century was, in Europe and its immediate peripheries, a golden age of vernacularizing lexicographers, grammarians, philologists, and litterateurs."[16] Yiddish literature produced earlier in the century was written out of an Enlightenment desire to reach the people in their native tongue; however, Yiddish's lack of status and perceived hybrid, and therefore ugly, character earned it the name, *zhargon* or jargon, by those who spurned Yiddish literature. The relationship of intellectuals to Yiddish through most of the nineteenth century was one of discomfort or even revulsion, and the literature written in it had, according to Dan Miron, an "aesthetics of ugliness." Its practitioners utilized its perceived ugliness to write literature that tended toward parody, satire, and farce. The move toward Yiddish language reform came only after the discourse around Yiddish shifted, when potential reformers deemed it worthy of reforming, since reform meant making Yiddish more modern and more beautiful.[17]

Reform took a leap forward when Yehoshua Lifshits, often considered the first Yiddishist, published the first Yiddish-German-Yiddish dictionary in 1867. He did so in an era of rising nationalisms throughout the Russian empire. In the same year, Emelian Partychky compiled the first general German-Ruthenian (also known as Ukrainian) dictionary as the modern Ukrainian language movement gained momentum.[18] During the same period, as the result of pioneering work by nationalist scholars, three distinct literary languages were formed in the northern Balkans: Slovene, Serbo-Croatian, and Bulgarian.[19] The publication of a dictionary was a momentous occasion in the history of a language reform, and in the history of a particular group's national identity, since a dictionary served as a unifying authoritative source for questions about language, and also marked one language as distinct from others. Once a language was codified through a dictionary, reformers could then consider further modernization.

A central part of reforming and beautifying Yiddish was its orthography, how words are written. Yiddishists of the late nineteenth and early twentieth centuries wanted to use Yiddish's close association with German to make it a language of "high culture." Yiddish orthography began to absorb spelling patterns of its more beautiful and cultured cousin.[20] Many Yiddish words began to be spelled "germanically." For example, the Yiddish word *zeyer* was spelled z-e-h-r (in German, the equivalent is *sehr*, meaning "very"). The "h" was an extraneous letter, but represented Yiddish's close connection to German. According to Moshe Shulman, a Soviet Yiddish linguist, the dominance of German was strong even among Russia's Jewish revolutionaries, who were heavily influenced by their education in German universities and by the dominance of the German socialist party as a model for other socialist movements.[21]

At the 1908 Czernowitz Conference, Yiddish language reform was a central issue. The invitation to prospective conference participants listed Yiddish orthography, grammar, foreign words, and a dictionary as the first four issues to be discussed.[22] Yiddish reform became more important as the politicized relationship between Hebraists and Yiddishists intensified. In 1909–10, the journal *Life and Scholarship (Lebn un Visnshaft)* devoted a special section to language issues and language reform, and even included early proposals to write all Hebrew root words in Yiddish phonetically, and even to abandon the Hebrew alphabet in favor of the Latin one.[23] The most important publication in the debates about language reform came out in 1913, when Shmuel Niger and other Yiddishists decided that the field of Yiddish language studies needed its own professional journal in which to debate philological issues.

In 1913, under the editorship of Niger, the first journal dedicated to Yiddish philology, *The Register (Der pinkas)*, appeared in Vilna. The opening article was written by Ber Borochov, the political and spiritual leader of the Jewish socialist Poalei Tsion movement, and a man whose interests spanned many fields, including Yiddish linguistics. Borochov's article, "The Tasks of Yiddish Philology," became an instant classic, and is often cited as the article that laid the foundation for the entire field of Yiddish linguistics and philology. In the opening sentence, Borochov argued that "[o]f all the areas of scholarship, philology plays the largest role in the national revival of oppressed peoples."[24] Borochov then linked the development of Yiddish philology with the Jewish national movement. "As long as the people remain 'illiterate' in their native tongue, we cannot speak of a national culture. National culture is not just about works of poetry, but is first and foremost about giving the people the opportunity to speak and write in their language properly. . . . The Yiddish language must become a means to refine and cultivate a national culture both for the people and for the intelligentsia."[25] Borochov agreed with later Soviet reformers that language standardization was the path to modern nationhood.

Although he differentiated between the intelligentsia's use of Yiddish – refined and literary – and the common people's – raw but real – he argued the two must come together synthetically to produce a new modern Yiddish befitting a modern nation. Soviet reformers echoed this argument as they strove to create a new Soviet Jewish culture – a synthesis of the high culture of the literary élite with the popular culture of the Yiddish speaking masses – and like Borochov, they thought this could be achieved only with a modern synthetic language.[26]

Borochov's article also gave Yiddish a linguistic history, and by showing its past, also anticipated its future. "Our great poets understood the need to enrich and develop the simple people's language, even without using the resources of scholarly philology. Mendele Moykher Sforim is the Columbus of the Yiddish language and Y.L. Perets is its Napoleon: the first discovered it, and the second brought the European world to it. . . . Mendele *nationalized* our language; Sholem Aleichem beautifully *popularized* it, and Perets *humanized* it."[27] In this passage, Borochov brought European history to Yiddish, while telescoping 400 years of that history into one generation of Yiddish prose writers. Mendele's genius, according to Borochov and others, was his ability to create living speech in text, thereby capturing "the folk" in written language. Sholem Aleichem made quality Yiddish literature accessible to a wider Yiddish-reading audience. And Perets, who was known at the time not for his mimetic representations of raw living speech but for introducing aesthetic criteria into Yiddish literature, made Yiddish a human, perhaps more "Renaissance" and Western language and literature – the final step in the process of making Yiddish respectable.

These notions of national identity fit into a pattern of nationalism suggested by Ernest Gellner, who argues that "[I]f nationalism prospers it eliminates the alien high culture, but it does not then replace it by the old local low culture; it revives, or invents, a local high (literature, specialist-transmitted) culture of its own, though admittedly one which will have some links with the earlier local folk styles and dialects."[28] Yiddishists needed to invent a Yiddish-based local high culture. Despite Borochov's initial equation of the folk speech with national language, in the above passage he, like Gellner, shows that national language is created not by the masses with their tongues, but by writers with their pens.

Borochov was both of his time and ahead of his time. His was the first article in the first Yiddish philological journal, and he articulated many of the ideas of Yiddish language reformers. But Soviet linguists found his ideas about reform more salient than many non-Soviet reformers. In the words of one Soviet linguist, "Only after October did his primarily linguistic reform proposals become the basis for orthographic reform that was later implemented in Yiddish print."[29] But the question remained, how to move from theoretical discussions of language reform to practical implementation. Who would decide what reforms would be enacted? How would those reforms be disseminated to the literate Yiddish public?

REFORM FROM THE PERIPHERY

Shortly after the October Revolution, Russian-language orthography under-went radical reform. As in the case of Yiddish, the Russian orthographic reform plan had been developed in pre-revolutionary Russia and just needed the power of the state to introduce it. The initial desire to reform Russian at the turn of the twentieth century came from schoolteachers, the ones most aware of the problems encountered in learning to read and spell; and it was teachers, and later linguists, who drafted reform plans that would be implemented in the Soviet period.[30] A.V. Lunacharsky, Commissar of Enlightenment, issued two decrees, one in December 1917 and a second in October 1918, making eleven orthographic changes in Russian, most significantly the elimination of four "antiquated" letters, with the goal of modernizing Russian.[31]

Like Russian reform, the initial drive for Yiddish reform came from teachers and political activists. For teachers in the Pale of Settlement, the motivation to reform Yiddish was pedagogical. They wanted to create a Yiddish that could be used in the Yiddish-language school system that had emerged in the Russian Empire before World War I.[32] Independent Jewish teachers' organizations in various cities were simultaneously calling for Yiddish language reform; however, each group of teachers had a different set of recommendations for reforming the language.[33] One reason for the variations in the teachers' reform plans was the existence of various Yiddish dialects throughout Eastern Europe, primarily the two competing dialects of Lithuanian Yiddish (centered in the Northeastern parts of the Russian Empire) and Polish Yiddish (known in Yiddish as Galician Yiddish).[34] Nonetheless, the desire to reform, and the haphazard nature in which it was occurring, encouraged some to consider centralizing the reform effort and creating a standard Soviet Yiddish.

At the same time, editors of several socialist periodicals began using a re-formed Yiddish in their publications. One of the most radical reforms that both the teachers in Yiddish schools and the editors of socialist periodicals authorized, and one that had been proposed as early as Czernowitz, was writing out Hebrew root words of Yiddish phonetically, thus eliminating their special status. The first periodical to actually use this spelling reform in print was *Latest News (Letste Nayes)*, which used a form of phonetic spelling from 1916–18. More important, however, were the reforms undertaken by the Kiev-based socialist newspaper, *New Times (Naye Tsayt)*, whose new standard spelling influenced other Yiddish periodicals.[35] Gradually the reform spread to Soviet-sponsored publications.

In August 1918, the Communist Party's central Yiddish-language newspaper, *Emes*, was established, and in one of its first editions, the editors sent out a notice to its correspondents explaining how they wanted submissions written and formatted. Included was the following request: "Use the orthography that we use in the paper. Learn the rules: *op* instead of *ob*; *ant* instead of *ent*; *ba* instead of *be*; drop the extra "h" as in the word, *zeyer; oy* instead of *oh;* use the letter *khet* only in Hebrew words."[36] The *Emes'* editors call for reform was made for practical reasons. Tireless editors often had to spend more time correcting the correspondents' Yiddish than actually editing the articles. The standard they were calling for attempted to separate Yiddish from German by getting rid of those extra "h"s and using the "a" sound in prefixes rather than the Germanic "e". The desire to decouple Yiddish from Hebrew would happen one year later, when the general proposal to standardize Yiddish fused with the specific reform of phoneticizing the Hebrew components. Reading through 1918 editions of *Emes* shows that, despite calls for standardization, there was no standard, nor was there a consensus on how certain words should be spelled. Language reform and standardization had barely moved beyond theory, and there was no centralized implementation of these reforms.

The first Soviet publication to mention the more radical reform of Hebrew root words in the context of standardizing Yiddish was the 1918 journal of the Jewish Subdivision of the Commissariat of Enlightenment, *Culture and Enlightenment*.[37] In the October 1918 edition of the journal, Y. Mitlinsky linked the reforms going on in Russian to Yiddish language reform.

Hebraists are always quick to point out that you can't really know Yiddish without knowing Hebrew. And once, at a meeting of a cultural society in Kiev, I heard a hysterical scream from a Hebraist in the audience who said that children of one Yiddishist school wrote the word Torah phonetically. The holy word *Torah* written out as *toyre* [*tet vov yud resh ayin*]! The Russians have just completely reformed their orthography to make it more approachable. And we are supposed to teach our kids a second language, just so they can read [Yiddish] orthography! I think it's time we reformed our language as well. [...] It might be time to carry out a revolution in our orthography, and write *toyre, balebos, sreyfe* [phonetically].[38]

Mitlinsky argued that if Russians could put pedagogical concerns before seemingly antiquated attachments to outmoded letters, so too should Jews.[39] He
invested political and emotional energy into the debate over orthography, especially with his portrayal of the hysterical Hebraist. He fused the practical
concerns of the *Emes* editors with the anti-Hebraist politics of Yiddishists, but
he also tempered those political emotions by showing that in theory there were
practical reasons to de-Hebraize Yiddish – to make it easier to read. Mitlinsky's
article was only the first in *Culture and Enlightenment* that gradually made the
more radical version of Yiddish reform the standard accepted in all Yiddish-
language Soviet institutions.

In November 1918, the Jewish Commissariat passed a resolution to begin
publishing *Culture and Enlightenment* with the more radical, de-Hebraized orthography, and to adopt the new orthography in Jewish classrooms.[40] Nonetheless, like *Emes*, which demanded a standard orthography of its contributors, but
did not maintain one itself, the journal's editors continued publishing Hebrew
root words non-phonetically. At least now the state body dedicated to Jewish
culture had passed a resolution on the subject. From now on, linguists, scholars,
and teachers would have to interact with Jewish representatives of the state to
enact reform, to move from theoretical discussion to practical implementation.

Some linguists began calling for a central state body to oversee and implement Yiddish language reform. In fall 1919, Moshe Shulman proposed to the
Collegium of the Enlightenment Commissariat to establish a scholarly board
to oversee Yiddish language reform.[41] Like the teachers, Mitlinsky, and the
editors of *New Times,* Shulman chose Hebrew root words as his main target
in reforming Yiddish. Phoneticizing these words, he thought, would break the
interdependence of Yiddish and Hebrew and allow for Yiddish alone to define
Soviet Jewish culture. Shulman envisioned an institution to maintain the new,
improved Yiddish. He proposed making the Jewish Subdivision of the Enlightenment Commissariat in Moscow the authority on Yiddish language issues,
centralizing the whole question of language reform.

Although Shulman petitioned the Collegium of the Commissariat for the
finances needed to establish this three-person language board, the future of
Yiddish reform would be in Jewish hands, and scholarly ones at that. There
is no mention of Communist Party oversight or of other state interference in
his proposals.[42] In 1919–20, the Jewish subdivision heeded Shulman's advice
and established the Yiddish Philological Commission – the final arbiter in the
language reform disputes raging on the pages of *Culture and Enlightenment* and of
the Party publication, *Communist World (Komunistishe Velt)*. The commission's
reform plan, based on Shulman's vision of a standard Yiddish, was officially
approved at the First All-Russian Jewish Culture Conference in July 1920,
establishing the first state-sponsored standard Yiddish in history.[43]

Shulman's plan was more moderate than many other proposals. Shulman claimed that he had seen one proposal to replace the entire Hebrew alphabet with the Latin one. And in 1920–1, Avrom Veviorke, another central figure in Soviet Yiddish language reform, was part of a group of radical linguists that proposed creating two entirely new letters for the Yiddish alphabet – one to replace the "two *vovs*" letter that made a "v" sound and the "two *yuds*" letter that made an "*ey*" sound.[44] Soviet Yiddish reform could have been much more radical than it was.[45] Moreover, the Russian language and the Cyrillic alphabet had already been radically reformed with the elimination of a number of letters, and there was even talk of eliminating Cyrillic entirely. In January 1920, the general scholarly body overseeing language work announced a meeting at its offices, to which the head of the Jewish Subdivision was invited, to discuss the introduction of a single Latin script for all languages of the Russian Republic.[46] A language revolution was underway, and Yiddish was part of it. Even in the United States, the expressionist writer's group *Introspectivism (In Zikh)* used phonetic spellings for Hebrew root words, very similar to the orthography that came to be used in the Soviet Union.[47]

ITSIK ZARETSKY AND THE PROFESSIONALIZATION
OF YIDDISH LINGUISTICS

The early debates of Yiddish language reform were dominated by new names among Yiddish cultural activists. Although Niger and his brother, Daniel Charny, edited *Culture and Enlightenment*, most of the linguistic contributions were made by relative unknowns: Shulman, Mitlinsky, and a linguist named Itsik Zaretsky. Jewish cultural activists in Moscow recruited Zaretsky in 1919, at a time when people were fleeing the cities for the countryside. Cultural activists were in short supply and great demand, and Zaretsky had proven his credentials in the Volga city of Samara, where he headed the local Jewish division of the Enlightenment Commissariat.[48] The Jewish Commissariat in Moscow sponsored Zaretsky's trip to Moscow. While in Moscow he briefly served as the highest-ranking state Jewish cultural activist, head of the Jewish Subdivision of the Commissariat, and was given a room in a state-controlled House of Soviets near the Jewish Subdivision's offices in Moscow.[49] Zaretsky played a large role in placing Yiddish language reform and Yiddish language research at the center of Jewish cultural activity in the capital. From 1919 until his departure in 1921, Zaretsky's presence was so important for Yiddish language reform that when he left Moscow for Kharkov, the Moscow-based philological commission that he and Shulman helped set up fell apart.[50]

Zaretsky's first published article appeared on the pages of *Culture and Enlightenment* in 1920. He showed not just why the old orthography was insufficient for the needs of modern Yiddish, but also why the old orthography appeared as it did. Zaretsky endeavored to explain why Yiddish had incorporated the Hebrew spelling of Hebrew root words in the first place.

As was the case with other national groups, the orthography was monopolized by the more educated, and our educational system was monopolized by the bourgeoisie. The intelligentsia, the *maskilim*, both secular and religious, who created the orthography, was primarily closer to Hebrew than to Yiddish. Hebrew, at the time, had the quality of fixedness, uniqueness, while Yiddish was considered chaotic. Finally, learning Hebrew was a sacred duty for every Jew, and whoever didn't know Hebrew was an *amorets* [a simpleton or ignoramus].[51]

Zaretsky cleverly incorporated Marxist categories into his linguistic analysis, and synthesized Soviet discourse about language reform with the specificities of Jewish internal bilingualism.

He then systematically countered each argument that opponents of the reform had put forth. First, he addressed the "sentimental-reactionary" resistance to reform, based on Borochov's Romantic nationalism, which came from those attached to the "thousand-year tradition" of Yiddish. In Zaretsky's words, "All revolutions interrupt 'holy' traditions." He took more seriously the second critique of the new reform, that it would take Yiddish writers and readers too long to assimilate into everyday parlance, and would not achieve its goal of simplification. Zaretsky believed that the transition would be relatively easy, and used the example of the recent Russian reform to show that the fears were more pronounced than the actual problems of adapting to a new spelling system. Finally, some argued that the variety of possible phonetic spellings of the Hebrew root words would lead not to standardization but to linguistic chaos; each speaker would spell the words however s/he pronounced them. Zaretsky responded by calling for a standardized form of all Hebrew root words, which would then be disseminated to the Yiddish-reading populace through Yiddish publications and schools.[52]

He finished the article by outlining the reasons for going ahead with the reform:

1. To make reading easy, and writing even easier for the largest majority of Jews. Remember that the times are long gone when we Jews were all "people of the book" when we all were educated, smart, and all knew Torah.

2. It will make teaching Yiddish orthography to children easier. . . . It will bring the school closer to real life and will free it from outmoded traditions.

3. The reform will make the fight with Hebrew in the schools (although this issue is less important) easier.[53]
4. The reform will give us the opportunity to rationalize the alphabet, to free it from letters that don't appear except in Hebrew words (*sin, taf, sov, khet*).[54]

Zaretsky placed the battle with Hebrew as the least important reason for reforming Yiddish, and made modernization and rationalization his guiding principles. His quixotic comment about Jews no longer being "people of the book" was both a reminder that not all Jews knew enough Hebrew to decipher the Hebrew root words of Yiddish, and a poignant way of describing linguistic and cultural assimilation, the consequences of which were the need to reform the language. This programmatic outline shaped all subsequent debates about reform.

The article launched Zaretsky's career as the chief Soviet Yiddish reformer. Unfortunately for Zaretsky, after the initial round of reforms, which de-Germanified Yiddish orthography and phoneticized Hebrew root words, Yiddish language reform went into hibernation. As civil war continued to rage, and resources became more scarce, language reform was no longer a priority; the central newspaper used the new standard orthography, but even large regional Yiddish papers used their own orthography well into the mid-1920s.

ESTABLISHING AUTHORITY

In 1921, Zaretsky left Moscow for Kharkov, where he founded a new center for Yiddish language research. He published his *Rules for Yiddish Spelling* in Odessa with the goal of establishing himself as the main authority on Yiddish language reform.[55] In July, he and other Yiddish scholars founded a philological commission at the Central Jewish Bureau of the Ukrainian Enlightenment Commissariat. The same state organization also sponsored a Yiddish section at the Linguistics Research Institute in Kharkov. The commission dealt with problems of spelling, terminology, and grammar, and in 1923, published a linguistic collection called *Yiddish*, with more than half of the articles written by Zaretsky himself.[56] Soon after its publication, both the commission and the smaller research center broke up, and Zaretsky returned to Moscow to work at the new Jewish department of the Second Moscow State University.

The goal of establishing an authoritative body of professional Yiddish reformers took a giant step forward in 1925, after an infusion of state resources into building Yiddish-language institutions and publications as a result of the new nativization policies enacted at the Twelfth Party Congress. Even before nativization, in 1921, the Belorussian government began discussions about an institute for Jewish culture in Minsk, which started operating in 1924–5.[57] The climate in Belorussia was ripe for Jewish scholarship, thanks to the simultaneous Belorussian and Yiddish nativization movements. The Jewish department at the Institute for Belorussian Culture attracted scholars from across the Soviet Union and abroad.[58] The department was divided into three primary sections, each headed by a well-known Yiddish scholar. Israel Sosis, who had been a historian in St. Petersburg, became director of the historical commission, and Nokhum Oyslender, a literary critic, headed the literary commission.[59] The philological commission was led by Mordechai Veynger, who, unlike most members of the Soviet Yiddish intelligentsia, had been a Party member since the Civil War. He became the Party Secretary of the Central Asian University in 1922, and moved to Minsk to join the Institute for Belorussian Culture in 1924–5. Veynger was also a long-time Yiddish linguist, who had published a highly technical article in Niger's *The Register*.

Veynger's philological commission developed an impossibly ambitious plan. After its first year, the institute's bulletin advertised the following projects: producing an academic Yiddish dictionary; rationalizing Yiddish script and spelling; establishing a standard orthography for publishing houses of Yiddish material; compiling terminologies for mathematics, physics, agronomy, law, and administration; working on a geography of Yiddish dialects; and creating a Yiddish-language atlas.[60] The academy's most visible success was the creation of terminologies used in the new institutions of Soviet life (such as courts, agricultural collectives, and schools) that were being conducted in Yiddish.

The crowning moment of the Minsk institution came in 1926 with the publication of what is still considered one of the best collections of Yiddish philological work – the Minsk *Tsaytshrift*. The first volume was 640 pages and had twenty-six articles, compared to the forty-eight pages of *Yiddish* just three years earlier. The fact that the State Publishing House of Belorussia was willing to designate such a large number of its limited page allocation to *Tsaytshrift* shows how important the publication was, not only to the scholars involved, but also to the publishers and cultural commissars, who recognized that Soviet Yiddish scholarship was a world leader.[61] It included work from Yiddish philologists throughout Eastern Europe, from Max Erik and Max Weinreich to Nokhum Shtif and Nokhum Oyslender. Soviet reviewers heralded its publication as the appearance "not just of a book, but of a historical event." Both Shtif and Leyme Rozenhoyz lauded its appearance as "the first scholarly work to be supported, not by private sponsors, . . . but by state institutions."[62] The *Tsaytshrift* was also momentous in the history of Yiddish orthographic reform for its scholarly legitimization of the newly reformed Yiddish language, which was both used in the publication and studied in a number of the articles.

Linguistic research also continued in the other centers of Soviet Jewish culture – Kharkov, Kiev, and Moscow. Zaretsky had moved back to Moscow to help found the Jewish department of the Second Moscow State University in 1924, whose purpose was "to prepare teachers of Yiddish and Yiddish literature in schools and in teacher training institutes where Yiddish is the language of instruction."[63] Unlike the Minsk institute, the Moscow-based institution focused on training more than on theoretical research. Nonetheless, Zaretsky used the Jewish department in Moscow as his institutional base to establish himself as the leader of Soviet Yiddish linguistics. He propagated a vision of Yiddish language reform that would rival Veynger's work throughout the 1920s.

THE YIDDISH LANGUAGE, THE FIRST PERIODICAL DEDICATED EXCLUSIVELY TO YIDDISH PHILOLOGY

The Jewish division of the Institute for Belorussian Culture was important for being the first Soviet Jewish scholarly institute, and for showing other Soviet republics that nativization could successfully foster both the dominant nationality's culture and those of its own minorities. Despite its location at the center of the Soviet Union, in the 1920s the small department at the Second Moscow State University was an outpost of Jewish linguistic research.[64] The real center of Jewish research in the Soviet Union was in Kiev, which, more than Minsk or Moscow, had been a center of Jewish culture and politics even before the revolution, and also had a very large Yiddish-speaking population.

Within the Jewish cultural world, Kiev was considered a worldwide center of secular Yiddish culture. It was the home of Sholem Aleichem, David Bergelson, and more avant-garde Yiddish literary groups of the early post-revolutionary period. Independent Ukraine was the first country in the world to establish a Minister for Jewish Affairs, showing that Jews were always politically prominent in Kievan politics and culture.[65] After the Soviet invasion of Ukraine in 1918, Kharkov replaced Kiev as the Ukrainian capital, which is the reason Soviet Yiddish culture developed in this city, despite its distance from the historic Jewish heartland.[66] But Kharkov had to struggle to be seen as a Jewish cultural center. Mikhail Levitan, chair of the Central Jewish Enlightenment Bureau (CJEB) of the Ukrainian Enlightenment Commissariat, located in Kharkov, wrote this description of the city to the chair of the Central Bureau of *Evsektsiia,* Alexander Chemerinsky, in Moscow: "You must not forget that Kharkov is in the mind of the Jewish activists a complete wasteland [*midber*]. There is hardly anyone to turn to for help in this or that area of culture."[67] Kiev was always seen as the true cultural center of Jewish life in Ukraine; Kharkov was the home of the state and Party headquarters.

The establishment of an Institute for Jewish Research at the Ukrainian Academy of Sciences, the center for scholarly research in Ukraine, coincided with the introduction of a professional philological journal called *The Yiddish Language (Di Yidishe Shprakh)*. Both the institute and the journal were officially founded in 1926, but the journal was not published until early 1927. Like the founders of *The Register* thirteen years earlier, the initiators of *The Yiddish Language* recognized the need for a periodical dedicated to Yiddish language philology if Yiddish was to develop its own professional language establishment. A journal functioned as the forum for debates, the place where official reform could be published, and the primary resource for teachers and anyone else interested in "improving" their Yiddish. A philological journal would also be the key to creating a standardized Soviet Yiddish orthography, a goal still unrealized. Finally, a professional journal could provide work for linguists and writers searching for ways to finance their scholarly research.

Concrete plans for producing a philological journal initially came from the CJEB. The CJEB had been receiving correspondence about a philological journal since 1925 from the Central Bureau of *Evsektsiia* and from Nokhum Shtif, a well-known Yiddish linguist and scholar. Shtif, one of the cofounders of the Vilna-based Institute for Jewish Research (YIVO) – the most important center for scholarship on Yiddish – petitioned several Soviet organizations for work in the burgeoning network of state-sponsored Jewish institutions. The CJEB recognized the match between Shtif's skills and the need for philological work.[68] The director, Levitan, wrote to the chairman of the Council of National Minorities (*Sovnatsmen* – a higher-level state organization) to bring his attention to the dearth of publications about the Yiddish language. He pointed out that the collection *Yiddish* was the only philological publication to come out in the years since the early heyday of Yiddish language reform.[69] *The Yiddish Language* grew out of negotiations over a collection of essays that were to be published in Kiev by the *Culture League* publishing house in 1926, not too long after the CJEB petitioned *Sovnatsmen* to use some of its allotted pages for Yiddish linguistic work.

The process by which the journal came into being involved careful negotiations between the CJEB and *Culture League*. The CJEB had proposed a heavy degree of state oversight, but the publisher was not happy with state interference in language reform.[70] Levitan reassured the editor-in-chief of *Culture League*, B. Marshak, and the future editorial staff of the journal that state oversight would not interfere with the professionals' work of language reform.[71] Despite the rancorous negotiations that took place between the CJEB and *Culture League*, a Yiddish philological journal began appearing in March 1927.

Two introductory articles in the first issue presented the mission and set the tone for future Yiddish language reform. The editor, Nokhum Shtif, who moved to the Soviet Union to take the job, was particularly interested in mapping out the linguistic history of Yiddish as a written and spoken language.

Since the Jewish workers' movement made Yiddish a language of social-political life and of cultural work, three styles of language have become evident: (1) the living people's language, as we hear it from our elders, and as it was fixed by writers since Sholem Aleichem; (2) the high cultural language of the new literature based on the people's language (for example, the master of language, David Bergelson); and (3) the genuine cultural language, whose most important tone setter is the press. It's clear that this third one is an independent style. Cultural language cannot be based merely on the people's language, which is too poor in its means of expression and is too suffused [*ongezapt*] with religious and spiritual, not to mention economic, life. On the other hand, it [cultural language] is not completely tied to the language of artistic prose, which has completely different goals.[72]

In this outline of the social and cultural levels of Yiddish, Shtif cleverly accomplished a number of goals. First, he opened with a nod to the political climate by crediting the Jewish labor movement with reinvigorating Yiddish and making it into a respectable language. Next, he created a taxonomy of Yiddish that incorporated both the rhetoric of Soviet language politics and the history of Jewish language debates.[73]

Shtif also charted the linguistic territory in which this new professional journal would operate. He believed that Soviet Yiddish must be enriched by the living language of the people, while using the literary devices and crafted language of élite culture, as represented by Sholem Aleichem on the one hand, and David Bergelson on the other. *The Yiddish Language* would chart this new territory for its readers.

Shtif also argued that the social context of post-revolutionary Russia in which Yiddish was developing – in theory, the eventual classless society – would make the polarization between "vernacular and written" and "popular and high" Yiddish obsolete. In the past, he suggested, intellectuals produced high culture and the masses produced vernacular culture. (However, given his reference to Sholem Aleichem's genius of textualizing orality in the first statement, it is evident he doesn't believe in such a simple dichotomy.) But in the Soviet Union, "We no longer have intellectuals and publicists. We have the man of the masses [*masn mentsh*]."[74] After outlining Yiddish language politics and analyzing the various strata of its users, Shtif then came to the point about the need for the new journal.

Yiddish's ability to express [thoughts and ideas] is not sufficient to meet our current language needs. We need to create a language laboratory, in which our real cultural language can be critically tested. It should be refined; it should be enriched by collecting and then systematizing new material, and [it should] include new suggestions and improvements.[75]

Shtif then outlined the nine areas that the journal would cover, ranging from questions of practical Yiddish language studies and critical analyses of the use of Yiddish in Soviet publishing to the creation and standardization of new lexicons for Soviet Yiddish. The journal worked toward a standard orthography and included book reviews and a section for readers' questions.[76] More broadly, the journal published articles to generate debate about language use and language creation, and served as a forum for Yiddish language professionals. Under Shtif's six-year editorship, until his death in 1933, *The Yiddish Language* (later named *On the Language Front*) accomplished many of the goals set out by its founders.

A STANDARD ORTHOGRAPHY

Although *The Yiddish Language* was successful as a forum for professionals, it did not institute reform; it only disseminated it. The real sources of linguistic change were the linguists, writers, and researchers, along with the state and Party supporters who participated in these reforms. All of the constituents involved in Yiddish language reform met to finalize a standard orthography at a special conference during the Second All-Union Jewish Cultural Congress of April 1928.

Cultural conferences and their larger cousins, cultural congresses, were a regular facet of Soviet culture. On the one hand, such events provided people in a given field the opportunity to come together to debate and share ideas on subjects of concern, and served as a means of professionalization. On the other hand, they also provided a forum for state and Party officials who oversaw a given field to disseminate an official vision to a broad audience. Soviet Jewish cultural conferences started as soon as the state began sponsoring and organizing Jewish cultural activities in 1918. But the first All-Union Cultural Congress (meaning that participants came from all republics of the Soviet Union) took place in 1924. At a time when nativization was just getting off the ground, language reform specifically and academic research more generally were not the most pressing concerns. General institution building was the main agenda item. Schools, newspapers, and other Jewish cultural institutions needed to be created before developing a professional establishment to staff these places. According to one participant, the first conference approved three very minor reforms in Yiddish spelling.[77] But between the first All-Union Jewish Cultural Congress and the second one, the scene changed dramatically.

Three Jewish academic institutions were founded during this period, each with a special division devoted to the study of Yiddish language. In 1926 the

Jewish division of the Institute for Belorussian Culture proposed an all-Union philology conference to create a single standard Yiddish orthography.[78] At the request of the research institutions, in early 1926 the CJEB asked the Ukrainian-based Yiddish Party newspaper *Shtern* and the Belorussian Yiddish newspaper *Oktyabr* to begin including a special column addressing Yiddish orthography.[79] Avrom Veviorke, a Moscow-based member of the Soviet Yiddish intelligentsia, published a series of articles criticizing the work of Veynger's language commission in Minsk. Veviorke, who had been a radical language reformer in the early days of Soviet Yiddish reform, suggested that the pace of reform needed to slow down, lest it threaten the basic stability of the existing Yiddish writing system. In addition, he argued that this reform had to fit the changed social and political context. By this he meant that while the early radicals could have fantastic visions of Yiddish's future due to the radicalized nature of Civil War society, the NEP period of institution building called for a more pragmatic approach. In other words, Veviorke was calling for language reform instead of a language revolution.[80]

A number of articles in *Oktyabr* attacked Veviorke for being "too bourgeois" in his modest proposals. The writers of these articles called for the formation of an all-Union commission to enable them to force through their more radical proposals.[81] However, as head of the linguistic division, Veynger established the official Minsk position.[82] To simplify the writing system, he proposed eliminating duplicate letters that represented the same sounds such as *taf-tet*, *sin-samekh*, *kaf-kuf*, and *khet-khaf*.[83] Second, Yiddish had very strong and independent dialects that posed challenges for creating a standardized writing system. Veynger believed there already existed a more-or-less universal literary Yiddish, which was a synthesis of various Yiddish dialects. But the orthography did not match this literary Yiddish, and speakers of different dialects pronounced existing letters in different ways. How could a standard Yiddish eliminate this ambiguity except by reeducating all Yiddish speakers to a standard Soviet Yiddish pronunciation in linguistic jargon? Veynger argued that spelling could not be dependent on dialects, otherwise standardization would be impossible.[84] Finally, Veynger believed that a standardized Yiddish would make publishing in Yiddish simpler and more efficient, and would lower the prices of Yiddish books, making them more accessible to poor Yiddish readers.[85]

Zaretsky responded to Veynger by denying that there was a "standard literary Yiddish" to which the writing system needed to be matched, and challenged the idea that language reform needed to follow historical developments. He accused Veynger of being simplistic by thinking that orthographic reform alone would create a standardized Yiddish. He argued that reformers needed to recognize dialectical differences and create a writing system that reflected those differences. As for the trajectory of language reform, while Veynger thought the work of

Soviet Yiddish language reformers was to follow the natural historical process of language evolution, Zaretsky saw the language reformer's job as forcing the hand of history. History, Zaretsky argued, had muddled the Yiddish language with non-phonetic spellings, a special status for Hebrew root words, and an orthography so non-standard that each of the three major Soviet Yiddish newspapers spelled words in its own way. Rather than following history, he maintained, language reform was about shaping history, or correcting historical mistakes. For Zaretsky it was the job of the language reformers to create a new writing system and then have it become a historical reality through the instruments of dissemination – schools, books, and the press.[86] Language reformers would be the vanguard of modern Yiddish.

While the debates among linguists were raging in the Soviet Yiddish press, representatives of the Jewish divisions of the Enlightenment Commissariats convened a meeting in 1927 to plan an orthographic commission that would be empowered by the state to standardize Soviet Yiddish,[87] with the commission's decisions eventually becoming state policy. The list of those invited included teachers, editors, publishers, and linguists, in addition to the representatives of the Enlightenment Commissariat who were planning the event.[88]

The conference opened on April 9, 1928. According to one participant, "the greatest Yiddish linguists . . . and lots of teachers" all gathered in Kharkov.[89] The commission broke down into two polarized positions that one reviewer termed "right" and "left," using the political rhetoric of the time. In the late 1920s, "right" elements were perceived to be more nationally oriented, those who aimed for preserving existing forms, and for a generally slower pace of reform. "Left" elements were more radicalized, wanted to force change rather than wait for historical developments, and tarred their rightist opponents as nationalists.[90] The reviewer argued that Shtif, Litvakov, and Veviorke – the "right" elements – thought about the present needs of Soviet Jewry, and thus, were more concerned about adults' use of language. (Although the reviewer did not include Veynger, he was also part of the "right" element.) Because of this, they favored moderate reform. This group thought that radical change might cut off Soviet Yiddish publications from foreign readers, and would cause a break between the international Yiddish intelligentsia and the Soviet one. Litvakov was quoted as saying, "We can't use our readership to carry out experiments. Orthography should unify people, not drive them apart."[91] The "left" group, including Zaretsky and other younger linguists, believed that a radical operation would be less painful and in comparison with a gradual move toward standardization, would be more useful in the end.[92] Party affiliation did not determine group alliance. Litvakov, a high ranking Party member and de-facto official Yiddish cultural commissar, voted with non-Party members in favor of moderation.

The commission passed a number of moderate reforms early in the proceedings, but encountered a major controversy over the proposed elimination of the five final letters from the Yiddish alphabet, a reform Zaretsky had been publicly advocating since the 1923 publication of *Yiddish*.[93] The final resolution reflected Zaretsky's more radical proposal. It created a standardized orthography in thirty-five cases where there had either been ambiguity or where the conference decided to move forward with reform. The most significant change, and the one that came to define Soviet Yiddish as opposed to non-Soviet Yiddish, was the elimination of the five final letters. Those opposed to this move thought that by eliminating the letters, and thus implementing a radical reform in the visual appearance of the language, Soviet Yiddish and its practitioners would be establishing a standardized Yiddish that the rest of the Yiddish-speaking world did not recognize. Soviet Yiddish would be erecting a wall between itself and the international Yiddish that was slowly being standardized at the Institute for Jewish Research (YIVO), the competing Yiddish institution just across the border in Vilna.[94]

The orthography commission recognized that creating an official orthography and implementing it were different matters. For this reason, many disseminators of Yiddish were invited to the conference. If publishers, editors, and teachers supported the new orthography, it could be implemented more easily than if the decision had been made by linguists at the academy and presented to publishers and teachers as a fait accompli. The conference participants wrote an implementation plan that reflected the ways language specialists thought language change diffused through Soviet society. All reforms aside from the elimination of the five final letters were to be implemented at the start of the 1929–30 school year. As for the most radical reform to the new alphabet, the first to transition were the publications of the Kiev Institute, and its philological journal, *The Yiddish Language*, as well as pedagogical journals, teacher training books, and books for first and second graders.[95] Next were the two Ukrainian Yiddish literary journals and then the popular newspapers, which introduced the reform gradually by having a special section devoted to the new orthography. Literature, for the most part, was expected to shift over quickly; for older students in high schools and professional programs, the plan gave them an extra school year with the old orthography, assuming that it would take this stratum of people longer to become used to the lack of final letters. By 1932, there would be no final letters left in Soviet Yiddish publications.

To make the reform state policy, *Glavlit*, the censorship organization, signed it, and said that publishers and editors who did not implement the new reform in a timely fashion might encounter problems getting censor's approval for their publications.[96] As a result, publishing houses often put clauses in their contracts with writers stating that manuscripts had to be written according to the new writing rules: "The original manuscript must correspond to academic writing standards and terminology. In case of deviating from these standards, the publishing house will make all necessary corrections at the author's expense."[97] After the January 1, 1932, deadline, publishers used financial pressure to force writers to utilize the new orthography. The new reform was implemented with little overt resistance. Through centralization, state sponsorship, and the concentration of publishing in fewer and fewer places, the new reform process took place quite rapidly. By 1930, all Yiddish publishing houses were using reformed Yiddish.

The 1928 Second Cultural Congress created the Central Orthographic Commission (COC) to continue the work of the orthography conference. After Veynger's death in February 1929, Shtif and Zaretsky – the two who faced off at the orthography conference – continued the reform process. In 1932, they put together the *Orthographic Dictionary*, which codified more than ten years of language reform. With the "right" and the "left" well represented, the COC oversaw the process of propagating modern Soviet Yiddish.

LATINIZATION – THE FINAL FRONTIER OF SOVIET YIDDISH LANGUAGE REFORM

After de-Germanification and de-Hebraization, the next radical step in reforming Yiddish orthography was to eliminate the entire Hebrew alphabet and "Latinize" Yiddish, a proposal that had been made by Yiddish reformers in the past, but one that had remained on the fringes of debate until the late 1920s. Latinization, or the replacement of an alphabet by the Latin/Western alphabet, became a somewhat common practice in the 1920s after the first wave of decolonization following World War I. In 1928–9, during Ataturk's modernizing revolution in Turkey, the Ottoman script was replaced by the Latin alphabet. The move was meant to highlight Turkey's Europeanness and to represent visually the large-scale secularization that Ataturk had initiated in the 1920s.

Latinization was also on the agenda inside the Soviet borders from 1922 until at least 1932, although the case of Yiddish will show that Latinization was an issue as late as 1934.[98] There were proposals as early as 1920 to Latinize all Soviet languages as a means of bringing to fruition the call for the proletariat to unite.[99] Latinization of Soviet national minorities' languages occurred first among ethnic groups that used the Cyrillic alphabet. The Yakuts in 1920 and the Ossetians in 1923 abandoned the Cyrillic script for Latin.[100] As a large-scale movement, however, Latinization began in Azerbaijan, and initially spread in republics that had been using Arabic script, or as it was called "the Turko-Tatar alphabet." There was particular focus on the languages that used the Arabic alphabets because of Arabic's connection to Islam. The desire to Latinize languages with an Arabic script would not only modernize these languages by making them more European, but would also break the power of Muslim clerics.

The Latinization movement in the Soviet Union began independent of the central Soviet government. According to Samed Agamaly-Ogdy, a high-ranking member of the Azerbaijani central executive committee and one of the leading proponents of Latinization in Azerbaijan, the movement began as early as 1919, before Azerbaijan even became part of the Soviet Union. He dates the beginning of Latinization to the publication of a Latinized textbook and its presentation to the Azerbaijani parliament. In 1922, Agamaly-Ogdy convinced the newly Sovietized Azerbaijani government to form a Committee for a New Turkic Alphabet and establish a Latinized Azeri newspaper. In a similar way that the Soviet Yiddish intelligentsia brought the suppression of Hebrew to the central government, Azeri intellectuals introduced Latinization as a pedagogical and political issue to Soviet politics. In 1926, a pan-republican congress was called to discuss Latinizing all Turko-Tatar alphabets, and the proposal was well received. Participants at the Congress agreed that Latinization would open up their cultures to more Western influence, and would raise the cultural level of the people. It was only at this point that the state and Party officials in Moscow began to take a larger role in overseeing Latinization for alphabets with Arabic script. Latinization was still seen as a radical step. Other voices in the Caucasus and Central Asia were calling for the reform, rather than replacement, of Arabic script into a single, modern alphabet.[101] Latinization was not the only road to modernizing "backward" cultures. But it was seen as the quickest way.

Latinization began to spread beyond the part of the Soviet Union dealing with Arabic script. In 1926, at the Belorussian Language Reform conference, the Latinization of Belorussian was on the conference agenda, although was not implemented.[102] Latinization also affected Soviet German language activists. In 1927, a reviewer of German-language texts complained that most German books in the Soviet Union were still published in Gothic, rather than Latin, script that made reading more difficult. He advocated switching all Soviet German publishing over to Latin.[103]

As Latinization gradually moved to the center of Soviet language reform, the central state apparatus in Moscow took an increasing interest in how to support and oversee its spread. In connection with the direction Latinization was taking among Turkic languages, the Council of People's Commissars (*Sovnarkom*) began to provide funding for the official New Turkic Alphabet Commission.[104] By mid-1928, all of the Turkic republics had legislatively accepted the new Turkic alphabet and begun its implementation.[105] In a resolution from August 1929, the Presidium of the All-Union Central Executive Committee agreed to expand an initial edict to Latinize Arabic script alphabet to include other alphabets.[106] By 1930, according to the Central Executive Committee, thirty-six nationalities and more than 3,500,000 people had shifted their languages' alphabets to Latin.[107] These included three Mongolian languages and seven Iranian languages including Judeo-Tat, the language of Dagestani Jews, and Judeo-Tadzhik, both of which abandoned the Hebrew alphabet.[108] Statistical tables representing the distribution of Latin typeface throughout the Soviet Union show Latin letters being sent to Chinese territory, Korean territory, and Karelia, an ethnically Finnish area. In the year 1932 alone, the high water mark for Soviet Latinization, sixty-six languages switched to the Latin alphabet.[109]

Not surprisingly, there was some support of Latinization among Yiddish linguistic circles, especially given the initial rationale for Latinization – to undermine religious influence over language and to make all languages mutually legible. Yiddish had already reformed away from the Hebrew root words and written them out phonetically, and several reformers had commented on the Hebrew alphabet's inability to represent the diversity of sounds (phonemes) in Yiddish. Latinization could be seen as the conclusion to the process of modernization.

Yiddishists themselves had proposed Latinization ever since the Yiddishist movement began in the first decade of the twentieth century. The earliest example of Latinized Yiddish was the work of the Romanian Yiddishist, Jacob Sotek, who wrote linguistic articles in a Latinized Yiddish at the turn of the century.[110] One anonymous author in the journal *Life and Scholarship* proposed Latinization in 1910, although apparently readers did not receive his proposal well.[111] In 1912, a New York Yiddish journal called *Our Script (Unser Shrift)* was published once, using Latin letters, and in 1923, a Vienna-based journal called *Beginning (Unhojb)* did the same.[112] Finally, in 1926, Chaim Zhitlovsky, one of the conveners of the Czernowitz Conference and a well-known socialist Yiddish activist, called for the Latinization of Yiddish on the pages of the New York newspaper *The Day (Der Tog)*.[113]

Latinization had never been very popular among Soviet Yiddish language reformers. The idea had been broached at various times during the 1920s, but it had never been taken seriously until 1930, when it became the dominant trend in general Soviet language reform.[114] That year, Zaretsky began supporting the idea, a shift from his earlier opinions. Zaretsky had come out against Latinization in 1926, and, even at the Second All-Union Cultural Congress in Kharkov in 1928, Zaretsky noted that "someone made a proposal for Latinization, but the proposal was laughed down."[115] In his 1928 preparatory remarks for the Congress, Zaretsky stated that "as for changing the Yiddish script for a Latin one, there will probably not be any discussion [at the Congress]."[116] Complete Latinization was not part of his own, more radical agenda.

Nonetheless, if one followed the theory behind Yiddish language reform (simplicity, uniformity, accessibility, lower publication costs) and the trajectory of Soviet language policy, then Latinization was the obvious next step. The Central Orthographic Commission created a unified Latin system to be used when transcribing Yiddish words, but this was intended only as a research and publication tool. It was the Soviet-wide trend toward Latinization, a reform movement initiated in Azerbaijan, that put it on the Yiddish agenda. Latinization marked the shift from language reform inspired by Jewish socialists and their visions of a future Jewish culture to reform shaped primarily by Soviet-wide policies.

In December 1929, Moshe Kamenshteyn published an article in the Kharkov newspaper *Shtern* in favor of Latinizing Yiddish. He argued that Soviet Jews should Latinize because everyone was doing it: Germans were moving from Gothic to Latin letters, Arabic-script languages were being shifted, and there was even talk of Latinizing Russian. He also suggested that there were very practical problems that Yiddish culture faced because of the strangeness of the Yiddish alphabet. "Recently I was at a meeting of the Book Union publishing house (*Knihospilka*) at which we discussed Yiddish book distribution, and they told me that in smaller provincial towns, bookstore workers were not Jewish, and they simply could not read the lists of Yiddish books or the titles of the books."[117] Finally, he pointed out that the Jewish alphabet had structural limitations that Latin did not have. Yiddish had many letters that looked nearly identical; it had no capital letters; and when writing Yiddish, one had to lift the pen from the paper in between each letter, making writing much slower than with Latin letters. Last and most importantly, the right to left system of the Hebrew alphabet created an array of problems for publishing houses.

Authoritative calls for Latinization were not heard until 1930 when the Central Orthographic Commission officially endorsed it, a move that was clearly in harmony with the general trend throughout the Soviet Union. "Latinization of the Yiddish alphabet will assist in the cultural revolution of the Jewish masses (and to a certain extent also in the cultural revolution in the Union overall)."[118] The commission then listed seven reasons why Latinization made sense:

1) Latin script is better than Yiddish script. Yiddish comes from Hebrew script that was created for a Semitic language. The script has never really fit the Indo-European character of Yiddish.
2) Latin script goes from left to right. This would make fusing Yiddish texts with those of other languages, with mathematical formulas, with musical notes, easier.
3) Latin letters are better designed than Yiddish letters. No extra marks are needed.

4) We will be able to use the illustrations [from publications using] languages written left to right.

5) It will be easier to print Yiddish materials since every press has Latin typeface, especially after the Latinization of the Central Asian languages.

6) Yiddish will be more accessible to non-Jews. Scholars in Yiddish never have their work read, because no one can approach it.

7) Ideological reasons – breaking ties with the Hebrew language.[119]

The first five points were all part of the modernization process of Yiddish. Points six and seven had overtly political implications. If Yiddish were Latinized, it would not look so foreign to scholars and others who wanted to approach Yiddish texts. This point goes along with the first one – the Latin alphabet was easier to learn because it was familiar and thus, less intimidating. Most intellectuals and scholars already knew the Latin alphabet, and many knew German, which was potentially similar enough to Yiddish to allow non-Jewish scholars access to Yiddish scholarly work. Latinization would serve two functions. It would remove the Jewish appearance of Yiddish making it less alien to others and making it have less in common with Hebrew. It would also bring Yiddish scholarship into closer contact with European scholarship. Latinization could be perceived as simultaneously anti-national – it sought to get rid of the historically distinctive appearance of the language – and very national, because Latinizers hoped to make Yiddish language scholarship more well-known, respected, and modern. Point seven fit in with both the intra-Jewish politics of de-Hebraizing Yiddish, because of Hebrew's association with the petty bourgeoisie, Zionism, and religion, and with the original discourse of Latinization about breaking the power of religion.

So why did Yiddish Latinization never happen in the Soviet Union, especially since other Soviet Jewish languages such as Judeo-Tadzhik were Latinized? In 1931, the COC was scrapped in favor of an All-Union Orthography Conference in Kiev. At the conference, there was little mention of Latinization. Instead, the concern was that the COC had not "carried out its earlier work efficiently." The report from the conference showed that the members agreed that rather than carrying out any further radical reforms (such as Latinization), they should further the work of the Second All-Union Jewish Cultural Congress, implement that conference's edicts, and continue working on linguistic details that had not been discussed at the original conference. The 1932 *Orthographic Dictionary* made no mention of Latinization. Language reformers were continuing to focus on implementation of old reforms rather than carrying out new ones. Ironically, most of the orthographic reforms did take place, and Soviet Yiddish publications no longer used final letters.

Moshe Shulman, one of the original Soviet Yiddish reformers, attributed the perceived failures of the COC to its chairman, Litvakov, whom he accused of sabotaging its work. He asserted that Litvakov was an "enemy of the people." The rhetoric Shulman used reflects the language of Party purges of the late 1920s and early 1930s in which Litvakov, a Party member since late 1920, was caught. Shulman's accusations may or may not have been based in fact, although it is unlikely that Litvakov would have worked against the reforms he agreed to in 1928. However, since Zaretsky and Litvakov had been on opposite sides in the 1928 orthography debates, when Litvakov lost, it seems reasonable that as chairman of the new COC, he might do what he could to slow down the pace of reform. It is also likely that Litvakov used his influence to prevent Zaretsky's Latinization campaign from taking effect. In addition, other linguists who had been against Zaretsky's more radical reform movements, most notably Nokhum Shtif, who was still the editor of *The Yiddish Language*, continued to come out against any further radicalization in Yiddish language reform.[120] Therefore, although the 1930 articles by the Central Orthographic Commission and Zaretsky were convincing and seemed official, two major cultural activists were staunchly against the plan.

Another factor in Latinization was the role played by Semen Dimanshteyn, an important state-level figure in the general Soviet Latinization campaign, a long-time Bolshevik, and founder of the Yiddish Party paper *Emes*. Dimanshteyn, a member of the Council of Nationalities, was a key figure in the Central Asian Latinization campaign. As liaison between the Soviet Yiddish intelligentsia and the Communist Party, he also ensured the continued existence of Yiddish language cultural activities. Since Dimanshteyn had the power to push through Latinization for other languages, the fact that he did not use this power on Yiddish shows that he used his influence to prevent it from taking place.[121] With Litvakov and Shtif's (and most likely Dimanshteyn's) influence, Latinization was taken off the agenda just as quickly as it was put on. The issue was addressed once more in February 1932, in an article by Shtif and Elye Spivak who came out against Latinization, and by Zaretsky who published an article in a Russian-language journal favoring Latinization.[122] The issue then died.

In 1934, long after the discussion of Latinization of Yiddish and in the Soviet Union more generally had passed, the only Yiddish book to be published in the Soviet Union appeared.[123] That same year, Ben Tsiyon Ben Yehuda (also known as Itamar Ben Avi), the son of Eliezer Ben Yehuda, considered by some as the father of modern Hebrew, began publishing a Hebrew newspaper in Jerusalem in Latin letters.[124] The Latinized Soviet Yiddish book, *The Folklore of Yiddish Music (Jidisher Muzik-Folklor)*, was published by the Institute for Jewish Proletarian Culture in Kiev under the editorship of Meir Viner, who took over after Shtif died. The author offered an explanation for the choice. "This book is appearing in two languages – in Yiddish and Russian. In Yiddish we are printing it with a Latin transcription, because in the given circumstances, it is technically easier. Aside from that, we had in mind the decision of the Central Orthographic Commission that said that scholarly publications must gradually adopt the new Latin alphabet."[125] Since music was a special case when Latinizing made the most sense, it is easy to understand why the only Latin Yiddish book was a book of songs. But the editors also Latinized to make a statement, and their reference to a COC decision suggests that this might have been a last ditch effort to prove that Latinization could have worked. By 1934, the Soviet Union was moving away from Latinization. The moment for a Latin Yiddish had passed.

Yiddish language reform and the modernization of Yiddish in the Soviet Union put into practice many ideas that were part of both Soviet discourse about language and pre-revolutionary Yiddish philology. The shape of Soviet Yiddish language reform was informed by several ideologies: Yiddishist concerns that to modernize Jews, Yiddish too had to be modernized; Soviet nationalities policy, which conceived of Yiddish as the means for the Soviet Jewish nation to develop a Soviet Jewish culture; and the animosity between Yiddishists and Hebraists that led the drive toward a Jewish nation with a single national language. In the late 1920s, Soviet politics became more important than the national concerns for Yiddish's future. Yiddish linguists on the other side of the border were lambasted in Soviet Jewish publications and reforms were done in the name of politicizing language. Through the 1920s, though, language reform was implemented for the reasons Borochov set out in 1913 – to create a simple, standard Yiddish that could bring together high and low, city and shtetl, intelligentsia and folk, to create a modern national language used by the modern Soviet Jewish nation.

4

Who Owns the Means of Cultural Production?

The Soviet Yiddish Publishing Industry of the 1920s

The increase in book production is the best sign of the growth of our culture.
–Aaron Makagon, Soviet Jewish Cultural Critic, 1925

In May 1921, the Central Bureau of *Evsektsiia* reported a rather bizarre crime – the midnight theft of reams of paper that had been earmarked for producing Soviet Yiddish books. The evidence included the obvious masses of missing paper from the Yiddish publisher's warehouse in central Moscow, as well as broken doors and windows. The police were called to investigate this property crime. But given its unusual nature (who steals reams of paper?), the local police division called in the Peasants' and Workers' Inspectorate (*Rabkrin*), the Soviet organization charged with ensuring the political health of the new state. Was the theft of paper also a political crime? The fact that the political machinery of the state was mobilized suggests that it was. The culprit could have been desperate enough for paper that s/he would steal it from anyone, or it could have been someone who did not want this particular publishing house to produce its books. Some on the *Evsektsiia* suspected that anti–Semitism was the motive. Perhaps, they thought, given the very tight supply of paper in the early Soviet period, which was under strict paper rationing, someone thought that Soviet Yiddish books and newspapers were not worthy of paper. The *Evsektsiia* insinuated that someone was sabotaging the production of Soviet Jewish culture. The investigation, however, turned up no suspects, and no arrests were made.[1]

The Soviet Yiddish intelligentsia won the battle to make Yiddish the language that defined Soviet Jewry and, over the course of the 1920s, reformed Yiddish into a modern, standardized language. But to begin the process of cultural transformation that would foster a Soviet Jewish nation, that language needed to be disseminated and internalized. At the heart of this cultural revolution were publishing houses – the institutions that turned ideas and concepts into printed words and images that were the building blocks of this new culture. Print was the single most important means of circulating knowledge in the Soviet Union during the 1920s and 1930s; other means of disseminating ideas, such as radio and film, lacked the necessary institutional infrastructure to play such an important role.[2]

Theoretically, the Soviet state was encouraging the production of ethnic minorities' print culture in order to bring the modern ideas of the Soviet state and the Communist Party to its multiethnic population. Because of this, publishing houses that worked in ethnic minorities' languages produced many translations of Lenin and Marx, textbooks for new Soviet schools, and other material that was meant to create a particularly Soviet culture in an ethnic group's native language. Since Yiddish was the language of Soviet Jewry, Soviet publishing houses produced Yiddish Party newspapers, Yiddish translations of the Marxist classics, science textbooks in Yiddish, and other material that would create Yiddish-speaking Soviet citizens.

But the Soviet Yiddish intelligentsia, which was empowered to produce Soviet Yiddish print culture, had its own ideological visions of remaking the Jewish people. According to Terry Martin, during the 1920s, the central Soviet state and Communist Party encouraged each ethnic group to produce its own version of Soviet culture in its native language based on its own socialist traditions. Ukrainians, Georgians, and others imagined a new culture based on their own literary and cultural traditions all within the framework of building the Soviet state. The Soviet Yiddish intelligentsia was no exception. In the 1920s, like their linguist colleagues who reformed Yiddish, the writers, editors and publishers within the Soviet Yiddish intelligentsia had relative autonomy to create Soviet Yiddish print culture. And the intelligentsia produced propaganda that supported the state. It was exciting for many Jewish intellectuals to imagine an entire bookshelf of modern science in Yiddish or to produce the best translation of Lenin in Yiddish. But the intelligentsia also published modernist poetry, nineteenth-century Yiddish plays, Jewish demography, and histories of the Jewish working class movement.

Not only did the Soviet Yiddish intelligentsia have ideological space to shape Soviet Jewish culture in its own image, it also had institutional space. Until 1928, unlike many other ethnic minorities, Soviet Yiddish publishing took place primarily in establishments dedicated exclusively to Yiddish publishing, such as the burglarized publishing house. The state and Party bureaucrats who regulated Yiddish publishing were also members of the Soviet Yiddish intelligentsia, who had long been interested in creating secular Yiddish culture.[3]

YIDDISH PUBLISHING IN EASTERN EUROPE

The printed Yiddish word has a history that stretches back to the years immediately following the explosion of vernacular print after Martin Luther published the Bible in German.[4] The oldest extant printed Yiddish text is a translation of the Passover poem *Adir Hu*, from a 1526 Prague edition of the haggadah. The oldest printed book, Rabbi Anshel's *Mirkevet ha-mishneh*, was published in 1534 in Krakow, Poland. Although these examples come from the newer Yiddish-speaking communities in Eastern Europe, Yiddish publishing actually originated in Germany and in Northern Italy, the historic origins of Yiddish and Ashkenaz, but these texts did not survive.[5] Due to the language hierarchy within Jewish culture, early Yiddish literature tended toward low-status genres, such as popular literature, romances, morality books for women, and Yiddish translations of Hebrew-language religious texts for the "simple reader."[6] However, the development of a Jewish publishing industry did lead to the birth of the first Yiddish newspaper, *Di Kurantin*, in Holland, which was printed twice a week in 1686–7.[7]

Throughout its history, the Jewish publishing industry was always shaped by its economic, political, social, and cultural surroundings. First, every publishing house had to have a source of income – a single patron, a private family donor, income on book sales, or state or crown subsidies – and publishing houses were always constrained by the interests of these benefactors. Second, all publishing houses had to work within legal and political limitations that shaped what and how material could be published. From harsh nineteenth-century tsarist restrictions on Jewish publishing – which pushed the industry away from Russia and toward the Kingdom of Poland, especially Warsaw, and the Austro-Hungarian empire – to the Soviet era during which the state literally left its mark on every publication, non-Jewish political powers always shaped the Jewish publishing industry. Third, all publishing houses had to work within the ideological, political, and religious biases of the publishers, editors, and writers. Fourth, specific to Jewish publishing, Yiddish and Hebrew are printed in the Hebrew alphabet, so Yiddish books could only be produced at places that had Hebrew typeface. Because of this, the production of Jewish print culture generally happened within specifically Jewish institutions. Finally, Yiddish-language publishing had to work within the parameters of the Hebrew-Yiddish language hierarchy. When print culture in the vernacular Yiddish did not have high status, Yiddish literature tended to concentrate on low-status genres, while publishers produced large numbers of Hebrew books like Torahs, Talmuds, and other rabbinic literature. Compare that with the situation in the Soviet 1920s, when Yiddish was the high-status language. Yiddish book production expanded dramatically, and the publication of Talmuds and Torahs ceased.

As the restrictions of the earlier tsarist period and the cultural taboo against Yiddish waned over the nineteenth century, Yiddish publishing became an industry, and publishers – especially large trade publishers in Warsaw – turned a profit.[8] Warsaw's Yiddish publishing industry reflected the dominant trend of late tsarist Russian-language publishing that catered to a burgeoning mass reading public. In the fifty years before World War I, the Russian empire witnessed a boom in Russian-language publishing. In 1825, there were only 583 titles produced in the Russian Empire, 323 (55 percent) of which were in Russian. By 1860, the total number of books had risen to 2,085, and by 1895, there were 11,548 titles published in the Empire, 8,728 (76 percent) of which were in Russian.[9]

The Yiddish publishing market was small in comparison to the Russian one, but large in comparison to other ethnic minorities in the Russian Empire. For example, in 1908, all Ukrainian periodicals combined had a total circulation of 20,000, serving an estimated Ukrainian-speaking population of thirty million.[10] In 1906, there were already five Yiddish daily newspapers and three weekly ones with a total circulation of more than 120,000 in Warsaw alone, serving a tsarist empire Jewish population of five million (according to the 1897 census).[11] In 1911, the first Eastern European large circulation (over 100,000 copies) dailies, *Today (Haynt)* and *Moment (Moment)* appeared in Warsaw. There clearly was a large market for Yiddish publications in Poland and other parts of the Pale of Settlement.

Unfortunately for the Soviet Yiddish intelligentsia, the two most important Yiddish publishing centers – Warsaw and Vilna – and the two largest Yiddish book markets – Poland and Lithuania – ended up on the wrong side of the border after the Polish-Soviet War of 1920–1. The most important Yiddish publishing center that remained in the Soviet Union was in Kiev, which blossomed as a Jewish publishing center after the 1905 Revolution because of its role as a political and cultural center for Jewish socialists and nationalists.[12] Kiev was also a center for Yiddish modernists, who had difficulty getting their work published in Warsaw's big publishing houses. The famous Yiddish writer David Bergelson could not find a publisher for *At the Train Station (Arum vokzal)* and had to get Nachman Mayzl, a wealthy patron of Yiddish culture and a cultural critic, to intercede on his behalf with the Warsaw-based Progress Publishing House to publish his book, the first impressionist novel in Yiddish.[13] To break Yiddish writers' dependence on the economies of scale of the Warsaw houses, Mayzl opened his own publishing house in Kiev, Art Publishing House (*Kunst farlag*).

With the outbreak of World War I, Yiddish publishing suffered a general downturn as resources were diverted for other uses. Yiddish was doubly targeted due to both restrictions on non-Cyrillic publishing in the borderlands, and the July 1915 ban on printing books using the Hebrew alphabet in the areas adjacent to the front line, which included virtually all of the Pale.[14] In the first year of the war, eighteen periodicals, including eight dailies, were closed down.[15] After the February Revolution of 1917, the provisional government lifted the World War I-era restrictions on Jewish publishing, and work in both Yiddish and Hebrew instantly proliferated.

SOVIET YIDDISH NEWSPAPER PUBLISHING

In the anarchic political world of revolutionary Russia, every group was competing for followers, and each one produced its own newspapers, pamphlets, posters, and other forms of propaganda. In the days following the October Revolution, three Jewish Bolsheviks petitioned the new heads of the government, V.I. Lenin, and the head of the All-Russian Executive Committee, Yakov Sverdlov, for resources to publish a Yiddish-language Bolshevik newspaper modeled after the Party newspaper, *Pravda*. Even though it had many Jews within its leadership, the Bolsheviks as a political movement had never catered to a specifically Jewish audience. As Bolsheviks moved from underground agitators to state builders, these activists felt that the Party needed to inform Jews about the ideas of the new ruling party and to encourage them to support the new regime.

Soviet Yiddish newspapers, which began appearing in 1918, were an outgrowth of the twenty-year history of socialist Yiddish newspapers. Bundist intellectuals had struggled with the material, political, and ideological challenges of publishing a Yiddish-language newspaper for Jewish workers.[16] Most of its leaders were socially and culturally a part of the Russian socialist intellectual milieu. Many of them looked down on Yiddish for its lower cultural status within Jewish enlightenment culture, and, more practically, were not as comfortable working in Yiddish as they were in Russian. Publishing a socialist Yiddish newspaper came from a practical need, in the tradition of the *maskilim*, to bring new ideas to the Jewish masses in a language they understood. But it also came from the populist, nationalist desires of many Jewish socialists, who wanted to develop a new kind of Jewish culture based on the people's language, Yiddish. Many Jewish socialists who became leaders of the Soviet Yiddish intelligentsia had extensive experience editing and producing non-Communist socialist Yiddish newspapers. Moshe Litvakov had been editor of the Kiev *New Times (Naye Tsayt)*; Esther Frumkina edited the Minsk *Alarm (Der Veker)*. In addition to the political and ideological similarities between Bundist and Communist Yiddish newspaper publishing, there were also similar material challenges, such as lack of finances and paper, weak distribution networks, and the fact that the majority of the intended readership lived far away from where the intelligentsia lived and produced the newspaper.[17]

The didactic and propagandistic purpose that underlay Bolshevik newspapers can be traced back to Lenin's statement that the newspaper was a "collective propagandist, a collective organizer of the masses around the Party, and an invisible bond between the Party and the working class."[18] It was the voice of the vanguard Party to its constituents, and it was also a means for Party members to talk to each other. Newspapers needed to be both of the people and for the people, as well as of and for the intellectual and political vanguard.

TYPES OF SOVIET NEWSPAPERS

The Bolsheviks were excellent propagandizers and understood that not every Soviet citizen needed the same kind of newspaper. Some people were accustomed to reading a morning newspaper, while others were barely literate and needed to have the news presented to them in different ways. To best reach a diverse reading audience, the Bolsheviks established an array of newspapers that aimed at a different stratum of the literate, and sometimes illiterate, public. Each large Soviet national minority, including Soviet Jews, had a newspaper network in its native language. At the bottom of the hierarchy, directed at illiterate Jews or Jews who did not read newspapers, were live newspapers (*lebedike* or *mundlekhe tsaytung* in Yiddish, *zhivaia* or *ustnaia gazeta* in Russian), an oral form of disseminating news and educating and entertaining listeners.

Local Jewish activists convened an "editorial board" to read through the news from wire services or other newspapers, and then to write articles that served as the live newspaper's script. This script presented the news, analysis, and political propaganda in an entertaining way, and it was then performed to a public gathering. Although people began producing live newspapers during the material crisis of the Civil War period, when there wasn't paper to produce a real newspaper, some argued that live newspapers could actually give a listener more information than traditional newspapers, because the live newspaper could provide gestures and visual cues to the audience to assist them in interpreting the news. Live newspapers could also reach the illiterate. Critics advised using music and creative set designs to enliven the productions.[19] At the Fourth All-Russian *Evsektsiia* conference in August 1921, Frumkina stated, "under no circumstances should a live newspaper simply be read like a standard newspaper. It must be living, its articles short and striking."[20] In Kiev, the newspaper *Communist Banner (Komunistishe Fon or Komfon)* claimed to attract 200–300 workers to its live newspaper presentations, but only if the readings were followed by a concert. Without the concerts, attendance dropped off precipitously.[21] In 1923, on the twenty-fifth anniversary of the Russian Social Democratic Workers Party, the entire *Communist Banner* editorial board, including the editor-in-chief, Henekh Kazakevitch – who attracted large crowds to his live newspaper readings, because he was known as a good public speaker – presented a celebratory live newspaper.[22]

Above live newspapers on the Soviet journalistic hierarchy were wall newspapers, single-sheet large format texts aimed at Jews who had no more than a few minutes to glance at a newspaper on the wall in the workplace. Wall newspapers were cheap and easy to produce, and so they began to appear in the Civil War period when most localities were cut off from larger regional newspapers, and when there were not local resources to produce a circulating newspaper. Most of the early wall newspapers were just translations of the Soviet wire service *Rosta* (which later became *TASS*, the Telegraphic Agency of the Soviet Union), and were plastered on walls and in institutions around town to inform local residents of the latest news. Wall newspapers were also produced in factories and were intended to solidify a factory's collective identity with articles written by factory workers.[23]

The most important part of a wall newspaper was its visual appearance. Wall newspapers were illustrated with cartoons and photographs, and if there was no money to hire an artist, as there often was not, editors "occasionally cut out pictures from other newspapers creating new montages with a pair of scissors."[24] Throughout the 1920s and into the 1930s, the wall newspaper expanded as an institution, with the goal of having a Yiddish wall newspaper in every institution, enterprise, or factory with a significant number of Yiddish readers.

Above the wall newspapers were locally circulating newspapers. The Bund had experimented with local newspapers in its early years as a way of attracting more readers, but there were significant conflicts between the local and central Bund newspapers over content and authority, similar to the issues the Soviet Yiddish newspaper network faced.[25] These conflicts between peripheries and center complicate the hierarchical newspaper structure described by scholars of the Russian-language press of the 1920s. According to Matthew Lenoe, provincial Russian-language Party newspapers did not publicly attack central ones.[26] Unlike the Russian-language press, the Bundist tradition of open public conflict between the periphery and the center continued throughout the 1920s in the Soviet Yiddish press with frequent fights between the central Moscow newspaper, *Emes,* and regional Yiddish papers, especially the Minsk-based *October (Oktyabr)*.

Above local newspapers stood the large republic newspapers whose intended audience was the entire Jewish population of a given republic. In Ukraine, *Communist Banner (Komunistishe Fon)* was published in Kiev from 1919 until 1924, and was replaced by the Kharkov-based *Star (Shtern)*, which started appearing in May 1925. In Belorussia, the Bund's daily newspaper *Alarm (Veker)* became Communist in 1921 and changed its name in 1925 to *October*.[27] At the top of the Soviet Yiddish newspaper publishing hierarchy sat the Moscow-based *Emes* (*Pravda* or "The Truth"), which set the tone and content for all other Yiddish newspapers.[28]

THE FIRST COMMUNIST YIDDISH NEWSPAPER IN HISTORY

Emes was born out of the Yiddish newspaper *Varhayt* ("Truth" in German), the newspaper the three Jewish Bolsheviks – Dimanshteyn, H. Tartsinsky, and Nokhum Bukhbinder – got permission from Lenin and Sverdlov to publish. According to Dimanshteyn, it was named the German *Varhayt*, because *Emes* was too close to the name of the Vienna-based Hebrew periodical *Ha-emes*. In its August 1918 reincarnation, the newspaper was renamed *Emes* to reflect the move away from a Germanized Yiddish toward a more "authentic" Yiddish.

Varhayt first appeared on March 8, 1918, International Women's Day, and was published out of the Marinsky Palace in St. Petersburg where the Jewish Commissariat had a small office. The newspaper was a labor of political drive, but it was not an object of high literary standards – it had three editors who wrote and proofread most of the articles, which were usually not well written, and the newspaper had a shoddy appearance, reflecting the poor resources available at the time. According to Shmuel Agursky, a leading Jewish Communist, writing on the tenth anniversary of *Varhayt*'s first appearance, "It was poor both in content and in appearance. Why? Because the newspaper was first put out by a small group of people who had more revolutionary passion than they had experience in writing articles and publishing a newspaper."[29] *Varhayt* only appeared twelve times and closed down in May after it was moved to Moscow.

The front-page articles of the inaugural edition included a manifesto called "Our Program," which informed readers why, for the first time, they were seeing a Yiddish-language Bolshevik periodical. The article explained who Jewish Communists were and how the Bolshevik Party was going to free the Jewish laboring masses from the tyranny of capitalist oppression. The other front-page article, given more space than the manifesto "Prepare for War" proclaimed, "Every worker and peasant, male and female must learn how to fire a gun!" clearly a slogan the editor had taken from other Bolshevik newspapers.[30] *Varhayt* was full of such exhortations, exclamatory headlines, and calls to arms.[31] Other non-Bolshevik Jewish periodicals were also calling on the Jewish masses to arm themselves during the violent Civil War period, but in most cases, the battle lines were seen not through a class lens of peasants and workers against the bourgeoisie, but through a national lens of Jews fighting against "Petliura's pogromists," in reference to the Ukrainian pogroms of 1918–19. *Varhayt* also contained a number of articles propagandizing against Zionism.

In addition to the propagandistic articles on the front page, the first edition included poetry by the American Sweatshop Yiddish poet Joseph Bovshover, and a political and literary analysis of his poetry by Agursky.[32] Bovshover's reputation as the quintessential Jewish worker's poet made him important to Jewish socialist movements who were looking to create a proletarian Yiddish literary history by finding past exemplars of worker writers. By publishing Bovshover in *Varhayt's* opening edition, the editors canonized him as a founder of a Jewish worker's literary history, and also made Yiddish poetry an inherent part of the Soviet Yiddish cultural project. The editors included Bovshover's poetry in three of the twelve editions of *Varhayt*.

In August 1918, the Jewish Commissariat and the *Evsektsiia* resurrected *Varhayt* under its new name, *Emes*, whose first issue focused on the question of Jewish particularity. The lead article exposed the "problem of a Jewish psychology," by which the authors meant a particularistic Jewish worldview, against which Bolshevism would work. On the one hand, the editors told readers that Jewish particularism was nationalistic, yet they were making this argument in a Jewish newspaper published in Yiddish, emphasizing Jewish difference. Another article on a similar theme was "Why the Jews have an 'exile mentality.'" The authors blamed "bourgeois Zionists" for fostering Jewish nationalism, which in turn inflamed anti-Semitism. The editors accused Zionists of fostering an exile mentality in their attempt to encourage Jews to leave Soviet Russia for Palestine.

Despite the fear of particularism, the editors were interested in identifying what, if anything, made Jews different from other ethnic groups. In the Soviet conception of national difference, the primary characteristics that defined a national group were its language, territory, and a group's "national culture."[33] Other differentiating characteristics were remnants from a previous era that were doomed to fade away as the socialist era brought all nationalities together. According to *Emes*, aside from the difference in language, which *Emes* itself was fostering by publishing in Yiddish, all characteristics that differentiated Jews from others were part of a "Jewish psychology," and psychology was something that could be educated away. At its first All-Russian Congress, the *Evsektsiia* leadership identified the linguistic and psychological differences between Jews and Russians as the two primary factors distinguishing these two nations.[34]

By resorting to psychological explanations, *Evsektsiia* and *Emes* wielded a sword that cut both ways. On the one hand, psychology was something that would change over time, and eventually render particular Jewish cultural expertise (theirs in particular as the developing Soviet Yiddish intelligentsia) unnecessary. On the other hand, psychology was something that needed great care and attention at the moment, and thus demanded the attention of those knowledgeable about the Jewish psyche. *Emes* was justifying the need for a separate Jewish section of the Party and separate Jewish cultural institutions by saying that the differences between Jews and others went beyond mere linguistic distinctions.

Although the authors were the same as those who wrote in the earlier *Varhayt*, the issues had changed – the "fire" that made *Varhayt* so propagandistic was subdued in *Emes*. The newspaper maintained a balance between what might be called Party-initiated news, such as the call to arms or the daily update on the status of Lenin's health after an assassination attempt in August 1918, and particularly Jewish stories, such as literature by Daniel Charny or regular updates on pogroms in Ukraine. There were advertisements for other non-Jewish Soviet publications placed next to ads for a new Vilna-based Yiddish weekly publication, *The Week (Di Vokh)*, edited by A. Vayter and S. Niger, showing the broad reach of Soviet Jewish culture in its early years.

Civil War conditions in Moscow became so dire that in early 1919 *Emes* closed.[35] In its place, a temporary bi-weekly journal called *Communist World* (*Komunistishe Velt*) appeared until *Emes* could start up again.[36] The Third All-Russian *Evsektsiia* conference in 1920 resolved, "It is necessary to expend all forces to establish printed *agitprop* [agitation and propaganda] on a solid base, and put an end to the chaos that reigns in this area of our Communist work."[37] *Evsektsiia* recognized that the re-establishment of *Emes* was dependent on the creation of a publishing network that would support a daily newspaper. To concentrate publishing resources in Moscow, the conference recommended closing down regional newspapers in Vitebsk and Gomel and transferring their staffs and printing materials. "These newspapers do not satisfy the needs of the broad layers of the Jewish working masses for the following reasons: since they are regional organs, and given the current conditions, they have in fact become purely local organs of this or that city and have lost the interest of more distant, but important, places."[38]

Evsektsiia believed that a central newspaper was so important that it was willing (and seemingly eager) to sacrifice the relatively successful regional newspapers coming out of Vitebsk and Gomel – two centers of Bundism where, one would think, Communist propaganda would be deemed a high priority. The material demands of centralization and rationalization of Yiddish publishing and the political desires of the activists to make Moscow both the Soviet and the Jewish cultural center made the re-establishment of *Emes* the highest priority. Moreover, they believed that establishing a single central Yiddish Party newspaper would allow these activists to spread their ideas beyond the Soviet borders, "in surrounding states, in America, England and other areas with strong leftist Jewish communities."[39] To assuage local activists' fears that the elimination of local papers in favor of a central one would mean cutting off the rural Jewish population, the activists called for the establishment of a network of wall newspapers that could provide basic news to a large number of people at minimal cost.

Emes reappeared on November 7, 1920 – the anniversary of the Bolshevik Revolution on the new Westernized calendar – was published thirty-seven times, and then stopped production again until September 1921. The newspaper encountered so many publishing difficulties in its first three years that the editors published regular apologies to its readers explaining why it stopped appearing for days or weeks at a time.[40]

THE RESOURCES TO BUILD SOVIET YIDDISH PUBLISHING

Until 1921, there were immense material pressures working against the continued flowering of a Soviet publishing industry. From a high of 34,630 book titles published in all languages in the Russian Empire in 1912, the number dropped gradually throughout the war, and then plummeted with the outbreak of the Civil War in 1918. In 1920, the weakest year for publishing in Russia since the nineteenth century, there were only 5,300 titles printed. Soviet publishing would not reach its prewar levels until 1928. To lay the groundwork for the struggling state-sponsored Party-allied Yiddish-publishing industry, the nascent Soviet Yiddish intelligentsia needed to acquire the resources necessary to produce books, newspapers, and other texts that would form the basis of Soviet Jewish culture. One particular challenge was the conflicting geographies of Russian and Soviet culture, on the one hand, and Jewish geography, on the other. Moscow, the new capital of Soviet Russia, became a wasteland during the Civil War when food and other consumer goods shortages caused residents to flee the city. Moscow had never been a center of Jewish publishing the way Warsaw, Vilna, Odessa, Kiev, and St. Petersburg were, and did not have a large Yiddish writer base. In addition, the capital was located far from most Yiddish readers, making distribution difficult, particularly when distribution networks were being used to transport soldiers and supplies to the front lines. Over time, Soviet Jewish activists attempted to bring Jewish geography in line with Soviet geography by making Moscow the center of Soviet Jewish culture.

Some of the material challenges of Soviet Yiddish publishing were universal problems of Civil War society. According to Agursky, "Transport was in a terrible state; counterrevolutionaries had destroyed train lines. At the time, to go from Odessa to Moscow would take one month!! For these reasons, central newspapers could not go anywhere; therefore each city and shtetl began to publish its own newspaper."[41] There were not enough qualified people to publish newspapers and books. Finding proficient writers was a huge obstacle to early Russian-language publishing during the Civil War, a time of mass emigration of the Russian intelligentsia.[42] Publishing houses and newspapers needed editors who were good writers and careful readers; knew how to run a large operation;

were politically savvy; and, preferably, were members of the Communist Party, to ensure the political correctness of the newspaper. The Eighth Communist Party Congress resolved, "Only the most responsible, experienced Party cadres should be nominated to become newspaper editors, because editors must 'lead' their papers."[43] Russian newspapers were in need of qualified editors and writers, but the problem was particularly acute for national minority languages that did not have a Bolshevik journalistic tradition, such as Yiddish. Yiddish publishing needed Yiddish editors, writers, and proofreaders, as well as a printing house with typesetters who had Yiddish typefaces and knew Yiddish.

During the Civil War, *Evsektsiia* created its own publishing house, the Communist World (*Komunistishe Velt or Komvelt*) in Moscow. Its first editorial board – Avrom Merezhin, Shakhne Epshteyn, and Avrom Cheskis – was made up entirely of former Bundists who joined the Communist Party in 1918–19.[44] Communist World attracted an extraordinary level of talent to serve as writers and editors, jobs that provided salaries and sometimes benefits like warm coats and boots, luxuries during the Civil War. David Hofshteyn, the modernist Yiddish poet, co-edited the literature and art division; Der Nister, another well-known Yiddish modernist, edited the children's and youth division; and other high-level Jewish socialists such as Alexander Chemerinsky, demographer Yakov Leshtsinsky, and Moshe Litvakov, also served as editors.[45] The first Moscow-based Communist Party Yiddish publishing house was established and run by writers, editors, and critics who had envisioned a new form of Jewish culture before the Russian Revolution and were now given access to state power to realize their visions.

In the case of the periodical *Communist World*, the Jewish Commissariat went against the rules outlined in the Party resolution about newspaper editors and recruited Daniel Charny, a non-Bolshevik, to be the editor-in-chief.[46] The *Evsektsiia* and Jewish Commissariat were so desperate for talent, Party-affiliated or otherwise, that as late as 1920, they considered having Litvakov, another non-Communist, edit the newly reincarnated *Emes*.[47] Of the twenty-nine *Emes* employees listed on an official employee roster in 1920, only two were Communist Party members. There were two Bundists, and the rest were unaffiliated.[48]

A general cause of personnel shortages was the Red Army draft. People were called up to fight on the front, and those with journalistic skills were recruited to report from the front lines.[49] The draft affected everyone including the editors, although they could often arrange exemptions due to their "important political work." Typesetters, however, who did not generally receive exemptions, were sent to the front lines; and, the loss of a single typesetter could prevent the publication of a newspaper for days or weeks until a new one could be found.[50]

There was also a high degree of turnover in editorial leadership. Dimanshteyn left his post as editor of *Emes* sometime in 1919 after it temporarily ceased publication. Charny took over editorship of the *Communist World*, and

in 1920, Shakhne Epshteyn became editor of the new *Emes*, but left for the
United States in 1921 to work on the future American Communist newspaper,
Freedom (Frayhayt).[51] Many editors and writers left the Soviet Union in 1920
and 1921, when prospects appeared better in other parts of Europe, causing
great turnover in the *Emes* staff. To be sure, like the Communist World publishing house, *Emes* had a wealth of talent – David Hofshteyn, Der Nister, Jacob
Leshtsinsky, Epshteyn and Litvakov, and others who contributed to the newspaper in these years – Charny, Shmuel Niger, and Perets Markish.[52] But of these
figures, only Litvakov remained on the editorial staff through 1921.

PAPER – THE MEANS FOR SPREADING ENLIGHTENMENT

The severe paper shortage was the most significant material problem ever to
plague the Soviet publishing industry. The bizarre theft shows how paper became a scarce, and therefore valuable, commodity. There simply was not enough
paper to meet publishing demands, which meant that this scarce resource had
to be rationed.[53] Soviet Yiddish publishing encountered the additional problem that paper was often allocated first for Russian-language publishing. This
lower priority sometimes led the Soviet Yiddish intelligentsia to accuse others
of anti-Semitism, as it did after the Moscow paper theft.

Paper shortage shaped both the form and content of the entire Soviet publishing industry. For example, Russian-language publishers issued Tolstoy's short
stories rather than his grand novels, because they did not want to use up paper
producing *War and Peace*.[54] Throughout the 1920s, paper was the most pressing
material limitation on the grandiose visions of Yiddish publishing, as a 1924
Evsektsiia report shows: "Paper is one of the most basic elements in the cost of a
book, and at our current average print run of 10,000 copies, the cost of
paper can equal 50 percent of the cost of printing the book."[55] During the
Russian Civil War, Yiddish materials were printed on any kind of paper at
hand including recycled posters, old packaging, and other poor-quality paper.[56]
According to the report, the annual per capita paper consumption in Russia
dropped from six pounds in 1908 to a meager one pound in 1921. (In the
United States in 1908, per capita paper consumption was 65 pounds.)[57] A 1927
article in the Soviet Yiddish newspaper *Shtern* noted concerns about the lack
of paper that resembled those made in 1924, and added, "Paper is the most
important substance. Without it we could not spread enlightenment."[58]

Unlike a printing press, paper was not something to be confiscated, unless one
was dealing with a clever thief. Paper was rationed by those who controlled paper
production and supply. In the Soviet case, it was the state, first through its paper
commissariat and, after 1919, through the State Publishing House (*Gosizdat*) that
controlled paper supplies for the Soviet publishing industry. The centralization
of paper allocation in the hands of non-Jewish paper rationers at the State

Publishing House concerned many state Jewish activists, because it was the most basic way of regulating publishing, and the Soviet Yiddish intelligentsia liked to keep that kind of control in its own hands.

Members of the intelligentsia generally thought that non-Jewish, paper-allocating bureaucrats had no sense of what kinds of Jewish publications should receive higher priority – Hebrew versus Yiddish, religious versus secular, primary or secondary school texts, impressionist or expressionist poetry. There was also the lingering fear that these bureaucrats might not consider Jewish publications important enough to receive paper at all. The intelligentsia wanted to be sure both that Jewish publications received their fair share in comparison to other ethnic groups and that the intelligentsia published Soviet Jewish material, rather than non-state allied Jewish publishers – like non-Communist Jewish socialists, before their incorporation into the Communist Party, or Zionists who still lurked on the fringes of Soviet society. In 1920, the *Evsektsiia* complained that the State Publishing House had given the "right social democratic" Bund permission to publish a Yiddish-language brochure, and had provided the group paper "at a time when we Communists cannot receive even a minimum quantity of paper for our Communist publications."[59] At the Third All-Russian Conference of *Evsektsiia* in July 1920, the executive board passed a resolution calling for the Jewish publishing division – rather than the paper committee – of the State Publishing House, to become the official distributor of paper to all publishing houses dealing with material in Jewish languages.[60] This was an attempt by the *Evsektsiia* and other Jewish cultural activists to keep institutional control of Jewish publishing in their hands and to maintain autonomy for the production of Soviet Yiddish culture.

SOVIET YIDDISH PRINTERS

Although paper is the foundation of publishing, books cannot be produced without a print house – a place that had the technical and human resources to turn a text that a publisher had laid out into a printed Yiddish product. The struggle to find a regular place to print confounded Yiddish activists throughout the 1920s. In the first years after the October Revolution, they printed books and periodicals wherever they could, which often meant sending books that had been conceived of, written, and laid out in Moscow, to be printed in provincial Jewish cities with Jewish-language printing facilities such as Vitebsk or Berdichev, or sometimes even abroad.[61] The Jewish Commissariat also confiscated Zionist printing facilities in Moscow and Petrograd and made them part of the Soviet publishing industry.[62]

The same *Evsektsiia* conference at which activists attempted to assert Jewish control over paper distribution also established the goal of creating a central Jewish print house in Moscow to lower printing costs and allow for increased Jewish Communist Party oversight of the Soviet Jewish publishing industry. A large scale Yiddish print house could print on an economy of scale and lower the astronomically high cost of printing.[63] It would also keep the last step in the publishing process under control of the Soviet Yiddish intelligentsia.[64]

In Moscow, the general Sixteenth State Print House produced Yiddish-language materials; however, the Soviet Yiddish intelligentsia found the reliance on non-Jewish print houses slow and frustrating. In general, printers were overburdened with publishing requests, and the Sixteenth often had trouble getting Yiddish-language publications out on time. In August 1921, Alexander Chemerinsky, chair of the Central Bureau of *Evsektsiia*, wrote a harsh letter to the Party's Agitation and Propaganda Division: "The print house . . . is systematically sabotaging our work. Work that is ready for printing sits there without moving, and the Director refuses to print them. . . . This director behaves in such a manner that, once we collect the materials, we plan to refer this matter to the commission for Party Purging."[65] Chemerinsky accused the print house of impeding the production of Soviet Jewish culture, and called for the director's expulsion from the Party. Chemerinsky was subtly reinserting anti-Semitism into the debate about control over cultural production. Because the Communist Party made the fight against anti-Semitism in the 1920s and 1930s an important state policy, key Party officials frowned upon anti-Semitism among petty bureaucrats and generally sided with the Jewish activists. Nonetheless, the lingering suspicion of anti-Semitism is one reason why *Evsektsiia* and other Jewish organizations wanted to have control over the powers of Jewish cultural production. With financial support from the Party's Central Committee, Soviet Jewish activists finally opened the *Emes* print house in 1923.[66]

Having the print house was one thing; finding people to operate it was another. Typesetters were in short supply in all spheres of the Soviet publishing industry, but publishing in ethnic minority languages with non-Cyrillic or non-Latin alphabets made the search for qualified typesetters even more challenging. Yiddish typesetters were in such demand that Moscow-based print houses taught the Hebrew alphabet to Russian-speaking typesetters so they could print Yiddish-language publications. Exacerbating the shortage was the fact that, compared to other typesetting jobs in Soviet publishing, Yiddish typesetting jobs offered fewer material benefits, a problem dating back to the Civil War era.[67] In 1923, the Central Bureau established a Jewish printers' school in Moscow to train future Yiddish typesetters.[68] In all aspects of the publishing process, Jewish activists attempted (and through most of the 1920s, usually succeeded) to maintain control over the production of Jewish culture by overseeing paper allocation, establishing print houses, and training their own printers.

PUTTING THE PIECES TOGETHER: SOVIET JEWISH
PUBLISHING HOUSES

During the Civil War, the *Evsektsiia* organized the Communist World (*Komunistishe Velt*) publishing house in Moscow, but the largest ventures in Jewish publishing took place in Kiev. Kiev was so central to the early development of Soviet Jewish culture that in 1920, 65 percent of all Soviet Yiddish publications came out of Kiev.[69] The most important publisher in Kiev, and the only one that survived the Civil War and the 1920s, was the Culture League (*Kultur Lige*), a network of publishers, writers, and cultural centers founded by Jewish cultural activists in 1918. The final Soviet takeover of Ukraine did not happen until 1920. Since Culture League was the largest Yiddish-language cultural network, the new Soviet Ukrainian government needed its resources, and after much negotiation about editorial oversight, financing, and the role of the Party, in November 1921, it became an official Soviet organization and state publisher of Yiddish materials.[70] Like other publishers and publications in the Civil War period, Culture League's executive board was made up of many important members of the Soviet Yiddish intelligentsia, such as Frumkina, Litvakov, Marc Chagall, David Hofshteyn, and the director of the State Jewish Theater, Alexander Granovsky.[71]

In Moscow, several Jewish activists established the School and Book (*Shul un Bukh*) publishing house in November 1923 with Moshe Litvakov as editor-in-chief. School and Book positioned itself as the chief publisher of Yiddish books and journals in the Russian Republic, and balanced its budget by exporting Yiddish books for hard currency.[72] The founders stressed that the foreign book market was vital "both from an ideological and from a commercial standpoint," demonstrating that material, political, and ideological concerns always intersected when it came to the production of culture.[73] School and Book also raised revenue by importing foreign books and selling them on the Soviet Jewish book market.[74] School and Book and the *Evsektsiia* also served as the coordinator of Yiddish book publishing throughout the Soviet Union to prevent the publication of duplicates of the same title, known as parallelism, or overproducing in one area while underproducing in others.[75] This kind of central planning came about for economic reasons, but also resulted in a more tightly regulated Soviet Jewish publishing industry.

Alongside the Jewish publishing houses such as Communist World, Culture League, and School and Book, the State Publishing House was also involved in publishing materials in languages other than Russian. In the years shortly after the revolution, it did not make ethnic minorities' publishing a high priority, especially since smaller nationality-specific publishing houses, like Culture League, were doing most of the work. In January 1921, the State Publishing House spun-off ethnic minorities' publishing and created a "Central Division for Publishing Foreign Literature," by which was meant the literature of national minorities of the Russian Republic. Each national minority had its own editorial, publishing, and organizational divisions to separate technical issues from content ones and to keep the production of culture in the national minorities' hands. Eventually the division split and became two publishing houses: the Central Publishing House for National Minorities of the West (CWP) and one for National Minorities of "the East." The CWP incorporated those minorities considered "Western" (that is to say, European): Latvian, Estonian, Lithuanian, Jewish, Polish, German, and Finnish.[76]

The CWP was dedicated primarily to publishing translations of Marxist classics and other Party literature from Russian into dozens of languages.[77] It published very little original work. In this way, the CWP created a generic Soviet canon translated into national minorities' languages, and thus put into action the notion of "national in form, socialist in content." While most ethnic minorities' publishing was concentrated in centralized publishing houses, suggesting that their cultural development was based on this definition of Soviet culture, Jewish publishing and the production of Soviet Jewish culture in the 1920s was more independent and took place primarily in Jewish enterprises.

The CWP existed for one year and produced very few titles: four in German, four in Polish, three in Latvian, six in Estonian, and five in Yiddish, in addition to three newspapers and journals, none of which were in Yiddish.[78] In June 1924, the Secretariat of the Central Committee approved the creation of the Central Publishing House for Peoples of the Soviet Union (*Tsentroizdat*) with Dimanshteyn as editor-in-chief.[79] There was a member of the Soviet Yiddish intelligentsia in the highest echelons of publishing power, presumably to ensure Soviet Jewish culture its fair share of resources in the multinational publishing house.

THE NEW ECONOMIC POLICY AND PROBLEMS OF PRODUCTION, CONSUMPTION, AND MARKETABILITY

With the harsh wartime conditions behind it, Soviet Yiddish publishing should have stabilized. Russian-language book publishing had its worst year in 1920.[80] Since Yiddish publishing was not dispersed in many places, it managed to continue producing on a local basis through the Civil War and did not collapse until 1923.[81] The post–Civil War era, known as NEP, ushered in new financial challenges. During NEP – a set of economic policies that attempted to jumpstart the flailing economy via market mechanisms – the state passed a law on economic self-sufficiency, known as *khozraschet*. In November 1921, the Council of People's Commissars (*Sovnarkom*) issued a decree stipulating that as of January 1, 1922, all economic enterprises, newspapers included, had to pay for themselves or they would go bankrupt and close down. Publications would no longer be given away as free propaganda literature, but would be sold, with the price determined by production costs.[82] The consequences of this decree on the periodical publishing industry were swift and fierce. On January 1, 1922, there were 802 newspapers published in the Soviet Union with a total circulation of 2.6 million. Seven months later, on August 1, there were only 299, with a total circulation under one million. This period of consolidation came to be known as the Press Crisis.[83]

Most locally circulating Soviet Yiddish newspapers shut their doors between 1921 and 1922, and those that did not immediately go bankrupt were closed down by Party decree as the Yiddish newspaper industry was forced to restructure and centralize for economic reasons. As for publishing houses, of the several publishers operating during the Civil War, only Culture League managed to survive the economic belt-tightening.[84] Publishing houses and newspapers were closed down, not for violating political maxims, but for failing to meet economic standards established by the Planning Commission. But the allocation of scarce resources was and always is a political act; the choice to focus on supporting the central and republic-wide newspapers, and let regional and local ones die, shows the Party's new interest in the centralization and rationalization of the publishing industry.

How could publishers increase revenues to be able to balance their budgets? Starting in 1921, people had to pay for subscriptions or purchase individual issues to receive Soviet newspapers. The prices of books also went up. Publishers recognized that one of the major problems facing their industry was poor distribution, which prevented those who wanted books to purchase them. Another way publishers increased revenue during NEP was by soliciting advertising. Some groups also acquired loans or grants from Jewish organizations in the United States. Cooperatives such as the Jewish Social Committee (*Evobshchestkom*) or the American-based *Joint* (*Agrojoint*) raised money from leftist intellectuals and workers primarily in the United States, and funneled the money to Soviet Jewish culture building activities including publishing.[85] Finally, publishers could continue soliciting money from the state. Under the NEP austerity program, publishers went from receiving complete subsidies to none at all in one year. In early 1922, there was an unsuccessful proposal before the Organizational Bureau of the Central Committee to cut off funding and force *Emes* to close down, as had happened to local Yiddish newspapers throughout Ukraine and Belorussia.[86] The Soviet Yiddish intelligentsia, which successfully lobbied for continuing subsidies, was even more successful than Russian-language cultural activists, which did not receive emergency subsidies until July.[87]

Yiddish publishers and newspapers were not alone in having to restructure under NEP. In June 1922, the National Minorities Subdivision of *Agitprop* set self-sufficiency rates for all national minority periodicals. *Emes* was to achieve a

35 percent self-sufficiency rating, which reflected a 65 percent Central Committee subsidy. The Latvian and Polish central newspapers needed to reach 20 percent self-sufficiency in the same time.[88] Even with this new gradual plan for each national minority's publications, all periodicals still had trouble publishing regularly. The Polish publications *Tribune (Tribuna)* and *Hammer and Sickle (Mlot i Serp)* experienced interruptions in publication throughout the NEP period.[89]

Despite economic austerity, the Soviet state invested extensive resources in publishing national minority newspapers. In 1913, there were only fifty-nine newspapers in ethnic minorities' languages circulating in the Russian empire. By 1928, in the Soviet Union, there were 321.[90] Among national minorities, Yiddish newspapers were supported more extensively than other groups' newspapers. For example, in one publishing house in Moscow, nine different national minority newspapers employed a total of fifty-five employees, one-third of whom were employed by *Emes*.[91] In addition, in quantitative terms, *Evsektsiia* published more periodicals than any of the other ethnic minorities' sections did. Starting in the Civil War period, in 1920–1, *Evsektsiia* oversaw thirteen Yiddish newspapers in the Soviet Union, five of which were dailies. In contrast, the Polish and German Bureaus, the next largest ones, each published only eight periodicals, none of which was a daily.[92]

MAKING MONEY AND APPEALING TO CUSTOMERS

Soviet Yiddish books and newspapers only fulfilled their role as a propagator of Soviet Jewish culture if someone read them. Among newspapers, *Emes* took the lead in finding new ways to make itself more appealing to Jewish readers. By appealing to Jewish readers, it could guarantee itself a more stable revenue stream from subscriptions. One part of the newspaper that could serve several purposes was advertising. Advertising was relatively unfamiliar to the socialist editors of *Emes*. Throughout the Civil War period, there were news and event listings, but no commercial advertising in Party-sponsored newspapers. The only time commercial advertising ever appeared in the Soviet press was during the eight years of NEP.[93] Advertisements for Soviet Jewish organizations begin appearing in the early NEP period. The State Jewish Theater, *GOSET*, placed small advertisements to publicize new productions; Yiddish-language publishing houses advertised new publications; and journals and newspapers advertised new subscription rates on each other's pages.[94] Most advertising was for consumer goods such as soap, toothpaste, and food.[95] *Emes* also ran advertisements for shipping lines that had regular passage to the United States, a kind of advertisement that appealed primarily to Jewish readers, many of whom had relatives in the United States and were contemplating making the trip themselves (Illustration 4.1).[96]

Publishers' financial dependence on advertising created a lingering fear that they would become beholden to their advertisers. Because of this, not all ads were permitted in Soviet periodicals, although the editor of each newspaper was the one responsible for the tastefulness and political appropriateness of any published advertisement.[97] In addition, no more than 25 percent of a newspaper's copy could be devoted to commercial advertising, and all advertising had to be placed on one of the last two pages of the newspaper.[98] By regulating advertising, the Party hoped it could control advertising's unseemly effects on the gullible reader. That said, through 1922, advertisements occupied a larger percentage of *Emes'* copy. Ironically, in *Emes'* special ten-page edition commemorating the October Revolution, three of the ten pages (30 percent) were devoted exclusively to commercial advertising.[99]

To effect real financial change and to fulfill its propagandistic role, *Evsektsiia* knew that the circulation of Soviet Yiddish newspapers and the distribution of books had to increase.[100] The average daily circulation of *Emes* between its high in early 1921 until 1923 was a dismally low 3,000 copies. For the central Party Yiddish-language newspaper trying to reach an estimated Yiddish-reading public of three million Jews, it was obviously not reaching its target audience.[101] In book publishing, between 1921 and 1924, publishers produced fewer Yiddish books than were produced in 1919 alone.[102]

These fears of low circulation and low book production plagued national minorities publishing in general. In 1924, well after the Press Crisis had passed, the Latvian newspaper in Moscow had a circulation of 4,500 (only 3,900 of which were paying subscriptions), and was published only three times a week. The Moscow-based German newspaper *Work (Die Arbeit)* had a meager circulation of 1,500 (only 1,100 to 1,200 of which were paying), because Soviet Germans had their own local newspapers in the Volga region where most Germans lived. The Mordovian newspaper *Yakstere Teshte* had a respectable circulation of 2,000, but only 130 people actually paid for the newspaper.[103] *Emes* was in fact more successful than most.

There were many impediments to increasing circulation. Distribution networks were still unreliable. Distributing a newspaper meant getting it from the print house to the postal center in Moscow for distribution to the provinces, and transport of the newspaper to its intended destination, usually by train. Once it reached the city, town, or village to which it was intended, it had to be delivered to its recipients, usually Soviet Jewish institutions and occasionally individuals. All publications had distribution difficulties that often came down to an inefficient postal system.[104] Books had to get to bookstores or libraries where Yiddish readers could purchase them or check them out. Hundreds of copies of books and newspapers sat on warehouse shelves due to distribution difficulties.[105] Some Jewish publishers complained that their publications were placed at the bottom of the postal system's delivery priority, a problem some editors, not surprisingly, attributed to anti-Semitism.[106]

One other reason for the low circulation of *Emes* in particular was competition from other Yiddish Party periodicals and from Russian-language newspapers. Since the implementation of economic self-sufficiency laws, *Emes* and the Central Bureau demanded that all provincial Jewish sections of the Party conduct advertising campaigns to increase the number of *Emes* subscriptions in their locality. The problem was that many places in Ukraine and Belorussia already had either a local newspaper (until the Press Crisis of 1922) or a republic newspaper competing with *Emes*. *Emes* had a monopoly on Party Yiddish newspapers only in the Russian Republic (RSFSR), for which *Emes* was both the "republic" and the "central" newspaper.[107] As Avrom Merezhin, chairman of the Central Bureau, put it, "Can people really be expected to read two newspapers daily?"[108] Fortunately, the self-sufficiency decree and the Press Crisis put three of *Emes*' five Yiddish competitors out of business.[109]

The marketing campaigns for *Emes* reached absurd levels in 1923–4 as the newspaper struggled to meet its quotas and gain financial security. The newspaper sponsored various "best" competitions – best cultural activist, best Soviet Jewish schoolteacher, best Jewish farmer – and highly publicized the events to garner reader interest. One of the most popular campaigns was one to sponsor an "*Emes* airplane." Throughout 1923–4, notices with pictures of an airplane, an image new to many readers, called on people to "Sponsor your *Emes* airplane." Shortly after the campaign began, *Emes* campaign organizers broadened its target audience by including all major Soviet Yiddish newspapers, and began calling for people to sponsor the "*Emes, Veker, Komfon* airplane."[110]

Books did not have similar mechanisms of self-promotion. Publishers such as School and Book took out advertisements in *Emes* to publicize new books by well-known Yiddish writers, the latest edition of a history of the Party, or other new works set to hit the shelves. Unlike newspapers, which had to find individual readers, the primary markets for books were Soviet Jewish schools and libraries, which had required reading lists or purchasing lists and had the money to purchase books in the post–Civil War period.

WHAT PUBLISHING HOUSES PUBLISHED

Given the ideological framework in which Soviet Jewish publishing occurred, propaganda, education, and politics were three of the main areas of Soviet Yiddish publishing. The Soviet Yiddish intelligentsia had been empowered by the state to remake Soviet Jews, and books and newspapers were some of the most important tools for effecting such a change. It meant creating materials for children in their new schools, giving adults new kinds of

poetry to replace traditional forms of Jewish literature. It meant providing
Jews with the tools to make themselves economically productive Soviet citizens as the shtetl's economy continued its precipitous decline. Jews needed
to learn how to be factory workers, farmers, and good Party members. To
accomplish the dual goals of making Jews into Soviets and of creating a new
Soviet Yiddish culture, the Soviet Yiddish intelligentsia would need to create
a print culture that addressed all these aspects of social, economic, and political
change.

The project started with Jewish children. In the early NEP years, textbooks
were in high demand as more Soviet Jewish schools opened.[111] In 1923–4,
Culture League, the dominant Yiddish book publisher until the second half
of the 1920s, printed twenty-seven Yiddish titles, more than half of which
were textbooks. These ranged from Yiddish grammars, which used the new
Soviet Yiddish spellings, to biology and mathematics textbooks translated from
Russian. The second most popular area of Yiddish publishing was children's
literature. The only problem with the almost exclusive focus on children in the
dearth years of Yiddish publishing was that Jewish adults were being culturally
neglected. To be sure, many Soviet Jews were buying Russian books (and some
of them were even buying Ukrainian or Belorussian books). The intelligentsia
wanted to make sure that Soviet Jewish adults were also invested in the creation
of Soviet Yiddish culture.

Publishing exploded over the next two years, both in Yiddish-language work
and in Soviet publishing more generally. Culture League more than doubled its
list, producing fifty-eight titles; and all categories of literature showed increases,
especially political literature and fiction, which each grew more than three-
fold.[112] Political literature included not only translations of the Marxist classics,
but also original Yiddish-language works, like Frumkina's *October Revolution* and
Lenin and His Work, or Agursky's *The October Revolution in Belorussia*. Culture
League's sales increased as well, more than doubling in one year.[113]

After 1925, once textbook production was under control, Soviet Jewish publishers turned their attention to Jewish adults and doubled their production of
original Yiddish fiction. This was clearly the area of publishing over which the
avant-garde Soviet Yiddish intelligentsia, the only ones capable of producing
these original works, had the most power. People like Frumkina and Agursky
may have written original political tracts, but most of the members of the intelligentsia, following in the traditions of the Russian intelligentsia on which
they modeled themselves, saw themselves as writers as well as political activists
(and tended to produce better poetry than they did original political philosophy). The increasing publication of Yiddish fiction eventually attracted many
of the old Yiddish avant-garde who had left the country shortly after the revolution. It was, in many ways, the most successful period of the Soviet Yiddish

intelligentsia's cultural project, making Moscow and the Soviet Union one of the centers of international Yiddish culture.

With the new interest in Jewish adults and with other Soviet publishers producing more Yiddish books, Culture League's textbook and children's literature production actually dropped from its 1925 high. This was due in part to increased Yiddish-language publishing at the Central Publishing House for National Minorities.[114] The drop was also caused by an industry-wide depression that lasted from 1925 until late 1927.[115] By 1928, with the Central Minorities' Publishing House focusing on translations of Russian-language textbooks, political literature, and other didactic materials, Culture League had completely shifted focus and was publishing more fiction than textbooks.[116] The Central Minorities' Publishing House list did not include any fiction, but had a large number of textbooks and social/political literature. [117]

In its first full year of operation, School and Book produced dozens of titles, including several textbooks, children's literature, an extensive list of political literature, and a wide selection of fiction.[118] The publishing house also printed the Yiddish works or the Yiddish translations of Hebrew-language writers Chaim Nachman Bialik, Uri Gnessin, Yosef Brenner, in addition to the work of the cultural Zionist Ahad Ha'am.[119] It seems strange that the same Soviet Yiddish intelligentsia that repressed Hebrew and Zionist culture would publish these Hebrew writers. In the first three cases, each one was considered a great modern Jewish writer, contributing to a Jewish literary canon. Bialik, more than the others, was also considered a Russian Jewish writer, having left the Soviet Union in 1921. There is little to explain the odd publication of the Zionist Ahad Ha'am.

Although publishing modern Jewish literature was a goal in and of itself for the intelligentsia, making Soviet Jews into productive Soviet citizens was the reason the project received so much support. This mission led to the creation of a new genre of Yiddish literature – popular science. These books included how-to books, basic science books, and eventually grew to include popular science newspapers and periodicals. The library of popular science in Yiddish included such gripping titles as *Shoes and Galoshes: How They are Made*. The intelligentsia also created special newspapers for new social groups, the most important of which was the new class of Jewish peasants. Its newspaper was called, not surprisingly, *The Jewish Peasant (Der yidisher poyer)*, and it taught Jewish farmers about planting cycles and crop rotation, and also included fictional literature about farming and life in the countryside. One article was titled "How to Find a Cow That Will Produce Lots of Milk" that included pictures of full udders and diagrams on how to distinguish good udders from bad ones, information that Tevye the Milkman of Sholem Aleichem's stories may not have needed, but the new Soviet Jewish peasant clearly did. The opening article told its readers that the Jewish peasant "needs to learn to fit into his new village surroundings. He is building socialism with his hands."[120] These books and newspapers also subtly worked against traditional Jewish culture, as in the title of an agronomical article, "Corn Plus Pigs Equals Cheap Sausage *(farzhankes)*." Encouraging Jewish farmers to work with pigs and make sausage was clearly a way to work against Jewish dietary laws.

The *Jewish Peasant* was marked as Jewish certainly by the language in which it was written, but its articles were at times also aimed specifically at Jews. There was an article commemorating the death of the classic Yiddish writer, S.Y. Abramovitch, and another one about the old Bundist, Hirsh Lekert. It also mentioned repeatedly the development of specifically Jewish agriculture and of specifically Jewish territory in the Soviet Union. After 1928, *The Jewish Peasant* added a lengthy column devoted to the Jewish autonomous region, Birobidzhan, and Jewish agricultural areas like Kalinindorf. Even popular science was shaping both the Soviet Jew and the Jewish Soviet citizen.

FROM JEWS TO JEWISH SOVIETS

If *The Jewish Peasant* was targeted specifically at peasants, the central Party news-paper, *Emes*, aimed at all Yiddish readers, was trying to enlighten, excite, and ultimately, convert them to a new way of thinking. In this task, *Emes* was doing nothing new. Jewish journalism was historically driven by Jewish intellectuals' desires to transform their Jewish brethren into their own self-image.[121] In order to accomplish its primary tasks, *Emes* simultaneously discredited existing forms of Jewishness and advertised new ways of being Jewish. Throughout the 1920s, the battle between the old and the new raged on the pages of *Emes* and in dozens of books. Religious leaders, Hebrew instructors, religious institutions, and Judaism itself were attacked with a proud vigilance. In their place, the Soviet Yiddish intelligentsia created an alternative, using Yiddish as the primary marker of Jewishness.

In the immediate post–Civil War period, *Emes* told its readers about the woe and misery in the shtetls.[122] The overall picture was a bleak one – famine killing off people by the thousands, bandits roaming the area that made up the former Pale of Settlement, refugees crowding temporary housing centers, and a large number of Jews emigrating from the area. Throughout the fall of 1921, the paper devoted a special column to the famine, to discuss both its widespread devastating effects and the various sources of aid available to its victims. The Soviet Yiddish intelligentsia wanted to highlight the violence tar-geted at Jews and lay blame squarely on "reactionary," "counterrevolutionary" or "bourgeois" forces, and encourage readers to support the Soviet Union. By the end of 1922, however, talk about the violence that had plagued Jews since 1918 virtually stopped, and in its place, the focus turned to building Soviet culture in the shtetls.

The narrative *Emes* created in its early years was "from death to life," from decaying shtetls to vibrant Soviet villages, towns, and cities. The newspaper gave its readers the impression that the population remaining in the shtetls consisted of orphaned children, abandoned women (known as *agunot*), widows, and elderly people, showing that violence and emigration had taken a terrible demographic toll, especially on the young able-bodied male population. In this representation, everyone was surviving off foreign aid from family and friends or the state's support.[123] Shtetls did undergo massive demographic restructuring and economic collapse as a result of war, famine, and the Soviet Union's economic focus on large-scale production. This economic crisis was one of the issues that prompted Soviet state leaders to invest political and financial capital in resettling Jews on the land. But the exaggerated image of a place lacking "working" or "productive" people created the impression that shtetl society was dead.[124] Yiddish fiction of the time created literary images of the dying shtetl made up of, in the words of the Soviet Yiddish poet, Izi Kharik, "all the graying fathers/Who have not extinguished your days – /Who left you to your silence and to your waiting! – ."[125] The editors and writers also used the metaphor of generations to show the movement from the aging shtetl population to the vibrant youth of the new Soviet Jewish culture. By portraying the shtetl as a dying institution, Soviet Yiddish culture legitimated the implantation of new social and cultural institutions, which would create a new form of Jewish identity.

In addition to attacking the shtetl, both the socio-economic place and the literary image, Soviet Yiddish culture aimed at traditional Jewish forms of authority in the "anticlerical campaign." In the portrayal of the battle between the nascent secular Soviet Jewish culture and a traditional religious one, Jewish activists used a variety of tactics. The one that reached the largest audience was the anti–Jewish-holiday campaigns, which used the very time and space of Jewish holidays to undermine them.[126] The campaigns, which happened throughout the 1920s, focused on the more popular and important holidays, such as Passover, Rosh Hashanah (Jewish New Year), and Yom Kippur (Day of Atonement). The campaigns against specific holidays consisted of newspaper articles attacking the religion on ideological grounds, followed by news of various marches, special readings, and protests that attacked the holiday physically "on the streets."[127] The overall goal of the antiholiday campaign was to combat the traditional practices that surrounded a holiday and simultaneously create alternative practices during these intense periods of Jewish communal activity. For example, M. Altshuler published the "Passover Haggadah in Yiddish (*Hagode shel pesakh af ivre taytsh*)," which was subtitled the *Communist Youth*

Haggadah (Komsomol Hagode). The cover depicted an evil-looking rabbi with a long beard and hooked nose standing next to a young worker. The first section of the haggadah, the "Search for Leavened Bread (*bedikas khomets*)," read: "before the first Komsomol Passover, the whole working class of Russia, together with the peasantry, searched for *khomets* in the whole land. They cleaned out all remnants of aristocratic and bourgeois domination, and took power in their own hands, and appropriated the aristocrat's land." Each part of the Komsomol Haggadah took the skeleton of the original story and put it in a Soviet Russian context. Altshuler repeatedly talked about the backwardness of Judaism, the evil of the Biblical God, and called for everyone to take up class conflict.[128]

The reworking of Jewish time and space was a key method the Soviet Yiddish intelligentsia used to remake Jewish identity in the Soviet Union, and *Emes* played a leading role. The newspaper publicized meetings in which workers voted to abolish Jewish holidays; it told stories about frustrated children running out of their family Passover seders to join parades on the street.[129] Rather than reading the prayer book during the holidays, *Emes* told its readers, Jews should be convening in workers' reading rooms to discuss Soviet Yiddish literature.

Within the context of antiholiday campaigns, *Emes* targeted the leaders of the traditional Jewish community, the rabbis, cantors (ritual singers), and *melameds* (Jewish teachers), by representing them as old, evil men who wielded a mysterious power over "unenlightened" Jews. In an article about a real trial of four *melameds* who were accused of teaching religion to underage children, *Emes* described the defendants as "deaf, blind, hunched over," and concluded by saying that they "give a horrible impression."[130] Such anti-Semitic characterizations, like the one on the cover of the haggadah, tried to convince Jewish readers that their educators were decrepit men indoctrinating their young, impressionable children with religion. In contrast, images of Soviet Jewish activists showed young, smiling healthy activists – the future of Jewish culture. In another trial, four *melameds* were prosecuted for using corporal punishment in the classroom.[131] The traditional Jewish establishment was portrayed paradoxically as a group of old men who nonetheless oppressed the Jewish masses mentally, psychologically, and physically with their power.

The years 1924–5 were a turning point in the construction of Soviet Jewish culture on the pages of *Emes*, as a response to the expansion of nationalities policies. A 1925 Politburo decree officially implemented nativization by requiring "the maximum formation of national councils [*soviets*] and national schools, an increase in the national press, the promotion of national officials, and the strict punishment of all chauvinists."[132] The establishment of the state-sponsored Central Publishing House for National Minorities was part of this new investment in ethnic minorities' cultures.

The Yiddish books and newspapers produced after 1925 reflected the belief that shtetls were no longer the primary home of Soviet Jews or of Jewish culture. Jews now lived in cities, on agricultural colonies, or after 1928, in Birobidzhan, and worked in factories, on farms, and in other places of productive labor. Jews attended Soviet cultural conferences, went to Soviet schools, and read Marx, Lenin, and by the late 1920s, Stalin. The Jewish population was no longer categorized as orphaned, widowed, and elderly. Soviet Yiddish books and newspapers portrayed Jews in new Soviet social categories. Jewish workers and peasants were the first and most obvious social groups, and the ones toward whom much of Yiddish-language cultural activity was directed. By the late 1920s, the dominant image Yiddish newspapers presented to their readership was the transformation of traditional Jews into Soviet Jewish citizens.

MAKING YIDDISH NEWSPAPERS MORE INTERESTING

Soviet Yiddish newspapers portrayed a world the editors and writers wanted Yiddish readers to see, but Yiddish readers would only see it if they read the newspaper. In addition to increasing circulation and improving production, publishers tried to expand their readership by creating a more interesting product and responding to readers' desires. Maurice Friedberg has shown that during NEP, "Soviet readers and buyers of books could influence publishers to bring out specific authors and titles by indicating their willingness to buy specific types of literature."[133]

Beginning in 1923, one of the most visible ways editors tried to make newspapers more appealing was by including images to accompany text. That year was also the worst in Yiddish book publishing and the height of the campaign to increase *Emes'* circulation. Book publishers had been incorporating visuals into texts since the beginning of Yiddish modernism, a movement that envisioned text and image as aspects of a single cultural product. Yiddish literary journals from the Civil War period always had sketches, drawings, and even typography that reflected the aesthetics of constructivism, futurism, expressionism, and other modernist movements.

Newspapers were slower to incorporate visuals. Advertisers were the first to use images to attract readers, and over time, newspaper editors began incorporating them as well. Soviet Yiddish newspapers began by including photographs to accompany articles on such topics as Party conferences, union meetings, and other large-scale institutional activities. In keeping with the overall goal of portraying a particular vision of the world, editors chose edifying photos – happy activists, individual heroes, brave Jewish farmers – and other images that projected the image of the Jew involved in the construction of Soviet society.

These photographs appeared during the debates about how to increase *Emes'* circulation, and were part of a broader campaign to gain popularity for the newspaper, a phenomenon that was occurring simultaneously in Russian-language journalism.[134]

The members of the Soviet Yiddish intelligentsia who produced newspapers were also part of the modernist movements that fused text and image in Yiddish books. (*Emes'* editor-in-chief, Litvakov, first made his reputation as a modernist literary critic.) The inclusion of photographs also reflected a new trend in the Soviet visual arts – the use of photography and graphics as an expressive medium by Suprematists and Constructivists.[135] Two of the most important artists in the Constructivist movement, Alexander Rodchenko and El Lissitsky, incorporated photography and graphics into the presentation of texts. Rodchenko's first printed photomontage dates to 1923, the same year *Emes* began including photographs on its pages; and Lissitsky was personally affiliated with the Soviet Yiddish intelligentsia through his illustrations of Soviet Yiddish texts.[136]

The push to make *Emes* more accessible by including visuals reached new heights in 1926, when the editors began publishing a picture-book weekly supplement to the newspaper called the *Emes Journal* (*Emes zhurnal*). It contained dozens of pictures in each edition and also included poetry and art. The journal produced an iconography for Soviet Jewish culture. There were sketches of the Paris Commune and its heroic fighters, a favorite image of early Soviet culture more generally; photographs of Syrian freedom fighters in the Middle East, providing an alternative image to "imperialist" Zionist pioneers; pictures of Soviet Jewish agricultural workers, as opposed to their "nationalistic" kibbutz counterparts in Palestine; and other symbols of the new Jewish proletarian world order.

Along with photographs, *Emes* began running satirical cartoons that were usually a form of commentary on the daily news. Unlike photographs, which were institutional, serious, and celebratory, the political cartoons were irreverent, politically sharp, funny, and at the same time, like the photographs, they propagated Soviet ideology. They usually appeared on page one, next to the international news, and commented on the international story of the day. The use of political satire was quite popular during NEP as a way of using humor to lambaste politically questionable groups while also transmitting the politics of the Soviet state. In the words of Litvakov, "Satirical cartoons . . . attract the reader; they give the newspaper a nicer appearance, and they develop a taste in art."[137] Litvakov's first two explanations point to the marketing use of flashy cartoons, but his final comment points to the newspaper's enlightening role of teaching Soviet Jews how to cultivate a proper taste in art.

For satire to be effective, readers needed to understand the content as well as the cultural frame of reference. Like Altshuler's antireligious haggadah, *Emes* often used images of traditional Jewish culture and reworked the content of the image to make a political point.

The "*Bris* in Locarno" depicts the most traditional Jewish scene – the circumcision of an eight-day-old son (Illustration 4.2). As any Jewish reader at the time would understand, the ceremony is called a *bris*, which translates as "covenant," and is the ritual act by which a Jewish baby boy is "covenanted" into a relationship with God (Genesis 7:10–14). The *bris* scene was the final cartoon in a series on the Locarno Agreements of 1925, which called on France to withdraw from the Rhineland region and guaranteed the integrity of Germany's western borderlands. In effect, it brought Western Europe into political and military concert after seven tense years following World War I. The picture shows the German foreign minister, Gustav Stresemann, being circumcised by the ritual circumcisers (*mohels*), Austen Chamberlain and Aristide Briand, British and French foreign ministers respectively. The Eastern European leaders and Mussolini were standing on the sidelines, watching with disappointment, because the agreements did not include guarantees of Germany's Eastern borders. The article that accompanied the cartoon explained the politics of the Locarno Agreement from a Soviet perspective, and the cartoon visualized those politics by satirizing the Jewish covenant scene.

Cartoons appeared periodically throughout the second half of the 1920s and often used Jewish themes to make political points (Illustration 4.3). This cartoon from late 1929 is a sharp critique of the capitalist relations that produced Yiddish culture in the United States. This multidimensional cartoon, titled "Oh, So That is the Madam of Broadway," shows the Yiddish writer Avrom Reyzen dressed in drag as an aging prostitute seducing the "john," the profitable Yiddish daily newspaper *Forward (Forverts)*, represented as a fat and stereotypically Jewish-looking capitalist. The cartoonist was criticizing Reyzen for "prostituting" himself to popular Yiddish newspapers rather than holding himself to a higher aesthetic or political standard the way Soviet Yiddish writers did. The cartoon was part of the break up of the international Yiddish intellectual community of interwar Europe under the pressure of radicalizing politics that pushed Communists to call socialists "fascists," and prompted American and other Yiddish intellectuals to harshly criticize Soviet writers for supporting Stalin's regime and the culture produced in the Soviet Union.

In addition to photographs and cartoons, *Emes* used other means to improve the visual appearance of the newspaper, such as higher quality paper, better ink, and new typeface. Like modernist book publishing, the newspaper began experimenting with typography. *Emes* first used Constructivist typeface in

ILLUSTRATION 4.2: A cartoon appearing in *Emes*, October 22, 1925. The titles reads: "Treaty in Locarno." The subtitle reads: "The Bris in Locarno." The figures in the image are: bottom row, from right, Ramsay Macdonald, British Labor Party leader, Emile Vandervelde, Belgian socialist party leader; Austen Chamberlain, secretary of foreign affairs, serving as the mohel; Gustave Streseman, German foreign minister; Aristide Briand, French foreign minister; second row, from right: Alexander Skrzynski, president of Poland; Alexander Tsankov, Bulgarian premier; Eduard Benesh, Czechoslovakian premier; and Benito Mussolini, Italian fascist leader.

פרייטיק, 15־טער נאיאבר 1929 יאָר.   № 263(2592)

אָט דאָס איז די דאַמע פון בראָדוויי

ILLUSTRATION 4.3: A cartoon appearing in *Emes*, November 15, 1929. The title reads: "So That is the Madame of Broadway," referring to the figure on the left, Avrom Reyzen. On his right is a fat capitalist holding the American socialist Yiddish newspaper, *Forward*.

ILLUSTRATION 4.4: An advertisement for the Soviet Yiddish youth journal, *Young Forest* (*Yungvald*) that appeared in *Der Emes*, March 26, 1923.

March 1923 in an advertisement for the new youth workers' journal, *Yungvald* (Illustration 4.4).[138]

Interest in the visual quality of language through type began in the pre-revolutionary era within the Suprematist and Futurist movements, but became central to the Constructivists of the 1920s, who saw a text as both an aural and a visual experience.[139] It is not a coincidence that the quintessential example of Constructivist print, the design for Vladimir Mayakovsky's *For the Voice* and the Constructivist-leaning literary journal *LEF*, came out in 1923, the same year *Emes* switched from a standard typeface to a self-consciously Constructivist, sans-serif typeface. The most notable theorist of Constructivist print and the designer of Mayakovsky's book was none other than Lissitsky, the Jewish graphic artist, member of the Soviet Yiddish intelligentsia from Vitebsk, who worked closely with Marc Chagall and Kasimir Malevich to unite art and the revolution. Although she overstates the point, Camilla Gray argues that "It was from this Jewish tradition that the first post-revolutionary experiments in typeface, which are among the first examples of 'modern' typographical design, were done."[140] Soviet Yiddish newspapers used their connections with modernism to improve their own visual appearance. The new move toward the visual met the needs of the producer and the consumer, of the highbrow Soviet Yiddish intelligentsia needing to be part of new artistic trends and of the average reader needing to be stimulated.

IMPROVING THE CONTENT OF SOVIET YIDDISH NEWSPAPERS

It was difficult for Soviet Yiddish newspapers to improve their news coverage. Without a network of international correspondents, *Emes* took most of its front-page news stories from the Soviet news wire service, *Rosta/TASS*. Established in September 1918 by the All-Union Central Executive Committee, *Rosta* was the first national agency responsible for the press. It oversaw the publication of Russian-language provincial newspapers, a function that *Evsektsiia* handled for Yiddish-language regional newspapers. *Rosta* was also the wire service for all smaller Soviet newspapers, providing the majority of their news stories.[141] During the lean Civil War years, many localities simply translated *Rosta* wire stories into Yiddish and published them as wall newspapers. After the Press Crisis and the newspaper consolidation in 1922, *Rosta* was used almost exclusively as a wire service for larger newspapers. The result was that most Soviet newspapers ran the same international news stories. That said, editors could commission independent commentary on news stories, publish political satires, or use other means of analysis to reach a newspaper's particular goals and reading audience, such as the satire of the Locarno Agreements.

In addition to the wire service, Soviet Yiddish newspaper editors turned to the many newspapers to which they subscribed for main themes and for story ideas. First thing in the morning, "the editor bathed himself in a sea of fresh-smelling newspapers" to see what happened the day before. The primary source of information was the wire, which editors referred to as "a newspaper's bread." The first wire stories started coming in around 10 A.M. "One finds speeches of Party leaders, news about a train wreck . . . a decision made by the state. . . . This is all material for the department called 'Information' which we must [first] rework, then give titles to all of these special news stories, sort the material into various divisions, and decide what gets the headline and what goes into a corner."[142]

New technologies changed the way editors were able to obtain information. Editors and writers used the radio, but even more important was the telephone. "In some ways it is more important than radio: on a telephone you can ask questions; on the radio you have to listen and write very quickly and don't have a chance to check facts, ask questions. With the telephone, you can investigate things, find things out for yourself, get clarifications if something is unclear, unlike the radio, which just gives you information." Technology changed and improved the nature of newspaper writing, and as the editors stated, gave the power of journalistic investigation back to those creating the newspaper.

As important as these resources were, they could not provide local news, which republic, regional, and wall newspapers included. For this material, newspapers relied on personal, human resources. "Every day, the editorial staff of *October* had dozens of visitors, 'living people' who came with different questions for the editors." These "living people" were informers, local gossips who brought stories about squabbling husbands and wives or other juicy material that would add color to often dull newspapers. Each newspaper had its regular informers.

Beyond the town gossip, starting in 1922–3, all newspapers developed circles of "worker correspondents" and later "village correspondents," who provided regional news stories to republic and central newspapers. The gossips and worker correspondents made the newspapers more interesting, and more relevant to local readers, showing how consumer demand could shape content.[143] With new technology, local gossips, and worker correspondents, Soviet Yiddish newspapers could develop a bigger readership and better fulfill its task of being the voice of the state, the Party, and the Soviet Yiddish intelligentsia to Soviet Jewry.

SOVIET YIDDISH PUBLISHING IN UKRAINE AND BELORUSSIA

Although by the mid-1920s, Moscow had become the center of Soviet Yiddish cultural production, most Yiddish-speakers lived nowhere near Moscow. This tension between centralized cultural production for ethnic minorities and cultural production taking place where the ethnic groups actually lived lingered throughout the 1920s and into the 1930s. For most ethnic groups, the tension was between cultural production in Moscow and in their national territories, like the Volga region for Germans or Karelia for Finns. But Yiddish-speaking Jews did not have their own territory. It was not until the 1930s that Jews were given Birobidzhan, which, despite its official designation as the Jewish Autonomous Region, never became the home of a majority of Soviet Jewry in the way that the Volga region was the home of Soviet Germans and Karelia, Soviet Finns. Despite the lack of official recognition, Soviet Yiddish cultural production did take place where Jews lived, in Ukraine and Belorussia, and after its establishment, to a lesser extent in Birobidzhan.

In Ukraine, in the early 1920s, Culture League had a virtual monopoly on Yiddish publishing. After all, Kiev was the historic heartland of Jewish publishing in Ukraine, and in the years 1918–21, had served as the incubator for a socialist Yiddish cultural establishment. Moshe Litvakov founded the All-Ukrainian Literary Committee, which attempted to publish book-length Jewish literature in Kiev.[144] The People's Publishing House (*Folksfarlag*) was founded in Kiev in 1918 by some of the biggest talents in Jewish literature – David Bergelson, Der Nister, David Hofshteyn, Shimon Dubnov, Leyb Kvitko, Chaim Nachman Bialik, the literary critic Baal Makhshoves, and others.[145] In addition to the independent Jewish publishing houses, the Soviet state established a Jewish division of the Ukrainian Central Executive Committee's general publishing house, which was dedicated to publishing Jewish literature (almost exclusively in Yiddish) in war-torn Ukraine.[146] However, the capital of the Ukrainian Soviet republic in the 1920s was not Kiev, but Kharkov, which was the center of general ethnic minority publishing in Ukraine, but which was historically not a center of Jewish culture. Henekh Kazakevitch, the initial editor of the Kharkov-based Yiddish journal, *Red World (Royte Velt)*, bemoaned Kharkov's lack of literary resources that were needed to produce a Yiddish journal. Hersh Smolar, a Jewish Communist youth activist, complained that "Kharkov seemed to be such a foreign, cold city."[147] Nonetheless, politics shaped Jewish cultural geography, and Kharkov became a center of Soviet Jewish culture.

To accomplish the goals of creating Soviet Jewish print culture, publishing houses throughout the Soviet Union had to work together. However, because of the dire financial conditions of NEP, each publishing house was trying to survive by increasing revenues and lowering costs. The Main Bureau of the Ukrainian *Evsektsiia*, the highest Jewish Party body in Ukraine, and the Central Jewish Enlightenment Bureau (CJEB), the state body overseeing Jewish cultural work, took responsibility for developing a coordinated plan for all publishing houses working in Yiddish. One way to increase the production of Yiddish texts was to encourage publishing houses outside the Jewish cultural network to publish in Yiddish. In April 1924, the CJEB called on the Ukrainian State Publishing House (*Gosizdat Ukraine*) and the Path of Enlightenment *(Put' prosveshcheniia)* publishing house to increase their Yiddish publishing efforts.[148] The State Publishing House agreed and began subsidizing several national minority newspapers including Yiddish.[149] In early 1925, the Main Bureau began specifying what kind of literature different publishing houses should produce.[150] The Main Bureau realized that a more efficient production system would bring the most books to market, and having each publishing house specialize in certain spheres of literature was one of the best ways to achieve this. By January 1926, there were four publishing houses – Book Union (*Knihospilka*), Ukrainian Worker (*Ukrainskii rabochii*), Ukrainian State Publishing House, and Culture

League – producing Yiddish materials in Ukraine alone.[151] Culture League focused on fiction and textbooks, while the others printed political and propaganda materials. The downside to encouraging non-Jewish publishers to produce Yiddish texts was that it threatened the power of the Soviet Yiddish intelligentsia over Soviet Jewish cultural production.

As publishing houses began coordinating with one another, the Central Bureau of *Evsektsiia* in Moscow acquired more power to oversee Union-wide Jewish publishing. By late 1928, all publishing houses working in Yiddish needed to receive permission from the Central Bureau to proceed with their plans. Having to get Central Bureau approval often slowed down the production process, since it took time to submit plans, then for the Central Bureau to review, alter, and approve them for implementation. Publishing houses, especially the non-Jewish ones, often complained about production delays.[152] Although some were frustrated, this system of control kept Jewish publishing in Jewish activists' hands until the closing down of *Evsektsiia* in 1930.

Ukraine and Russia were the two largest centers of Jewish publishing in the Soviet Union. In contrast, Yiddish book publishing in Belorussia – home to one of the largest Yiddish-speaking communities in the world – was so underdeveloped that it completely dried up in the years 1920–1, when only one small brochure of 500 copies was produced.[153] Contributing to the problem was that unlike Ukraine and Russia, which had Culture League and School and Book respectively, there was no large Jewish publishing house in Belorussia. Activists had to rely on the Belorussian State Publishing House, which meant that they did not have the leverage necessary to play one publisher off the other as Jewish activists had in Ukraine and Russia. In 1925, Belorussia's capacity to publish in Yiddish improved with the production of thirty-eight titles at ten different publishing houses.[154] In the year 1926–7, although Jews made up 8 percent of the Belorussian population, 12 percent of all publications were in Yiddish, compared to less than 4 percent printed in Russian or Polish.[155]

Belorussian Yiddish newspaper publishing was more important than book publishing. In 1927, the Belorussian Communist Party produced three newspapers in Belorussian (highest circulation 7,100), one in Russian (circulation 12,300), one in Yiddish, *October (Oktyabr)* (circulation 7,150), one in Polish (circulation 4,100), and one in Lithuanian (circulation 2,000).[156] *October* was an outgrowth of the old Bundist newspaper *Alarm* that Frumkina had edited. The 1925 switch from the Bundist *Alarm* to the more Communist sounding *October* and the new investment in ethnic minorities' culture in general led to a dramatic increase in the newspaper's circulation. In its first year, *October*'s circulation jumped more than 50 percent from 4,139 in 1925 to 6,400 in 1926.[157] Despite the similarities between the central newspaper *Emes* and *October*, the republic newspapers had different content that catered to a regional audience.

Both *October* and the Ukrainian *Star* had local film and theater listings (for Minsk and Kharkov respectively). In addition, even though *Emes* was the central newspaper, setting the tone and politics for the Soviet Yiddish newspaper network, *October* sometimes openly criticized *Emes'* political stance or coverage of a particular story. The relationship between the two newspapers revealed lingering tensions between center and periphery and between central Soviet institutions in Moscow and republic ones in Minsk or Kharkov.

THE REGULATION OF SOVIET JEWISH PUBLISHING

The regulation of newspapers and books in the Soviet Union is usually understood within the paradigm of "censorship," the repression of harmful or forbidden ideas. In the words of Herman Ermolaev, the Soviet censorship agency, *Glavlit*, "removed the undesirable truth from manuscripts and books."[158] But regulating texts was as much a productive act of creating meanings as it was a suppressive act to restrict them.[159] Editors and publishers, who oversaw the production of a book, worked with authors to guide them in positive directions, both ideologically and aesthetically. Their role as regulators often meant convincing Jewish state and Party representatives to fund projects, just as often as it meant cutting funding from those they wanted to suppress.

Underlying the Soviet state's attitude toward the regulation of ethnic minority publishing in the 1920s was the belief, encouraged by ethnic minorities' intelligentsias, that general publishers like the State Publishing House simply did not have enough knowledge to regulate non-Russian publishing properly. In late 1921, the Communist Party's Central Committee explained: "The general units of the State Publishing House are not really in a position to judge the market for books in national minority languages. It is inconceivable that the general State Publishing House apparatus could master the languages, the cultural specificities, the social makeup of each nationality, and for some nationalities, one would have to examine a foreign book market as well."[160] Because of this attitude, ethnic minorities' publishing houses were regulated by their own institutions, separate from and sometimes with more authority than general Russian-language institutions. The Soviet Yiddish intelligentsia regulated Soviet Yiddish publishing.[161]

From very early on in Soviet history, the Central Bureau of *Evsektsiia* had a relatively tight grip over Yiddish publishing, more so than its Russian-language equivalent had over Russian publishing. In a 1921 report, *Evsektsiia* boldly, but not completely correctly, claimed that it had "totally concentrated publishing in the Central Bureau's hands, and in Ukraine, in the hands of the Main Bureau of Ukraine."[162] Despite the hyperbole of the claim, the Central Bureau did have quite a bit of control. After the 1920 controversy, when the State Publishing

House put out Zionist Hebrew-language calendars over *Evsektsiia*'s explicit rejection of Hebrew-language publishing, the Central Bureau was awarded oversight for all publishing requests involving Jewish languages. The State Publishing House needed permission from Jewish activists to publish Jewish material.[163] Centralizing the Yiddish publishing industry also meant that unlike Russian-language publishing houses, which did not coordinate their plans until the second half of the 1920s, Yiddish publishing was already working toward coordination soon after NEP began.[164] In January 1922, the Central Bureau established a special commission to work out a plan to mitigate some of the financially harmful effects of the economic austerity program and to remind Yiddish publishers that Jewish Party officials in Moscow had a say in what was published.[165]

Even the 1922 founding of the state censorship agency, *Glavlit*, did not radically affect the intelligentsia's oversight. Although there were a few minor structural changes, *Glavlit* frequently turned to the Central Bureau for advice on dealing with Jewish-language publications.[166] In 1923, Pavel Lebedev-Poliansky, *Glavlit*'s chairman, asked the Central Bureau whether or not it was appropriate to import and distribute Bialik's work in Russian translation, recognizing that even though it was a Russian-language translation, Bialik was known as a Hebrew-language cultural figure and, therefore, was under the purview of the Jewish Party apparatus. Although *Glavlit* had final oversight, it relied on the expertise of each ethnic minority to carry out its regulatory functions.[167]

Jewish organizations may have had control over the actual production of texts, but they were expected to work within general Soviet guidelines set by the Central Committee of the Communist Party, the Council of People's Commissars (*Sovnarkom*), and the state's Central Executive Committee (*VTsIK*). For example, in 1924, the Central Executive Committee called for the publication of more popular literature in ethnic minorities' languages. Publishers were expected to follow this lead. What kind of material, who published it, and how much was published was ultimately up to the publishing house and the state and Party apparatus regulating Jewish publishing.[168] As Alfred Greenbaum has argued, "Cultural policy on the local level was based on local interpretations of the 'general party line.'"[169]

The process by which a book came into being was complicated. To give an example of how the system worked, in March 1922, the Main Bureau of the Ukrainian *Evsektsiia* decided to produce a Yiddish translation of Y. M. Steklov's Russian-language book, *Studies on the History of the International*. *Evsektsiia* requested and received permission from its non-Jewish political overseer, the *Agitprop* division of the Central Committee of the Ukrainian Communist Party. Next, the bureau needed funding to pay a translator, so it turned to the State Publishing House for an advance of fifty million rubles, then used the money to pay Moshe Litvakov to translate the text. Finally, it needed to find a place to print the text, and in 1922, the Yiddish-language printing capacities of the Kharkov-based State Publishing House were insufficient to produce the book. The State Publishing House agreed to publish and finance the project, Culture League in Kiev to print it, and the whole project happened on the impetus of the Jewish section of the Party.[170]

As for content, writers brought their book proposals either to a publishing house directly or to the state agency overseeing Jewish culture. The Yiddish poet, Ezra Finenberg, for example, pitched his idea for a poetry collection to the Enlightenment Bureau,[171] while the writer, Itsik Kipnis, sent a complete manuscript for a children's story to Culture League.[172] Ultimately, for a text to appear, both the publisher and the state bureaucrat had to support its publication.[173] Writers were also well aware of resolutions passed by the Central Committee or the Central Executive Committee about literature, because they read newspapers produced by *Evsektsiia* and were part of writers' groups that gave direction to writers. Most importantly, it was members of the Yiddish intelligentsia, people like Litvakov and Frumkina, who defined the standards of Yiddish literary political correctness.

In shaping the text, both the publisher and the Enlightenment Bureau made editorial comments about style, language, and ideological viewpoint. Sometimes they would edit manuscripts themselves; other times they sent the piece out for independent review. The editor played a large role both in shaping the author's original text and in politically and ideologically contextualizing it for the reader by, for example, commissioning introductions. Politics and ideology were only two criteria editors and publishers used. One author complained that his one-act play was not getting published and inquired as to whether it was rejected because of ideological problems. The chair of the CJEB, Mikhail Levitan, responded unambiguously, "Your play was rejected, not because it is ideologically problematic or dangerous. It was rejected because your one-act play has no plot, is terribly disjointed, and is boring, not to mention that your approach to the question is completely superficial."[174] Bad literature, even politically appropriate literature, would not get published.

The publisher also coordinated the production of a text. As the biggest publisher of Yiddish books in Ukraine, Culture League negotiated publishing deals with the bureaucracies that regulated Jewish culture. It also turned to members of the Soviet Yiddish intelligentsia working for state and Party organizations to encourage distribution, to help expedite the approval process for manuscripts, or to secure state funding for publishing.[175] Throughout the 1920s, the *Evsektsiia* and state enlightenment bureaus were coordinating publishing lists, and publishers were ferrying a text into print, and sometimes they disagreed. For example, in negotiations over the publication of the journal, *The Yiddish Language,* Culture League wanted a single editor-in-chief, while the Central Jewish

Enlightenment Bureau wanted an editorial board, a battle the publishing house won. There were also different plans of how to finance the journal, one suggesting higher subscription prices, the other, increased state funding.[176] The relationships among writers and editors, who had the necessary skills to produce the work, the publisher, who had the vision and technical support to bring it to life, and the state and Party activists, who could secure funding and approval from all the necessary agencies were complicated, but at least in the 1920s decisions were not simply "handed down" to publishers, editors, and writers.

By 1927–8, the power relationships that produced Soviet Yiddish culture began to show signs of hierarchy and bureaucratization. One sign was that by 1928, much of the official correspondence between Levitan and B. Marshak, editor-in-chief of Culture League, was no longer in Yiddish, but had switched to Ukrainian, the official bureaucratic language of the Ukrainian Republic. It was a sign that the more intimate internal Jewish affairs that produced Yiddish books in the first half of the 1920s were giving way to more bureaucratic processes of literary production governed by non-Jewish politics. There was an increasing distance between the state and Party activists in the political capital, Kharkov, and the publishers and writers in the historic cultural capital, Kiev, with the balance of power shifting toward Kharkov. As of 1928, Culture League, like other publishers, needed to have advanced reviews of all of its manuscripts, reviews that were solicited and organized by the Enlightenment Bureau, not the publishing house. The advanced review was a new step in the publishing process, and it gave greater control to the state apparatus, which chose the reviewer and gave him/her instructions on how to review.[177] The balance of power continued to shift toward the political center as The Central Publishing House for Ukraine's National Minorities in Kharkov began publishing more Yiddish literature, often at the expense of Kiev-based, and exclusively Jewish, Culture League. But even then, Yiddish publishing was still a negotiated venture, as is evident in the establishment of the Yiddish pedagogical journal, *Soviet Enlightenment (Ratnbildung)*, which began publication in 1929. The terms of the publishing agreement divided power between the Enlightenment Bureau and Culture League.[178]

The final organization to regulate publishing was the official censor – *Glavlit* and its regional affiliates – which asserted its role by actually rejecting publications that had been approved by a publishing house and a state or Party activist. The Yiddish censor for the Kiev region, Comrade Levin, developed a reputation for refusing to approve books in Culture League's *Jewish Writer (Yidishe Shrayber)* fiction series. Levin did not approve publication of *1863*, a book about the 1863 Polish uprising against the Russian empire by the socialist Yiddish (but not Soviet) writer, Joseph Opatoshu. Marshak was not pleased that a petty censor was interfering with the publishing house's well-defined and pre-approved plans. This was, in fact, the second time Levin had turned down a *Jewish Writer* publication, after earlier refusing Bergelson's *The Severity of the Law (Midas hadin)*. His reason for rejecting both publications: "they come across as mystical [*klingn mistish*]."[179] Because of these refusals, the publishing house was falling behind schedule and would not carry out its annual publishing plan. More frustrating was that the Main Bureau of the Ukrainian *Evsektsiia* and the CJEB had already approved Culture League's book list. Who was Comrade Levin to tell the state, the Party, and the publishing house that they were wrong? Marshak suggested, perhaps ironically, "Maybe we will send the books directly to Kharkov, since the approach over there will not be as provincial." (If anything, most Yiddish writers thought of Kharkov as more provincial than Kiev.) But Marshak did not really trust the Kharkov censors either. He asked the Enlightenment Bureau to tell Levin to approve the manuscripts.[180] With pressure on Levin, the books were eventually published, showing that in the late 1920s, the publishing house could still triumph over the censor.

THE END OF AUTONOMY

The shift from Kiev to Kharkov, from Jewish publishers to general ethnic minorities' publishers, and from regional newspapers to republic ones, were all part of the process of centralizing cultural production and incorporating it into the overall project of Soviet state building and Party development. During NEP, all nationalities were fighting for their own publishers and newspapers, all of them were running deficits, and all of them were at the material whims of other sources of power. Jewish cultural production had the additional problem of being centralized in Moscow and Kharkov, both distant from their traditional cultural centers.

The tension between centralization and regionalism was not isolated to Yiddish publishing. The Moscow State Jewish Theater was almost relocated to Belorussia twice, once in 1925 and again in 1926, on the grounds that the theater's real audience was in Belorussia, not in Moscow.[181] The issue persisted throughout the 1920s, and many non-Jewish cultural activists thought that the Moscow-based Soviet Yiddish intelligentsia was overreaching in its persistent attempts to maintain control over Soviet Yiddish culture. As early as November 1920, the executive board of the State Publishing House recommended against funding a Moscow-based Yiddish newspaper, *Yedies*, because "newspapers in Yiddish must be published in the provinces."[182] The non-Jewish central administration was concerned about the negative effects of centralization, especially centralization that was controlled by former Bundists and radical Yiddish cultural critics.

In 1926, a dramatic attempt to close down *Emes* revealed the underlying strains between regionalism and centralism, and the overlap between economics and politics in building Soviet Yiddish culture. The Communist Party carried out a financial audit of the *Emes* print house and newspaper, and presented its findings at a local Moscow committee of the Workers' and Peasants' Inspectorate (*Rabkrin*), the same organization that investigated the paper theft. The meeting strayed from a discussion of finances to an argument about the need for a central Yiddish Party newspaper. Some of the members asked, "Why does this newspaper exist at all?" or "Shouldn't it be located where Jews live, out in the provinces?" "And what language is it written in anyway – 'Biblical' or 'Jargon?' And if it's written in jargon, doesn't that mean it contains Bundism?"[183] This line of questioning showed that political and material pressures were working against centralized Jewish cultural production. According to Litvakov, the meeting's key speaker, the tone of the discussion was mocking, if not anti-Semitic. The *Rabkrin* discussion continued "in a spirit of complete ignorance and, dare I say, provincialism that was absolutely inappropriate for a Party organization in the capital." The questions asked, however, show that these "ignorant provincial" bureaucrats were aware of Jewish language politics and of the historical polemics between the Bund and the Bolsheviks, in which "Bundism," meant bourgeois separatism and nationalism over workers' internationalism. There was suspicion among some, perhaps even some Russified Jews on the Inspectorate, that the Yiddish language itself smacked of Jewish separatism.

The Regional Inspectorate recommended closing down *Emes* because "the newspaper circulates primarily in Belorussia and western Ukraine, and it is unprofitable."[184] Moscow-based Jewish activists defended the newspaper, citing the political reasons for *Emes*'s existence. Semen Dimanshteyn and Alexander Chemerinsky wrote to *Rabkrin* arguing that "*Emes* is the oldest existing Communist Yiddish newspaper in the world. It is patterned on *Pravda* and is the organ of the Central Bureau of *Evsektsiia*. . . . It is the best Yiddish newspaper in the world. . . . One single notice abroad about the closure of *Emes* will be judged by the bourgeois press and the Zionist counterrevolutionaries within the country as a rupture in Jewish politics in the USSR."[185] Dimanshteyn waxed about the triumphs of *Emes* and emphasized its international political importance. To heighten fears about the dangerous political ramifications of the closure, Chemerinsky wrote under separate cover to the executive board of *Rabkrin* that "Moscow is the headquarters of two dangerous Jewish parties, which put out two legal, dangerous newspapers: *Proletarian Thought (Proletarskaia mysl')* and *The Pioneer (Gekholuts)*," each of which was a publication of quasi-legal socialist Zionist organizations still operating in the Soviet Union.[186] These letters caused many to rethink the regional *Rabkrin* decision. In the end, all interested groups sided with *Emes* and *Evsektsiia*. The Central *Rabkrin* ruled that transferring *Emes* to the provinces was "not appropriate at this time."[187]

Shortly after this crisis, *Emes* found itself under attack again for being a continued financial drain on state resources. In late 1927, the People's Commissariat for Finance wanted to reduce the 130,000-ruble subsidy – up from 80,000 rubles in 1926 – to 30,000 rubles, and publish a monthly Yiddish journal in place of a daily newspaper.[188] The incident generated discussion about continuing subsidies for ethnic minorities publishing in general. The *Emes* editors argued that with a circulation of 12,000, *Emes* was the largest national minorities' newspaper in the Soviet Union. Closing it down would set a bad precedent.[189] To investigate the issue, the Central Committee Secretariat established a five-person commission (including Dimanshteyn) that after its two-week inquiry, recommended continuing the full subsidy for *Emes*.[190] The Commissariat agreed to the commission's findings, but called on *Emes* to double its circulation, leading to a new round of marketing campaigns to find subscribers.

Emes faced another financial crisis in 1928 when one of its leading financial supporters, School and Book publishing house, was closed down. During its four-year existence, the publisher had provided large financial subsidies for *Emes*, for the Yiddish youth journals *Yungvald* and *Pioner*, and from a distance, supported the two republic Yiddish newspapers, *October* and *Star*.[191] The reasons for School and Book's closure rested on the restructuring of the Soviet economy as a whole – away from NEP economic liberalization and toward a state-centered economic apparatus. In May 1928, the Communist section of School and Book (the Party committee of School and Book employees, whose job was political oversight of the institution) met to pronounce "the continued existence of School and Book as a commercial operation is not possible, and as quickly as possible, it must be liquidated." There was discussion about shifting publication of *Emes* to the Central Publishing House of National Minorities, which had already taken over publication of the Ukrainian Yiddish daily, *Shtern*.[192] Such a move would have put all of Jewish publishing into centralized non-Jewish establishments. In the end, the Communist section decided against this, and instead, in August 1928, established a new Yiddish publishing house in Moscow, renamed Emes, although Emes's autonomy was circumscribed.[193]

Centralization took its toll on the cultural production of ethnic minorities when all Party sections were closed down in 1929–30 and *Evsektsiia* was disbanded in 1930. At the same time, the entire publishing industry was consolidated, and even the Central Publishing House of National Minorities fought to maintain its autonomy as publisher for the Soviet Union's ethnic minorities. Culture League was officially closed in 1931, leaving only the Emes house in Moscow as an exclusively Yiddish publisher. The consolidation meant that the intelligentsia no longer had control over the creation of Soviet Yiddish culture.

THE UNIQUENESS OF SOVIET JEWISH CULTURAL PRODUCTION

In many ways, Soviet Yiddish publishing fit the overall pattern of Soviet cultural production. The 1920s were a time when each ethnic group's intelligentsia had power to create culture, something that made many central Party and state authorities anxious, but was nonetheless something they supported. The Cultural Revolution and the 1930s were a time when these established intelligentsias had their power circumscribed by a centralizing state that was turning its attention to industrialization and collectivization.

But quantitatively and qualitatively, the production of Soviet Jewish culture was different from that of other ethnic groups in the Soviet Union. Jews were a highly educated, highly literate, non-landed national minority with a deep socialist tradition. The fact that Jews were "non-landed" often posed administrative problems, since most ethnic minority political and administrative structures were based on territory, but also sometimes created institutional space for the Soviet Yiddish intelligentsia to produce its own culture. Ukrainians, Georgians, and others had their own "state" publishing houses in their republics, but there was no Jewish state publishing. Even with the founding of a Jewish territory in Birobidzhan in 1934, Jewish publishing never developed its own state apparatus on its own territory.[194]

In the 1920s, Yiddish culture, more than that of other national minorities, was produced in exclusively Jewish establishments that did not raise the specter of nationalism in the way that Belorussian or Ukrainian state publishing houses did. If members of the Soviet Yiddish intelligentsia were accused of nationalism, it was other members of the intelligentsia who made the accusations. In terms of sheer numbers, Jewish culture also received a disproportionate quantity of state resources. In 1924 in Ukraine, Yiddish-language publishing was quantitatively behind only Ukrainian- and Russian-language publishing based on the total number of pages printed and total number of publishing houses active in Yiddish-language materials. Ukrainian and Russian dominated the Ukrainian publishing establishment, making up more than 90 percent of all publishing in Ukraine. Yiddish made up 8 percent, while the next most popular language for Soviet publications in Ukraine, German, made up only 0.8 percent; but Jews only accounted for 5.4 percent of the population.[195] The statistics for 1925–6 were virtually identical. In the Russian Republic and Belorussia, Yiddish publishing also received significant state resources. For the 1923–4 year, the Commissariat of Enlightenment allocated one thousand printer's pages for Yiddish-language publications, the largest number of any non-landed national minority in the Russian Republic.[196]

In addition to the quantitative dominance of Yiddish publishing among non-landed national minorities, the production of Soviet Jewish culture was not qualitatively like that of other national minorities, even into the 1930s. Although the 1932 statistic showing that 62 percent of all Yiddish books were translations might have seemed surprisingly high, that number declined throughout the 1930s. By 1939, only 46 percent of Yiddish books were translations or by authors outside the Soviet Union, and the remaining 54 percent were original Soviet Yiddish publications. In comparison, German-language publishing that year counted eighty-three titles, sixty-nine of which were translations, and seventeen of which were by German authors outside the Soviet Union. There were no original German works by Soviet Germans.[197] As late as 1939, Soviet Yiddish publishing was based on original works by Soviet Jewish authors, while Soviet German publishing, and therefore the Soviet German cultural project, was made up exclusively of imports and translations. Soviet Germans did not produce their own distinct Soviet culture. The Soviet Yiddish intelligentsia did.

Producing texts always involves a complicated negotiation among publishers, writers, editors, and critics, and texts are regulated by myriad social, political, cultural, and even professional pressures. Matthew Lenoe has shown that the Soviet publishing industry of the 1920s was always working at the intersection of material limitations and ideological goals, but that Russian-language Party periodicals were always strictly controlled by central institutions.[198] Although the Soviet Yiddish intelligentsia was very much a part of (and not suppressed by) Soviet power, it was also far enough on the edges of that system to be able to determine what Soviet Jewish culture would look like. It was not until the late 1920s that Soviet Jewish cultural production began taking place predominantly in general non-Jewish state publishing houses, and that general writers' organizations, such as the Russian or Ukrainian Associations of Proletarian Writers, began taking a larger role in educating writers about the production of texts. As time went on, the intelligentsia's cultural and political space were constricted and eventually eliminated as both the special sections of the Party devoted to national minorities and the publishing industry were consolidated during the 1928–32 Cultural Revolution.[199]

5

Engineers of Jewish Souls

*Soviet Yiddish Writers Envisioning the Jewish
Past, Present, and Future*

In 1932, the Central Committee of the Communist Party consolidated all existing literary groups and, in their place, created the Union of Soviet Writers
as the official literary organization in the Soviet Union. Two years later, at the
first Congress of Soviet Writers, the Union made Socialist Realism the official
form of Soviet culture. Until that time, Soviet Yiddish writers, the backbone
of the Soviet Yiddish intelligentsia, had organized themselves in competing literary groups and had published in diverse journals, each defining itself through
a combination of aesthetics, ideology, and politics. This diversity mirrored developments in Soviet Russian literature in the 1920s, which, more than in
Yiddish literature, were marked by a large number of writers' groups and much
internecine fighting. Soviet Yiddish writers understood that literature was an
integral part of the construction of a new Jewish culture, society, and nation.[1]
Although the intelligentsia's writers produced prose, poetry, and literary criticism, this examination of the intelligentsia's aesthetics and ideology focuses on
poetry, which in the 1920s was the site of much ideological and aesthetic experimentation. As the ones who built Soviet Jewish culture with their pens, these
writers and their literary groups and journals revealed many ways the Soviet
Yiddish intelligentsia imagined Soviet Jewish culture and the Soviet Jewish
nation. Just as the Yiddish publishing industry became institutionalized and incorporated into the central Soviet publishing system, literary groups, writers,
and aesthetics also moved toward greater institutionalization within the Soviet
structure of cultural production as Yiddish writers became a more integral and
integrated part of the central Soviet literary establishment.

THE MANY TRENDS OF SOVIET LITERATURE

Until 1932, there was no consensus on what Soviet literature was or should be,
let alone what Soviet Yiddish literature should be. Some writers argued that

Soviet literature was marked by its support of the Communist Party; others thought it required a revolution in writing by making the simple worker the writer of his/her own literature; and still others thought the revolution was a time for literary revolution and radical experimentation. These debates led to the formation of many literary groups, each with a vision of how literature should look after the revolution. A group known as *The Smithy (Kuznitsa)* moved toward Lenin's idea of proletarian culture, defined by its political stance and support for Communism. Many of *The Smithy's* writers used lyric poetry to describe the creation of a new society.[2] Out of *The Smithy* came the group *October (Oktiabr')*, whose name connected the group to the politics of the regime. *October* served as the basis of the proletarian literary movement in the Soviet 1920s, and the model for proletarian organizations of other nationalities.[3] *October's* manifesto called for a "strengthening of the Communist line in proletarian literature and the organizational strengthening of the All-Russian and the Moscow Associations of Proletarian Writers [MAPP]," the writers' groups established to organize proletarian writers.[4]

In the first half of the 1920s, Russian-language Soviet writers' groups kept splintering. In 1923, *On Guard (Na postu)* was established as a reaction to the rise of writers' groups not explicitly grounded in Communist ideology and advocated that Communist ideology needed to define proletarian literature.[5] These writers whom Lev Trotsky termed "fellow travelers," grew out of groups such as the *Serapion Brothers*, who, in 1921, proclaimed the independence of art and the creation of a new aesthetic.[6] The Futurist *LEF* group followed the *Serapion Brothers'* call for more literary experimentation, but charged the group with appropriating and diluting their devices while "flavoring them with symbolist spices."[7] So-called Russian fellow travelers grouped around the literary journal, *Red Virgin Soil (Krasnaia Nov')*, which Alexander Voronsky edited during its entire existence from 1921–27. And these were just some of the trends in Russian Soviet literature.

Writers' groups of Soviet ethnic minorities were also a part of these trends. In Ukrainian literature, the early 1920s were marked by debates over the relationship between aesthetics and politics. Like Yiddish and Russian writers, Ukrainian symbolists were the "first wave" modernists, the pre-revolutionary writers who broke with realist traditions of the nineteenth century and made Ukrainian literature part of European modernism. They published in the years immediately following the abdication of the tsar, putting out the collection *Muzahet* in 1919, which was patterned on Andrei Belyi's symbolist group, *Musaget*.[8] There were Ukrainian Futurists, symbolists, neo-classicists, and alongside these more modernist trends appeared the Ukrainian version of the realist and proto socialist-realist proletarian culture. In 1919, the Ukrainian proletarians published two issues of *Stars of Tomorrow (Zori griadushchego)* and the

Soviet state sponsored a journal edited by the Futurist Mykhail Semenko titled *Art (Mystetstvo).*[9] In the mid-1920s, Ukrainian literature also developed
its own fellow traveler group known as *The Link (Lanka)*, founded in Kiev
in 1924.

Despite Yiddish writers' involvement in Russian language trends, Yiddish
literary history diverges from the histories of Russian and Ukrainian literature. In
the first half of the 1920s, writers of the Soviet Yiddish intelligentsia consolidated
rather than fragmented, and, unlike Ukrainian and Russian modernists who
made their aesthetic affiliations with a particular "–ism," Yiddish modernists did
not mark themselves with explicit allegiances to a given trend. Soviet Yiddish
journals tended to incorporate writers with varying aesthetics and politics.
Aesthetic labels were an ascribed identity given to a writer by others as part of
intergroup polemics.

MODERNISM AND SOVIET JEWISH LITERATURE

The radical literary experimentation of the 1920s is most often associated with
the era of modernism, in which Jewish writers played an integral role. Dozens
of Jewish writers writing in Jewish and non-Jewish languages across several
continents experimented with literary movements – such as Symbolism, Impressionism, Expressionism, Futurism, and others – both through personal interaction in cultural groups in such places as New York, Berlin, Paris, and
Moscow and through textual interactions by reading and studying contemporary modernisms in Yiddish, Hebrew, German, Russian, English, and French.
European Yiddish modernism began in war-torn Eastern Europe in 1917–18
with the *Our Own (Eygns)* group in Kiev and with multicultural avant-garde
literary circles in Moscow. Some of the Yiddish modernist writers migrated
to Lodz, Warsaw, and Berlin and set up new modernist groups like the *Young
Yiddish (Yung Yidish)* movement, *The Gang (Khalyastre)* group of expressionists in
Warsaw, and the members of the Kiev Group in Berlin, who put out the journal *Pomegranate (Milgroym).*[10] During the Civil War, with chaos and pogroms
raging in Ukraine generally and Kiev specifically, most Yiddish writers fled for
other centers of literature in Eastern Europe, especially Berlin, Warsaw, and
Moscow. Those who ended up in the Soviet capital created the journal *Stream
(Shtrom).*

Critics of Yiddish literature have had a difficult time conceiving of a Soviet
Yiddish modernism, of aesthetic movements within the Soviet Yiddish intelligentsia that wanted to challenge and redefine literary conventions. When talk
ing about writers in the Soviet Union, Chone Shmeruk, Seth Wolitz, and other
scholars of Yiddish modernism refer to the object of their study as Yiddish literature in the Soviet Union, never as Soviet Yiddish literature. *Stream* is referred

to as a "Moscow" journal or a "successor to *Our Own*," rather than as a Soviet journal, even though the Enlightenment Commissariat subsidized the journal.[11] If the term "Soviet Yiddish literature" is used, it usually refers to the antimodernist socialist realist literature, the saccharine Yiddish ballads about factories, or the paeans to Stalin of the 1930s.[12] This most common understanding of Soviet Yiddish literature obfuscates the presence of competing tendencies and the many ways in which the intelligentsia used Yiddish literature to imagine the Soviet Jewish future.[13]

There is a similar trend in histories of Ukrainian modernism, which also resist putting radical modernism and Soviet state building together. For many Western and émigré scholars, Ukrainian literature was supposed to work in the service of Ukrainian nationalism. Those modernist trends that did not conform to these national goals or that were supported by the Communist Party were ignored or disparaged. For example, "Futurism remained reprehensible for its purported political conformism and acquiescence to the Soviet regime."[14] Scholarship on Ukrainian and Yiddish literary modernism in the Soviet Union, and therefore on the politics of Soviet ethnic intelligentsias, both suffered from the seeming incompatibility of nationalism and Communism, between art in the service of the revolution and art in the service of the nation. Perhaps because of this, scholars of Russian-language Soviet literature have had less trouble seeing modernism and the Soviet state together.

It is true that Soviet Yiddish literature, both its modernist and non-modernist varieties, was part of the Soviet state building project of incorporating ethnic minorities into the Soviet Union. It is also true that Soviet Yiddish writers and critics were very good at and obsessed with defining groups and categories, and at creating and re-creating their own literary histories as politics changed around them. They marked the very concrete delineation between such groupings as proletarians and non-proletarians, between "the émigrés" who went to Berlin and Warsaw and returned and those who never left the Soviet Union, between the "old" generation and the "new" generation, and between Party members and fellow travelers. What becomes clear in examining these groups is that, more than aesthetic manifestos, Party affiliation, or age, what defined literary groups and Soviet Yiddish literature was the writers' and critics' own polarizing rhetoric.[15] The common presumption that Communists were necessarily proletarian writers was by no means the case. Calling oneself a "proletarian" writer also did not necessarily imply an antimodernist aesthetic, despite the fact that proletarian manifestos proclaimed so. In examining the aesthetics, ideology, and politics of the Soviet Yiddish intelligentsia, it became clear that Soviet Yiddish literature was simultaneously part of a state-building process and defining and redefining what Jewish literature and culture should be.

IN THE BEGINNING . . .

The drive to form groups in order to gain political and literary power began independently of the Soviet Union.[16] In 1918, David Bergelson and Der Nister, considered the first writers to create a Yiddish modernist prose, founded the Yiddish writers' group known as the Kiev Group and the journal *Eygns*, marked as the first "institution" of European Yiddish modernism. *Eygns* means "Our Own," and the journal reflected the sense of optimism in the immediate post-revolutionary era, before the full force of anti-Jewish pogroms swept through Ukraine in 1919. David Hofshteyn's "Springtime" is the most overtly optimistic poem with images of sunshine pouring forth from the skies that "mixes with magical wine in a goblet of joy." The final stanza puts the poetic voice in the center of this joyous scene:

> How many times has it been? I won't count—
> Today I was girded up by sunshine,
> I walk without fear in all the dark caves
> of the world and am. . . .[17]

Alongside Hofshteyn's exuberance, Yehezkiel Dobrushin's "In shtetls" also revels in sunshine as it "illuminates the shtetl's rooftops and market places." Perets Markish, a newcomer to Yiddish poetry, included a poem titled "Dawn," again expressing the feelings of hope that the Jewish intelligentsia in Ukraine had after the collapse of the tsarist empire. All three use images of the sun and light – traditional images of the en*light*enment that emphasized the beginning of a new, modern era – to portray joy.

Although, according to Bergelson, *Our Own* was poorly received when it first came out, Nachman Mayzl, literary critic and participant in the Kiev Group, called it the first "free Yiddish word" in Russia.[18] Despite its oppositional stance, it was explicitly not aligned with any political party. But aesthetically, *Our Own* is usually associated with the modernist trends of Symbolism and Impressionism because of the leadership of Der Nister and Bergelson. *Our Own*'s poets, however, were primarily newcomers to the Yiddish literary scene. Hofshteyn created his literary persona in the journal, which also included works by Leyb Kvitko and Markish, each of whom was experimenting with Expressionism. This aesthetic movement was a new direction in European literature that reflected the internal crises writers portrayed after the horrors of World War I. But from the beginning, Yiddish literary institutions, and the Soviet Yiddish intelligentsia, would incorporate diverse aesthetics and politics. *Our Own*'s literary critics included Yehezkiel Dobrushin and Moshe Litvakov, who also became important members of the Soviet Yiddish intelligentsia.

What brought these intellectuals together to form the Kiev Group? There was little consensus, since at least two different conceptions of *Our Own*'s aesthetic and political project emerged. Some have suggested that those like Bergelson who wrote in a Symbolist and Impressionist style, called for an "art for art's sake" stance to improve Yiddish literature and the Jewish reading public. Such a stance might be politically problematic if literature was to be in the service of a political and social revolution. At the same time, Litvakov wanted the Yiddish intelligentsia's aesthetic program to be grounded in political revolution, not the other way around. In Civil War Kiev, as the independent Ukrainian nationalists and Russian Red Army fought one another, such distinctions had political consequences – one implying a more nationalist stance, the other an internationalist one.

Ukrainian modernists were engaged in similar debates about how to re-make Ukrainian literature and the Ukrainian nation in a revolutionary world. Ukrainian symbolists, whose journal *Ukrainian Home (Ukraïnska khata)* served as the foundation of Ukrainian modernism through World War I, sharply criticized Ukrainian Futurists, like Semenko, whose goal, as they saw it, was aesthetic experimentation that took its cues from Russian literature rather than Ukrainian national development. The Symbolists called Semenko a "Muscovite," a lapdog of the Russian Futurists in Moscow and Petrograd.[19] The tensions among the impressionists, the proto-expressionists, and the futurists within Yiddish literature resembled these debates within Ukrainian modernism about the relationship between aesthetics and politics, and between national and international revolution.

Within the Kiev Group, there was no disagreement that Yiddish was the language of the Jewish people of Russia and that Jewish national renewal would happen in the "people's tongue." There was consensus that, as leaders of this renewal, the Yiddish intelligentsia needed to create a modern literature in the Jews' language that was modeled on European literature.[20] Politically, although non-aligned, the Kiev Group was generally socialist and non-Zionist, with little political consensus beyond that. Everyone in the Kiev Group was talking about the same problem – how to envision a modern Jewish literature and nation in the aesthetic and political universe of modernism and revolution.

As a response to the so-called art for art's sake stance of *Our Own*'s editors, the literary section of the Soviet Ukrainian Enlightenment Commissariat, the new Soviet body overseeing culture and propaganda in Ukraine, put out *Dawn (Baginen)* (July 1919), a competing journal that brought together the proto-expressionist trends of the Kiev Group while emphasizing explicit political engagement.[21] The cover of *Dawn* presented the tensions and fusions between nation building and revolution that *Our Own* reflected with a Picasso-esque image of a man blowing the shofar, and a beaming sun rising above the shtetl where the shofar-blower lives (Illustration 5.1).

ILLUSTRATION 5.1: The cover of the Yiddish journal *Dawn* (*Baginen*), Kiev, 1919. The text above the image reads: "Beginning: A Monthly Journal, First Issue" Below the image: "June 1919, Kiev." Across the handles of the Torah scroll reads: "Proletariat of the world, unite!" and at the bottom in the shadows, it reads: "Publication of the All–Ukrainian Literary Committee, Jewish Section."

The image shows both the modernist breakdown of realist representation and the simultaneous optimistic "dawn" of a new age, heralded by the call of the shofar and the rising sun. The title is written in sans-serif block letters, a modernist form of typography. Finally, the surrounding image shows a Torah scroll with the words "Proletariat of the World Unite" across the bottom scroll, again fusing the national with the international. The illustrator, Joseph Chaikov, was, along with El Lissitsky and Marc Chagall, one of the most important avant-garde Jewish illustrators in Russia at the time.[22] The Soviet government only used the best talent to create literature that represented its more politicized and very modernist vision of the future.

In addition to the fusion of Jewish national and Soviet socialist imagery, *Dawn's* poetry addressed the issue of Jews living in the modern world. David Hofshteyn's "City" (*Shtot*) opens with a triumphant call for Jews to become more modern, and he uses the city as the symbol of modernity: "City! You called me from afar with announcements from the wire. I have always seen you from a mountain top."[23] The trope of the tension between city and country, modernity and tradition, runs through Hofshteyn's poem and became a common trope for other Yiddish poets who followed him. Leyb Kvitko's "In a Red Storm" *(In roytn shturem)* depicts the speaker's family dealing with revolution, giving a human perspective to the broad generational change that was occurring.[24] *Dawn* and *Our Own* inaugurated Yiddish modernism in Eastern Europe, and established many of the themes and images that would define Soviet Yiddish literature of the 1920s.

Dawn was edited by A. Litvak, a Bundist editor who arrived in Kiev just months earlier.[25] All the great Yiddish poets of the time contributed to this official Soviet publication: Hofshteyn, Markish, Kvitko, and H. Leyvik, who was by this time in the United States. Sholem Ash and I.J. Singer contributed short stories and Dobrushin, the literary critic of *Eygns*, wrote an essay on Mendele Moykher Sforim (a.k.a. S.Y. Abramovitch). As with many aspirations of Kiev's Jewish cultural community, *Dawn's* founders intended the journal to be a serial, but only one issue was published before pogroms broke out in Kiev late in the summer of 1919.

Litvak picked up where Litvakov and Bergelson left off. In "Literature and Life," Litvak supported Litvakov's view that art was in the service of life, politics, and the revolution.[26] He argued that representations of Jews in Yiddish literature were lagging behind Jews' actual lives during and after the revolution. Jews had experienced a revolution, but Yiddish literature had not. He made the bold claim that "as for the new Jewish individual, we only have [Sholem] Ash. I'm not talking about these sweet, slick *(boymldik)* stories about every dirty worker's house, and this 'Oh, the proletariat. Boo, hoo, the proletariat.' These have nothing to do with art. We need the spirit of battle, the psychology of the great many-headed personality – the masses and the psychology of the individual."[27] Aesthetically, Litvak revealed a developing Futurist sensibility by the multiplicity of "I"'s within the individual and the masses, as a many-headed beast – a hydra – and in his vision of aesthetic interactions as "battle." Vladimir Mayakovsky, the quintessential Russian futurist, implied as much when he stated, "Today's poetry is the poetry of struggle."[28] He was obviously not a fan of proletarian poetry, the so-called boo-hoo, the worker poetry written by and for workers, and thought it was simply bad literature. Litvak, surprisingly, complimented Bergelson for having written about the decline of the old Jewish family, and insisted that the legacies of Mendele, Sholem Aleichem, and Perets were important for art, which needed to reflect the new reality of Jewish life and the reality of the Jewish intelligentsia: "If you scratch the surface of a Jewish intellectual you will find a *melamed* . . . and the old Tevye the Milkman can still be found. He doesn't sell cheese and butter, and doesn't crack a whip, and the verses that pepper his speech aren't from the Torah, but are from Marx or Herzl."[29]

He ends with the vivid metaphor that "the artist is not a tombstone engraver. He is a creator of life." Litvak's final statement shows the dual role of the artist in the new world of Revolutionary Russia. On the one hand, art needed to reflect life, to catch up as the real world changed around the artist. At the same time, however, the artist needed to "create life." The tension between reflection and creation was endemic to the Soviet conception of literature. Stalin is well known for having said, at the First Soviet Writers' Union Congress in 1934, that writers are the engineers of souls. While the writers were "engineering souls," they were also, in theory, responding to the social conditions of post-revolutionary Russia. Litvak revealed this tension in Yiddish literature as early as 1919. The "*melameds*-turned-Marxist revolutionaries" were the ones imagining and creating the Jewish future.

Our Own and *Dawn* were but two of several literary journals that the Kiev Group of socialist Jewish activists envisioned. What defined Soviet or non-Soviet, Communist Party or non-aligned Yiddish literature, was not at all clear. For example, *Ascent* or *Sunrise (Oyfgang,* 1919), another literary collection, was published in Kiev by the independent Culture League, the same publisher of *Dawn* and *Our Own*. This collection was officially supported by the Central Bureau of *Evsektsiia* in Moscow, which received money and paper from the State Publishing House to produce the literary collection.[30] *Sunrise* went back to *Our Own*'s roots by including poetry and prose from Impressionists and Expressionists. It also included material about Jewish visual arts and music, showing the development of a modern Jewish culture in many media, something that *Our Own* had not done. Dobrushin's piece "Three Poets" argued that poetry, not prose, was the literary form for the revolutionary age. The editors – left unnamed – also translated two German poets, Christian Morgenstern, known for his grotesque, fantastic poems, and Ludwig Scharft, a lyricist, and incorporated them into the nascent modern Yiddish canon.

Evsektsiia supported other modernist Yiddish literary efforts. At its July 31, 1919 meeting, the Kiev *Evsektsiia* suggested putting out another literary journal to express a "purely Party perspective," believing that Litvak's *Dawn*, although more Party-oriented than *Our Own*, was still not allied enough to the Party. The chair of the committee, Elyohu Kheyfits, proposed a new journal called *Battle (Kamf)*, echoing Mayakovsky and Litvak's calls for a "fighting literature," which was to include literary criticism, theory, prose, and poetry. He envisioned *Battle* as a "scientific literary journal that combines theory with Communist politics."[31] The Communist Party and Yiddish writers were finding a community of interests in the development of Soviet Yiddish literature.

Although Kiev was the breeding ground of Soviet Yiddish modernism, in Vitebsk, a group of writers came together in 1920 to publish a smaller journal that has been virtually erased from Yiddish literary history – *Waves (Khvalyes)*.[32] Unlike *Our Own*, which was politically independent, and even *Dawn*, which was state-sponsored but not Communist Party-sponsored, *Waves* was the first official Yiddish publication of the Communist Party.[33] *Waves'* masthead proclaimed that it was an organ of the Jewish Section of the Vitebsk Regional Party Committee of the Communist Youth League. It was not accidental that the Jewish Communist youth league published the journal – age had become ideologically significant in the polarized world of Revolutionary Russia. If the Kiev Group was known for its connections to earlier forms of modernism and was thus seen as an "older generation," *Waves* was breaking new ground because of its youth.

The opening, unsigned manifesto proclaimed the journal's purpose: "The young Jewish worker does not give any less of his strength, power, or blood [than other workers]. Thousands of lives have been lost on the battlefield. . . . Our organ has been called into being to add stridency and clarity to the young Jewish Communist movement."[34] The manifesto addressed the purpose of literature in the new society using the same categories established in Russian and Yiddish Soviet literary criticism. "*Waves* must reflect all aspects of the multicolored, stormy life of the young Jewish worker; it must blaze a trail in our joyous building and fight for freedom. . . . *Waves* must flow from our deepest depths, soul, and spirit. It must not express itself in the language of old Jews. . . . May the young Jewish worker grab a pen in his hand and write his red history, his fiery, flaming life story."[35] *Waves'* call for the worker to write his own history echoed the ideology of the Proletarian Cultural movement, known as *Proletkult*, under the leadership of Alexander Bogdanov, who wanted workers to become their own storytellers. In keeping with the proletarian ideal, there was no "authoritative" editor listed for the journal, although Moshe Yudovin was the contributing editor. *Waves'* aesthetics reflected the Futurist and Expressionist trends that were coming to Yiddish literature, and even the name "waves" had become an established Expressionist image conveying the tumult of a world torn by wars and revolutions. The journal also adopted the new phoneticized Yiddish orthography that had been debated among Yiddish linguists, cultural activists, and writers from 1918–20, and was officially adopted by the Soviet Yiddish linguists in 1920. The reformed orthography marked this journal as visually different from the Kiev journals, which used a more traditional one.

Dobrushin reviewed *Waves* for the Moscow *Emes*.[36] He used unflattering adjectives like "dry," "unoriginal," "sentimental," and ironically, "outmoded," to suggest that *Waves*, despite its rhetoric of youth and innovation, was working in an older tradition of Yiddish poetry of the "Sweatshop poets," who wrote similarly bombastic and, at times maudlin, poetry about the downtrodden working classes of America.[37] This is the poetic tradition Litvak referred to in his sarcastic statement about "boo, hoo, the proletariat" poetry. In addition, according to Dobrushin, *Waves* was not original, because "One feels the same type of mood that Der Nister created in his intimate revolutionary poem 'Unter di tirn' [Behind the Doors]." The irony was that while the *Waves'* writers might have tried to distance themselves from "first wave" modernists such as Der Nister, Dobrushin said that Der Nister was one of their most important influences. Dobrushin warned that "the youth must be careful in its literary experiments, because first and foremost it belongs to a genuinely devoted but inexperienced reading audience." He was expressing an emerging "generation gap," as younger writers working within a proletarian ideology presented a different path to the Jewish future.

OUT OF MANY, ONE: MOSCOW AND THE LITERARY JOURNAL *STREAM*

In 1919 in Kiev, with Anton Denikin's takeover and the outbreak of pogroms, Yiddish publishing came to a virtual standstill. Some of the journalistic apparatus stayed behind, but many of the writers and critics fled. Some, like the critic Nokhum Oyslender and his wife and poet, Mire Khenkina, joined the Red Army. Some were killed during the Civil War – Beynush Shteyman and Osher Shvartsman – and became martyrs of the Soviet Yiddish intelligentsia. But most left Ukraine. The result of these migrations was the remaking of the Yiddish cultural map with new centers appearing where the Soviet state apparatus could offer work – in Moscow, Kharkov, and Minsk. Perets Markish and Der Nister went to Moscow and worked for *Emes* in 1920 before leaving the Soviet Union in 1921 for Warsaw and Berlin, respectively.

In Moscow, a circle of socialist Jewish writers had been active since the early days of World War I. Daniel Charny, a Yiddish writer who had moved to Moscow to work with the *Folkspartay*, a Jewish socialist organization, and later to serve as editor of the *Communist World*, claimed that Moscow had become the center of the Jewish intelligentsia in unoccupied Russia as early as 1915. Moreover, after the February Revolution in 1917, which ended residential restrictions on Jews, "thousands and thousands of Jewish faces suddenly appeared on the streets of Moscow."[38] Moshe Broderzon, who founded the *Young Yiddish* group in Lodz in 1919, developed many of his modernist ideas in 1917 when he participated in Moscow's Russian modernist circles. [39] By mid-1918 those writers working in Yiddish formed their own group. In the first edition of *Emes*, in August 1918, the "Moscow Circle of Jewish Writers and Artists" advertised an evening of Yiddish cabaret.[40] In 1920, the Soviet state officially recognized the organization, and Charny was named secretary. The most important benefit of Soviet state recognition was financial – the Circle received a permanent subsidy from the Jewish subdivision of the Enlightenment Commissariat.[41]

With financial support and stable leadership, the Circle began to grow. It printed its own stationery, registered its members with the literature division of the Enlightenment Commissariat, and began to consider publishing on a larger scale. The group even had an "office," a rare commodity in famine-ridden Civil War Moscow, as well as a telephone, which it received only because Charny was the editor of a Party publication. Access to power had its privileges. The office, however, doubled as Charny's apartment located at Malaia Dmitrovka 29/3, and it also served as the salon of the Moscow Soviet Yiddish intelligentsia. This space was the home of Yiddish writers on the move during the Civil War. For one year, Charny, Hofshteyn, Der Nister, and Markish all lived there.[42] The Circle was a literary community both intellectually and physically.

The group's biggest achievement was the production of its literary journal *Stream* (*Shtrom*, which can also be translated as "Current" or even "Literary Trend"), which occupied an important role as the link between what Western Yiddish scholars consider the earlier "good" modernist literature of the Kiev Group and the "bad" literature that came with the rise of proletarian culture in the later 1920s. (Later, Soviet Yiddish critics put "bad" and "good" in opposite places, but they still put *Stream* in the middle as the link between the two.) The Central Bureau of *Evsektsiia* negotiated with the State Publishing House to publish the literary journal and received approval in early 1921.[43] It took a year for *Stream* to start appearing in February 1922, and its publication was advertised in *Emes*.[44] The Circle published 3,000 copies, a high number in comparison to later Soviet Yiddish literary journals, which had print runs between 1,000 and 1,500. Circle member Marc Chagall designed the simple cover, which like Chaikov's cover for *Dawn*, reflected a modernist aesthetic. Unlike Chaikov, however, Chagall used only the letters in the word *Shtrom* as illustrations, which included a disembodied person on the "R" and a factory with a worker entering the building as part of the "Sh."[45]

The journal's title was quite meaningful, and not just for its modernist self-promotion in naming itself "Literary Trend." The name of the journal came from an epigraph that appeared at the beginning of each issue, "But beneath the cliffs I hear a fresh stream, trickling and gurgling [*Nor unter felzn her ikh rint un rizlt frish a shtrom*]." The line comes from a poem by Osher Shvartsman, a modernist poet of the Kiev Group who was killed during the Civil War, making him the first martyr of Soviet Yiddish culture. By titling the journal with a statement from Shvartsman, *Stream* placed itself firmly within a developing modernist and Soviet Yiddish literary history. Unlike the Kiev Group and *Waves*, which both stated what was wrong with the existing literature, *Stream*, by its title and by its manifesto, stated what it was and would become. The name *Stream* also echoed the new Party-sponsored Ukrainian literary journal, *Gulfstream (Holfshtrom)*, which was dominated by the ever-present Semenko and other Ukrainian Futurists. *Gulfstream* and *Stream* were both published in early 1922, showing that the two journals and Yiddish and Ukrainian Soviet modernism were in dialogue with one another.

Not only did *Stream*'s title place it within a particularly Soviet Jewish literary tradition, but the journal ran advertisements for other Soviet literary enterprises, and did not advertise for journals or publishing houses outside the Soviet Union. There were advertisements for the children's journal *Cling Clang (Kling Klang)*, for *Emes*, and for *Culture League*. Although *Stream*'s aesthetics showed that it was part of an international literary community, its structure and the lineage it drew began defining a distinct Soviet Yiddish literary culture separate from international Yiddish modernism.

As for content, *Stream* included work by Hofshteyn, Aaron Kushnirov, Beynush Shteyman, Dvoyre Klyatskin, Shmuel Rosin, Lipe Reznik, Ezra Finenberg, and Chagall, as well as criticism from Dobrushin, Nokhum Oyslender, and Sholem Gordon. Many of them were former members of the Kiev Group. On the back page, *Stream* published its manifesto:

Stream – a literary, artistic monthly journal that appears in Moscow with the participation of the best Yiddish writers, poets, and artists in Moscow, Kiev, Warsaw, Berlin, and New York. *Stream* hopes to unify all responsible, artistic Yiddish forces that are forging the aesthetic values of our period. *Stream* hopes to become the forum for the creative expression of our new and constantly renewed active artistic aspirations. *Stream* hopes to instill consciousness into the already mature creative process of Yiddish artistic culture. With its first difficult steps, *Stream* has received help from all of the comrades presented here – writers and readers from all countries. . . . *Stream* is awaiting new work from Bergelson, Singer, Markish, Mayzl, Der Nister, Kvitko, Ravitch, and [the Moscow-based graphic artist] Ribak. *Stream* believes in working collaboratively with those American comrades, both writers and poets, who are near to us in spirit.[46]

Stream set itself up as an international journal and did not mention the Soviet Union or the Communist Party, but mentioned those "near to us in spirit." What "spirit" meant was not explained. It could mean political agenda, aesthetic ideology, or any combination thereof. Geographically, most of the contributors either lived in Moscow or had left Russia within the past few years. Was *Stream* a Soviet Yiddish journal or was it a Yiddish journal based in the Soviet Union? The financing, the ideologies, and even the advertising showed that *Stream* was trying to be both Soviet and internationally modernist. From a purely organizational point of view, *Stream* was part of the network of cultural institutions that made up official Soviet Jewish culture that referenced each other, and advertised for each other, showing the complexity of Soviet Jewish culture, and the fuzziness of the category.

Dobrushin further defined *Stream*'s literary project in his article "Our Literature," not specifying what or whom such a pronominal adjective included.[47] He suggested that Yiddish literature had only recently become part of the "great family of European world-aesthetic literatures," and at the same time was becoming part of the "fight for raising the world consciousness of the masses." He paid homage to the revolution in two ways – first by proclaiming the October Revolution as the liberator of Jews from an exile mentality, and second, by arguing that a "worker's mentality" underlay every creative act. In his words, "Creative mentality is now on the path toward embodying socialism. Socialism is science; it is the conscious organization of the powers of nature, the materialization, as it is said, of life's energies. . . . The writer is a builder, and like any builder, must know the whole picture and be looking outwards toward material reality."[48] No such proclamation of the greatness of October, socialism, and the worker appeared in the Kiev Group's publications – neither in *Our Own*, nor in *Dawn*. Dobrushin ended by showing that the new trends in literature to which he referred can be found most notably with Bergelson, in his *After All is Said and Done (Nokh Alemen)* and in Der Nister's *In the Wilderness (In Midber)*, showing that symbolists and impressionists were still considered part of the Soviet Yiddish literary family. Dobrushin's transformation from *Our Own* and *Beginning* to *Stream* shows that the definition of Soviet Yiddish literature was constantly changing. A few years later, Der Nister would be branded as a bourgeois individualist for the Symbolism and decadence in works such as *In midber*.

The journal was reviewed quite positively by Aaron Gurshteyn, a rising Soviet Yiddish literary critic, who wrote for the Russian-language publication of the Commissariat of National Minorities, *The Life of National Minorities (Zhizn' natsional'nostei)*.[49] Gurshteyn sang the praises of the former Kievan poets – Hofshteyn, Der Nister, Markish, Reznik, and Finenberg – and lauded the journal's literary criticism. In his review of the third *Stream* collection, Gurshteyn added that "*Stream* is fighting for a faithful, precise Jewish art, and this basic premise underlies all the critical work in *Stream*."[50]

Gurshteyn's final comment about Jewish art reminded readers that *Stream* was not only negotiating the geographic and ideological boundaries of the Soviet Union and international modernism, but was trying to chart a path for a future Jewish culture at those intersections. Much of the poetry wrestled with the question of Jewish culture in the age of revolution. Perets Markish's poem "Hunger," which appeared in *Stream* no. 2, presents images of Civil War, pogroms, and famine using traditional Jewish and Christian imagery. "Hunger" is part of a longer epic poem called "The Land of Pain" (*Veyland*), and the fact that *Stream* republished parts of the poem told its readers that the particularly Jewish issues raised by pogroms and anti-Jewish violence were still part of modern Jewish culture.

Unlike much of the optimistic poetry appearing in the Soviet Union immediately after the revolution, Markish portrayed contemporary Eastern Europe as a civilization in decline, a place of destruction and despair where "sadness grows on trees." The poetic voice, using powerfully dark images, accentuated the moral chaos and violent mayhem that dominated contemporary Europe, the "land of pain." Markish specifically directed his anger at Christian Europe and its treatment of Jews. In one stanza the speaker presents Christian women simultaneously as madonnas and as cannibals, "And let each of you give birth to Yoyzl [Jesus] / To devour on holidays." The image of the devouring mother echoed the Biblical passage in Lamentations that shows mothers eating their young. Markish and other members of the Soviet Yiddish intelligentsia were still reeling from the pogroms that swept through Civil War Russia, and despite the universalism and internationalism of the revolution, still saw the world as one of Jews and non-Jews.[51]

Stream's publication of Markish's poem gave the journal a dark character, because of both its expressionist aesthetic and the themes of destruction and violence. Such dark poetry was seemingly out of character for the optimistic mood of 1920s Soviet Russia, but fit the dominant aesthetics of European modernism still responding to World War I. It is also important to note that Markish excerpted *Veyland* in the Warsaw expressionist journal *Albatros,* showing that *Stream*, while structurally Soviet, was in literary dialogue with international modernism.

In the same edition, the editors included Hofshteyn's "Ukraine," another poem expressing the tense relationship between Jews and the land they inhabited. The poem was addressed to Ukraine itself, the land of bloodied and disappeared shtetls, and of beautiful blue open skies. It was one of Hofshteyn's responses to the destruction of the war. He dedicated each section of the poem to a different poet who influenced his own writing; part I to Ukrainian poet Yakiv Savchenko, a symbolist known for writing grim, mystical poems about the destruction following World War I and the Revolution; part II to David Bergelson, leader of Yiddish modernism in Eastern Europe; part III to Chaim Nachman Bialik, who was probably the most significant poetic influence on Hofshteyn, and who left Russia for Palestine in 1921; and, part IV to Sergei Esenin, known both for his nostalgic poetry about the Russian countryside of his childhood as well as his wild poems about postrevolutionary youth frolicking in the cities. Hofshteyn and *Stream* were thus very much invested in the question of how Jews were to be part of, and still apart from, the Russian cultural and political landscape. With Hofshteyn's dedications to Ukrainian, Yiddish, Hebrew, and Russian writers, the journal – and by extension, the Soviet Yiddish intelligentsia – demonstrated it was part of the developing, multilingual canon of Soviet Jewish modernist literature.

In *Stream* no. 3, Sholem Gordon reviewed Hofshteyn, the only one of the three major Kievan poets still in the country, since Markish and Kvitko had left. Gordon referred to Hofshteyn as "one of our young poets."[52] Ironically, two years later, Hofshteyn would be widely referred to as a "father" of Soviet Yiddish poetry. Soviet critics were caught between competing pressures: in the age of revolution, to be young and new, while at the same time participating in a nation-building project, which required the development of a literary canon and a literary history. *Stream*'s own self-image was caught in the same conundrum, trying to remain at the crossroads of old and new: "We stand on the threshold of this new literature hopeful with optimistic prospects."[53] Because it was on a threshold, *Stream* and the Soviet Yiddish intelligentsia had to look forward and backward simultaneously.

In the course of its two-year publication history, the editorial board began including more "new" poets, who had not belonged to earlier modernist writing circles, poets whose style did not seem to resemble the obvious movements that the "old new" Yiddish literature had incorporated. The fifth and final issue of *Stream* highlighted the tenuous position of the journal. Its circulation had dropped from 3,000 to 1,000, and it took more than a year for the last issue to appear. The list of contributors included names that were not well known among the international Yiddish modernist circles – Itsik Fefer, Izi Kharik, Shmuel Halkin, Daniel Meyerovitch, Zelik Akselrod, and others – all of whom would later become important members of the Soviet Yiddish intelligentsia.[54]

To expand its writer base, the circle added Kharik, Avrom Veviorke, Shmuel Persov, Shmuel Rosin, Avrom Shoykhet; kept some of the "old" faces, including Oyslender, Dobrushin, Reznik, Finenberg, Charny; and rounded out the circle with theater artists such as Alexander Granovsky and Shlomo Mikhoels.[55] Emblematic of the Moscow Circle's shift to a more explicitly Soviet and less internationalist stance, was the official greeting that the group sent to the 1924 *Evsektsiia* conference, a public statement supporting the Party and the state. The idea that the group needed to show official support at the Party's meeting indicates a new meaning to the group's status as a Soviet journal. The Circle had never sent official greetings to Party meetings before 1924. More telling, perhaps, was the statement itself: "Dear Comrades, The Union of Jewish Writers in Moscow greets the *Evsektsiia* meeting. The Yiddish artistic word was created from the fertile glow of the Jewish working masses. The creative spirit of Yiddish literature increased with each victory of the worker's mentality. The October Revolution nourishes Yiddish literature." Yiddish writers were following the trends of Russian modernism, which by 1923, were moving toward an explicit union of Soviet politics and modernist aesthetics. The Soviet futurist group, *LEF*, proudly proclaimed in its manifesto, "Working at strengthening the conquests of the October Revolution by strengthening leftist art, *LEF will agitate for art with the ideas of the commune* and open for art the road to tomorrow."[56] At the same time, the Circle was charting a path for Yiddish literature, which worked on behalf of the Jewish working classes. The Jewish national and Soviet state building projects were still working in tandem.

Charny had temporarily returned from Berlin, and Dobrushin was *Stream's* leading critic, showing some sense of continuity in personnel. The two editors-in-chief were Aaron Kushnirov and Avrom Veviorke. In addition, the management included one prose writer, Shmuel Godiner, and one poet, Izi Kharik, both of whom represented the non-Kiev generation.[57] The tensions within the group became too much to hold it together. *Stream* no. 5–6 was the last volume to appear; Charny relocated to Berlin, and the Moscow Circle broke up shortly thereafter.

IN KIEV, A NEW GENERATION

Although the Moscow Circle attracted many who fled from battle-scarred Kiev after the final Soviet takeover in 1920, Yiddish writers returned to the city. Kiev became home to a new literary grouping and to the largest Soviet Yiddish publishing house of the 1920s – Culture League. Yitzhak Nusinov, who had been involved in integrating the Yiddish cultural apparatus in Kiev with the Communist Party, joined David Hofshteyn and Nokhum Oyslender to launch a new Yiddish publishing house called *Lyric (Lirik)*. The next year this publishing house established a literary imprint for young writers, *Aftergrowth (Vidervuks)*.[58]

The new imprint fostered a literary group by the same name and was made up of members of the "new" generation who were not part of the original Kiev Group. The name of the group suggested its position at the crossroads of Jewish history and contemporary modernisms. The Yiddish *vidervuks* derives from the Hebrew *safiach*, in English, "aftergrowth," a second, spontaneous growth after a harvest; and its use here, like Markish's allusion to Lamentations, drew explicitly on Biblical themes.[59]

In Leviticus 25:5, God instructs the Jews to let the land rest in the seventh year. One way to do this was "not to harvest the aftergrowth." *Aftergrowth* was that which was growing again from the same stalk as that which had come before, but was something new and spontaneous. *Aftergrowth* was part of, but something new in, Jewish literary history. Metaphorically, it had a ring of newness similar to *Stream*, which "gurgled freshly beneath the cliffs." But *Stream*'s name referred back to Shvartsman, a modern Soviet writer; *Aftergrowth* alluded to a Biblical text. At the same time, the idea of aftergrowth resonated with a Russian word used by Communist youth, *smena*, which also means "aftergrowth." Communist youth then were also showing their roots in the past while "spontaneously" paving a new path.

Poets such as Ezra Finenberg, who was part of the Kiev Group, but did not publish in its journals, and Moshe Khachevatsky, who first published in the Kiev *New Times* in 1918, remained in Kiev to publish with *Aftergrowth*. This group of writers worked with *Culture League* and *Lyric* to put out books of poetry by each *Aftergrowth* writer. The most visible figure, Yitzhak (Itsik) Fefer, published his first book of poetry, *Splinters (Shpener)*, in 1922 with *Vidervuks*. David Hofshteyn wrote an introduction to Fefer's book describing how "fresh experiences could be expressed with word names [verter-nemen], but always with a sense of deep feeling."[60] Hofshteyn used such Romantic literary phrases as "free spirit" and "artistic creation" to describe Fefer's work. In addition to receiving Hofshteyn's blessing in the foreword, Fefer incorporated himself into the developing Soviet Yiddish literary canon by dedicating several of his poems to fellow writers: Hofshteyn, Reznik, Shoykhet, Kushnirov, Nusinov, Khachevatsky, and the Ukrainian Futurist, Mykhail Semenko. He also dedicated one to his sister, Chava, and the last poem in the thirty-page book, to himself. By honoring both writers from the Kiev Group and the "new" poets, Fefer brought the two movements and the two generations together.

Fefer's opening poem, "In Our Times" (*Hayntike teg*) takes many of the motifs of violence that filled the pages of *Stream* and presents them using what Fefer calls *naked speech* (*nakete reyd*), a simple, spare language.

In Our Times	Hayntike teg
In our times	Hayntike teg,
The pains of today!	Hayntike veyen!
Where did someone see	Vu hot men gezen
Such a mess of blind screams	A plonter azoynem fun blinde geshreyen
Of naked speech . . .	Mit nakete reyd . . .
Who really has ever seen,	Ver hot gor gezen,
Who really has ever seen	Ver hot gor gezen
On ruins	Af khurves,
On ash—	Af ash—
Such great joy!	Aza groyse freyd!

The sentences are all short and many rhyme; the vocabulary is relatively simple. Such poetry reflected the call to bring poetry out of the symbolist "ivory tower" and back down to the factory floor, where workers could read – and maybe someday even write – it. Simple speech was also an aesthetic form used in several poems in *Albatros*, the Warsaw Yiddish journal that published the minimalist poetry of Esther Shumiacher, and also the collection of Melekh Ravitch's poems titled *Naked Speech*.[61] Fefer charted a new aesthetic stance for Yiddish literature specifically, and Soviet Jewish culture more generally. He referred to images that all Jewish writers had in common – the destruction of pogroms – while presenting those images in simple speech that fit the aesthetic demands of modernist minimalism and the proletarian command to write poetry accessible to the common worker. And like other Soviet Yiddish writers, he showed the joy that could come out of such destruction.

By July 1922, *Vidervuks* published four first-time authors: Fefer's *Splinters*; Khachevatsky's *Thirst (Dorsht)*; Shoykhet's *Assault (Ongrif)*; and Avrom Velednitsky's *Suffering (Layternish)*, each title reflecting the negativity of postpogrom Soviet Jewish culture.[62] *Aftergrowth* made plans for an entire series that included established members of the Kiev Group such as Hofshteyn and Reznik.

The sense of newness and oppositionality were reflected in the first review of *Aftergrowth*, which appeared in the Kiev *Communist Banner* in July 1922. Nusinov, literary critic and future leader of the Jewish literature department at the Second Moscow State University, praised *Vidervuks* for bringing choice into Soviet Yiddish poetry. "Hofshteyn, Markish, and Kvitko used to be the only 'game in town.' With *Vidervuks*, that has all changed." What Nusinov liked about Fefer and Shoykhet in particular was their ability "to synthesize the individual with the collective" to create a new kind of Yiddish poetry.[63] By

1923, *Vidervuks* had published Itsik Kipnis's and Shmuel Halkin's first books, and the group produced a journal of its own, *Uphill (Barg Aroyf)*, once in 1922 and again in 1923.[64]

The first negative criticism of *Aftergrowth* came from the competition, *Stream*, and one of its literary critics, Nokhum Oyslender.[65] Oyslender did not give high praise to the aesthetics of these new poets: "It is obvious that the poets' lack of initiative ... impelled them to follow the path where they would meet the least amount of opposition ... It is clear that the proper unfolding of *Aftergrowth* can come only when the group frees itself from foreign poetic examples and develops within itself ... a healthiness by being true-to-oneself." Oyslender defined *Aftergrowth* as a group with a particular aesthetics, not a particular politics. But what did Oyslender mean when he said that *Aftergrowth* was not being "true to itself"? Not Jewish enough? Not modernist enough? Perhaps both.

Despite *Aftergrowth*'s literary success, 1923 was the worst year materially for Yiddish publishing. If publishing resources were being maximized, so too were literary resources. As part of the process of consolidation and centralization within the Soviet Yiddish intelligentsia in 1923, *Aftergrowth* and *Stream* merged, and by 1924, *Stream* had published all of the *Aftergrowth* writers.

THE ARRIVAL OF THE PROLETARIANS

As *Aftergrowth* and *Stream* charted a modernist future for Jewish culture, a third trend appeared in Yiddish literature that patterned itself on the Russian-language *Proletkult* movement. *Proletkult* wanted to fuse "life with art," a call heralded by *Waves,* by having workers come together in collectives to become the creators of their own art. The Yiddish writer most associated with infusing this ideology into Soviet Yiddish literature was Chaim Gildin, whom the *Lexicon of Contemporary Yiddish Literature* calls the "leader of the holy war for Communism." Gildin, a former factory worker, joined the Communist Party in 1919. Party membership was significant for a writer because of the privileges and opportunities for advancement it afforded. However, joining the Party also exposed a writer to more rigorous criticism and the lingering fear of a Party purge, when members deemed not ideologically rigorous enough were expelled from the Party. (The Great Purges of 1936–9 were the most violent form of a general political cleansing process that began institutionally in the early 1920s.) In 1919, Gildin began contributing poetry to *Communist Banner*, and allied himself with *Proletkult*, which had a relatively large standing within Russian-language culture, but few adherents among Yiddish or Ukrainian writers.[66] Nonetheless, critics at the time recognized that Yiddish literature had its own tradition of proletarian literature in the form of the American Sweatshop Poets, who fused socialism, working class organizing, and literature at the turn of the century.[67]

At *Communist Banner*, although he was completely untrained for the task of editing, Gildin served as the only Communist on the editorial board, which made him a political asset to the newspaper. In July 1919, this former factory worker became managing editor of the newspaper, causing great upheaval and anger among the more experienced editors and writers.[68]

Although he was initially marginalized from the Soviet Yiddish intelligentsia, which was immersed in modernist debates, Gildin was not marginal within the antimodernist proletarian movement. His first book of poems came out in 1921 in Gomel, and his book *Hamer Klangen*, reviewed quite negatively by Aaron Gurshteyn in *The Life of National Minorities*, was the first by a non-Russian writer to be published by *Proletkult* in Moscow.[69]

Many of Gildin's early poems had the bombastic flare of some of the *Waves* poems. "Step" (*Shpant*), which appeared in the first edited volume of proletarian Yiddish poetry titled simply *Poems*, revels in the destruction of revolution and uses overwrought imagery to describe it. Flaming hearts, beating drums, the sound of storms – all of these images herald the end of one world and the coming of a new one. This is not the gentle dawn of sunshine from the *Our Own* poets. "Proud witnesses of a world's decline/and rise."[70] The poem lacked the intertextual Jewish references that demonstrated how invested the rest of the Soviet Yiddish intelligentsia was in the creation of a new Jewish culture in a Soviet context. Gildin seemed to be all about revolution, although his repetition of the image of worlds going under and rising echoed other modernists' uses of the same image. Gildin's visions of upheaval continue in the next poem in the collection, "On the Path to Myself"(*Afn veg tsu zikh*).[71] The title suggests a more modernist, self-reflective stance, and the opening line talks about relationships with the past:

Spit, spit, on your old holy ark	*Tseshpayen, tseshpayen, dayn altn orn*
And idols after idols smashed on your	*koydesh*
steps.	*Un gets, nokh gets, ba dayne trep*
	tseshtoyb.

Gildin shows literal rather than just figurative iconoclasm as the reader sees desecrated Jewish holy spaces and smashed god figures. This dark poem shows Gildin to be in touch with his Jewish past in his attempt to destroy it and its relics.

By 1924, proletarian literature had become less marginalized from the rest of Soviet Yiddish literature. Gildin sat on a commission with Litvakov – now editor of *Emes* – Shoykhet, and Oscar Strelits to begin forming a Yiddish proletarian literary organization.[72] The very makeup of this founding commission realigned the literary positions: Gildin the proletarian, Litvakov the Kiev Group critic, and Shoykhet from *Aftergrowth* came together to redefine Soviet Yiddish culture on proletarianism, but one that moved beyond the narrow definition of *Proletkult*. Even though Gildin was what one might call establishment proletarian literature, his vision of Yiddish literature was not "proletarian enough" for some. In a letter to *Emes*, a young proletarian writer complained that after coming to Moscow, he joined a Yiddish proletarian writers' group, which he called the "Gildin-Taytsh" group, named after Gildin and his fellow proletarian literary organizer, Moshe Taytsh. The young writer lauded the group for being ideologically distant from the "Kiev individualistic petty bourgeois word," but argued nonetheless, that the group was not connected to proletarian art.[73] Others in the Party reproached Gildin for not being supportive enough of Party politics. In a letter to the *Communist (Komunist)* club, the central gathering spot of Moscow's official Jewish culture, Strelits complained that Gildin gave a speech during a meeting of proletarian writers that was "against the *Evsektsiia*, against the leaders of the Party, and held political stances that under no circumstances should have been heard at a Communist club."[74] From all sides, Yiddish literature finally seemed to be splintering.

Despite these centrifugal forces, Soviet Yiddish literature began to settle into two groups, defined in opposition of one another. If the Moscow Circle was the legacy of Kiev, as they proudly claimed and as proletarians scornfully denounced, then Gildin, Litvakov, and others were the proletarian opposition. Organizing a group meant coming together both physically and textually. In 1923, proletarian writers began holding meetings at the *Communist* club.[75] At the same time, *Emes* announced a new literary journal devoted to proletarian literature called *Screen (Ekran)*, a title meant to suggest connections between the textual and the visual in the new genre of film. Avrom Veviorke, Aaron Kushnirov, and Shoykhet were to be the editors, and the main goals of the journal were to organize writers "who considered the revolution the basis of their work," who wanted ties between readers and writers, and who wanted to foster an "active, literary environment."[76] In January 1924, just months before the last edition of *Stream* was published, the *Ekran* group issued a manifesto outlining its literary goals, and the necessity for continued financial support from the Party. Its manifesto included complaints that the Party was supporting the "bourgeois" *Stream* at the expense of the proletarian and Party affiliated *Ekran*.[77] After receiving permission to publish, they began soliciting work from writers and artists both in the Soviet Union and abroad.[78] Despite their efforts, however, *Ekran* never made it to press.

There was another proposal for a journal called *New World (Nayvelt)* to be published by the newly formed Jewish section of the Moscow Association of Proletarian Writers (MAPP). The most surprising fact about this aborted attempt at creating a proletarian Yiddish journal was that Charny – the "old man" of the Moscow Circle, now living in Berlin and publishing his own journal, *Emigrant* – supported its publication. He wrote to Avrom Merezhin of the Central Bureau of *Evsektsiia* to discuss its publication: "Several unemployed or semi-employed writers have put out a new Party monthly journal, *New World*. The publisher is the same as the one that publishes *Emigrant*. . . . The editor is myself – Charny – and the contributors are all Yiddish writers in the USSR. You will undoubtedly have received an inquiry from *Glavlit* [the censorship bureau] about it. I need to tell you that the journal will, of course, be one dedicated to Soviet construction but in general, will avoid all politics."[79] In a surprising turn of events, Charny was supporting Yiddish proletarian writers out of material concern for his friends. And the lack of political engagement Charny called for also shows that in 1925, there were still no clearly defined groups within the Soviet Yiddish intelligentsia, which was still fostering union and consolidation in an effort to stave off political infighting and to prevent the waste of scarce financial resources. *Stream*'s final edition in mid-1924 was a union of proletarian and Moscow Circle literature. (Note that the proposed *Ekran* editors were all also editors of *Stream*'s final edition.)

Nevertheless, the Yiddish proletarian writers, including Litvakov and Gildin, came before the Party organization charged with overseeing publishing, the *Division of Print*, to request funding for a proletarian Yiddish organization once again.

Currently in Moscow there are 15–20 Yiddish poets, prose writers, dramaturges, and critics. Several of them (about 10) have grouped themselves around the journal *Stream*; the others are on their own. As for the social status of the writers, they were for the most part de-classed elements, despite the fact that at least two of them (Shoykhet and Gildin) are members of the Party. Moreover, all of them are on the side of the Soviet government, and many of them delight in our ideology. The work among Jewish writers is not only possible but is necessary. It can play an enormous political role among the Moscow, Ukrainian (especially Kiev), and Belorussian (especially Minsk) populations, and even abroad in America. From Moscow we must lead those proletarian and partially proletarian Jewish organizations . . . both here and abroad.[80]

The Division of Print took Litvakov's information under advisement and asked him and his team to hold a meeting of the Jewish proletarian writers to prepare an official group platform. The group prepared such a platform, which lamented the proletarians' lack of organization and criticized *Stream* for its lack of concreteness and lack of clear ideology.

We consider our goal to be the ideological and aesthetic leadership of Jewish literature and to awaken the aesthetic powers of the Jewish working masses. . . . To achieve this goal we contacted the Komsomol group of writers grouped around *Young Forest [Yungvald]* in Moscow and . . . groups of proletarian and Communist youth writers from Pinsk [sic.], Vitebsk, Kiev, Odessa, Kharkov, and Ekaterinoslav. And since Yiddish literature exists in all countries, we are making contact with proletarian groups in Poland, primarily in Warsaw, and in America with writers working for the New York Party paper, *Freedom [Frayhayt]*, and in Argentina. To start our literary activity, we request that you grant us the means to put out ten almanacs of 10 printers' sheets [160 pages] each with a circulation of 3,000 for the year 1925.[81]

The petition was signed by the management of the Jewish Section of MAPP: Shoykhet, Kushnirov, Gildin, Veviorke, and Yosef Rabin. Two groups within the Soviet Yiddish intelligentsia seemed to be emerging, but all writers were still in agreement that the new literature, whatever it looked like, would chart a path for Soviet Jewish culture.

THE PARTING OF WAYS

In 1925, with the *Stream* group falling apart and a proletarian movement emerging, journals reflecting this separation appeared. Self-proclaimed proletarian writers published *October*, named after the Russian proletarian journal by the same name. The non-proletarian *Stream* writers put out their alternative called *New Earth (Nayerd)*.

The two collections marked the outbreak of what one reviewer declared, in a moment of hyperbole, a "Civil War in Yiddish Literature." Ber Orshansky reviewed the two collections for the first edition of *Star (Shtern)*, a new Yiddish journal out of Minsk. His review sided with *October (Oktyabr)*, the official publication of the Jewish Section of MAPP, citing the group's declaration that "the history of literature is the history of class conflict." *New Earth*, Orshansky complained, did not have any kind of declaration at all. Orshansky equated this silence with *Stream*'s philosophy, which he described as an "intellectually moaning standpoint, the same old suave aestheticism and heavenly art," an implication that *New Earth* was still tied to the aesthetics and politics of Symbolism and Impressionism.[82] He accused *New Earth*'s literary critic, Nokhum Oyslender, of proclaiming art for art's sake, and Dobrushin of using "fancy terms like 'the content of words,' and 'the social lyric,' and we have no idea what he is talking about." Orshansky preferred the declarations by Veviorke in *October*, which were simpler and did not use abstractions.[83]

October's contributors were the same people who had appeared in the proletarian petitions as well as younger poets including Sh. Helmond, Y. Rabin, and Moshe Tayf. *New Earth*'s contributor list, however, was much more inclusive than its critics suggested, incorporating works by Fefer and Kharik, neither of whom were part of the original Moscow Circle. Although critics saw the "very obvious" differences between the two collections, the list of contributors does not reveal which collection was more Party affiliated and which was more proletarian. Shlomo Niepomniashchy asked a similar question in a letter to Charny in 1924, "So, who is a proletarian? Khachevatsky, no, at least as [Yashe] Bronshteyn has decreed; Dobrushin, of course not; Meyerovitch, in God's name no. That leaves "Yitzhak Yarnan" – Itsik Fefer. Itsik Fefer has a special talent that none of the contributors to *October* have – namely, a Party card."[84] By mentioning Fefer's Party membership and the fact that other so-called proletarians in *October* were not members, Niepomniashchy complicated the definitions of literary groups, at a time when some thought the boundaries were becoming clearer. Orshansky recognized this problem in his brief review of Izi Kharik's narrative poem, *Minsk Swamps (Minsker Blotes)*, which appeared in *Nayerd*. He said that Kharik published in the wrong collection: "It would have been an organic part of *October*, and in *New Earth* it is jewelry on an old bride."[85] He closed by saying "*October* is ours, and *New Earth* is with us," using a differentiation established within Russian-language circles of the proletarians and the "fellow travelers" – a term that, in 1925, was becoming common parlance.

Literary critics created the sharp delineation between *New Earth* and *October* as group definition and differentiation became more important in the second half of the 1920s. On the celebration of its five-year anniversary, the founders of the Jewish Section of MAPP wrote a history of their organization. In the history, the authors claimed that the founding of the Jewish Section of MAPP in 1925 inaugurated the second stage of Soviet Yiddish literature. Previously, "writers wrote for art's sake; content was not important. Most important were the qualifications and the form! That used to be their Torah, and the carrier of that Torah was the journal, *Stream*."[86] *Stream*'s breakup and the publication of *October* and *New Earth* were the first steps in the differentiation process, which happened very quickly.

BEYOND MOSCOW: WRITERS' GROUPS AND THEIR JOURNALS IN UKRAINE AND BELORUSSIA

After the breakup of *Aftergrowth* in 1923, it seemed that all roads led to Moscow. Izi Kharik and Zelik Akselrod, two young poets from Belorussia, were sent by the Belorussian Commissariat of Enlightenment to Moscow to train at the Briusov Institute for Art and Literature and to work with the literary greats of the Moscow Circle. The goal was that people like Kharik and Akselrod would return to Belorussia with their newfound talents and reputations to develop literature in their home republic. There was a clear sense that Moscow was the political and artistic center of the country, but that each Soviet republic needed to foster its own literary centers.

As early as 1923, members of *Evsektsiia*, notably Litvakov, had begun talk-ing about a state-sponsored Yiddish "thick journal" in Ukraine that would include literature, the arts, politics, society, and science. The concept of the "thick journal" was a well-known Russian cultural form connected to the in-telligentsia, something that Soviet Jewish activists wanted to bring into Soviet Yiddish culture.[87] Litvakov wanted *Evsektsiia* to sponsor such a journal to spur the development of Soviet Jewish culture and to give status to the Soviet Jewish intelligentsia.[88]

The founders named the journal *Red World (Royte Velt)*, an oblique reference to the fellow traveler journal, *Red Virgin Soil*, and located the journal in Kharkov, the developing center of Jewish culture in Ukraine.[89] *Red World* first appeared in September 1924 in a tiny run of 200, and was printed first by the non-Jewish publishing house the Red Path *(Chervonyi Shliakh)*, and later by the State Publishing House. The journal's editor, Henekh Kazakevitch, was a journalist and newspaper editor, and published *Red World* "with the close assistance of M. Litvakov and Esther [Frumkina]," both members of the Central Bureau of *Evsektsiia*.[90] From its inception, the new journal was tied to the Communist Party, making it all the more interesting that it explicitly shunned political affiliations. The first edition contained poetry by Fefer, prose from Shmuel Persov, a book review from Aaron Gurshteyn, and a translation of an article by Trotsky.

Its second edition appeared one month later, the first Soviet Yiddish liter-ary collection to come out as a monthly periodical, undoubtedly due to its Party support. The second *Red World* had a wider selection including work by Khachevatsky and Chana Levin. To emphasize the breadth of literary tal-ent, the editors published a notice of all the participants in *Red World*, among whom were most of the *Aftergrowth* writers such as Fefer and Velednitsky; the Belorussian poets, Kharik and Akselrod; some former Kiev Group writ-ers and critics such as Dobrushin, Reznik, and Nusinov; a few proletarian writers, Shoykhet, Sh. Godiner, and Veviorke; and Central Bureau members, Chemerinsky and Merezhin. Missing from the initial contributor list were the established Yiddish modernists who had left the Soviet Union: Hofshteyn, Bergelson, and Markish, among others. Over time, however, the journal would grow to incorporate their work; and by 1929, it published one of Der Nister's most famous mystical stories, *Under a Fence (Unter a ployt)*. *Red Earth* very quickly became the thick journal of Soviet Yiddish culture, a forum that was not defined by age, political affiliation, or aesthetic ideology.

In its early days, the journal struggled to overcome material obstacles, many of which were connected to *Red World*'s location. The journal had no managing editor, which meant that the day-to-day tasks of running the operation fell to the editor-in-chief, Kazakevitch. He complained that the journal's articles were written on a relatively high level and were only accessible to a very educated reader.[91] Kazakevitch had edited newspapers, never thick journals, so he had a different vision of Soviet Jewish print culture. However, the question of accessibility was not his alone. Many activists believed that the purpose of literature was to reach the "Jewish masses." That was, after all, the theory behind writing in the Jews' vernacular.

The Central Bureau dealt with the problem of management by naming Mikhail Levitan and Efraim Portnoy coeditors of the journal, and officially resolved that the journal should "orient itself to the mass, middle-educated reader." In addition, to make sure that *Red World* was not just a literary magazine, but a real thick journal, the bureau asked the editorial board to reserve one-third of the journal for belles-lettres, one-third for political literature, and one-third for popular science. Party sponsorship may have helped solve material problems, but it also meant that editorial decisions were taking place among both the editors and the Party supervisors.

Over time, the journal's editorial board grew, and it developed a reputation as the least politically aligned Soviet Yiddish journal. It also helped attract writers to Kharkov, including Chana Levin, Leyb Kvitko, and eventually Der Nister and Moshe Khachevatsky.[92] As late as 1930, it defined itself as "the organ for all Soviet Jewish literature." *Evsektsiia* was proud that the journal included material on Party issues, national and Jewish issues, economics, and the politics of literature, and in 1928, began a marketing campaign to increase its circulation.[93] The dialectical synthesis of national and socialist seemed to be working.

Just as *Red World* got off the ground, a group of writers in Minsk joined forces to put out their own thick journal. The journal *Star (Shtern)* first appeared in May 1925, and was edited by Shmuel Agursky, Ber Orshansky, and Elyohu Osherovich, only one of whom was a fiction writer. From its inception, *Star* had the reputation of being more Party affiliated and more proletarian than *Red World*. The first major review of *Star*, written by the proletarian writer Moshe Tayf, appeared in the Minsk newspaper *October*. As a self-defined proletarian writer, he suggested that the main goal of *Star* should be introducing the Jewish worker to quality literature. "The worker has many opportunities for political development, but very few for literary development."[94]

Y. Nusinov reviewed *Star* in *Red World* and was much harsher than Tayf. He criticized all of the literary contributions to the journal, calling Godiner's prose a "rough draft," and Yashe Bronshteyn's article on Marxist literary criticism "irresponsible."[95] With a lackluster beginning, *Star* had a hard time finding support, and in 1926, it was in serious financial trouble and nearly closed down.[96] *Red World* reviewed the journal again in September, and once again harshly criticized it. The reviewer found most of the political articles too difficult for the "mass reader," the economics section underdeveloped, and material on trade unions completely lacking. The venom of the reviewer, however, came out in his review of *Star*'s fiction. "As for the literature section, it seems that the greatest lack is the fact that the journal does not publish work from writers outside Belorussia. And I hate to say it, but Belorussia cannot take the place of Ukraine or Moscow. If one wants to have a serious literary section, there cannot be local patriotism, but must also publish material from 'abroad.'"[97] The only positive comment was toward Kharik's translation of Mikhas Charot, a young Belorussian poet.

The polemics between the two journals heated up. Orshansky responded to *Red World* in his 1926 review of the journal. He opened with a gesture toward camaraderie by calling on all people to support both journals, but then, went on the offensive. "We have never written about it [*Red World*] because until recently, the only good thing to say about it was that it existed at all." He expressed dismay at "politically problematic" material that appeared in the journal, and questioned whether the Communists on the editorial board were really doing their jobs.[98] Finally, Orshansky objected to the harsh review *Star* was given in *Red World*, and questioned the accusation that *Star* was only publishing Belorussian writers: "[Nusinov] accuses us of local patriotism. What chutzpah! Why is Ukraine more kosher than Minsk?"[99] If the battle lines in Moscow were between *October* and *New Earth* over the future (and not the legacy) of Yiddish literature, then the battle in the rest of the country was between the two thick journals, representing a different geography as well as a different ideology.

THE RETURN OF THE WRITERS

With two regularly appearing thick journals in Ukraine and Belorussia and literary collections coming out of Moscow, the Soviet Union was finally looking like a good place to be a Yiddish writer. Economic conditions were improving under NEP, and writers found more opportunities to earn a living as writers and producers of print culture. There also seemed to be a tense balance between the Communist Party's control of literature and writers' literary freedom. Through the 1920s, the Party was never sure precisely what its role was in shaping literary policy. Some groups had pushed the Communist Party to define Soviet literature as proletarian literature and give the proletarians a monopoly of state support. As a rebuttal, Trotsky came out against using political power in this way: "The Party does not lead in the domain of art."[100] His opposition to the proletarians' call for monopoly was based not only on his insecurity about using Party power in literature, but also on his dismissal of the concept of proletarian art. He argued that as the proletarian dictatorship faded away – as Marxism–Leninism said would happen – proletarian art would disappear too.

The Politburo ruled only once on the issue of literary policy in the first half of the 1920s. In July 1925, it passed a resolution "On the policy of the Party in the field of belles-lettres," against the position of the proletarian writers groups. On the one hand, the resolution supported an openness in literature by showing that fellow travelers were needed during the transition period to socialism. There was to be "free competition between various groups and trends" in the search for a "style appropriate to the epoch."[101] On the other hand, the resolution supported the idea that literature could not be politically neutral, and that proletarian writers were to be given material and moral support.[102] This second statement about political engagement reminded writers that literature needed to support the state and Party's politics and to be "in service of the Revolution," echoing the early debates in the Yiddish journals about the role of art in building a new (Jewish) culture and society. How writers did that was still up for debate.

Many of the Yiddish writers who had left the Soviet Union earlier in the 1920s as a result of the bleak economic and social situation considered returning. Most of them had been part of the Kiev Group or at least connected with the social and cultural scene of Civil War Ukraine, and several had continued participating in Soviet journals. The question of "return" raised the question of the definition of Soviet Yiddish literature that the Soviet Yiddish intelligentsia struggled with. And the stakes were high – defining Soviet Yiddish literature was in many ways also defining Soviet Jewish culture. *Stream* considered itself an international journal because it encouraged submissions from writers outside the Soviet borders who were sympathetic to *Stream*'s project. In fact, however, *Stream* almost exclusively published writers living in the Soviet Union, and the few exceptions were former Kiev Group writers: Bergelson, Markish, and Kvitko. *Star* was charged with petty patriotism for only publishing writers from Belorussia. Only in 1926 did it start publishing "foreigners" from outside the Belorussian border. *Red World* was more liberal in whom it published. The editors printed work from H. Leyvik, Z. Reyzen, and others "sympathetic to the Revolution," but interestingly, all of the non-Soviet writers published in *Red World* made pilgrimage trips to the Soviet Union. They also worked with the Communist Yiddish newspaper, *Freedom*, in New York.[103] Although Soviet Yiddish writers wanted to see themselves as part of an international Yiddish cultural community, they themselves defined their literature based on geography and politics, and created a separate path for Soviet Jewish culture well before the Soviet Yiddish intelligentsia parted ways with the international Yiddish intelligentsia in 1929–30.

Several well-known linguists and literary scholars, such as Nokhum Shtif and Max Erik, returned to the Soviet Union in the second half of the 1920s; and there was a similar trend among writers. Hofshteyn had been an active member of the Moscow Circle and on the editorial board of *Culture League* and *Stream*, but left the country in 1924 after being lambasted for using his position of power in the Soviet Yiddish intelligentsia to support Hebrew culture. He spent time in Berlin and then in Palestine where he wrote for several established Hebrew literary journals. In 1926, however, he requested repatriation to the Soviet Union in an open letter to *Emes*. "One year ago there was a rupture between myself and Yiddish writers and cultural workers in the Soviet Union because of mistakes I committed. The whole matter is, as they say, part of history. And I believe that these words of mine will eliminate any lingering arguments, so that I may take my place among those of you building a new life for the Jewish toiling masses of the Soviet Union."[104] Hofshteyn returned that same year. One year later, A. Tsvayg reviewed Hofshteyn's newest collection of poetry, *On Bright Ruins (Af likhtike ruinen)*, calling the collection Hofshteyn's ideological and aesthetic credo, and Hofshteyn "our greatest lyricist."

By 1927, Hofshteyn had regained his place in the Soviet Yiddish intelligentsia. Although his first year back in the Soviet Union involved negotiating new literary politics, he quickly understood that the proletarian writers groups were the rising source of literary power. In 1928, he became a member of the Jewish Section of the All-Ukrainian Proletarian Writers Organization (*VUSP*) and was a founding editor of the proletarian Yiddish journal, *Prolit*. He wrote to Charny in August: "I am now the jack of all trades at *Prolit*. . . . I am the secretary and publisher of the journal. . . . I have an assistant, an office, a telephone and more."[105]

Perets Markish left in the early 1920s for Warsaw, where he, Uri Tsvi Grinberg, Melekh Ravitch, and Esther Shumiacher founded the literary circle *The Gang*. At the same time, Markish published in the Soviet Union continuously during his five years out of the country, and was never really beyond the bounds of the Soviet literary community. Nonetheless, he had trouble adjusting to the political climate of literature in the Soviet Union. At one point in the late 1920s, he thought about leaving the Soviet Union again, but was warned by Litvakov that the physical boundary of the Soviet border had more meaning than it had earlier, and that leaving would put up a wall between Markish and Soviet Jewish culture. He chose to stay and became well established in the Soviet Yiddish intelligentsia.[106]

In February 1927 in Moscow, there was a party welcoming Markish back to the Soviet Union. In his speech, he emphasized the physical border that had come to define Soviet Jewish literature: "I am not a guest, because I never went anywhere. I never broke with Moscow, and I never joined any other place. I just went to a second chamber for a little while." Litvakov shouted sarcastically from the audience, "Where you could roam free?"[107] Markish claimed that his status as a Soviet writer – unlike that of Hofshteyn's – was unbroken.

Niepomniashchy confirms Markish's claim to unbroken Sovietness in a second letter to Charny: "Reb Markish is no reborn Soviet writer (*khozer be-tshuvah*) and so we do not lash out at him. He is one of our own." That said, he made sure to put Markish in his place as well. "You say, Comrade Markish, that you carried out revolutionary activities...in Yiddish? Well, a "heap" (*kupe*) is good, but it is also reminiscent of Bialik...." Niepomniashchy affirmed Markish for his modernist credentials, but also reminded him that Markish too had his time on the "other side of the border." Markish wrote poems, most notably his pogrom poem "The Ash Heap" (Di Kupe), in dialogue with Chaim Nachman Bialik, the writer most associated in Jewish literature with decadence and Symbolism, as well as with Zionism and Jewish nationalism.[108]

Bergelson's situation was slightly different. He left the Soviet Union with the other Kiev Group writers in 1921 and settled in Berlin, where he continued the Kievan literary traditions in the journal *Pomegranate*.[109] Over time, his writing became more overtly allied with Soviet politics, to the point that one of his most famous articles, "Three Centers" (*Dray tsentern*), published in 1926, proclaimed the Soviet Union as the future homeland of Jewish culture.[110] In 1926, as part of his reconciliation with the Soviet Union, he wrote an open letter to *Evsektsiia*, most clearly addressed to Litvakov.

I followed my conscience and came out against you. And now, as I once again follow my conscience, I am letting you know that I am sorry for my earlier expressions. . . . I am writing this letter to you in one of those moments, when I fear that my return to Soviet Russia is, by current relations, not really going to happen. . . . I do this because I am with you, with all of my heart, with this great Jewish undertaking that you are leading, and that will only become greater under the broad socialist skies, following the paths of the world-wide socialist revolution that I believe in. . . . I find that I so celebrated going into exile at that time, because I did not understand the difficult situation of the *Evsektsiia*. With respect and with comradely greetings, David Bergelson.[111]

The editors of the Kharkov newspaper, *Star (Shtern)*, in which the full text of the letter was printed, were not impressed with Bergelson's apology. They questioned his original motives for criticizing *Evsektsiia* and emphasized that Bergelson had never previously expressed problems with his exilic state.[112] In March, just a week after Bergelson's letter was published, Niepomniashchy commented on the stir that the letter had caused. This public recanting was the culmination of a longer correspondence between Bergelson and Litvakov about

Bergelson's reconciliation with the Soviet Union.[113] Niepomniashchy also said that there were two questions on everyone's mind: Was Bergelson coming to the Soviet Union to make his "pilgrimage," and more importantly, was he going to stop working for the *Forward (Forverts)*, the New York socialist newspaper that Communists considered the basest form of Yiddish populist journalism?

In April 1926, Bergelson stopped publishing in New York.[114] Soon after – with his apology letter, the "Three Centers" article, and his parting with the *Forward* – Bergelson achieved readmittance into Soviet Jewish letters. To mark the moment, he made a pilgrimage to the Soviet Union, spending time in Kiev, Kharkov, and Moscow. Soviet journals printed his work, and publishing houses produced his books, even though he did not join the Communist Party, and did not return permanently to the Soviet Union until 1934. For eight years, Bergelson defied the definitions of Soviet Jewish culture by living abroad as a Soviet writer while being a member of the Soviet Yiddish intelligentsia. In 1934, the year of his permanent repatriation, Bergelson was by far the highest paid Soviet Yiddish writer, quite an accomplishment for someone not in the Soviet Union.[115]

THE RISE OF POLITICAL AND LITERARY AFFILIATION

The 1925 publication of *New Earth* and *October* paved the way for the division of the Soviet Yiddish intelligentsia into two camps – those associated with proletarian writers groups, and those who were not. Organizations of Yiddish proletarian writers began appearing in major Jewish centers throughout the Soviet Union. In Ukraine, a Jewish section of the All-Ukrainian Proletarian Writers Organization, *VUSP*, organized in 1926. There was a sense within the Yiddish literary establishment in Moscow that while the spontaneous flourishing of proletarian groups was a positive development for making literature more political, it was also splintering writers' groups and devolving power from the center in Moscow to the peripheries in Ukraine and Belorussia. To regulate this movement, Frumkina, member of the Jewish Section of MAPP and of the Central Bureau, called for the formation of a Jewish Section of the All-Union Proletarian Group (*VAPP*) to coordinate the efforts of local groups throughout the Soviet Union. Writers and political activists in Moscow hoped to shape literary policy through a relatively narrow chain of command. By 1928, such a network was in place.[116]

The Ukrainian branch was initially led by two figures: Fefer, whose work in *Aftergrowth* and *Stream* had made him one of the most well-known and politically connected writers in the country; and Gildin, the perennial outsider who struggled to be taken seriously by the Soviet Yiddish intelligentsia. In a speech to the 1926 *VUSP* Congress, Gildin outlined a proletarian Yiddish literary history, which he hoped would come to define Yiddish literary history more generally. First, he referred to the three classic Yiddish writers (*di klasikers*) – Mendele, Sholem Aleichem, and Y.L. Perets – as the "mohicans" of Jewish literature, a past generation, but one that Gildin claimed was important to the development of Yiddish literature. He included a fourth mohican in the first generation – Bialik, "a man with great poetic talent, a man who created original images, but he portrayed the whole world through pogroms."[117] By the mid-1920s, Bialik's reputation among Soviet Jewish writers and critics had become tarnished, not as much for his Hebraist politics – although that of course was a black mark in his biography – as for having established the "pogrom poem" as a literary form on which Soviet writers based their work. It was too depressing a model for charting an optimistic Soviet Jewish future. After incorporating Bialik into the Yiddish literary canon, Gildin named the Kiev Group as the second generation – "Bergelson who showed how capitalism died away; Markish and Kvitko, who while talented poets are 'not connected to life.'" Markish's "The Heap" showed that "the whole revolution is a new crucifixion, new sufferings. The fight for socialism is all about the suffering of Jews."[118] Gildin relegated the Kiev Group to history.

Gildin then criticized *Red World* and called on proletarian writers to boycott the journal, because "it has not given us [proletarian writers] a single line. It has given space not to Soviet writers, but to foreign ones."[119] Finally, Gildin got to the real point: "I am one of the few true proletarian writers. I wrote a poem 'To Leningrad.' I won't talk about its artistic value. It was published in America and reprinted in Argentina, but in Russia I wasn't able to publish it for two years."[120] The quintessential proletarian Yiddish writer lamented the fact that in 1926, literary power still rested with others within the intelligentsia and not with him.

Another proletarian writers group known as *Young Worker (Yunger Arbeter)* formed in Minsk; and, unlike the Ukrainian Yiddish proletarians who had a hard time publishing in *Red World*, *Young Worker* writers published extensively in the Minsk *Star*. The Minsk group gained prominence once Kharik and Akselrod returned from Moscow. They had become well known throughout the Soviet Union and had studied, trained, and gained political and literary power through their associations with Litvakov, Dobrushin, and others in Moscow. [121] In 1928, Kharik, who had resisted overt affiliation and whose worked was liked by both sides, finally joined the Belorussian Association of Proletarian Writers (*BelAPP*), and soon after became editor-in-chief of the *Star*.[122]

To gain political standing, nonproletarian Yiddish writers organized themselves. Dobrushin once complained to New York–based writer H. Leyvik, that "in Moscow, we have MAPP. And we, that is Kharik, Meyerovich, Halkin, Khachevatsky, Akselrod, and others, who stand outside groupings are therefore ourselves a group. And all of these groups keep fighting each other. It is quite silly."[123] What may have been silly in 1925, when Dobrushin wrote this letter, was a more serious matter by 1927, something Kharik understood in his choice to join *BelAPP* in 1928. In 1927, David Volkenshteyn, David Feldman, Ezra Finenberg, Nokhum Oyslender, Noyekh Lurie, Lipe Reznik, and Leyb Kvitko, who had moved back to the Soviet Union in 1925, established an organization in Ukraine for those writers choosing not to join a proletarian organization – a Yiddish fellow traveler group. The organization took the name *Construction* (*Boy*, also translated as *Build!*) and was reminiscent of the Russian word for construction, *stroika*, which had come to signify the building of Soviet society on the land and in heavy industry. It also echoed with the Russian word "*boi*," meaning battle, another common trope both of literary modernism and of Soviet state building.

Construction's manifesto proclaimed that the duty of literature was "to artistically embody and portray in words and forms the great class battles of the proletariat."[124] *Construction* believed that "the writer must first and foremost work on himself, on his own political, social, and aesthetic culture, on his special skills and his craft." The manifesto differentiated *Construction* from the proletarians by emphasizing the quality of writing, rather than its political orientation, and the improved status of the writer. "The question of the financial situation of the writer must now be placed at the center of our attention." The most biting clause of the declaration suggested that writers must engage in a "battle against literary parasitism, against the cheapening and simplifying of the processes of the real world, against the talentlessness and intellectual poverty, that is often affixed to left-wing prose." The group was back to criticizing "Boo-hoo, the proletariat" literature, and aimed its barbs at the proletarians.[125] Finally, the declaration also included a paean to Yiddish itself, which "before the revolution, was persecuted and disfranchised, but has now become, like all languages of national minorities, the language of schools and state institutions. It has become the language of the ruling class and of its revolutionary battle." *Construction* clearly reasserted the national path of Soviet Yiddish literature by mentioning the language and its writers, rather than the working class, as the downtrodden. It also proclaimed the importance of the writer in creating Soviet Yiddish culture. Worker hack writers were not up to the task of building a new culture.

Red World published *Construction*'s manifesto as well as the declaration of the Association of Revolutionary Yiddish Writers of Ukraine, an outgrowth of the Jewish section of *VUSP*. The association's petition came out against "petty-bourgeois literature," placed Yiddish literature within worldwide proletarian literature, and took from great artists of the past that which could be used for the class goals of proletarian literature.[126] However, "the association will fight with all of its resources against any attempt to move away from reality, to rely on the slippery slope of literary tradition, to bury oneself within one's own 'I'. We reject the concept of free art. The only path for literature is the realistic representation of life."[127] The developing debate between the proletarians and the fellow travelers fell back on similar debates made in *Our Own* and *Beginning*. Those signing the proletarian declaration included Hofshteyn and his protégé, Fefer, as well as Itsik Kipnis, Velednitsky, and interestingly, three female writers who had never led a Soviet Jewish literary organization, Mire Khenkina, Dvoyre Khorol, and Anyuta Pyatigorskaya. For Hofshteyn and certainly for Khenkina, Khorol, and Pyatigorskaya, coming together as a proletarian organization was a means of accessing literary power.

PROLETARIAN GROUPS COME TO POWER

According to literary scholar, Katerina Clark, "the mid-1920s saw a shift to a more proletarian and tendentious art, but debates on the nature of Soviet culture were still fierce and its direction not yet set.... the principal VAPP organ, *On Guard (Na postu)* . . . had trouble with funding and paper and was able to secure publication for only five issues.... By contrast, the principal fellow-traveler organ, *Red Virgin Soil (Krasnaia nov')*, appeared monthly and enjoyed the largest circulation of any literary journal."[128] The debates about Soviet Yiddish literature displayed a similar pattern of politicization, in which the language of proletarianism infiltrated all literary debates even though proletarian writers and their journals struggled to gain power over the more established fellow travelers.

As early as 1926–7, joining a proletarian organization publicly established a writer's commitment to Soviet literature as much as becoming a Communist Party member did. Communist Party politics supported this shift toward proletarianism. An October 1927 resolution "On Improving the Party's Leadership in Print" was a clear step toward Party regulation of literary questions.[129] In December 1928, the Central Committee ordered publishers to give preference to those authors who were Communist Party members and, of these, to select the ones who were also members of proletarian literary organizations.[130] A new literary hierarchy was evolving as part of the Cultural Revolution.

During the Cultural Revolution, literature was expected to drive the transformation of the individual and the increased pace of constructing Soviet society. Those less willing to participate in this project were marginalized as "right deviationists," bourgeois nationalists, or worse.[131] Those who had been involved in the building of ethnic minorities' cultures were often accused of nationalism. People criticized each other vehemently in public, not just in private, and writers were expected to learn the art of self-censorship in the production of new works, and of self-criticism in relating to their past oeuvres. In

addition to the pragmatic goals of state and society building, the Cultural Revolution was also about definitively upending existing hierarchies – to supplant
the "old" writers' individualism and replace it with "young" writers' interest
in the masses.[132]

These changes in Soviet society affected literature in all languages. In 1927,
as a result of pressure from proletarian organizations, the moderate editor of *Red
Virgin Soil*, Voronsky, was removed. Similar pressures drove *Red World* to replace
Mikhail Levitan with Shakhne Epshteyn in 1929. In Ukrainian literature, Pavlo
Tychyna, the "poet of the Ukrainian Revolution," began publishing Symbolist
poetry in 1918 and continued throughout the first half of the 1920s. In 1925, this
Symbolist and so-called national poet joined the Ukrainian proletarian writers
organization.[133] The formation of Ukrainian literary groups mirrored those of
Yiddish literary groups. The *Free Academy of Proletarian Literature* (*VAPLITE*)
emerged in 1924–5, just when Yiddish proletarian groups were forming as well.
Like Yiddish proletarian organizations, *VAPLITE* welcomed a diverse group
of writers into its ranks – the old guard poets, Tychyna included, along with
young writers who had taken an oppositional stance to the more nationalist
verse of the revolution generation.[134] By 1927, however, the union of writers
under the umbrella of *VAPLITE* began to crumble. Along with other Ukrainian
Symbolists, Tychyna and Ukrainian writers were accused of national deviations,
and in response, the accused nationalists either renounced their earlier work in
the early 1930s or had their work banned.

In Yiddish literature, a new place of importance was given to the proletarian
writers groups and to criticism of non-proletarian literature. A. Abchuk, editor
of the new Yiddish proletarian journal *Prolit*, summarized these criticisms of
non-proletarian literature and non-proletarian writers in his article, "On foreign
paths (*Af fremde vegn*)."[135]

1. Writers cutting themselves off from real life and moving toward individualism and Symbolism (Der Nister, Lipe Reznik)
2. Idealization of the gradually disappearing classes with emotional investment in their fate (Noyekh Lurie)
3. A passive attitude toward our reality (Itsik Kipnis)
4. Epicureanism, glorifying the passing moment (Zelik Akselrod)
5. Lack of self-definition, neutralism, going along at a distance (a general
   problem)[136]

Abchuk's criticism summarized the proletarian critique of modernism in its
various forms: Symbolism in Der Nister, Impressionism in Kipnis for making
the writer a passive receiver of external stimuli, and a Esenin-like Imaginism in
Akselrod that "revelled in the moment." By 1929, the charges of mysticism and
Symbolism leveled against Der Nister came to define a new "-ism," *Nisterism*,

which was used negatively to refer to literature that was not proletarian. These general criticisms showed that a single definition of Soviet Yiddish literature and Soviet Jewish culture was forming, one whose criteria would be determined by literary critics, publishers, and editors in positions of power. Yiddish prose narratives about building factories and settling Birobidzhan would come to replace expressionist poems about mental and physical destruction.

THE INSTITUTIONALIZATION OF SOVIET JEWISH LITERATURE

Until 1928, *Red World* and *Star* were the literary forums in which Soviet Yiddish literature developed. Yiddish proletarian writers decided to form their own, explicitly proletarian journal called *Prolit*, an abbreviation for *proletarian literature*, which first appeared in early 1928. Fefer, Abchuk, Levitan, and Gildin were on the board. None of the women who founded the proletarian organization were on the journal's editorial board.

Star's editor, Orshansky, reviewed *Prolit* as soon as it appeared, proclaiming "We have been waiting for a journal like this."[137] The journal, he claimed, was to portray the worker (not the writer) artistically as the banner carrier of our era, seeming to come down in favor of the *Proletkult* definition of proletarian culture as that created by the worker. But he continued, "The *ideology* of the proletarian – that is what is important." Orshansky incorporated both social background and ideology into his definition of proletarian literature and of Soviet Jewish culture. He also reviewed several pieces of literature that appeared in *Prolit*: Gildin's *Fountains (Brunems)*, about which he says, "The thematics are definitely interesting and it is told in a lively manner. However, art must not just tell, art must first and foremost represent. In our opinion, this kind of representing is rather weak in Gildin's work."[138] He granted the highest praise to Hofshteyn and Fefer's lyric poetry, which "carry a heartfelt warmth."

Although Orshansky's evaluation of *Prolit* may have been positive, others were not as impressed. In a review for *October*, Litvakov complained about the lack of a unified ideological direction in Soviet Jewish literature even within proletarian organizations, an ironic criticism since *Prolit* was formed precisely to unify an ideological direction. "The first issue of *Prolit* had nothing on workers. It looks just like our other journals. This shows that we have weak ideological control."[139]

The Jewish Section of MAPP in Moscow also responded to the changing political climate. The organization established a union-wide group of Communist Jewish proletarian writers that first met in May 1928. Chemerinsky, chairman of *Evsektsiia*, and Litvakov organized the first meeting. Attending the meeting were the two organizers, Fefer, Shoykhet, Oscar Strelits, Yashe Bronshteyn,

Avrom Rivess, Gildin, and Yashe Goldman.[140] The meeting was a means for bringing the concepts "proletarian" and "Party" together within Soviet Yiddish literature, and to do so union-wide. Part of the reason for doing this was that Jewish proletarian writers groups were not very proletarian. There were only twenty-four members of the Jewish Section of MAPP, seven of whom were Party members, five in the *Komsomol*, and twelve were non-Party members. The group claimed that within the Jewish section of MAPP, there were six workers by origin/birth, three workers by profession, three peasants, and fourteen were what might be called white collar [*sluzhashchie*]. In other words, more than 50 percent of Yiddish proletarian writers were neither Party members nor proletarian in social class.[141]

In December 1929, the Jewish Section of MAPP passed a resolution outlining the history of Jewish literary politics in the Soviet Union. After situating MAPP at the center of intensifying battles "against foreign class powers" and on the side of "ideological hegemony for proletarian culture," the resolution praised its accomplishments and heralded the rise in "self-criticism."[142] The resolution then began its criticism of others. "The Jewish section has developed activities and initiative in the battle against ideological vacillation in Jewish literature and criticism, especially against the right dangers (Kvitko, Hofshteyn, and others). . . . As a result of this battle for the Party line in the area of literature, the Jewish Section attracted to the center the best Soviet fellow-travelers of Yiddish literature (Gurshteyn, Khachevatsky, and others)."[143] Even more important than converting fellow travelers was the petition's call to create a new generation of worker writers. With a new group of writers "untainted" by older models of literature and ideology, proletarian literature could become more proletarian. Through a change in social background of Yiddish writers and a new vigilance of Party regulation, these organizations could effect a change in Yiddish literature.[144]

In Kiev, the Jewish Section of *VUSP* was making plans to increase its dominance in Soviet Jewish literature.[145] In 1928, *Prolit* gave *Red World* a critical review claiming that there was too much emphasis on Yiddish literature's past and not enough on the creative work of contemporary Soviet writers.[146] *Red World* responded to the rise of politicized literature by introducing the "Word from the Editor" – a column in which the editors gave instantaneous feedback on the materials they had chosen to publish in a given edition, one manifestation of what Brian Kassof calls "visible censorship." Visible censorship, or the use of "problematic" material for didactic purposes, was a technique used throughout the publishing industry, especially during the Cultural Revolution. Cultural radicals found this tactic valuable because it made the literary enemy readily identifiable, and more importantly, showed the reader concrete examples of good and bad literature.[147] Despite *Red World*'s attempts, however, *Prolit* editors complained that "Word from the Editor" did more harm than good, because *Red World*'s editors ended up praising ideologically problematic literature more than correcting it.[148]

Red World continued to appear throughout the Cultural Revolution and never officially affiliated, but ideologically grew closer to *Prolit*. Fefer joined the board in 1929, and Gildin in 1930; it changed its format, added sections, and critiqued writers. *Red World*'s final issue, which appeared in January 1933, showed how far the journal had traveled. Although the editorial board included Fefer and Levitan, it also included Moshe Kiper, chairman of the Main Bureau of *Evsektsiia* Ukraine – a politician, not a writer. And the new editor-in-chief was none other than Chaim Gildin, who at last held the reins of the Soviet Yiddish intelligentsia, or so he thought. (Bergelson was still the highest paid writer.) If the high point of *Red World*'s openness was 1929, when it published Der Nister's symbolist story *Under a Fence*, then the final edition of the journal was the aesthetic opposite, made up almost entirely of ballads and epic poems in honor of the fiftieth anniversary of the death of Karl Marx, whose face adorned the cover.[149]

As for the *Star*, it had always been more closely allied with the Party and proletarian writers groups than *Red World*. It did not have as far to travel in accommodating the changing politics of literature. In 1930, the journal made an unofficial declaration that it would support proletarian writers. The declaration titled, "We are building a proletarian culture," informed readers that they would start seeing the incorporation of proletarian ideas into coming issues of *Star*. It proclaimed itself an organ of the proletarian movement, something that *Red World* never did.[150]

IN-FIGHTING AMONG PROLETARIANS

As more writers sought to ally themselves with proletarian organizations, there was a sense among die-hard proletarian writers that "proletarianness" was being diluted. In Russian literature, the left opposition formed the *Litfront* in response to the Russian Association of Proletarian Writers (RAPP), which it did not consider proletarian enough.[151] Many Yiddish critics similarly complained about the Jewish Section of *VUSP* in Ukraine. If David Hofshteyn – the Impressionist lyricist who just four years earlier had fled the country in shame for his unabashed support of the "nationalistic and clerical" Hebrew language – could serve on the board, then what made it proletarian? A group of young proletarians wrote, "There are two elements in the Jewish Section [of VAPP]: the older writers (older in years and literary status) and the youth (the genuine core of VAPP). The youth feels out of place and not at home in VAPP. VAPP does not satisfy this group, neither ideologically nor formally."[152] The youth felt disfranchised by the old. This Yiddish version of *Litfront* complained that the older generation was not publishing them, and that the state had not established a journal dedicated to their work. On this count, Jewish Party leaders responded by helping the Jewish Section of *VUSP* form *Prolit* in 1928.

When the Cultural Revolution got underway in 1928–9, Communist Party organizations began purging their ranks of unworthy members. Within the writers' groups, the first to be expelled were ironically these young gadflies, the ones who had joined the Party out of conviction, but who never had power. Moshe Tayf, the proletarian writer who was the most outspoken critic of VAPP, found himself on the defensive during the purge. In 1928, Tayf was a member of the Jewish Communist proletarian group, but at the group's 1929 meeting, an announcement was made that "because his activity has led to demoralization, Moshe Tayf has been excluded [from the organization]."[153] Tayf pleaded his case and admitted that in the early years of proletarian organizing (1925), he was frustrated by the "foreign elements" that had entered proletarian groups and confessed that the petition he circulated against VAPP might have been made in haste. Tayf, however, then went on the attack, lambasting Litvakov for his "right deviations" and anti-Party views, and reminding Litvakov and others that the Party never gave the proletarian organizations a monopoly on proletarian literature. This was one of the few times the decision against a proletarian monopoly was lauded by a Yiddish proletarian writer.[154] Tayf did not try to make peace, and instead asked Chemerinsky to reprimand Litvakov for his anti-Party attitude. *Evsektsiia*, not surprisingly, sided with Litvakov, and Tayf was removed from the Communist group before the April 1929 meeting.[155] In an era of politicization, everyone was vulnerable, and the future of Soviet Jewish culture and the Soviet Yiddish intelligentsia seemed to be up for grabs.

THE KVITKO AFFAIR

One particularly public event crystallized the literary politics of the Cultural Revolution within Yiddish culture: the Kvitko Affair. Leyb Kvitko, a poet and member of the Kiev group who had joined Bergelson and Der Nister in Berlin, returned to the Soviet Union in 1925.[156] Not long after, he was given a position in Kharkov as an editor of *Red World*, which granted him a stable income and a forum for publishing his work. Kvitko aligned with the fellow traveler Construction group, rather than the proletarian writers.

In the May–June 1929 edition of *Red World*, Kvitko published a cycle of poems, *Purge (Reynikung)*, part of a larger series called *Portraits (Portretn)*, which satirized various aspects of Soviet literature. Some thought it was Kvitko's response to criticism of *Red World*'s overt stance for literary autonomy. The cycle included a short satire called "The stinkbird Moyli" (*Der shtink-foygl Moyli*), which was also published in Kvitko's collected works, *Struggle (Gerangl).*

"The Stinkbird Moyli"
Recently, every night
The stinkbird Moyli comes
And sits on our roof

The bleating of his beak is thin
Scrapingly thin, each sound is a
  spider.
Recently, every night,
On the roof, he sits in the moonlight
And drops spiders on us,
On the thin weave of our sleep.

It seems to us, seems to us – he stands
  on the roof

And stretches out his beak, reaches
Into the room, and makes a smell.
The resentment is great, the woe is
  great
We can't reach out of bed
To the roof of the house
To catch the stinkbird,
On the roof, up on his high place.

The next day –
Where we bring our power,
Like usual, to weave
Taffeta out of weeks.

Our nose feels it.
The stinkbird Moyli was here.
And he left his odor behind . . .

"Der shtink-foygl Moyli"
Di letste nekht, yeder nakht,
Kumt af unzer dakh
Der shtink-foygl Moyli

Der mrik fun zayn shnobl iz din,
Iz ripedik din, yeder klang iz a shpin.

Di letste nekht, yeder nakht,
Er shtelt zikh avek afn dakh
Un lozt af undz di shpinen op,
Af dinem geveb fun undzer shlof.

Undz dakht, undz dakht – er shteyt
  afn dakh
Un tsit oys zayn shnobl, derlangt
In shtub, vert a geshtank.

Iz groys der fardros, der veytik groys:

Mir kenen fun bet nit derlangen
Tsum dakh funm hoyz,
Tsu pakn dem shtink-foygl dort,
Afn dakh, af zayn hoykhn ort

Dem tog dernokh, –
Vuhin mir brengen undzer kraft,
Vi geveynlekh, tsu vebn
Fun vokh dem taft

Iz do, oykh do, derfilt unzer noz, –
Oykh do iz der shtink foygl moyli geven
Un hot do zayn reyekh gelozt . . .[157]

Litvakov read this poem about the stinkbird Moyli (read *Moyshe Litvakov*) as an attack on his position in Soviet Jewish culture; Kvitko thought it was appropriate satire. In a July 13, 1929, article in *Emes*, Litvakov came out against Kvitko's "anti-Soviet remarks" and went so far as to call Kvitko a "dangerous element."[158] Kvitko responded: "I wrote the poem in the beginning of winter. A few leading Party activists heard it, and I read it out loud at a party in Kharkov, and no one jumped on me and suggested that it was dangerous.... For any objective person who reads *'Portraits'* it will be clear that I wanted to portray various types: a devoted Communist, who gave so much of his body and soul to the process of socialist building that he didn't notice that he was suffering physically from it. In the second poem I wanted to portray an arrogant Communist, a braggard, who uses his Party card for his own purposes."[159] Kvitko explained the satire of each personality in his poems, and showed that there was no particular gossip about any actual person in his work. What Litvakov read was not what Kvitko intended.

Kvitko concluded, "I am happy to repent for my poem *'Purge,'* if an objective critic can show me the parts that are dangerous to the state and the Party. I vehemently protest, however, such crippling and mistranslating of my poem, and the trashing of my name, when my entire literary work over the last few years ... has responded to, taken part in, and strengthened the fight for and the achievements of the workers' revolution."[160] Kvitko argued neither for artistic freedom nor against a proletarian monopoly in literature. He claimed his position within the new literary political structure and suggested that Litvakov was, in fact, the one outside of it.

The articles set off a firestorm. If the accusations Litvakov made against Kvitko were true, how was it that such a right deviationist, anti-Soviet writer could sit on the editorial board of the most important Yiddish journal? The Jewish Section of *MAPP* took up the issue at its fall 1929 meeting. Yosef Rabin, a longtime proletarian Yiddish poet, said that the incident highlighted the problem of reintegrating "emigrants" back into the Soviet Yiddish intelligentsia, underscoring the distinction between Soviet and non-Soviet Yiddish literature.[161] He also suggested that the fault for anti-Soviet remarks lay, not just with Kvitko, but also with the editors of the publishing house that put out *Red World* (which was Kvitko himself) and the editor of Kvitko's book *Struggle*, which included the *Portrait* poems. Rabin called for Kvitko's removal as editor, and a reprimand of Henekh Kazakevitch, editor at the Central Publishing House for National Minorities (*Tsentroizdat*), for publishing *Struggle*. Others at the meeting, including Aaron Kushnirov and Shmuel Rosin, also came out against Kvitko, calling for an end to "trash drama and *Stream* poetry." Kushnirov's remarks remind us that, by 1929, *Stream* had become a part of pre-Soviet literary history, another irony considering Kushnirov himself had edited *Stream*'s last edition. Avrom Veviorke, also a former *Stream* editor, was more reserved in his criticism, and doubted whether Kvitko's satire was actually politically motivated. Nonetheless, the *MAPP* resolution accused Kvitko of right deviations, of writing petty-bourgeois literature, and of anti-Soviet accusations, and called for his removal as editor. It passed unanimously.[162]

The Jewish Section of *VUSP* had a similar discussion about Kvitko with Fefer commenting that *VUSP* was "not calling for an end to his publishing career. . . . We just want him off the editorial board."[163] The newspaper *October* in Minsk also supported the charges against Kvitko and called for his removal.[164] The Main Bureau of the Ukrainian *Evsektsiia* – the first Party voice to weigh in on Kvitko – also called for his and Kazakevitch's firing.[165] The intelligentsia seemed to be telling one of its own that internal dissent would no longer be tolerated. The Central Bureau upheld the Ukrainian Main Bureau's decision to remove Kvitko from the editorial board.[166]

The affair is seemingly straightforward. Litvakov, as cultural commissar, dictated the proper response to Kvitko's work, and everyone followed. But this presumes that Litvakov had authoritative control over the intelligentsia, and was unscathed by the political changes around him. (The charges by Moshe Tayf mentioned earlier prove that this was not the case.) It also presumes that the Cultural Revolution and rise of the proletarian groups brought an end to dissent. Several writers came out publicly in defense of Kvitko: David Hofshteyn and other contributors to *Red World*; and two proletarian writers – Hershl Orland, whose novel *Hreblies* is often considered the first example of a Yiddish socialist realist novel, and Daniel Meyerovich, also a newcomer to the Yiddish literary scene.[167] The editors of *Star*, who published Orland and Meyerovitch's defense, noted that "the editorial board considers the defense of Orland and Daniel [Meyerovitch] to be an attempt to distort the political perspective on the Kvitko Affair" – an example of visible censorship. Public dissent happened, sometimes as part of the process of visible censorship and criticism, but sometimes because people simply disagreed.

Meanwhile, just as Litvakov criticized Kvitko for right deviations, others from the far left were criticizing Litvakov for his "right deviation" support of the poet Shmuel Halkin. Halkin's 1929 book, *Pain and Courage (Vey un Mut)*, contained work that was interpreted as pessimistic about the condition of Soviet Jewry. Some critics also thought Halkin's poetry was too liberal in its allusions to traditional Jewish literature, something that made him suspicious in the eyes of many proletarian Yiddish critics, who sometimes understood the allusions and did not like them. Litvakov, a consistent supporter of Halkin's work since the early 1920s, wrote a positive review of Halkin's book. In the new climate of literary politics, those who wanted to overturn the hierarchy of power went on the offensive. The Minsk group of proletarian critics and newspaper editors – Yashe Bronshteyn, Khatskel Dunets, and others – accused Litvakov and other members of the Central Bureau of "masked Jewish nationalism" for their support of petty bourgeois and nationalistic writers such as Halkin. No one had a monopoly on dictating the future of literature or of Soviet Jewish culture – not Litvakov and the Moscow group, Bronshteyn and the Minsk group, nor Fefer and the Kharkov group.[168]

THE FINAL CONSOLIDATION OF LITERARY GROUPS

The proletarian writers groups had political power and were the literary center of Soviet literature for only four years until 1932, when the Central Committee abolished the umbrella proletarian organizations. Prior to that, the politics of literature had become more vituperative and divisive. The rise of self-criticism, visible censorship, and political denunciations, along with targeting fellow travelers and Party members alike, continued into the early 1930s. In private correspondence, writers such as Markish and Der Nister expressed frustration with the changing politics, the decline in literary experimentation, and the rising importance of socialist realism. At the same time, many writers transformed themselves and became part of the dominant structures of Soviet Jewish literary culture. Hofshteyn did this shortly after his return to the Soviet Union, and in a series of letters, Markish revealed his own transformation. In a January 1929 letter, Markish decried the rise of the proletarians, calling Avrom Veviorke, for want of a more polite term, a "shit head" (*Govno Veviorke*) and gave an angry description of Litvakov's and Nusinov's harsh reviews of his book, *One Generation Goes, Another One Comes (Dor oys dor ayn)*.[169] In a November 1929 letter, however, Markish expressed different feelings: "no one is forcing anyone to become Communist. Each does what he wants," showing that although aesthetic affiliation in the form of socialist realism had become less a matter of choice, in Markish's opinion, political affiliation still was.[170] By 1931, Markish waxed poetic about how wonderful life had become in the Soviet Union, where bread was cheaper and the working class stronger, in his mind, a stark comparison to the Depression-ravaged world outside in which his Yiddish colleagues lived.

If an individual's own literary past and relationship to the Soviet present could change, so too could a group's or journal's history. In the same way that *Stream* went from a positive literary father of Soviet Jewish literature to its negative pre-history, the organization Construction went from being a benign group of fellow travelers organizing to support non-proletarian writers to being a "nest of Trotskyite subterfuge." If the charge of *Nisterism* in the late 1920s was a warning to a writer about his/her symbolist aesthetics, the charge of Trotskyism could end a writer's career. In 1931, the founder of Construction and former editor of *Red World*, David Feldman, publicly recanted his association with the group, using the language of political polarization that had taken hold of Soviet culture, and doing so in a Russian-language journal, not a Yiddish one:

In 1927, on my initiative, a literary group was established called *Construction (Boy/Stroika)*. At the time I was a Trotskyite, and we organized in the interests of creating a "national cultural" group dissatisfied with the correct Leninist line on the national question... Although my anti-Party line (Trotskyism plus national deviation) was not an official platform of *Construction*, the characteristics were the same.[171]

Once Feldman defined Construction as Trotskyite, everyone formerly associated with that group was tainted. In a February 1932 editorial in the Kiev Yiddish newspaper *Proletarian Banner*, the Communist and proletarian literary critic Max Viner tarred the entire Construction group, naming Feldman, Lurie, Oyslender, and Finenberg as former Trotskyites, which led to their ostracism from Soviet Yiddish literature.[172] The charge of *Constructionism* (*Boyism*) in the early 1930s became as potent as the charge of *Nisterism* had been in the late 1920s; both were marks of a writer's allegiance to a personal aesthetic over political imperative. If in the 1920s, as Kvitko found out, individual artistic *expression* tarnished a writer's reputation, in the 1930s past and present literary *associations* could end a writer's career – a dangerous shift.

Public divisiveness came to an end in April 1932, when the Communist Party declared that "the framework of the existing proletarian literary and artistic organizations is becoming too narrow and is hindering the proper development of literary work."[173] The Communist Party's action to abolish RAPP in 1932 and consolidate all writers into the Union of Soviet Writers was prompted by a desire to end factionalism and to reestablish Party control over literature.[174] There was a clear sense that the politics of literature under the proletarians had become too publicly divisive, and that in the Stalinist era of state building, literature needed to serve the state. The Union of Soviet Writers abolished the idea of literary groupings based on ideology, aesthetics, or politics, and established an "official aesthetic," Socialist Realism. The institutionalization of Socialist Realism, an aesthetic or cultural form often described as "portraying life as it should be," brought with it the end of many aspects of modernism – much literary experimentation, public debates among writers, dialogue with Yiddish literature from abroad.

The rise of Socialist Realism did not mean the end of the careers of Yiddish modernists. Bergelson moved back to the Soviet Union in 1934; Perets Markish received the Order of Lenin, the highest state honor awarded "to individuals or groups for their achievements in the building of socialism"; Der Nister published his famous epic novel, *The Family Mashber*, in 1939. The Soviet Yiddish intelligentsia changed with the times, as it had done since the first years after the revolution, and in the 1930s became an integral part of the Soviet literary establishment even as it continued producing a Jewish vision of Soviet culture.

6

Becoming Revolutionary

Izi Kharik and the Question of Aesthetics, Politics, and Ideology

In poem after poem Kharik develops the strained, creative feeling of construction
that both destroys and builds worlds.

– Yehezkiel Dobrushin, 1926

Even before they come to build the new, the old had already been destroyed in a
thunderous storm.

– Micah Berdichevsky

The life and work of Israel (Izi) Kharik embody many of the phenomena of
Soviet Jewish culture and the Soviet Yiddish intelligentsia. As a high-ranking
member of both the Communist Party and the Writers' Union, he was a
quintessential product of the system of Soviet cultural production. At the same
time, he had an extraordinary ability to break conventions and avoid literary labels despite his position as a central, exemplary Soviet cultural figure
and writer.[1] His poetry has been interpreted as some of the most politically
motivated Yiddish literature to appear in the 1920s, according both to contemporaries who reviewed his work and to the few scholars who have examined
Kharik's poetry.[2] But contemporaries also recognized how invested Kharik was
in envisioning a Soviet Jewish future and how involved he was in debates about
Jewish aesthetics and politics. His poetry exposed the nostalgia and pain associated with the destruction of the Jewish past (and the literal destruction of
many Jews during the Russian Civil War) and the ideological exuberance of
the generation of the Soviet Yiddish intelligentsia that became writers after the
revolution.

Kharik was a member of proletarian literary groups, and he edited
Communist journals. On the other hand, he only joined the Communist Party
in 1930 and wrote nihilistic expressionist poetry about the shtetl that worked
against the more dominant realist poetry of other proletarian poets. There was

no maudlin sweatshop poetry in Kharik's oeuvre. In other words, Kharik's life and work showed how the polarized categories of Soviet Jewish literary groups and aesthetic affiliations and the ideologies that defined them were much more fluid than contemporary rhetoric allowed and than later critics have supposed. Kharik's work was as much in dialogue with Jewish literary forms and tropes as it was arguing for a Communist utopia, and Kharik's life revealed the tensions and ambivalences in ideology that drove the Soviet Yiddish intelligentsia to create a Soviet Jewish culture in Yiddish.

IZI KHARIK OF ZEMBIN, BELORUSSIA (1899–1937)

Kharik studied in a *heder* for several years, and then moved to a Russian school.[3] Before he became a professional writer, Kharik was a "jack of all trades"; he supported himself as a baker, an optician, a druggist, union activist, and even a medic. While a medical student, he began publishing Yiddish and quickly gave up his medical studies to train to be a full-time Yiddish poet, a profession seemingly possible only in the Soviet Union.[4] Kharik started publishing after the revolution, making him a member of the "second generation" of the Soviet Yiddish intelligentsia. He did not participate in the Kiev group, and he developed his aesthetic and political ideologies in the destructive aftermath of the Civil War, which colored much of Yiddish poetry with a dark expressionism. Like many other modern Yiddish writers, Kharik wrote under a pseudonym for his earliest publications in Communist journals, both in Moscow and in Minsk. Shmuel Agursky, editor of the *Communist World*, published Kharik's first works, apparently without the author's knowledge, under the pseudonym A.Z. Zembin.[5] In 1920, Kharik published "Beneath Red Banners" (*Unter royte fonen*) in *Waves*, the Belorussian Yiddish literary journal that set itself up in opposition to the Kiev journals of 1918–20.[6] He published a poem in *The Alarm*, the Bundist–turned–Communist newspaper of Belorussia, and his first book of poetry, *Trembling (Tsiter)*, came out in 1922, the same year *Aftergrowth* began publishing second-generation writers in Ukraine. The success of his early poetry and his interest in Communist Party publications led the State Commissariat for Enlightenment (*Narkompros*) to encourage Kharik to move to Moscow to study at the Briusov Institute of Literature and Art, where up-and-coming writers and artists went to study the arts under the auspices of the Soviet state.[7] Kharik and his friend, the poet Zelik Akselrod, moved from Minsk to Moscow and rented an apartment not too far from the Briusov Institute. To pay his rent, Kharik initially worked at the Central Jewish Library, but by 1925, after more than two years at the institute, Kharik earned enough money writing and quit, becoming one of the first young Soviet Yiddish writers to be a full-time writer.

Kharik's literary career skyrocketed as part of the Soviet Yiddish intelligentsia not only because of his talent as a writer, but also through his association with the Moscow Circle of Jewish Writers and Artists.[8] The important figures of Moscow's Yiddish cultural scene were impressed enough by Kharik that in 1924, he joined the group's executive board.[9] He had already published a few short poems in *Emes* in 1923 and early 1924, and he made a name for himself as an international Yiddish writer with a poem he published in *Stream*.[10] Kharik's other big 1924 publication was his narrative poem (*poema*), *Minsk Swamps (Minsker Blotes)*, stanzas of which appeared on the pages of *Emes* and in the literary collection *New Earth (Nayerd)*.[11] The narrative poem portrays the transformation of a shtetl during the revolution, and was heralded as one of the first Yiddish works to depict Jewish life, instead of death, during the Civil War.

By 1925, Kharik had become an integral member of the Soviet Yiddish intelligentsia in Moscow. He was on the editorial board of *New Earth*; a regular contributor to the Moscow youth journals, *Young Forest (Yungvald)* and *Pioneer (Pioner)*; and the secretary of *Nayerd's* literary competition, the anthology *October (Oktyabr)*. In addition, he wrote articles for *Red World* and *Emes*.[12] After he completed his studies, the Briusov Institute wanted to bring him and Akselrod to Leningrad, not an exciting prospect for a new member of the Soviet Yiddish intelligentsia.[13] Shlomo Niepomniashchy remarked that "our literary family cheered up Kharik, who is now going off to the 'Exile-Institute' in Leningrad, as it seems the Briusov Institute has relocated. Zelik Akselrod, our Benjamin, also has to go."[14] By referring to Akselrod as "our Benjamin," the youngest of the Biblical Jacob's twelve sons, Niepomniashchy was making him and Kharik the youngest siblings of the new Soviet Yiddish literary family and was also implying that the entire family had a responsibility to take care of them. Kharik and Akselrod pleaded for assignments in Moscow in order to stay in the new Jewish cultural center of the Soviet Union. In the end, they both returned to their native Belorussia and became central cultural figures in Minsk, big fish in a smaller pond. In Belorussia, they were no longer "Benjamins" in the literary family.

In 1926, Kharik published his first major collection of poems, *On the Land (Af der erd)*, which was reviewed by all the major Soviet Jewish publications.[15] Yashe Bronshteyn, a second-generation Yiddish literary critic from Belorussia, wrote the review for the Minsk literary journal, *Star*, and the Minsk newspaper, *October*. In Ukraine, the Kiev critic Yehezkiel Dobrushin reviewed the book for *Red World*, and Avrom Veviorke, for *Emes*. Bronshteyn praised it for "rehabilitat[ing] simple poetic language and the language of real human interactions...."[16] Veviorke described Kharik's poems as "grounded in time and place," as opposed to the "abstract, stylized poems" of the Kiev generation modernists.[17] And for Dobrushin, the most established Soviet Jewish literary critic, "Kharik is more than a lyric singer, but is also a describer and a constructor himself. His poetry is a part of the great post-October rebuilding work, but more importantly, it is really a part of his own, internally experienced unrest that comes from the struggle."[18] These reviews stressed that Kharik's work was unlike that of the important poets of Yiddish modernism such as David Hofshteyn, Perets Markish, and Leyb Kvitko, who wrote poems that according to the critics were abstract and too complicated for the common reader and spoke only to an elite Yiddish reading audience. All three reviewers touched on the relationship in Kharik's poetry between "the shtetl," in this case a metonymy for all traditional Jewish life, and the city, which represented revolutionary culture, youth, and the Party. In other words, the poems that earned Kharik a reputation throughout the Soviet Union expressed the ambiguous and tortured relationship between the Jewish past, present, and future; between tradition and modernity; between memory and imagination.

Shortly after his return to Minsk, Kharik became secretary for the Minsk literary journal *Shtern*, and received the 1926–7 Sholem Aleichem stipend of Belorussia, given to the most promising Yiddish writer.[19] He began editing for *October* and gave lectures throughout the Soviet Union. His most important contribution to Soviet Jewish literature, his 1928 narrative poem *With Body and Soul (Mit Layb un Lebn)*, was widely reviewed and received great acclaim. Kharik portrays the life of the Soviet Yiddish intelligentsia through the eyes of a young Jewish teacher, whose grand hopes for rebuilding the shtetl are dashed. Despite the overwhelmingly dark themes of the work, the reviewers lauded Kharik for portraying "real Soviet life" and for showing the reconstruction of Soviet society. One reviewer called it "the embodiment of 'now,'" and suggested that finally Soviet Yiddish poetry had moved on from the dominant motif of the early 1920s – the lament for a world destroyed. The same reviewer, however, pointed out that *With Body and Soul* was primarily about the difficulties of bringing the shtetl into the modern world, and how the burden of this cultural work ended up destroying the protagonist. Even in 1928, when triumphal proletarian poetry began its reign and Socialist Realism was first coming into its own as a dominant mode of cultural expression, Kharik was praised for writing poems expressing ambivalence about the Soviet project.[20]

In December of that year, Kharik applied for membership in the Belorussian Association for Proletarian Writers (*BelAPP*), finally taking on the institutional persona that critics had been ascribing to him; and two years later, he joined the Party.[21] A contemporary of his suggested that as a member of the Belorussian Communist Party Central Committee, Kharik was the highest-ranking Yiddish cultural figure in Soviet Belorussia by the mid-1930s.[22] By all accounts, at the time he was considered the most important Yiddish poet in Belorussia and was a member of the prestigious Belorussian Academy of Sciences. He was celebrated in poetry readings, special book dedications, and other rites that conferred importance on Soviet writers. Kharik was the paragon of the Soviet Yiddish intelligentsia – a modernist poet deeply invested in the Jewish future and simultaneously committed to building socialism in the Soviet Union.

IDEOLOGY AND AESTHETICS: WHERE JEWISH HISTORY AND SOVIET CULTURE MEET

This study of Kharik's literary biography and his work raises the question of the relationship between ideology and literary tradition and how both shaped the building of Soviet Jewish culture. To understand the various ideological and aesthetic traditions in which Kharik and other poets wrote, it is vital to examine their work within the context of both Jewish history and literature, and Soviet culture and politics. The work of many poets was in constant dialogue with Jewish literary history ranging from Biblical allusion in nearly all Soviet Yiddish poets' work and nineteenth-century Jewish enlightenment literature, to the classic writers, and up to the Yiddish modernist fellow travelers such as David Hofshteyn.[23] Their work also engaged contemporary literary trends, such as German Expressionism, Russian Imaginism, and the Futurism of Vladimir Mayakovsky and Mykhail Semenko. Kharik is historically and literarily interesting precisely because he was, more than almost any other writer, a product of the Soviet cultural apparatus and was interested in modernist aesthetics as well as the past, present, and future of Jewish literature. He blended the utilitarian ideology of Yiddish culture inherited from nineteenth-century *maskilim*, who saw Yiddish as a means to the end of enlightening Jews, with a modernist aesthetic he developed as part of the interwar Jewish literary milieu, which used Yiddish as a means of expressing collective angst and ideological triumph. As much as he would have resisted the label, Kharik was a Jewish nationalist looking to a vibrant future for Soviet Jewish culture.

Kharik followed a long tradition of Jewish cultural activism that began in the nineteenth century and established the mission of using state power to enlighten Eastern European Jews and to prepare them for the modern world. For some enlighteners, the Eastern European *Haskalah* was fraught with tensions similar to the ones Communist Yiddish activists and writers thought they faced: how to bring an ideology to a people opposed to the goals of this ideology; how to reach them if they do not speak the lingua franca; how to be both part of the enlighteners group by claiming to represent Jews to non-Jews, yet apart from the group by dedicating themselves to remaking the Jewish people in their image? Starting at the turn of the nineteenth century a number of *maskilim*, from Mendel Lefin to writers such as S.Y. Abramovitch, turned to the language of "the people," Yiddish. In this ideological guise, Yiddish was meant as a means to the end of inculcating modern, European values (either bourgeois liberalism or, in Kharik's case, communist socialism) in a seemingly benighted group of people.[24] The literary critic, Shmuel Niger wrote in 1934, "The work during the *Haskalah* period is similar to that of Soviet Yiddish literature in two ways. First, they both believed that literature was not an end in itself, but rather was a means to the end of a specific socio-economic and cultural reform program, and, second, they were both opposed to the existing Jewish way of life."[25] Niger recognized the utilitarian role literature played within a revolutionary project. Soviet Jewish scholars were themselves aware of their connections to the *maskilim*.[26] During the 1920s, Jewish literary scholars and historians, such as Meir Viner and Max Erik, published a number of academic works examining the *Haskalah* as a bourgeois version of their own modernizing project.[27]

Despite the similarities, Niger overlooked the fact that Soviet Yiddish literature was both a means and an end, a means to a new society and an end in a new Jewish literature. The Soviet Yiddish intelligentsia was not just involved in a utilitarian project to bring ideas to the masses in a comprehensible language. They were creating a new Soviet Jewish culture in Yiddish as an end in itself. Not only were they interested in taking part in the Soviet call to build new national cultures, but they were also elevating the previously lowly Yiddish language to a "language of high culture." Unlike the *maskilim*, who wrote in Yiddish with a bitter taste in their mouths because its use was seen as a step backward in the modernization process, Soviet Jewish writers wrote proudly in Yiddish because it was the language of the Jewish working class.

Kharik's work revealed the tension between means and ends. Generically speaking, his poetry primarily uses the first person singular "I," suggesting that he worked within lyrical poetic traditions that had become widespread in Soviet Jewish literature. By using "I," Kharik also blurred the boundaries between writer and poetic subject, between autobiography and fiction. Most interesting about his work is that it revealed an ambivalence about the building of socialism, an ambivalence uncharacteristic of self-consciously proletarian poetry, of socialist realist work, or of the futurist writing of poets such as Mayakovsky. For Kharik, the revolution was a creative process that left a wake of destruction in its path. This ambivalence illuminated the struggle to create a new culture on the ruins of an old one. Not only did activists like Kharik have to rebuild society to create socialism, but they also had to transform themselves to create a new socialist person. Kharik's work provided a window on the process of becoming, rather than being, a revolutionary, while accepting the revolution as socialist construction and social destruction, as well as the simultaneous psychological processes of self-creation and self-destruction.

KHARIK'S SHTETL POEMS (MOSCOW, 1924–1925)

The period in which Kharik wrote the shtetl poems, the New Economic Policy (NEP), was considered a time of relative pluralism in artistic production (compared to the late 1920s and 1930s). It involved a limited dismantling of the centralized Civil War economy and a loosening of state cultural controls. It was the heyday of cultural diversity in Soviet literature, when writers such as Kharik were publishing in the same journals as émigré poets such as Perets Markish, and private publishing houses produced literature next to state-run publishers.

Stylistically, at the time of his shtetl poems, Kharik was part of the transnational Jewish literary scene that engaged the contemporary trends of European modernism. Kharik was most interested in Expressionism, the dominant poetic trend of young Yiddish modernist poets at the time.[28] The themes of darkness, apocalypse, and self destruction, which all permeated Kharik's poetry of this period, shaped the poetry of the best-known figures of Yiddish modernism, most notably Uri Tsvi Grinberg – who later moved to Palestine and switched to Hebrew – and Perets Markish.[29] Yashe Bronshteyn attempted to differentiate Kharik's modernist work from that of the most important Soviet Yiddish poet of the time, David Hofshteyn, by showing their different allegiances to contemporary Jewish modernist trends. Hofshteyn's nature poems were "lyric, pastoral, impressionist. The most important subject in his poems is the light." Kharik's poems, according to Bronshteyn, were "hard and rough, expressionist – disheveled and fleshy. He always writes about the joy of birth, and shows that the earth is a sensual place. He's elemental." Moreover, the darkness that colored all post–World War I expressionist poetry permeated Kharik's grim shtetl poems, and according to Bronshteyn, "Despondence [*umru*] is Kharik's normal disposition."[30] Dobrushin revealed the similar use of dark imagery in Kharik's and Markish's work when he reviewed Kharik's *On the Land*: "He has a few words or concepts that he repeats over and over again – 'restlessness,' 'wind,' 'hands,' and 'head.' He uses the word 'despondence' at least 50 times; wind – 40 times; hands and head – 30 times. This combination of words resembles that of Markish in his first book *Thresholds [Shveln]* (1919), in which he used the same words as Kharik. Perhaps this is a sign, if not of poetic relationship, then of the same elemental forces, of unrest, of a hot-tempered grasping with the hands and the head...."[31] Soviet writers and critics saw Soviet Yiddish literature within the general modernist literary trends of the time.

Given the atmosphere of NEP and the productive transnational relationships among Yiddish poets at the time, it is not surprising that Kharik wrote poetry expressing ambivalence and even darkness about the revolutionary project. It was during NEP that some Soviet Yiddish poets wrote nostalgic poems about their lost homes and the dying cultural world of the shtetl. One contemporary critic, looking at this period retrospectively, called the period of early Soviet representations of the shtetl "*kupe ash*" (ash heap), a reference to a 1921 Markish poem cycle *The Heap* (*Di Kupe*) about pogroms that destroyed shtetls throughout Ukraine, and a phrase that emphasizes the remnants of destruction from the early revolutionary years.[32] But Kharik's poetry was more than "ash heap" nostalgia; it was at once mournful, at the loss associated with destruction, and at the same time, fiery in its passion for what the destruction meant – building a new world.

Kharik wrote his shtetl poems in 1924–5, when he was living in Moscow. They grappled with the relationship between the shtetl and the modern Jew, and with the relationship between the poetic voice and his past. In reading Kharik's early work, his poetic subject should be read both as a lyrical "I" and as a fictionalized mediator between two worlds that cannot speak to one another directly for cultural and political reasons.[33] Like the *maskilim* of the nineteenth century, this modernist poet who had broken the shackles of his benighted, tradition-bound Jewish ancestors could not engage the shtetl in a dialogue directly, but his poems about the shtetl and the poetic voice within them could. Kharik's poems were also in dialogue with those of other "revolutionary lyricists," which described the self as part of a revolution. These dialogues, both with the past and with the self in the present, reflect a personally ambiguous feeling about the effects the poetic voice's actions have had on the shtetl (past) and, more introspectively, the effects his actions have had on himself and on the future.

The literary scholar, Dan Miron, who exposed a similar tension that *maskilim* faced in the nineteenth century – the need to create a mediator who could initiate dialogue – also pointed out that the literary shtetl became a dominant symbol of a dying world in the work of the classic writers, Sholem Aleichem and S.Y. Abramovitch. He describes several common themes in their literary shtetls. Most important are the image of fire consuming the shtetl, the presence of a visitor who brings redemption, and in the end, the migration of the people to redemption in "the land."[34] Kharik's shtetl engages many of the same motifs, but he uses them differently from his predecessors.

> *Shtetl,* 1924
>
> I
> A stranger came to visit the shtetl.
> A stranger—
> With restlessness in his step . . .
> No one noticed his restlessness
> No one asked him, "Are you tired?"
> The blue sky was then drawn to dusk
> And the silence cried out for someone,
> All the shops closed up long ago

And no one needs to go home anymore . . .
Deep into the night through the shtetl's wasteland
The visitor walked alone
Didn't wait, didn't ask
"Open up"—
At the last door of a used up house.
He heard and could hear no more
That the shtetl lay broken behind a fence.
"Good," he said. "Let it burn."
And with that he left closed off and hard.
And up till dawn he heard
The winds wail hot with fire and with
Little shtetls.
He looked back one last time
And left and dawn came.

2

The last smoke covered my shtetl
The final smoke the wind was to visit
Oh till when, oh till when, I ask, will
"Shtetele, disappear."
In the middle of the road, between blue highways
You're still lying down and can't yet go away.
Woe to all the graying fathers
Who have not extinguished your days—
Who left you to your silence and to your waiting!—
May a heavy wheel ride over you
And shake you up through to your sick heart.
Step— after step . . .
I know: your days are numbered,
And each one is red with pain.
Oh, if I only were a believer and could chisel out a cross for you:
The last guardian of your death.

3

Deep in the courtyard, a harmonica is overcome
And turns itself off between cool walls.
When it restrains itself,
I cannot remember what once used to be.
Shtetl, shtetl, silent and mournful
Until the last roof, forlorn and alone . . .
Guess when, on the highest walls, your dry sobbing
Will reach me.
When I left your alleys for the first time,
My youth was still burning silently.

I thought – it is forbidden to forget you.
And you must always follow me into exile . . .
Away I went; bent over following after the wagon,
My whole life clinging to my body . . .
The city led me up to the highest of its floors, To the window:
    Stay!
It's good now to stand by the window to remember
And lightly wave my hand . . .
Hear the harmonica still drawn out,
As if it never was.

4
A night like all other nights, in blue
Like all other nights is restless and silent . . .
Today I cannot wail out my raw pain,–
I rise up airy and – swim.
A sky. A crazy moon
Gets all riled up and tears into me, harsh and hard
It tears my heart and talks like a thousand flags.
Like a thousand flags my needs are tearing into me.
I cannot calm down on a night like this.
When it pulls me away and carries on woe and wind.
Mother, mother, it's your son who's gone crazy
Flying around blue in the wind.
I peek in through the thirst of my eyes
And stretch my neck as long as it will go.
There used to be shtetls lying here
In quiet calm with quiet bread and salt.
I alone helped to destroy them
And sent them off in smoke.
I can already hear how the stars shudder
How it pulls me away and carries me into the heights.[35]

The earliest of his shtetl poems, called simply *Shtetl*, is a modernist exploration of the boundaries between past and present, self and other, fantasy and reality. Throughout the poem, Kharik plays with the boundaries between internal
and external selves; the reader is never sure if the speaker is actually journeying
to a dying shtetl or if these are "shtetls of the mind" that the speaker must
destroy. Nonetheless, both the shtetls of Eastern Europe and the shtetl mentality needed to be overhauled. The modernist aesthetic of blurring boundaries
provided Kharik the poetic tools to represent these social and psychological
transformations.

The poem opens with the image of an observer arriving in a shtetl to witness its destruction. As a visitor, the person is detached from the processes that have transformed the shtetl into an empty wasteland. Throughout the first of four sections, the visitor is referred to in the third person, emphasizing the distance between him and the shtetl. The first section recounts the visitor's entire journey, from his arrival and realization that there is nothing left alive in the shtetl, to his fiery pronouncement, "Good. Let it burn!" He then leaves the shtetl as he listens to "the winds wail hot/with fire and with/little shtetls." The first section closes with him looking back one last time "and dawn came."

This opening salvo echoes the tropes of other Yiddish writers' representations of the shtetl. As Dan Miron argues, "one realizes that all of the shtetl's unexpected visitors, no matter what their special guise, are depicted in redemptive terms, as harbingers of *geulah* [redemption] of one kind or another . . . [they] bring miraculous solutions to the insoluble problems of shtetl people – the community as a whole of individuals – by bringing wealth to the destitute, health to the sick, progeny to the childless," and, in Kharik's poem, socialism to the ideologically backward.[36] Kharik, however, turns the image of the harbinger upside down by having his redeemer see the shtetl already smoldering, and then leave in a torrent of flames.

In nineteenth-century literature, according to Miron, fire alluded to the conflagration that consumed the First and Second Temples in Jerusalem in ancient times and sent Jews off into exile, but Kharik's fire brings creative destruction, clearing the ground for the arrival of the redeeming ideology. Bronshteyn suggested that the obsession with destruction in his "early period" was shaped by the nihilistic drive of the expressionists. Kharik's *Shtetl* series is "an abstract symbol of an outmoded Sodom that would be transformed through smoke and fire." Kharik's own critics recognized his reliance on the aesthetics of expressionism and Biblical intertextuality. Like Miron, Bronshteyn too used Biblical imagery to situate Kharik's work within Jewish literature; however, his intertextual reference to the destruction of sinful Sodom rather than the destruction of the Holy Temple suggested that, in Bronshteyn's reading of Kharik, the shtetl was divinely doomed to die for its sins.[37]

The next three stanzas move from the third person "visitor" to the first person "I," which blurs both external and internal reality and the distinction between self and other. The "I" first sees "the final smoke the wind visited," and cries, "Oh till when, oh till when, I ask, will 'Shtetele disappear.'" The wind in the poem is destructive – it either burns the shtetl or brings pain to the speaker. But the word "wind" is also a trope within *Haskalah* literature. In Hebrew, the word for wind "*ruach*" also means "spirit" and came to symbolize the modern zeitgeist of Western thought that was blowing new life into Jewish culture. For Kharik who was drawing on *maskilic* as well as modernist aesthetics, the wind brings enlightening change, but only after being a destructive force.

As with other metaphors in this poem, the wind has an opposite – the wall. While the wind burns and, like a forest fire, creatively destroys the shtetl, the wall, which blocks the wind, is defensive, protective, cool, and enclosing. In one other antiredemptive moment, the speaker sees the shtetl apocalypse before him. "I know: your days are numbered, and each one is red with pain." But the speaker cannot bring redemption. "Oh, if I only were a believer and could chisel out a cross for you:/The last guardian of your death." The crucifix here symbolizes redemption and salvation, something that the poetic voice cannot bring for the suffering shtetl. It also shows Kharik in direct dialogue with other modernists of his age, in this case with fellow expressionist Uri Tsvi Grinberg, who two years earlier published a poem called "Uri Tsvi Before the Cross" (*Uri Tsvi farn tselem*). Not only was Jesus' crucifixion the theme of the poem, but Grinberg wrote the poem visually in the form of a cross. Unlike Uri Tsvi, Kharik's lyrical "I" cannot chisel out a cross, neither in life nor on the page.

In this same passage, the speaker introduces metaphors of color, starting with the image of the shtetl's numbered days "each one is red with pain," while the nights are colored blue. Red is connected with fire and with Communism, and blue was already a meaningful color used in Expressionist art and poetry, ever since Vasily Kandinsky and Franz Marc founded the *Blaue Reiter* (Blue Rider) group in 1911. In the group's color scheme, blue was the color of infinity, purity, and transcendence. And in Kandinsky's words, it was the "typical heavenly color."[38] Kharik had already introduced the color blue in images of the sky and then reintroduces it in the opening of section four. He does so in the canonically traditional Jewish line, "A night like all other nights, in blue" [*A nakht vi ale nekht, in bloyen*], reworking the most important question from Passover: Why is this night different from all other nights? Near the end of the poem, the speaker refers to himself as "blue in the wind," mixing the images of the calm transcendence with the destructive winds of Communism, thus placing himself at the crossroads of the past and the future, the ephemeral present.[39]

As the poem progresses, the stranger of the first section transforms into a speaker intimately connected with the physical surroundings he describes. The third section of the poem is about the speaker struggling to remember his past that lives in the landscape around him. When reflecting on the strange image of the silencing of a harmonica into cool walls, the speaker says, "I cannot remember what once used to be." In the past, the harmonica might have represented something different – nostalgia and warmth. By the end of the section, the speaker says, "It's good now to stand by the window to remember/And lightly wave my hand . . . /Hear the harmonica still drawn out,/As if it never was." He desperately attempts to obliterate these sounds from his memory.

The speaker, who wrestles with the indelible images of the past that surround him, feels the burden of this memory, and attempts to separate from it. "Away I went; bent over following after the wagon,/My whole life clinging to my body." Both the use of folk motifs (wagons and harmonicas) and verb combinations like "silencing oneself" and "life clinging to body" add to the expressionist aesthetics. From a visitor to a destroyed shtetl, the speaker has transformed into one fleeing the mental shtetl, the memories of a past. What freed him from this burden was "The city [that] led me up to the highest of its floors, To the window: Stay!" His metaphoric and realistic journey goes from the shtetl's alleys and wasteland to the youthful city, then back again to the desolate landscape that surrounds him.

The poem ends with the merger of self and other, of internal and external, of visitor and speaker. The speaker burned the shtetl to the ground, which leaves him feeling guilty and rootless as he is pulled into the sky. Read Romantically, his ascent into the clouds could symbolize his death. But given the modernist imagery of the rest of the poem, the ascent is juxtaposed with the image of the speaker being crushed down by the weight of memory. It is reminiscent of Chagall's many images of people floating to the sky, not in scenes of death and resurrection, but in flights of fantasy.

The trope of the speaker as a stranger in his own hometown recurs in *Bread* – a nineteen-part epic poem about the history of a shtetl, from the building of the local count's mansion to the establishment of Soviet agricultural cooperatives. In the introduction, Kharik returns to the image of the "native foreigner."

Bread

Bread (Introduction)
On empty, tired alleys
My footsteps fall not very light . . .
This morning a shtetl full of Jews
Called me, "Anti-Semite!"

All of them in wrinkles and in rags,
Kept pointing with their hands:
"There, there's the one – we know him, him and his parents,
But he left for foreign lands . . ."

They feel like going to him and saying:
"Listen up, comrade," this way is bad,
If we can all be beaten down,
Can things really be so glad . . .

It's hard to be, to die with the shtetl,
After all, you yourself once lived here,
Say,— who is going to save us now,
Who will hold up our heads?. .

"I took one look at them – all empty and dead,
Beards and beards, and more dead beards . . .
"Enough," I said, "with idle and the ready-made,"
"With land, to the land, and if not, well then . . . "

The little shtetl let out a scream feverishly
Each word and each step – a bite.
I still don't know why a little shtetl full of Jews
Called me "Anti-Semite."[40]

Unlike *Shtetl*, *Bread* opens in the first person with the footsteps of the speaker
coming down the shtetl's empty, tired alleys. All of a sudden, the speaker is
confronted with verbal violence as the shtetl residents call him an anti-Semite.
The Jews then yell at the speaker that he has become estranged from them. This
shocking opening and the recurring theme of the stranger-as-speaker fuses the
trope of the redemptive wanderer with an autobiographical voice, implying that
Kharik's poetic voice is the foreign redeemer. The young activist is a stranger
in his home – a frightening and alienating realization – and nonetheless is
personally responsible for modernizing the shtetls and at the same time for
estranging himself.

Nostalgia for a lost past was also a trope in the work of the Russian poet,
Sergei Esenin, whose Imaginist poetry longed for a lost relationship between
an urbanized bohemian poet and his traditional peasant village. Soviet Yiddish
poets openly discussed their relationship to Esenin and eulogized him widely
after his suicide in 1925. But the relationship portrayed in *Bread*, between a
young urban activist and his hometown past, is seen through the lens of expressionism, and is therefore dominated not by a Esenin-like nostalgia, but by
alienation.

The speaker's frustration mounts as he listens to the abuse that he cannot
understand. "You yourself once lived here. Say,—Who will save us? Who is
going to hold up our heads?" Their harping continues until all the speaker sees in
these people are "beards, more beards, dead beards. . . . " He does not understand
their anger at all as he closes the introduction: "I still don't understand why
a little shtetl full of Jews/Called me, "Anti-Semite." Ironically, the speaker's
representation of shtetl Jews as nothing but dead beards is itself an internalized
anti-Semitic trope that reveals to the reader why the shtetl was calling this
modernizer an anti-Semite.

The introduction to *Bread* lacks the vivid metaphors of *Shtetl*, but this
passage introduced a narrative poem rather than a shorter lyric. It does, however,

reflect on the persisting ambivalence the speaker feels toward the shtetl and its Jews. In this poem, the Jews are angry complaining subjects even though the speaker only sees the objectified images of dead beards hanging from their faces. The shtetl is not as dead or empty as the speaker may see it. By having the seemingly passive dead Jews respond so violently to the presence of this young speaker, and then by having the speaker say that he cannot understand their hostility, we see the divide between fantasy and poetic reality, between what the young modernizer wanted to see in the shtetl and what actually confronted him.

The struggle to communicate becomes violently frustrating in the poem, "Pass On, You Sad Grandfathers." The title suggests the speaker's antagonistic feelings toward the "grandfathers," who represent a former, more traditional, generation of Jews.

Pass On, You Sad Grandfathers (Fargeyt, Ir Umetike Zeydes), 1924–1925

Pass on, pass on, you sad grandfathers
With terrified beards all run through with snow!
In the last disaster, in the last wail,
You survived, the last witnesses,—
Pass on, pass on, you sad grandfathers!

O, woe to your whole shtetl
Trampled in pain and hunger . . .
For every ravenous bite of bread
You had for long to smile and beg.
O, woe to your whole shtetl.

And now you look terrified and tired,
Your knees are shaking and knocking.
—"Who knows, who knows if
If our sons will still be Jews?"—
Your knees are shaking and knocking.

And we, the ones who still call you grandfathers,—
We also know that this won't be needed much longer,—
We rise like the first bell clap
Like the first sound of the approaching joy.
We, the ones who still call you grandfathers.

It's good to look into sad eyes
When the pain of your beards seems so foreign
We, this one and that one, . . .
We are destined
We are destined never to bow down again.
Pass on, pass on, you sad eyes.[41]

After the initial command to pass on (*fargeyn*), the speaker refers to the grand-fathers as "the last witnesses," who are the remnants of the "shtetl trampled in pain and hunger," that we meet in the second stanza. The speaker sees the grandfathers as the final remnants – the last generation – of Jewish identity as it was. The grandfathers are also the sole survivors of the latest destruction to sweep Jewish life, thus placing them in an ambiguous position at the crossroads of past and present.

The third and fourth stanzas introduce a train of thought unique to this poem – the speaker's explicit discussion of Jewish continuity. After reflecting on the downtroddenness of the grandfathers, the speaker describes fears that are more fundamental than the poverty and hunger in the second stanza – the threat of Jewish discontinuity, not fear of their own mortality, has the old men shaking. And interestingly, these "grandsons" are referring to their own fathers when they speak to the grandfathers about "your sons." The process of transforming Jewish identity is already one generation old, and is focused on the male line of Jewish descent. Kharik's use of the grandfather–grandson relationship to describe cultural upheaval echoed that of the early Zionist Hebrew writer Micha Berdichevsky, who wrote, "We can no longer solve the riddles of life in the old ways, or live and act as our ancestors did. We are the sons, and the sons of sons, of older generations, but not their living monuments."[42]

The speaker then addresses the nature of their relationship. He reminds the older generation that their position as grandfathers is solely dependent on the existence of grandsons such as the speaker. Throughout this poem, Kharik uses the plural, when speaking both of the grandfathers in the third person and of the grandsons in the first person. All his other shtetl poems are about the journey of a single person, while in this poem he switches to the plural to broaden the voice of the modernized Jewish youth. No longer is Kharik writing about one confused soul being called an anti-Semite by his former shtetlites; the notion of Jewish continuity between male generations affects many and cannot be considered a lyric reflection on one's relationship to the past.

The final stanza suggests that despite the biological relationship between the modernized youth and the traditional shtetl grandfathers, the grandfathers' existence is nonetheless evanescent. If the middle three stanzas suggested that the youth empathized with the fate of their grandfathers, the final verse returns to the image of a broken relationship. These genetically and culturally connected groups have become completely estranged from one another. The grandfathers, in fact, are no longer people. They have been reduced to lonesome eyes, echoing the dead beards of the previous poem, both of which are metonymies for this dying Jewish generation.

The estranged youth, however, has not completely freed itself from the personal attachment to the past. In a short untitled poem, Kharik turns the dialogue between two generations into a monologue that takes place within one modernized young Jew's consciousness to explore the anguish he feels at confronting his past.

Flee? I can't. I don't want to flee
But it is becoming impossible to stay here any longer.
The destruction was laid out across the courtyards
In the window panes – extinguished droplets of sparkle.

Nothingness and void. Wasteland and winds
A still extinguished hour hangs here . . .
I walk, but I sense – I'm being followed.
I turn around – no one is there.

I walk slowly; but it wants to chase me.
My step reverberates frightened upon the earth.
I turn around and beg: Let the day break.
Let the day break, let the day break! I can't anymore."[43]

From whom is the speaker fleeing? Is it from the mysterious ghost that haunts him in the second and third stanzas? The speaker hears nothing and only sees a void. Kharik's speaker finds himself in the proverbial "*tohu va-vohu*," the empty voids where God's presence rushed before Biblical Creation. The allusion to the void before Creation places the poem in the context of creative destruction. But this poem suggests that creation and destruction are dialectically related. First, there is a scene of destruction, and then the Biblical pre-creation void. The final plea for the day to break, echoing God's pronouncement, "Let there be light," is *not* followed by the Biblical phrase, "And there was light." There is no light of creation. The speaker is left in the void before dawn, haunted by a specter.

He cries out as he is being chased, that if the dawn would come, the specter, one assumes, would disappear. At the most superficial level, the specter could be the memory of that part of him that had been destroyed – the piled-up ruins. The dawn, a metaphor Kharik used in several of the shtetl poems, is the "dawn" of Communism – a common trope of the Soviet 1920s. But it also echoes the many "dawn" images of the Kiev journals like *Dawn* and *Ascent*. It also hearkens back to "dawn" metaphors of nineteenth-century *maskilic* culture, two of whose journals were *Ha-shachar* and *Rassvet*, which mean "dawn" in Hebrew and Russian respectively. In Kharik's world, the light of Communism, rather than that of the "enlightenment," brings on the dawn not in Hebrew or Russian but in the Jews' national language, Yiddish. Once the day breaks, the reader presumes that the speaker will have transcended the dead part of his identity that haunts him through the dark night. But the specter is also temporal, the haunting of a past without the redemption of a future.

This interpretation leaves out the first line: "Flee? I can't. I don't want to flee." Like the earlier *Shtetl*, there is an ambivalent relationship between the desire to flee from, and the desire to hold on to, the specter of memory. This ambivalence reflects on the relationship a modernized Jewish youth had to the memories of childhood, a struggle Jewish intellectuals had been wrestling with since the nineteenth century. Kharik was only in his mid-twenties when he wrote these poems – fresh from the shtetl experience, which, although it may have been oppressive, was still a part of his identity. The shtetl poems complicate the notions of remembering, of forgetting, and of nostalgia.

The critic Bronshteyn went even further in his analysis of the ambivalence in Kharik's presentation of the shtetl's destruction. "The shtetl doesn't disappear abruptly, in a catastrophe. It disappears dialectically, separating out its own gravedigger," who is perhaps the speaker in Kharik's poetry. Bronshteyn then contrasts Kharik's work with that of Itsik Fefer – Kharik's contemporary and the other paragon of Soviet Yiddish poetry at the time – by showing that Kharik's shtetl poems were more self-destructive, nihilistic, and therefore expressionist, than Fefer's. "Fefer mentions the Jews in the shtetl who read *Der Emes* or who want to join the *Evsektsiia*. Kharik doesn't mention these differentiating processes at all. Because of this, Fefer can paint such an idyllic scene – a type of civil peace between fathers and sons. Kharik, on the other hand, flees from the shtetl cursing it by saying "May you burn!"[44] In 1924, while Fefer's shtetl poems portrayed the happy and smooth transformation of shtetl Jews into good Jewish Communists who read the Yiddish Communist newspaper, Kharik saw only destruction.

> *In Your Little Houses (In dayne hayzelekh),* 1925–1926
>
> I
> Not because of the throngs,
> I would come to you, my little shtetl,
> Once again to see you long
> In quiet and transparent sadness.
>
> What did I want from you, little shtetl?
> Why did I argue with you, little shtetl?
> I wanted to dress you up in stone and steel,
> Little shtetl of mine.
>
> I wanted each one of your houses
> To reach proud heights.
> I did not want you to be silent about
> Your years full of life

Not because it's becoming milder,
As May spills out on to the streets,
I feel quiet and light-hearted
And you, little shtetl, I cannot hate.

You too must be experiencing May.
Although you must call it Sivan,
But, even so, the sky remains blue over everything that remains . . .

2

The whole shtetl – a holiday candle,
Burns its silent wax that drips with honey,
I expire here with a peaceful look on my face.
Today I am filled with the silence of remembrance . . .

A little boy here once lived
And that boy did not know of worry.
Little houses used to lift up their heads
And quietly greet him: "Good morning."

It wasn't good, it wasn't bad.
It simply just was . . .
In the star-studded sky of white nights
He played in the streets, as a boy does.

With eyes open, with an open heart
He woke up covered in dew
And he didn't know how one could love hate
How one could despise with a blessing . . .

. . . Now the boy would not have recognized.
And I probably wouldn't have recognized either
It's good that within the peace of these walls,
Still lives our sad mother.

3

I bow down my young head here in silence
But my heart can find no peace.
Shtetl, little shtetl, my dried up branch,
Will you once again turn green?
I walk around, a quiet guest, in silence.

And I so regret, I so regret.
I'm so envious of Esenin.
I would also have liked to come in song
And call you: "Mother."
Oh, you shtetl, how I so regret.

I feel as if I were standing at your end
And it often seems to me that you do not want to stand bent.
Your little houses, like sheep just waking up,
Open their round eyes after a peaceful summer sleep.

Shtetl, little shtetl, my childhood once-upon-a-time,
I wanted to see you while you were burning
But whoever cursed you back then,
Will already have to know you cursed.
Shtetl, little shtetl, my childhood once-upon-a-time.

4
August. I arrived in the shtetl.
Cool is August, and transparent, and blue.
By evening a smiling sadness rises like smoke
At dawn the shtetl rises in dew.

It's light and airy in the summertime fog.
From elevated distances in warmth and light
The air smells of wine-bright apples
And the heart becomes wine-like and tight . . .

Not long ago I cursed and spited you.
Now you lie down, shtetl, silenced . . .
While I wander in this flowery, fruity smoke
And August lies here, transparent and cool.

(August 1925)[45]

The final poem in this examination of Kharik's shtetl poetry I have called *In Your Little Houses*. I based my translation on a complete four-section poem by that title in a Soviet edition of Kharik's work.[46] The oldest section, the fourth one, was written in August 1925, and appeared in *On the Land* as a three-stanza untitled poem. The other three sections came out separately in 1926, and later were edited together into this complete poem. *In Your Little Houses* is Kharik's most sentimental, most personally anguished poem.

It opens with a touching explanation of why the speaker is in the shtetl. "I would come to you, my little shtetl/Once again to see you long/In quiet, transparent sadness." There is nostalgia in the speaker's voice, especially in the endearing address to his personal shtetl along with the reminder that the shtetl is on the verge of death. From sentimentalism, the speaker moves to a series of introspective inquiries examining the painful effects his actions have had on the shtetl. The speaker is explaining or rationalizing his actions in this dialogue, where he takes responsibility for the sad empty shtetl's destruction. This confession is reminiscent of the first poem, *Shtetl*, but here critical contemplation and mournful nostalgia replace expressionist destruction. He has foolishly attempted to transform the physical landscape of Jewishness into a socialist utopia made "in stone and steel."

He says bluntly, "And you, little shtetl, I cannot hate," and concludes the first section: "You too must be experiencing May/Although you must call it Sivan. / But, even so, the sky remains blue over everything that remains. . . . " Sivan is the month on the Jewish calendar that usually corresponds to May on the Gregorian calendar. In addition, the month of Sivan contains the Jewish holiday Shavuot, the time when observant Jews remember the giving of the Torah – the source of truth, law, and wisdom – to Moses and the Jews at Mt. Sinai. Kharik uses this cultural reference to suggest that the month of May, which begins with May Day, the holiday of labor, might be the time of year for the Jews to receive a new kind of Torah, a new source of truth that will supplant the one associated with Sivan.[47] The speaker recognizes the inherent differences between the culture of the shtetl and his own; but at the same time he concludes with the transcendent blueness that can unify the two, the same blueness of Passover from his earlier *Shtetl* poems.[48] Bronshteyn wrote that this poem represented a new period in Kharik's work, the period of "reconciliation."

Section two introduces a second level of dialogue – between the speaker as a grown man and as a boy. Kharik opens with an image of the speaker witnessing the shtetl as a holiday candle dripping its silent wax as he walks around "filled with the silence of remembrance. . . . " Following this ellipsis, the speaker segues into a fairy tale about a boy who once lived a carefree life in the shtetl. The ellipsis that concludes the fairy tale suspends the reader between the mind of the speaker and that of the boy, as Kharik switches into the third person pronoun, "he," to create the ambiguity between the two. It is both the boy and the speaker who enjoyed the streets of the shtetl and who questioned the desire for the shtetl's destruction.

The second section closes with the elliptical separation of the boy and the speaker, but then Kharik reveals that the two have the same mother and are in fact the same person. The two could not see themselves in the other, except through the image of their mother who sleeps, as if she were dead, in the tomb that is his past. She rests peacefully with these memories, while he only feels torment.

At this point, the young speaker expresses his despondency that, unlike his mother, he cannot be at peace in these silent surroundings. He wonders to himself, "Shtetl, little shtetl, my dried up branch, / Will you once again turn green? / I walk around, a quiet guest, in silence." This torment pushes him to look for hope in a rebirth of the shtetl, but this nostalgic yearning reminds him that he is just a guest. As he reveals in the next lines, he can only be comfortable at "home" in the silent recollections of his childhood, as he begins to feel longing for the shtetl – a nostalgia similar to the one expressed in the opening. He is in fact envious of other artists who managed to feel at home in two worlds, such as Esenin, whom the speaker mentions explicitly in the poem.[49] The speaker may also mention Esenin together with despondency as a reference to Esenin's 1925 suicide that shook up the Soviet literary community. His ambivalence reaches a fevered angst in the final stanza of the section.

Kharik closes with the speaker reflecting on the universality of nature and on his confused, nostalgic, regretful mood, and then returns to the themes in the opening section – the arrival of the speaker in the peaceful shtetl. What strikes the reader is that the summer has passed as we have gone through the four sections of the poem. While the first reflections took place in the late-springtime mildness of May, the closing scene is surrounded by the cool, late-summer blue of August. Kharik focuses on the natural landscape in this section, on the sights, smells, and sounds, but in modernist guise using oxymoronic word combinations such as "smiling sadness" or the unusual senses evoked in the use of the Yiddish adjective *vaynik*, winelike or winey. It is not the sweetness, nor romantic drunkenness that wine brings on, but it is its clarity (*klore*) and its thickness (*gedikht*), again seemingly oxymoronic descriptions.

Kharik, however, does not leave the reader on a note of sensory perception. In the final stanza, the speaker turns back to the curse and to his anguish that lingers in the perfumed air. All that remains of his shtetl is the sweetened smoke of apples and August. Kharik introduces the image of "pleasant-smelling smoke (*reyach nechoach*)," a Biblical reference to the burnt offerings at the Temple. The reference appears repeatedly in Leviticus and Numbers to describe the pleasant odor that emanated from burnt offerings for God.[50]

This was not the first time Kharik had introduced the image of smoke. It also appeared throughout *Shtetl*, where its meaning was ambiguous since it resembled both an offering and the remnants of destruction: "I alone helped to destroy them / And sent them away in smoke. . . ." In both poems, the speaker contemplates his romanticization of and revulsion toward his childhood, his memory, and ultimately, his identity. With the introduction of the Biblical reference to burnt offerings, the reader sees the speaker's destructive act as a divine command to bring on redemption. There is lingering sweetness in his pile of rubble (an image from another of his poems), but all that remains is the transparency of August (not Av, nor Elul, the equivalents on the Jewish calendar and the time of year for Jewish soul searching). All that remains, then, is time itself.

The poem and the *Shtetl* series could not have ended on a more ambivalent note. Kharik's shtetl is Sodom, a place burned for its sins; a burnt offering, an object destroyed to please God; and the Temple, a holy place whose burning caused the dispersion of the Jews.

The process of modernizing the shtetl invariably results in its destruction; however, it is ambiguous what the motivation for its destruction is. What the "natural" process of progress has not passively destroyed, the speakers of Kharik's poetry have had to destroy actively. And in doing this, the speaker feels the pain of guilt at having to destroy a part of himself to be true to redemptive ideals. Dobrushin thought that the pain and anguish in Kharik's *Shtetl* cycle, although a part of Soviet construction, were more importantly seen as a part of Kharik's own despondency that came from destroying himself.[51] Kharik's sensitive rendering of this personal and political dilemma poignantly encapsulated the paradox in building a new Soviet Jewish culture and, through this culture, a Soviet Jewish identity. To "enlighten" those who had not yet seen the light, the young, modern activist had to destroy all that was connected to the "old" culture and the "old" identity. And in doing this, the radical modernizing project of the Soviet 1920s demanded of its adherents that they destroy the part of themselves that still identified with this past life.

WITH BODY AND SOUL (MINSK, 1928)

"In this narrative poem, Kharik expresses the suffering and yearnings of our Soviet Jewish folk intelligentsia. He expresses doubt and woe."
– Khatskel Dunets, 1929

The year 1928 was a turning point in Soviet culture. It marked Stalin's consolidation of power and the inauguration of the first Five-Year Plan, which directed the economy and society toward a program of crash industrialization and agricultural collectivization. In the cultural sphere, the period 1928–32 marked the heyday of the proletarian cultural activists, whose organizations were given the state's blessing to set cultural norms and the cultural agenda in art and literature. Finally, the period, also known as the "Great Break," showed the Party's emergence as the single source of truth in all spheres of life. In this context, the proletarian-dominated cultural world of the Soviet Union was a different place from that of the mid-1920s when Kharik's shtetl poems appeared.[52] Thus, it is all the more interesting that despite the increased official emphasis on building socialism, the ambivalence that permeated his earlier poetry continued to define his work in 1928.

With Body and Soul (Mit Layb un Lebn) tells the story of a Soviet Jewish teacher from a big city who is sent to smaller shtetls to set up Soviet Jewish schools, teach Yiddish, and work with local Jewish activists. Well before the book was actually published by the State Publishing House of Belorussia, Kharik held prepublication poetry readings to advertise his new work. One reading in February 1928, at the Minsk Jewish Lenin Club, "attracted a large crowd. The hall was full; everyone wanted to hear him." The reading was "a resounding success," because it proved that "writers [were] getting closer to their readers, and to other writers.... The reading lasted 45 minutes, and the audience listened attentively. After the reading, there were discussions about the work."[53]

The audience, made up of both well-known poets and critics such as Aaron Kushnirov and everyday patrons of the Yiddish club, gave their responses to *With Body and Soul*. Kharik then incorporated the audience's feedback into the final draft of the poem before it went to print. Kushnirov called the work a "colossal success of form. *With Body and Soul* is a joyous call of the new generation that is just now beginning in the USSR – a generation of great works with complicated content that are, at the same time, comprehensible to a broad reading audience." Others who attended the reading echoed Kushnirov's statement that Kharik successfully made high poetry accessible to the masses. No one offered any serious criticism.[54]

According to one critic, the publication and reception of *With Body and Soul* was also very successful. "Usually, a book reaches the editors, then writers and critics, and after they have made their evaluations, a new book usually goes straight into the abyss [*in di tifenish*]. Kharik's narrative poem went straight into the city and the shtetl. The editors have been getting letters about disputes over the poem that took place at intelligentsia meetings."[55]

In November 1928, after the book came out, there was a reading at the Jewish Teacher's College in Gomel, and the correspondent covering the event gave unattributed quotes that reflected the generally positive opinions expressed at the reading.

"Although everything is real, there's no role for the Communist youth league in the shtetl."
"It's a real slice of life. The shtetl is portrayed as it really is – naturally."
"*With Body and Soul* is a breakthrough in Yiddish literature. We have, for the first time, a Jewish teacher as the central character. ... The narrative poem is beautiful, attractive, and interesting and displays Kharik's lyricality and softness. His main character, the teacher, is quite stark. He really gets into her soul."[56]

At one other public reading in Vitebsk, a teacher in a shtetl pointed out that the poem makes it seem as if the protagonist is alone in her fight for reconstructing the shtetl.[57]

Despite a climate in which literature was expected to positively represent the building of socialism, and a climate of increasingly public criticism of literature, no one painted *With Body and Soul* – a dark portrayal of the trials of culture building – in a negative light. According to a survey taken of the readers at the Central Minsk Jewish Workers' Club library, it was the most popular Soviet Yiddish poem for the year 1928–9.[58]

The title of the poem, loosely translated as "With Body and Soul," on the surface suggests a call for complete investment in the building of socialism.[59] Such proclamations to socialist construction were pervasive in literature of the time, which was mobilized to reflect the new socialist reality of an industrializing country and collective agriculture, all with the goal of building socialism in the Soviet Union. The poem opens with the epigraph, "I wanted to dress you up in stone and steel, oh shtetl of mine" – a line from his earlier shtetl poem. The epigraph reminds readers of a continuing ambivalence about this cultural and political project. On the one hand, a shtetl in stone and steel is an image suggesting the modernization of rural and semirural areas across the Soviet Union, but by using the verb *to dress up* (*onton*), Kharik implies that the remaking of the shtetl is a superficial process of putting the old in new garb. "Dressing up" suggests a masquerade; it does not imply changing the internal workings of the shtetl. At the same time, it also reminds the reader that the abstract process of industrialization means destroying very personal parts of one's past, especially with the endearing address "oh shtetele of mine."

Kharik opens with a phrase in Russian, "We, the young guard [*My, molodaia gvardiia*]." *Molodaia Gvardiia*, the young guard, was one of the proletarian poets' organizations to which a number of Yiddish poets belonged. This opening call is a political and ideological statement to the reader that the poem should be read against the background of proletarian poetry. The opening lines describe a scene in the outdoors, and a familiar theme of poetry – the autumn, a time associated with partings and endings. The first section finishes with another familiar image of a passenger talking with a carriage driver, and asking him if he knows a song from the Sholem Aleichem play, *200,000*, that was popular on the Soviet Yiddish stage.[60] Kharik alludes to contemporary Soviet Jewish culture and attempts to create new intertextual references within it, not just with prerevolutionary writers and with traditional Jewish texts. By 1928, Soviet Yiddish culture had been sufficiently developed to have a textual history of its own, as the titles of the narrative poem's next sections show.

The following scene opens with "a shtetl with lanes and streets / you can go through the whole town in twelve minutes...." This impressionistic tour through the old shtetl mentions *melameds* and *heders* – the traditional Jewish teachers and schools that went underground in the 1920s after Soviet Jewish activists attempted to destroy traditional Jewish education and replace it with a Communist Jewish one. At this point the reader is introduced to the protagonist, the "she" whom the narrator has referred to since the opening chapter. "She" is a Communist teacher, unnamed in the text, who has been sent to this unnamed shtetl to "Sovietize" it, which meant to battle religious recidivism and to train the younger generation in new forms of Soviet Jewish identification. The first encounter the activist has is with a *melamed*. Traditional Jewish ideology reserved formal religious education for boys. The dialogue between the male *melamed* and the female teacher undermines the traditional sexual separation between males and females that was a foundation of Jewish culture and a site of satire and criticism by modernizing cultural activists. Kharik also uses this interaction to show the hardships the shtetl has undergone. The *melamed's* family is poor and hungry, placing the cultural battles within the context of socio-economic transformation. The Soviet attack on traditional forms of education and the economic destruction of shtetl society forced *heders* to readjust their teaching methodology and invite girls who could pay tuition to study.

Kharik continues the subversion of gender separation in the first chapter's final passage. The teacher is walking through the streets of the shtetl when someone calls out, "Hey everyone, look, a boy! Look, short hair means short on brains," a reference to the fact that as Jewish men aged and grew "wiser," their hair and beards got longer. The teacher responds confidently, "Good morning, boys. A good morning to you," as she passed by and smiled. In traditional Jewish culture, short hair, as the Soviet Jewish teacher had, was a sign of immaturity and a lack of masculinity. The children, though, had no idea how right they were in accusing the "boy" of not being a man. In Soviet Jewish schools, long beards and hair were signs of benighted tradition. Kharik shows in this scene and the next how hair reflected one's Jewish and gender identity and how others used hair to interpret identity.

Placing a woman (masquerading as a boy) as the protagonist was also a transgressive move in Jewish literature, in which the modern, estranged intellectual was always male. The image of the wandering male intellectual originated with the autobiographies of the nineteenth-century *maskilim* and developed in early twentieth-century Hebrew literature in the form of the *talush* – the estranged, uprooted intellectual (male) who could call no place home.[61] The woman as poetic persona had become a more common move within modernist Jewish literature, especially in the work of figures such as David Fogel and David Hofshteyn. Although her appearance is transgressive within Jewish culture, in the Soviet 1920s, the woman as protagonist was a way of showing Soviet society's enlightened attitude toward gender, and was thus conventional by radical Soviet literary standards. So by centering this poem around a woman, Kharik broke with Jewish tradition by using an established convention of both Jewish modernism and Soviet ideology.

The second chapter opens with the shtetl preparing for the upcoming holiday of Yom Kippur. The young woman's identity is finally revealed to the characters in the poem – she is a teacher in a Soviet Jewish school, and she wanders the empty streets in silence on the eve of Yom Kippur, when the Kol Nidre prayer is chanted. She continues walking as she sees a group of Jewish Communist youth members arguing with each other about their failure to put on an evening antireligion program, which had become the typical Communist youth counteraction to traditional Jewish holidays. The teacher leads the group in singing (as opposed to praying) and in doing so, she become one of them.

She resembles the speaker in many of the earlier shtetl poems – a lonely revolutionary who cannot be a part of the traditional world that she, presumably, has left; nor is she completely a part of the Communist youth planning an upcoming antireligion event. Her character is further complicated by the title of this section, "If Not Higher." The Y. L. Perets story by the same name centers on a *rebbe*, the leader of a hasidic community, in a small shtetl who leaves home every Friday morning to do mysterious tasks. One day, a skeptical rationalist Jew follows the rebbe and finds that he spends this time posing as a Christian peasant, chopping firewood to keep a poor woman warm. The story, relying on the Kabalistic idea of descending into the world in order to raise one up spiritually, emphasizes the rebbe's higher spiritual calling and his ability to be of various worlds to accomplish his holy tasks. In the end, the rationalist becomes one of the rebbe's disciples. Unlike Perets's hero, the Communist woman in Kharik's poem has structured her life to be in the Communist world and does not succeed in bringing redemption for herself or for others; she fails to fit into any world comfortably.

Bronshteyn argued that Kharik's allusion to traditional Jewish texts and forms – in this case the Perets story – was simply a clever way of parodying traditional culture. By implying that Kharik's reference to Jewish literature was a farce, Bronshteyn was trying to bring Kharik's work into the dominant narrative strategy Soviet Jewish cultural activists used to describe the traditional Jewish past – satire.[62] However, in this particular case, Kharik is not parodying, but wants to imbue the idea of a "higher calling" with more ambivalence and complexity and does this by drawing on the spirituality and social critique of the Perets story.

As the narrative picks up in chapter three, the teacher has a nightmare. In it, she is in a room during a snowstorm feeling that the shtetl is becoming an abandoned prison. Kharik focuses on her cell walls – "on her narrow walls, Mendele and Lenin are both smiling." In this image, the reader sees the schoolteacher's two icons. The "patron saint" of Yiddish literature in this case is S. Y. Abramovitch (also known as Mendele). The "grandfather" of Yiddish literature and the master of *maskilic* satire, Abramovitch was an appropriate choice for a Soviet Jewish activist's icon corner.[63] Earlier Yiddish *maskilic* writers had neither Mendele's talent nor his iconic status, and later Yiddish writers did not have his biting satire and social criticism. Lenin's presence is perhaps less noteworthy. By 1928, he had been deified by Stalin, given a mausoleum on Red Square, and had become revered by all as the successor to Marx and Engels in the pantheon of Communist ideology.

One of the most anguished scenes in the poem comes when the teacher takes the children on a tour of the old shtetl: "Come with me, little children, come and I will show/how in the shtetl live hungry old men with beards hanging low." She begins the tour of broken old stores, houses falling down, and something hits her, something Kharik incorporated in all of his poems related to the shtetl. "She thought for a while, the time passed very slow. 'You know children, I think, we've come to the end of our show.' Such sadness in the shtetl the children should not know/happy tales and legends now need to grow." Kharik's schoolteacher feels a similar ambivalence about the destruction of the shtetl, and in this case, the pain of raising small children on the ashes of the past.

This scene raises another question – the creation of an alternate reality of happiness and joy, a hallmark of socialist realism. Socialist realist writers portrayed a new "reality" in which the building of a socialist society and the industrialization and collectivization of the socio-economic system were described as joyous events. Although many historians have documented the brutality of the first Five-Year Plan, the literary representations of these events and the Soviet discourse in which these representations fit created a world of popular support, happy toilers, and socialist harmony.[64] The teacher does not want the children to see the destructive reality of the Communist project, but rather wants to turn their attention to the joyous building of socialism. Kharik portrays the moment when, for the teacher, participating in the socialist realist creation of an alternate reality supersedes grim reality. Critics also commented on the distance between reality and representation. Khatskel Dunets, a proletarian critic who reviewed the poem, claimed, "She dreams of one thing, but sees another in reality." As with the picture of the teacher trying to shield the children from the naked reality of poverty in the shtetl, Dunets recognized the distance between the hopes that the shtetl would someday be "dressed in stone and steel" and the reality of a dying way of life.[65]

The fifth chapter cuts away from the actions of the schoolteacher – which include long descriptions of natural landscapes and even a love affair with a man in the shtetl – and introduces a brief correspondence relating to an earlier section of the poem that describes the migration of Jews from shtetls to Moscow. The letters are simply titled "Letter from Moscow" and "Letter to Moscow."

Letter from Moscow
In the beginning I'd like to let you
know
That thank God we're actually
quite rich.
We are not in any way reaching
for the stars
But here in Moscow we feel equal
to everyone else.
I manage to pray close by with a
whole minyen
And every minyen is packed
beyond full.
"God bless that old Kalinin."
They say he protects our
synagogue.
My business does as well as when I
was in the shtetl.
And no longer, thank God, do I
feel want.
Come to us, don't make us beg.

Hey by the way, do you too have a
satiating piece of bread?

Letter to Moscow
On the date when the Torah portion
"Vayehi" is read in synagogue
To . . . and . . . May his light continue to
shine.

To this day I still feel very weak

I will already have to live out my years
here
For it's too late for me to live in a big city

One shouldn't wish downfall on anyone
Not even on the worst Bolshevik.

I work hard in a Soviet Jewish school

And nothing. At least I have this much
luck.
I thought that my little world was
coming to an end,
I would have to move on, with a sack
over my shoulder.
Now in my old age, I've become
A guard and a comrade in the union
I know that you won't want to hear
about that,
Soon you'll think I've become a goy.
My children have become pioneers.
So what? So nothing. Just like that.
Enough already. I'm running out of
paper.
Please say hello to your spouse, and be
well.
From me.
Oh, they say that in Moscow you can
Freely go see how
Lenin is still lying there in his tent,
untouched.[66]

These two letters embedded in Kharik's poem are a metonymy for larger social, psychological, and cultural experiences that shaped Kharik's work. Within the text, the letters represent the dialogue between the urbanizing Jews and those who remained in the shtetl. Kharik first introduced the theme of Jewish migration in the section of the poem "All the Generations of Moscow" (*Ale Toldes Moskve*), which reads like a Biblical rendering of the various social types who had left the shtetl and headed to Moscow: "And this is the number of people who have gone to Moscow: Four shopkeepers, one slaughterer, eight girls, who went there to study. Teachers, three or four, and twelve boys who went there for work ... and even the rabbi, yes the old rabbi, also got himself to Moscow, but he came back with gifts in his hands. . . . " Thus, the teacher is not the only connection the shtetl will have to the big city – everyone seems to know someone there.

The "Letter from Moscow" describes a good life of trade, prayer, and a sense of well-being. Not only is the writer comfortable in his social and economic status, he is also clearly comfortable with the new language rules of Yiddish that were established throughout the 1920s. The Yiddish in the first letter falls tightly within the parameters of reformed Soviet Yiddish. The only Hebraism he uses in this letter is "minyen" – traditionally the minimum number of Jewish men it takes to make a prayer quorum – and he spells out the word in phonetic Soviet Yiddish spelling. He also includes a reference to Soviet leaders, in this case to Kalinin, the president of the Soviet Union who was an outspoken advocate for Jewish cultural autonomy. The addition of the adjective *altitshke* or old man makes the statement somewhat tongue-in-cheek and more colloquial as the expression *altitshker Kalinin* or in Russian *Starosta Kalinin,* which was a widespread way of referring to the ever-present figurehead leader of the Soviet state. Interspersed throughout the letter, Kharik includes exclamations with religious origins (*Thank God, Got zay dank*, for example), and the remark about the freedom to pray, emphasized with the iterative construction "*davenen davn ikh*" (I pray my prayers). Overall, this letter gives a sense of the freedom in Moscow under NEP and makes Moscow the place of vitality and creativity – even for traditional Jewish practices – in contrast to the second letter and its dreary portrayal of life in the shtetl.

"A Letter to Moscow" depicts at the broadest level the failures of Soviet Jewish policies in the shtetls. The letter reveals the story of an older man, stuck in the shtetl, who has decided to do what he can to survive there and to participate in the process of Sovietization, which includes new Soviet Jewish schools and collective farms. He is clearly dissatisfied with his life. He feels weak, is growing old, and doesn't even have enough paper to finish writing his letter. As a worker in a Soviet school whose children are both Communist Pioneers, this character could have been proud and boastful of this new life.[67]

Rather, Kharik portrays him as a pathetic depressed old man, lamenting his situation.

The use of language in the second letter is also radically different, with a strikingly high percentage of Hebrew root words. The letter opens with a Hebrew language address and closes with the Hebrew word *zugatekha* (your partner or spouse). Hebrew root words like *krakh* (city) or *mapole* (downfall) stand out at the end of lines, and the Hebrew spelling of the word *khaver* (*khet, vet, resh*) was not politically correct by 1927, since the phonetic Soviet spelling had become standard parlance in all publications.

Even beyond the letter, language politics play a large role throughout the poem. In the sixth chapter, the teacher attends a meeting to establish a Jewish council (*soviet*) in a village. Delegates at the meeting argue about how to refer to the council: "After the teacher spoke, one guy asked her, 'Which is more correct – *rat* [Yiddish for council] or *sovet* [Russian]?'" And she answered him: "*rat*." Although Yiddish speakers and most English speakers refer to these councils as "soviets" – from the Russian *sovet* – in the poem, the teacher insists that it is more proper to use the Yiddish word. Later, she trains other activists how to translate familiar Soviet terms into Yiddish.[68] In the description of this meeting and in the letters' diction, Kharik placed the question of language at the center of Soviet Jewish culture building.

As the "Letter to Moscow" progresses in its litany of complaints, the writer reaches his climax with a statement questioning his very identity: "You might even mistake me for a *goy*." This statement, taken out of context, could easily be viewed as boasting about the level of assimilation that a Jewish Communist had reached. But given the context of this lament, he makes this statement to his Moscow Jewish friend out of shame. The relocated Jew, the trader in Moscow, is the one who prays in a minyen and has set up a comfortable Jewish life for himself. The Jew who did not move has lost himself in the Sovietization of the shtetl. The postscript is an envious remark about a dynamic Jewish life in Moscow and a somewhat sardonic comment on the politics of the regime, with the comment about the great leader, "lying in his tent." The "tent" was also a traditional structure of a Jewish grave thus placing Lenin in a Jewish context. It also sealed the relationship between these two men, between Jews in Moscow and those in the provinces, and in a larger sense, the relationship between Moscow and the provinces. As the title of each letter suggests, Moscow is now the center of Jewish life.

Embedded letters reappear farther along in the narrative, and once again, they paint a picture of happiness in the city, desolation in the provinces and shtetls. These letters are titled simply "To . . ." and "From. . . ." Unlike the first letters, these are going to and from a shtetl. The first letter is written by a seamstress, presumably living in Moscow, or at least some large city, as she asks her addressee,

"What's going on now in the provinces [*af di erter*]?" The seamstress is content and spends most of the letter describing the new technological wonders of her Selifakter sewing machine, which has made her life easy. Her friend, for whom "things are difficult," struggles to work the land and spends most of the letter complaining about how the shtetls are silent and covered in snow. These letters reinforce the idea that economic and Jewish cultural dynamism is situated in Moscow, death and stillness in the shtetls.[69]

This section of the poem concludes with images of socialist construction, although once again Kharik undermines what should be triumphant socialist realist imagery. The same teachers' meeting at which activists were arguing about *rat* or *sovet* concludes with a children's performance describing the building of a factory in the shtetl. The children curse the shtetl's "streets dusty and terrified," a similar image to the representations in Kharik's earlier cycle. In place of the old dilapidated houses rises a factory "taller than the highest wall." The children's performance closes with a song about the joy of labor. But the realism of socialist construction is actually fantasy – this is a children's performance, and the activists, the ones who should be building socialism, are the audience. Socialist construction is something the activists of the poem only witness; they don't actually participate.[70]

In the last sections, the narrator shifts between third and first person, between narrative and self-reflection. After the meetings in the shtetl, the teacher goes to Moscow for a Union-wide teachers' conference. While in the big city, she runs into an old friend on the streets, not a surprise given the strong connections between Moscow and the shtetl that have been established throughout the poem. At this point, the narrative flashes back to a "three-day conference in the regional capital." To undermine any semblance of heroism and joy in participating in these conferences, the teacher is described as arriving at the regional conference in the middle of the night, "silent and pale. She got out of the sleigh alone, reached the porch and smiled strangely. She could not make it all the way to the house." Our hero activist, who converted a shtetl, who trained younger activists in Yiddish, has worked herself sick. She collapses in the snow only to be helped by a peasant. This is the reader's segue into the grand all-Union teachers' meeting in Moscow.

The narrator describes a meeting of Communist teachers on the *yom tov* (holiday) of March 8 – International Women's Day. There are flags waving, people cheering, and the crowd of teachers is greeted with warm words from none other than Anatoly Lunacharsky, the Soviet commissar of enlightenment. The activist is at the highest echelons of cultural power. And just when the reader feels comfortable that the poem might end heroically, "at exactly 10:20 – at exactly 10:20 blood started spurting from her throat," presumably from tuberculosis, or whatever disease had caused her to be sick throughout the second half of the poem and collapse in the snow. The crowd panics; someone calls for a doctor, but he takes too long to come. As she lay there dying, she reflects on the children's play she had seen back in the shtetl. Her thoughts become more confused, her represented speech more broken. External time moves forward "1:30 P.M., 1:40 P.M.," but in her head, time goes backward. The woman dies at the meeting. Her last moan on the conference floor starts out in Yiddish, but concludes in Russian: "*Di na-akht vet haynt du-u-rkh-geyn be sho-o-o-lem. / Da-a-a. . . .* [This ni-ight will pa-as-s in pe-ea-ce. Yes.]" In her death, her identity only becomes more confused, between languages and cultures.

The next section, "At the Marketplace," moves the narrative from the urban Women's Day celebration and scene of death back to the shtetl as the caretaker (*shames*) of the Jewish cemetery decides where to bury the teacher. Emphasizing her ambivalent identity, the *shames* says, "We should bury her on the other side of the fence, and bury the body far away. / With her feet in a church! And with her head in the ground! We are not preparing a burial space for her." Her confused identity in life carried over into her death. The person standing watch over the body says *kaddish* – the traditional prayer over the dead – for the teacher and goes to her Communist funeral. Communist youth stand guard at the door as a klezmer band begins to play. They carry her body to the gravesite, close her eyes, and cover her with sand.

The final two stanzas repeat the image of the opening one – a beautiful clear day and a cart bumping along with a woman in the back, the same scene that introduced the first school teacher. This scene may be introducing a new teacher who is arriving in the shtetl exactly as her predecessor arrived. But here, there are two competing interpretations. Two contemporary critics saw the repetition of the first two stanzas as a reminder that, although the first comrade died under the burden of her work, another will always be there to follow. The building of socialism is unstoppable. This reading allowed the critics to draw a positive conclusion from Kharik's morbid ending. But the actual description of the approach of the second activist is more ambiguous: "She rolls around the cart/And scrunched together her dried up arms. She cannot lie there still and wait. / 'Let it go,' and she pulls away from the cart." Given the description of the girl "rolling around" in the cart, and that she "pulls away," along with the knowledge that the first activist was not in fact buried in the cemetery, one could interpret this image as the first schoolteacher's corpse being dumped by the side of the road, not as a new teacher coming to the shtetl.

Even if one accepts that the end portrays a "second activist," the description of her presence encourages multiple readings. In this final scene, Kharik portrays the shtetl Jews encountering this new activist and asking her why she isn't feeling well, clearly worried about her health given the fate of the first activist who

had worked there. But that seems to have been the only interaction people had
with her: "No one came to greet the new guest in town / No one expressed
words of joy. / She lay down in a little room and stared silently like an August
sun disappearing in the sky. / But soon craftsmen came and surrounded her
on every side. 'Hey, comrade, have no fears. We'll fix everything . . . /But you
remember that your health is precious. Hey, do you hear us?'" Her silent gaze
is eerily reminiscent of the death scene of the first activist, and to emphasize
the corpse-like state, Kharik never has this second activist speak. Perhaps she is
already dead upon arrival in the shtetl; perhaps she is just a ghost of the first
one. In none of these readings is there glorious heroism or the triumph of
socialism. Contemporary readers, even more than literary critics, recognized
this, and wrote to the editor complaining bitterly that the teacher should not
have died.[71]

The teacher gave both her body and soul (*layb un lebn*) to her Communist
activity, but was not treated to a hero's burial. Her ambiguous identity in life
carried over into her death. Is she Jewish or Communist, "with us" or "against
us," urban or rural? Kharik colors the entire story with images of death as the
shtetl's Jews greet her "replacement," a seeming corpse in her own right.

Dunets suggested that Kharik's poem could have portrayed the shtetl more
positively.

It is true: why shouldn't we demand that in addition to the 'houses that are drooping
on one knee' these traditional poor homes of people from [Avrom] Reyzen's and
even Mendele's times – we should also see the new houses in the shtetl, the newly
built electric stations, the new people's houses? . . . In fact, a writer should not just
reflect; we've moved beyond that. A writer should portray something new – should
shine a ray of light and lead us somewhere. . . .[72]

In one pithy statement, Dunets summarized what perhaps should have been the
dominant response to this poem – that it should have been a more appropriately
socialist realist portrayal of the glorious transformation of the shtetl. Dunets
included references to a contemporary, popular, non-Soviet Yiddish writer and
to a classic writer, both of whom depicted the shtetl in various negative guises.
Dunets concluded his review by showing how Kharik did in fact "shine his
poetic light" on the shtetl. He emphasized that although cultural work in the
shtetl is difficult, or in this case deadly, other activists were there to continue
the work, and that the shtetl would, eventually, be "dressed in stone and steel."

In this chapter, I have offered a number of intertwined themes and ideas – the
confluence of Jewish, enlightenment, modernist, and Soviet ideologies informing the process of Soviet Jewish cultural production; a more varied understanding of Soviet Jewish culture; and most important, the place of the revolutionary
in his own revolutionary program. Izi Kharik's poetry suggested that becoming

a revolutionary was not just about breaks with the past, in this case the past as represented by the shtetl, but was as much about the lifelong process of accepting the consequences of actions taken in the name of higher ideals.

Kharik was not alone in recognizing that ambivalence was a defining feature of the ideology that drove the creation of Soviet Jewish culture. Shlomo Niepom-niashchy, a Hebrew-Yiddish–Russian writer and journalist, wrote a letter about the generation gap between the old Yiddish guard and the new one. In it, he described a conversation he had with a young Communist Yiddish writer who had started publishing poetry in Soviet Yiddish journals. Niepomniashchy read this young man selections from Sholem Aleichem's *Children's Stories*, but according to Niepomniashchy, "the trouble is that our new mass-reader has not begun to understand the meaning of *agmes nefesh* [aggravation] or *yerat-shamayim* [piety] . . . and the whole *kheder-besmidresh* [traditional Jewish schools] life is completely exotic to them." Niepomniashchy points out to the same young writer a mistake in a Boris Pilnyak story that portrays a Jew laying *tefillin* (phylacteries) in the middle of the night. Niepomniashchy laughs at Pilnyak's mistake, since Jews do not put on tefillin in the middle of the night. But "the young boy did not understand the mistake at all." Niepomniashchy even suggests that future editions of classic Yiddish fiction will have to come out with explanatory notes to describe the "lost" Jewish culture of the texts.[73] "The feeling is that we are really epigones of a way of life that is dying out. It's an unsettling feeling. It keeps us all 'in discontent,' . . . because there are no more relations between yesterday and tomorrow."

This group of ideologically driven Jewish intellectuals, including Kharik, Frumkina, Litvakov, and others, wanted to create a cultural system in which Jewish intellectuals could become a Soviet Yiddish intelligentsia and in which Jews en masse would develop a secular Soviet Jewish identity. For a very brief period, they succeeded. In her oral histories of Soviet Jews who grew up in the late 1920s, Anya Shternshis found that young Jews did develop a secular Jewish identity that differed from the more traditional identities of their parents and from the more Russified identities of their children.[74] The young author who does not know what *tefillin* are, but writes Yiddish poetry, is a model of the Soviet Jewish future. The destruction of the shtetl in Kharik's poetry and the project to create Soviet Jewish culture created ambivalent feelings about all that was lost in the process of establishing this new way of life.

Afterword

How Does the Story End?

Everyone discussed in this book, from Izi Kharik to Esther Frumkina, approached Soviet Yiddish culture for his or her own reasons, and it would be inappropriate to attribute collective motivations to personal actions and decisions. But if there is one thing the members of the intelligentsia had in common, one word that captures how they related to this project, it is *ambivalence*. Ambivalence is not usually the first term that comes to mind when describing an ideologically driven group of revolutionaries. After all, these were people impassioned enough about their project to close down synagogues, arrest rabbis, open up publishing houses and schools, reform a language, and write Communist-inspired Yiddish books and newspapers. And to carry this out, they worked their way into positions of power.

In order to build new cultures and identities, the intelligentsia also had to destroy the existing ones; and the destructive side of their acts of creation aroused feelings of ambivalence. One can begin to understand this group of Jewish revolutionaries as ambivalent by examining the building of Soviet Yiddish culture as the *unfolding* of a revolution, and by studying the intelligentsia's ideology as a process of *becoming* revolutionary, rather than by looking at revolution as a single event with a clear "before" and "after." Revolutionary ideology does not always result from an epiphany or a moment of conversion. Throughout the 1920s, Kharik expressed ambivalence about the destruction inherent in revolution. He felt ambivalent about what Soviet Jewish culture would look like in the future and also how that future would be realized. He did not, however, see his commitments to both a socialist and a Jewish revolution as contradictory or paradoxical, nor did he hide the fact that revolution necessitated destruction.

This project was defined by ambivalence from all sides, from those directly invested in a new kind of Jewish culture and from those who saw the building of Soviet Yiddish culture primarily as a means to the end of the state-building project. Stalin and Lenin had to convince other members of the Communist

Party that supporting ethnic intelligentsias would actually bolster the larger ideological and political goals of the socialist revolution and the Soviet state rather
than undermine those very goals through a perceived "bourgeois nationalism."
The relationship between state power and the Soviet Union's ethnic minorities
changed over time as Stalin, other members of the Party, and the ethnic intelligentsias themselves reexamined what it meant to be a socialist state. These
changing attitudes had unintended consequences, and in the 1930s and 1940s,
the state's lingering ambivalence began to have profound effects.

Unlike the 1920s, when the intelligentsia had institutional and ideological
power to shape Soviet Yiddish culture, in the 1930s, most members of the
Soviet Yiddish intelligentsia felt their power waning, even if the volume of
Soviet Yiddish books, newspapers, schools, and theater productions increased
through the middle of the decade. It was a time when publishing houses were
consolidated, when modernist literature gave way to Socialist Realism, when
violent debate about aesthetics and ideology among Soviet Yiddish writers'
groups gave way to bland speeches at meetings of the Union of Soviet Writers.
The politics and ideology of the Cultural Revolution and the institutionalization of Stalinism in the 1930s made the Communist Party the only source of
ontological truths. As the Party came to dictate the shape of culture building, the Soviet Yiddish intelligentsia lost its ideological power. In addition, as
the state centralized and consolidated its bureaucracies, the intelligentsia lost its
institutional capacity to shape Jewish culture.

Despite the loss of ideological and institutional power, members of the Soviet
Yiddish intelligentsia held positions of power through the 1930s. The Soviet
Writers' Union held its first Congress in August–September 1934, and en-
throned Socialist Realism as that which would define Soviet literature in all
languages. The Congress was a grand affair – 590 Soviet delegates attended
twenty-six sessions over a two-week period listening to more than 200 speeches
and reports.[1] Among the 300 delegates with voting rights, forty-four were
Jews, eight of whom were known as Yiddish writers: David Bergelson, Yashe
Bronshteyn, Khatskel Dunets, David Hofshteyn, Izi Kharik, Perets Markish,
Itsik Fefer, and Leyb Kvitko.[2] Two of them served on the Union's board – Itsik
Fefer (representing Ukraine) and Izi Kharik (representing Belorussia) – making
them the two most politically connected Yiddish writers in the Soviet Union.[3]

By the late 1930s, though, the Party's ambivalence about culture building for
its ethnic minorities led it to dismantle many of the policies that had called for
culture building. As a result, Yiddish schools, newspapers, and the majority of
institutions dedicated to Yiddish culture closed down. In addition to the policy
changes that led to the dismantling of cultural institutions, Stalin's consolidation
of power also led to the Great Purges, in which the key power brokers of Soviet
Yiddish culture were killed.

During his reign as de facto Jewish cultural commissar and editor of *Emes*, Moshe Litvakov made countless enemies, many of whom attempted to remove him from the Party ranks in the early 1930s. Despite these challenges to his authority, he kept his position as editor and remained chairman of the Moscow Union of Soviet Jewish Writers until September 1937. One month later, the general Union of Soviet Writers voted to expel Litvakov "in connection with [his] unmasking as an enemy of the people." In addition, the union vowed to "liquidate the dangerous legacies of *Litvakovism* in all areas in which he worked, especially in Yiddish literary criticism and in his role at *Der Emes*."[4] Litvakov was arrested shortly after the denunciation and was killed a few weeks later.[5] His newspaper, *Emes*, was closed down in 1938.

For a short time, Kharik became one of the most powerful Yiddish writers in the Soviet Union. In 1935, the Writers' Union sponsored a festival to celebrate the fifteenth anniversary of his writing career, which attested to his impressive reputation within Soviet literature. I.K. Mikitenko, a writer who attended the gathering as the representative of Ukrainian literature, announced: "The name Izi Kharik is synonymous with our socialist culture, and with our great motherland. . . . I've been all over Europe, and the name Kharik was popular everywhere. And not just as a Yiddish poet, but as a Soviet poet. . . . [In fact] he's more than a poet; he's reached the status of the 'philosophy of an era.'"[6] As we can see from Mikitenko's effusive praise, Kharik was no longer regarded as simply a member of the Soviet Yiddish intelligentsia and a Jewish activist; he was seen as a Soviet socialist poet and even as a philosopher.

By 1936, Kharik's work was read in Yiddish schools throughout Belorussia and had been translated into other languages. He served as editor-in-chief of an important literary journal and not only achieved literary status, but also became a member of the Central Committee of the Belorussian Communist Party. In 1936, when Stalin proclaimed the new Soviet Constitution, writers praised their Great Leader. Given his importance in the Soviet literary establishment, Kharik participated in the propagation of the Stalin cult, announcing at a party in December 1936, "Long live the great genius of humanity, Comrade Stalin, who has created unending possibilities for literary creation."[7] Kharik was at the peak of his career as a Soviet writer, but less than a year later, in 1937, he too was arrested and killed. In addition to the violence that befell Kharik and Litvakov, the entire Jewish Party leadership was caught up in the Great Purges that wiped out nearly 60 percent of the representatives to the Seventeenth Communist Party Congress of 1937 and nearly 80 percent of the Party's Central Committee. Other Jewish Party members were arrested, including Esther Frumkina, Semen Dimanshteyn, and Alexander Chemerinsky.[8] Members of ethnic minorities' intelligentsias were targeted both as Party members and as ethnic leaders, especially those who – like members of the Soviet Polish and German Party leadership – had ties to foreign countries.[9] In the 1930s, a person could be elevated to the level of national hero and then, as Litvakov, Kharik, and others discovered, be suddenly cursed as a saboteur, wrecker, or "enemy of the people."

But most of the less politically active members of the Soviet Yiddish intelligentsia – such as Hofshteyn and Bergelson – and even a few of the very powerful – including Fefer – survived the Purges only to witness the atrocities of World War II and the Holocaust. Fefer, whose poetic inspiration came directly from David Hofshteyn, was on the editorial boards of all the major journals, and took the high road to power by enmeshing himself within Soviet Yiddish literary politics at its centers in Ukraine and Moscow. During World War II, Fefer served on the Jewish Anti-Fascist Committee, the central state body devoted to Yiddish culture and politics during the war. He worked for the state in a different capacity after the war – by denouncing fellow Yiddish writers as bourgeois nationalists and rootless cosmopolitans during the anti-Semitic anti-cosmopolitan campaign in 1948–52. His allegiance to the Party and the state at the expense of his friends in the intelligentsia did not save him. He too was shot in prison on August 12, 1952, more than three years after all the remaining state Yiddish cultural institutions had been closed down.

✡   ✡   ✡

"Pinchas smiled again, then fell, his head landing on the stockingless calves of Zunser. One of his borrowed shoes flew forward, though his feet slid backward in the dirt. Bretzky fell atop the other two. He was shot five or six times, but being such a big man and such a strong man, he lived long enough to recognize the crack of the guns and know that he was dead." –Nathan Englander, the last sentences of his fictional short story, "The Twenty-seventh Man"

"When the final curtain was lowered on the Yiddish stage, it fell with the force of iron." –Jeffrey Veidlinger, the last sentence of his book, *The Moscow State Yiddish Theater*

"By reducing Jewish nationality to a denationalized Yiddish language and by suppressing more than a thousand years of Jewish culture, the Bolsheviks insured that the march of History would not be interrupted." –Zvi Gitelman, the last sentence of his book, *Jewish Nationality and Soviet Politics*

Tragic stories end when heroes die. Many of the Soviet Yiddish intelligentsia's heroes were killed by the state that empowered them to build Soviet Yiddish culture. Historians and even many fiction writers, including Englander – whose short story both begins and ends this book – retell Soviet Jewish history through a tragic lens. Since tragedy is a compelling motif, the most straightforward way to close this book would have been with the deaths of the protagonists.

But tragedies have to have clear endings. For Englander, it was August 12, 1952; for Veidlinger, the closing of the Yiddish theater in 1949. But does the story of Soviet Yiddish culture really have such a clear ending? I end my narrative, more or less, in 1930, when institutional consolidation took power away from the intelligentsia, despite the fact that more Yiddish books and newspapers continued publication and more theater productions and schools were opening. A possible ending could have been in 1937, when Kharik and others were killed in the Purges, even if the most famous Yiddish writers continued to produce poetry. It also could have ended in 1948–9, when all state-sponsored Yiddish cultural production was halted, or on August 12, 1952, when the remaining members of the early generations of the intelligentsia were killed off. Although this narrative focuses on the 1920s, that is not an indication that 1930 should be considered an end or the moment marking "failure," but rather a time when power was taken away from the intelligentsia and when the process of cultural production changed.

The project to create a secular Yiddish culture and a people who identified with that culture succeeded in the 1920s.[10] Secular Yiddish writers penned poetry, school children studied Sholem Aleichem from a Marxist perspective, and Soviet judges conducted trials in Yiddish. But ultimately the project to make Yiddish the marker of Jewish ethnic difference in the Soviet Union did not succeed. By the late 1930s, Jewish children no longer went to Yiddish schools. Birobidzhan did not become the homeland of Soviet Jewry. And, after World War II, Russian replaced Yiddish as the dominant language of Soviet Jews. The overall project did not succeed, because the majority of Soviet Jews did not necessarily support it, and because Stalin had other ideas about the future of Soviet Jewry and the future of ethnic minorities in the Soviet Union. It seems everyone was ambivalent about this project.

The case of Yiddish shows that building Soviet culture took various forms in different languages depending on the needs and desires of the particular intelligentsia driving the project. By becoming part of the state and using the state's power, the Soviet Yiddish intelligentsia created the institutions, cultural products, and, ultimately, the people who embodied a particularly Jewish *Soviet* culture, and a particularly Soviet *Jewish* culture. The intelligentsia also used state power to suppress some forms of Jewish culture and identity while building new ones. But in the end, that same state power was turned against them, as Kharik, Litvakov, Frumkina, and nearly all the other members of the Soviet Yiddish intelligentsia eventually discovered. The story, like its characters, ends ambivalently.

Appendixes

Author's Note: All originals are taken from Izi Kharik, *Mit Layb un Lebn* (Moscow: Sovetskii pisatel', 1970) and I have transliterated based on the book's Yiddish spellings, which do not always correspond with YIVO's standard.

Shtetl

A fremder gast in shtetl iz gekumen,
A fremder gast –
Mit umru in di trit . . .
S'hot dortn keyner nit derkent zayn umru,
Un keyner hot im nit gefregt
Bist mid?. .

Dem bloyen himl hot getsoygn tsu farnakht dan,
Un shtilkayt hot nokh emetsn geveynt,
Ale kromen shoyn fun lang farmakht dort
Un keyner darf shoyn dort nit geyn aheym . . .

Biz tif in nakht
Durkh shtetldikn hefker
Gegangen iz der gast azoy aleyn,
Un nit gevart, un nit gebetn:
"Efnt" –
Ba letster tir fun opgenitster heym.

Er hot gehert un hern nit gekent mer,
Vi shtetl ligt farbrokhn hinter ployt . . .
—Gut, – hot er gezogt,—
Zol brenen!—
Un iz avek farshpart un harterheyt.

Un biz fartog hot er gehert,
Vi vintn
Heys hobn mit fayer un mit shtetele geklogt . . .
A letstn mol hot er a kuk getun af hinter,
Un iz avek, un s'hot getogt.

2

A lester roykh hot tsugedekt mayn shtetl,
Un letstn roykh hot ongeshikt der vint.
Oy, bizvan, un oy, bizvanen betn zikh:
— Shtetele, farshvind.

Inmitn veg, tsvishn bloye traktn
Ligstu alts un kenst nokh nit avek.
A brokh tsu ale grayze tates,
Vos hobn nit farloshn dayne teg —

Un dikh gelozt af shvaygn un af vartn!—
Shvererheyt zol durkhforn a rod
Un dikh tsetreyslen biz dayn krankn hartsn,
Trot – nokh trot . . .

Ikh veys: di teg zaynen getseylte,
Un yeder tog dayner iz oysgeveytekt royt.
Oy, ven kh'gleyb un ken dir oyshakn a tseylem:
A letstn shoymer af dayn toyt.

3

In tifn hoyf fargeyt zikh a harmonik
Un lesht zikh oys tsvishn kile vent,—
Farvilt zikh dan un kh'ken zikh nit dermonen,
Vos iz amol geven.

Shtetl, shtetl, shtilinks un fartroyerts,
Biz letstn dakh farlozn un aleyn . . .
Treft nokh ven, af hekhstn fun di moyern
Dergeyt tsu mir dayn trukener geveyn.

Ven kh'bin dos ershte mol avek fun dayne geslekh,
Mayn yugnt hot nokh shtilerheyt gebrent,
Gemeynt hob ikh – me tor dikh nit fargesn
Un shtendik muzstu nokhgeyn in der fremd . . .

Bin ikh avek geboygn nokhn vogn,
Dos gantse lebn tsugedrikt tsum layb . . .
Arufgefirt hot shtot af hekhstn fun di shtokn,
Tsugefirt tsum fenster: blayb!

Iz gut atsind bam fenster zikh dermonen
Un gringerheyt a makh tun mit di hent...
Hern shtil, vi s'tsit nokh der harmonik
Un lesht zikh oys, vi keynmol nit geven.

4
A nakht, vi ale nekht in bloyen,
Vi ale nekht iz umruik un shtil...
Ikh ken haynt nit mayn royen vey tseveyen,—
Ikh heyb zikh uf a luftiker un – shvim.

A himl. A meshugene levone
Tsitert uf un rayst zikh shtreng un sharf,
Es rayst dos harts un redt, vi toyznt fonen.
Vi toyznt fonen rayst zikh mayn badarf...

Ikh ken zikh nit in aza nakht baruikn,
Az s'tsit avek un s'trogt af vey un vind,
Mame, mame, s'iz dayn zun meshuge
Un flit arum a bloyer afn vint...

Ikh kuk zikh ayn durkh dorsht fun mayne oygn
Un lenger-lenger tsi ikh oys mayn haldz:
Gevezn zaynen shtetelekh farleygt do
In shtiler ru mit shtiln broyt un zalts.

Hob ikh aleyn geholfn zey tseshtern
Un opgeshikt zey alemen in roykh...
Itster her ikh shoyn, vi s'tsitern di shtern,
Vi s'tsit avek un s'trogt mikh in der hoykh.
Yun 1924

APPENDIX II

Broyt
(poeme)
Araynfir

Af geslekh leydike un mide
Leygt zikh nokh shtayfer mayne trit...
Haynt batog hot mikh a shtetele mit yidn
Ongerufn: antisemit!

Ale zey, in knetshn un in shmates,
Hobn alts gevizn mit di hent:
"Ot der, – mir kenen im, i im, i tate-mame,
Hot er zikh fun undz azoy farfremdt...

Vilt zikh tsugeyn, tsugeyn un im zogn:
Herstu, khaver, s'iz azoy undz shlekht,
Oyb me ken undz alemen dershlogn,
Volt ba undz zayn rekht . . .

Shver tsu zayn, tsu shtarbn mitn shtetl,
Host dokh oykh amol do ven gelebt,
Zog, – ver vet undz do retn,
Ver vet aynhaltn di kep? . ."

Hob ikh zey ongekukt: ale leydike un toyte,
Berd, un berd, un vider toyte berd . . .
— Genug, – hob ikh gezogt, – fun leydikn un greytn,
Mit erd, tsu erd! Ven nit – iz . . .

Hot shtetele tseshrien zikh in fiber,
Yedes vort un yeder trot – a shnit.
Veys ikh nit, farvos hot mikh a shtetele mit yidn
Ongerufn: antisemit.

APPENDIX III

Fargeyt, ir umetike zeydes . . .

Fargeyt, fargeyt, ir umetike zeydes,
Mit berd tseshrokene, farlofene mit shney! . .
In letstn brokh, in letstn vey
Zayt ir farblibn letste eydes,—
Fargeyt, fargeyt, ir umetike zeydes!

Az vind, az vey tsu ayer gantsn shtetl
Tsetrotenem in veytik un in noyt . . .
Tsu yedn hungerikn bisn broyt
Hot ir fun lang geshmeykhlt un gebetlt,—
Az vind, az vey tsu ayer gantsn shtetl.

Un kukt ir itst tseshrokene un mide,
Un s'tsitern un s'treyslen aykh di kni.
— Ver veyst, ver veyst, oyb s'veln di,
Oyb s'veln ot di zin shoyn blaybn yidn?—
Un s'tsitern un s'treyslen aykh di kni.

Un mir, ot di, vos rufn aykh nokh zeydes,—
Un veysn, az dos darf men shoyn nit lang,—
Mir geyen uf, vi ershter klang,
Vi ershter klang fun kumendike freydn,
Mir, ot di, vos rufn aykh nokh zeydes.

Iz gut araynkukn in umetike oygn,
Ven fremd iz ayer veytik fun di berd . . .
Mir – ot di un di, – s'iz undz bashert,
S'iz undz bashert shoyn keynmol zikh nit beygn.
Fargeyt, fargeyt, ir umetike oygn!

APPENDIX IV

Antloyfn? Ikh ken nit, ikh vil nit antloyfn,
Un s'vert shoyn do umeglekh vayter tsu zayn.
Es hot zikh der khurbn tseleygt af di hoyfn,
In shoybn – farloshene tropelekh shayn.

Gornisht un leydikayt.
Pustke un vintn.

Es hengt do a shtile, farloshene sho . . .
Ikh gey, un mir dakht zikh – me geyt nokh fun hintn,
Ker ikh zikh um, – iz do keyner nito.

Gey ikh pamelekh, un s'vilt zikh mir yogn . . .
Es hilkht do tseshrokn mayn trot af der erd.
Trog ikh zikh um, un ikh bet zikh: zol togn,
Zol togn, zol togn! Ikh ken shoyn nir mer.

APPENDIX V

In dayne hayzelekh . . .

I
Nit derfar, vayl do iz eng,
Volt ikh tsu dir, mayn shtetele, gekumen
Nokhamol a kuk tun, vi du benkst
In shtiln durkhzikhtikn umet . . .

Vos hob ikh, shtetele, fun dir gevolt,
Vos hob ikh, shtetele, mit dir getaynet,—
Ikh hob gevolt in shteyn un shtol
dikh ontun, shtetele du mayns.

Ikh hob gevolt, dayn yeder shtub
Zol oysvaksn in shtoltse gorns,
Un du zolst mer nit shvaygn shtum
Af dayne oysgelebte yorn . . .

Nit derfar, vayl, s'vert itst lind,
Un may tsegist zikh af di gasn,
Fil ikh zikh itst shtil un gring
Un ken dikh, shtetele, nit hasn.

Ba dir muz itster oykh zayn may.
Khotsh du must altst im rufn siven,
Un s'bloyt der himl sayvisay
Af altst, vos iz nokh do farblibn . . .

2

Dos gantse shtetele – a yomtevdike likht,
Derbrent ir shtiln vaks, vos trift nokh alts
                                        Mit honik,
Ikh gey do um mit ru af mayn gezikht
Un kh'ver haynt ful mit shtilkayt fun dermonung . . .

Do hot amol a yingele gelebt
Un s'hot dos yingele nokh nit gevust fun zorgn,
Hayzlekh flegn ufheybn di kep
Un shtilerheyt im entfern: – gutmorgn.

Un s'iz gevezn im nit gut, nit shlekht,
Es iz gevezn im nor glat azoy zikh . . .
In oysgesherntkayt fun vayse nekht
Hot er af geselekh gefreyt zikh.
Mit oygn ofene, mit ofn harts
Hot er toyiker gevakht do,
Un nit gevust hot er, vi libt men has,
Vi ken men bentshndik farakhtn . . .

. . . Itst volt dos yingele zikh nit derkent
Un nit derkent volt ikh im oykh mistome.
Gut, ven s'lebt nokh do in ru fun vent
Undzer umetike mame.

3

Ikh beyg do ayn mayn yungn kop un shvaygn,
Un s'ken mayn harts keyn ru zikh nit gefinen,
Shtetl-shtelele, mayn opgedarte tsvayg,
Vider vilstu onheybn tsu grinen.
Gey ikh do um a shtiler gast un shvayg.

Un s'tut mir bank, es tut mir zeyer bank
Un kh'bin azoy Eseninen mekane:
Oykh mir volt zikh dokh veln in gezang

Kumen un dikh onrufn: mayn mame,
Ekh, du shtetele, vi s'tut mir bank.
Oftmol dakht zikh mir, ikh shtey shoyn ba dayn sof,
Un oftmol dakht zikh mir, du vilst nit shteyn geboygn,
Un dayne hayzelekh, vi ufgevakhte shof,
Efenen di kaylekhdike oygn
Nokh a shtiln, zumerdikn shlof...

Shtetl-shtetele, mayn kindersher amol,
Ikh hob gevolt derzeen dikh in brenen,
Nor ver es hot gesholtn dikh a mol,
Vet shoyn muzn dikh farsholtn kenen,
Shtetl, shtelele, mayn kindersher amol...

       1926

4

Avgust. Ikh bin in shtetele gekumen.
Iz avgust kil, un durkhzikhtik, un bloy,
Tsu ovnt roykhert zikh a shmeyklendiker umet,
Un fartog geyt uf dos shtetele in toy.

S'iz luftik-gring in zumerdikn nepl,
Fun heykhn vayt mit varemkayt un likht,
Se shmekt di luft mit vaynik-klore epl,
Un in hartsn vert oykh vaynik un gedikht...

Ikh hob nit lang gesholtn un geflukht dikh,
Ligstu itster, shtetele, farshtilt...
Gey ikh arum in roykh fun tsvit un frukhtn,
Un avgust ligt do durkhzikhtik un kil.

  Avgust 1925

APPENDIX VI

A Briv fun Moskve	*A Briv keyn Moskve*
In Onfang kum ikh dir tsu lozn hern,	Parshe Vayechi
Az mir zaynen got-tse-danken raykh.	Lekoved ... un ... neyro yoir.
Mir khapn nokh fun himl nit keyn shtern,	
Nor mir filn zikh mit alemen tsugleikh.	Ad hayem fil ikh zikh nokh zeyer shvakh,
Davenen davn ikh do noent in a minyen	Ikh vel shoyn do derlebn mayne yorn,

Un di minyonim zaynen do farfult.
Gebentsht zol zayn der altitshker
  Kalinin, –
Me zogt, az er farhit dos undzer
  shul.
Handlen handl ikh nit erger, vi in
  shtetl,
Un fil shoyn nit, geloybt iz er,
  keyn noyt.
Kum tsu forn, loz zikh lang nit
  betn,
Hostu oykh a zatn shtikl broyt.

Shoyn shpet far mir tse lebn in a krakh.
Men tor af keynem gor nit betn keyn
  mapole
Un zol dos zayn der ergster bolshevik.

Ot arbet ikh pavolye in yevshkole

Un gornisht. S'iz nokh oykh a shtikl glik.

Ikh hob gemeynt, es endikt zikh mayn
  veltl,
Ikh vel shoyn muzn mit der torbe geyn.
Un itst bin ikh gevorn af der elter,
  a shoymer un khaver fun fareyn . . .
Ikh veys, du vest fun dem nit veln hern,
Du vest mikh bald shoyn haltn far a goy.
Di kinder mayne zaynen pionern.
Meynstu vos? Un gornisht. Ot azoy.
Nu, genug. Es klekt nit keyn papir.
Gris zugatekha, zay gezunt.
  mimeni . . .
Ye, men zogt, az dort, in Moskve, ken
  men
frank-un-fray geyn onkukn, vi Lenin
Ligt nokh alts in ohel nit gerirt.

Notes

Introduction

1. Baruch Glazman was an American Yiddish writer who made a "pilgrimage" to Poland and the Soviet Union in 1924. He published in Yiddish journals worldwide including several Communist ones. For the quote, see Mordechai Altshuler, ed., *Briv fun yidishe sovetishe shraybers* (Jerusalem: Hebrew University Press, 1980), p. 24.

2. Rebecca Goldstein, *Mazel* (Madison: University of Wisconsin Press, 2001), p. 365.

3. Nathan Englander, *For the Relief of Unbearable Urges* (New York: Vintage Press, 1999), p. 16.

4. Amos Funkenstein, *Perceptions of Jewish History* (Berkeley, Los Angeles: University of California Press, 1993), p. 34.

5. Michael André Bernstein, *Foregone Conclusions: Against Apocalyptic History* (Berkeley, Los Angeles: University of California Press, 1994), p. 16. Italics are in the original.

6. Gennady Estraikh, *Soviet Yiddish: Language Planning and Linguistic Development* (Oxford: Clarendon Press, 1999).

7. See Jeffrey Veidlinger, *The Moscow State Jewish Theater* (Bloomington: Indiana University Press, 2000), p. 3.

8. For one particularly powerful framing of the issue, see Elie Wiesel, *The Jews of Silence* (New York: Holt, Rinehart, and Winston, 1966).

9. For an overview of the historiography of Soviet subjectivity, see Anna Krylova, "The Tenacious Liberal Subject in Soviet Studies," *Kritika* Winter 2000 1(1): 119–46.

10. *Di ershte yidishe shprakh-konferents* (Vilna: YIVO Farlag, 1931), p. 2, as translated in Emanuel Goldsmith, *Modern Yiddish Culture*, (New York: Fordham University Press, 1997), p. 184.

11. Ester, *An entfer af di gegners fun yidish* (Czernowitz, 1922), p. 16. Esther Frumkina's name is complicated: Her pseudonym was "Esther," as in the Biblical queen; her given name was Maria; and she married a man whose last name is Frumkin. The "name game" is important to emphasize the fluid and ever-changing identities that these activists developed.

12. The Israeli historian Mordechai Altshuler situates the history of Soviet Jewish culture between the poles of Jewish national interests and Soviet politics. He traces the conflicted desires of Soviet Jewish cultural activists to be part of both Jewish nation-building and

Soviet state-building. See Mordechai Altshuler, *Ha-yevsektsiya bi- vrit ha-mo'atsot: beyn komunizm ve-leumiyut* (Jerusalem: Hebrew University Press, 1981).

13. Mikhail Levitan was head of the Central Jewish Enlightenment Bureau of the Ukrainian Enlightenment Commissariat and simultaneously an editor for the Soviet Yiddish journal *Di Royte Velt.*

14. Mikhail Levitan, "Di grunt problemen fun der idisher kultur boyung: 'Di yidishe shprakh': a zelbsttsvek oder a mitl," *Royte Velt* May–June 1926 (no. 5–6), p. 82.

15. Benedict Anderson, *Imagined Communities* (New York: Verso, 1991), chps. 3 and 4.

16. Partha Chatterjee, *The Nation and Its Fragments: Colonial and Postcolonial Histories* (Princeton: Princeton University Press, 1993), pp. 6–9.

17. Henry Tobias, *The Jewish Bund in Russia* (Stanford: Stanford University Press, 1972), p. 47. The new strategies worked. The Bund's membership went from 5,600 in 1900 to 30,000 in 1903.

18. Lawrence Silberstein, *The Postzionism Debates: Knowledge and Power in Israeli Culture* (New York, London: Routledge Press, 1999), p. 4.

19. For more on the role language played in constituting modern collective identities, see Benjamin Harshav, *Language in Time of Revolution* (Berkeley, Los Angeles: University of California Press, 1990).

20. Zvi Gitelman addresses these Jewish activists from the perspective of modernization theory – that Jewish activists created new cultural institutions as part of the Soviet project to modernize its minorities. Gitelman's was one of the first books to study the Jews' participation in building the Soviet system without judgment. Modernization alone though does not explain why Jewish activists were so interested in modernizing Jews within Jewish institutions as opposed to general Soviet Russian ones. Zvi Gitelman, *Jewish Nationality and Soviet Politics: The Jewish Sections of the CPSU, 1917–1930* (Princeton: Princeton University Press, 1972).

21. The most comprehensive treatment of language politics in the Soviet Union is Michael Smith, *Language and Power in the Creation of the USSR, 1917–1953* (New York: Mouton de Gruyter, 1998).

22. See Ronald Suny, *The Revenge of the Past: Nationalism, Revolution, and the Collapse of the Soviet Union* (Stanford: Stanford University Press, 1993) and Yuri Slezkine, *Arctic Mirrors* (Ithaca: Cornell University Press, 1994). See also Adrienne Edgar, "The Creation of Soviet Turkmenistan, 1924–1938" (Ph.D. diss., University of California, Berkeley, 1999), which examines the Soviet state's visions of its national minorities and the practices it used to manage its ethnic diversity. For a more literary, Saidian approach, see Susan Layton, *Russian Literature and Empire: Conquest of the Caucasus from Pushkin to Tolstoy* (Cambridge: Cambridge University Press, 1994).

23. Terry Martin, *The Affirmative Action Empire: Nations and Nationalism in the Soviet Union, 1923–1939* (Ithaca: Cornell University Press, 2000).

24. Daniel Brower and Edward Lazzerini, eds., *Russia's Orient: Imperial Borderlands and Peoples, 1700–1917* (Bloomington: Indiana University Press, 1997); Theodore Weeks, *Nation and State in Late Imperial Russia: Nationalism and Russification on the Western Frontier, 1863–1914* (DeKalb, IL: Northern Illinois University Press, 1996).

25. Most agree that the switch from native-language imperial policies to ones that emphasized Russian as the Soviet lingua franca happened in the middle–late 1930s. For twenty years, then, Soviet imperial policy was defined by its emphasis on fostering native-language cultures. The case of Soviet Yiddish culture will show that Russian

began becoming more important in culture-building for ethnic minorities in the mid-1920s. See chapter two.

26. Lenin expounds on his ideas about the relationship between capitalism and imperialism, which were influenced by the non-Marxist British economist J.A. Hobson, in *Imperialism: The Highest Stage of Capitalism* (Petrograd, 1917).

27. Francine Hirsch, "Toward an Empire of Nations: Border-Making and the Formation of Soviet National Identities," *Russian Review* April 2000 (vol. 50, no. 2), p. 203.

28. The desire to find Jews a piece of Soviet territory was policy both for Jewish activists and for the state more generally. For more on the question of Jewish territory, see Robert Weinberg, *Stalin's Forgotten Zion: Birobidzhan and the Making of a Soviet Jewish Homeland* (Berkeley, Los Angeles: University of California Press, 1998) and Allan Kagedan, *Soviet Zion: The Quest for a Russian Jewish Homeland* (New York: St. Martin's Press, 1994).

29. The Nuremberg Laws of 1935 defined Jews as a race by categorizing anyone with three Jewish grandparents as a Jew. But another definition noted that people affiliated with a Jewish community were also Jews. This ruling included converts to Judaism and broadened the racial definition of Jewishness. See Michael Burliegh and Wolfgang Wipperman, *The Racial State: Germany 1933–1945* (New York, Cambridge: Cambridge University Press, 1991).

30. See statistics on Jewish demographics in Mordechai Altshuler, *Soviet Jewry on the Eve of the Holocaust; A Social and Demographic Profile* (Jerusalem: Hebrew University Press, 1998) and Yankev Leshtsinsky, *Dos Sovetishe Yidntum* (New York: Poalei Tsion Press, 1941).

31. For a comparison on the socio-economic status of Jews in different Eastern European countries, see Ezra Mendelssohn, *The Jews of East Central Europe Between the Wars* (Bloomington: Indiana University Press, 1989).

32. See Francine Hirsch, "The Soviet Union as a Work in Progress," *Slavic Review*, Summer 1997, p. 263.

33. See Terry Martin, *The Affirmative Action Empire: Nations and Nationalism in the Soviet Union, 1923–1939* (Ithaca: Cornell University, 2001).

34. Ya. Kantor, *Natsional'noe stroitel'stvo sredi evreev v SSSR* (Moscow, 1935), p. 172.

35. S. Dimanshtein, *Itogi razresheniia natsional'nogo voprosa v SSSR* (Moscow, 1935), p. 200.

36. Ibid., pp. 83–4.

Chapter One

1. Isaac Babel did not work in Yiddish and, therefore, could not claim (nor would have wanted to) the role of cultural translator that the Soviet Yiddish activists could claim. As Soviet Jews shifted from being a predominantly Yiddish-speaking to a Russian-speaking ethnic group, the role of intermediary shifted to members of a Russian Jewish Soviet intelligentsia. Most important among these Russian Jewish intercessors was Ilya Ehrenburg. Mordechai Altshuler characterizes Ehrenburg's relationship to Jews: "Ehrenburg never turned his back on Jews, nor did he change his name as so many other Russian Jewish writers did. His relationship to Jews and to things Jewish was a mixture of love and hate, contempt and sympathy." See Mordechai Altshuler, Yitzchak Ara, Shmuel Krakovsky, eds., *Sovetskie evrei pishut Ilye Erenburgu* (Jerusalem: Prisma Press, 1993), p. 10.

2. Eli Lederhendler, *The Road to Modern Jewish Politics* (New York: Oxford University Press, 1989), p. 99.
3. See Michael Stanislawski, *Tsar Nicholas I and the Jews* (Philadelphia: Jewish Publication Society, 1983).
4. For one example describing Litvakov's role as a *shtadlan*, see RGASPI, f. 445, op. 1, d. 2, l. 41.
5. Joseph Stalin, "Marxism and the Jewish Question," as cited in Jacob Miller, "Soviet Theory on the Jews," in Lionel Kochan, ed., *The Jews in Soviet Russia* (Oxford: Oxford University Press, 1978), pp. 50–1.
6. See Terry Martin, *The Affirmative Action Empire: Nations and Nationalism in the Soviet Union, 1923–1939* (Ithaca: Cornell University Press, 2000), pp. 4–8.
7. Vladimir I. Lenin, "Kriticheskie voprosy po natsional'nomy voprosu," *Prosvescheniie* nos. 10,11,12, 1913, p. 26.
8. Lenin, "Kriticheskie voprosy," p. 42.
9. See Chone Shmeruk, "Ha-pirsumim be-yidish bi-vrit ha-moatsot be-shanim 1917–1960," *Pirsumim yehudiim bi-vrit ha-moatsot: 1917–1960* (Jerusalem: Society for Research on Jewish Communities, 1960), p. 111.
10. On the beginnings of large urban Russian-speaking Jewish communities in tsarist Russia, see Benjamin Nathans, *Beyond the Pale: The Jewish Encounter with Late-Imperial Russia* (Berkeley, Los Angeles: University of California Press, 2002).
11. Gennady Estraikh, *Soviet Yiddish: Language Planning and Linguistic Development* (Oxford: Clarendon Press, 1999), pp. 10–23.
12. Mordechai Altshuler, "Socio-demographic Profile of Moscow Jews," *Jews and Jewish Topics in the Soviet Union* 3(16), 1991, p. 34.
13. Terry Martin, *The Affirmative Action Empire: Nations and Nationalism in the Soviet Union, 1923–1939* (Ithaca: Cornell University Press, 2000) pp. 49, 50n.
14. The original from July 1923 reads "Yidish iz oykh parnose far yidishe kinder."
15. Altshuler is one of the few scholars to emphasize the genuine national desires of many Soviet Jewish activists, and his book remains the best source for charting the tortured relationship between the activists and their work. See Altshuler, *Ha-yevsektsiia*.
16. Altshuler, *Ha-yevsektsiia*, p. 145.
17. The Jewish Commissariat was formed in January 1918, shortly after the formation of the Polish Commissariat. For more on the Commissariat for Nationalities (*Narkomnats*) and Stalin's role as commissar, see Stephen Blank, *The Sorcerer as Apprentice: Stalin as Commissar of Nationalities, 1917–1924* (Westport, CT: Greenwood Press, 1994).
18. Hersh Smolar, *Fun ineveynik* (Tel Aviv: Perets farlag, 1978), pp. 98–9.
19. Yuri Slezkine, *Arctic Mirrors* (Ithaca, NY: Cornell University Press, 1994).
20. See Sheila Fitzpatrick, Alexander Rabinowitch, and Richard Stites, eds., *Russia in the Era of NEP: Explorations in Soviet Society and Culture* (Bloomington: Indiana University Press, 1991).
21. For more on Birobidzhan, see Robert Weinberg, *Stalin's Forgotten Zion: Birobidzhan and the Making of a Soviet Jewish Homeland* (Berkeley, Los Angeles: University of California Press, 1998) and "Birobidzhan," special edition of *Jews in Eastern Europe*, Fall 2002.
22. Altshuler, *Ha-yevsektsiia*, p. 171.

23. Smolar, *Fun ineveynik*, p. 111.

24. Daniel Charny, *A yortsendlik aza* (New York: CYCO, 1943), p. 193, emphasis mine. Charny's role in Soviet Jewish culture is discussed in chapters four and five.

25. On the relationship between Trotsky, Kamenev, other Jewish Bolshevik leaders, and Soviet Jews, see, for example, Joseph Nedava, *Trotsky and the Jews* (Philadelphia: Jewish Publication Society, 1972).

26. Zvi Gitelman, *Jewish Nationality and Soviet Politics: The Jewish Sections of the CPSU, 1917–1930* (Princeton: Princeton University Press, 1972).

27. RGASPI, f. 445, op. 1, d. 73, l. 84. When the report mentions the languages that various delegates listed, nowhere does it mention Hebrew. Surely, many of these activists had studied and even written in Hebrew, and several could probably speak a halting Hebrew. But by 1922, Hebrew had been suppressed in the Soviet Union. See chapter two.

28. See Smolar, *Fun inevenynik*, p. 238.

29. For biographical information about Frumkina, see Naomi Shepherd, *A Price Below Rubies* (Cambridge, MA: Harvard University Press 1993), pp. 137–71.

30. Shepherd, *A Price Below Rubies*, pp. 151–4.

31. Shepherd, *A Price Below Rubies*, p. 142.

32. Ester, "Eynike bamerkungen vegn natsionaler dertsiung," *Tsayt fragn*, vol. 1 (Vilna, 1909).

33. Smolar, *Fun ineveynik*, pp. 281, 315.

34. To compile this brief sketch, I used the *Leksikon fun der nayer yidisher literatur* [Lexicon of Modern Yiddish Literature], an eight-volume biographical encyclopedia of the history of Yiddish activism, the *Bol'shaia Sovetskaia Entsiklopediia* [Great Soviet Encyclopedia] of 1932, and the three-volume *Rossiiskaia evreiskaia entsiklopediia* [Russian Jewish Encyclopedia]. In addition, I included archival material that revealed new aspects of Litvakov's cultural and political activity.

35. See chapter four for more on *Kultur Lige*.

36. RGASPI, f. 445, op. 1, d. 2, l. 106. The report is from August 2, 1920.

37. The *Leksikon* mistakenly says that he began his editorship in 1924, when in fact, he became editor in 1921.

38. On Litvakov's role as military censor, see RGASPI, f. 445, op. 1, d. 78, l. 26. The proposal is dated July 21, 1921. On his role as *Glavlit* censor, see GARF, f. 1318, op. 1, d. 807, l. 49.

39. Litvakov also wrote a short autobiography in 1935 connected with a Party purge, in which he stressed moments of *bildung*, or cultural development, that shaped his overall life, and focused on his *bildung* within Russian culture, erasing his personal history within Jewish culture. During his activist period in Kiev, Litvakov states, "from the beginning of 1919, I found myself doing Soviet work," and leaves out his wide involvement in Jewish intellectual and cultural circles in Kiev. See TsDAODM, f. 386, op. 1, d. 7, ll. 147–8.

40. For more on the tensions between the "first generation" and the post-revolutionary generation, which became politically active after the revolution, see for example, Hersh Smolar, *Fun invenynik*, p. 189. Generational conflicts will be discussed further in chapters five and six.

41. S. Dimanshteyn, "10 yor komprese in yidish," *Oktyabr*, Mar. 7, 1928 (no. 57), p. 3.

Chapter Two

1. Shmuel Agursky, *Der yidisher arbeter in der komunistisher bavegung*, 1917–1921 (Minsk: Melukhe-farlag, 1925), pp. 44–5.
2. For more on the way Jews have referred to the language now called Yiddish, see Max Weinreich, *History of the Yiddish Language* (Chicago: University of Chicago Press, 1981), chapter 5.
3. Ibid., chapter 4. See also Benedict Anderson, *Imagined Communities* (New York: Verso, 1991) for more on the relationship between vernaculars and supra-national religious languages such as Latin and Arabic.
4. Weinreich, *History*, p. 279.
5. Shmuel Niger argues, "not only morality books and *tkhines* [women's private prayers] were written in Yiddish, but an entire religious literature was created in the vernacular language." See Shmuel Niger, *Bilingualism in the History of Jewish Literature*, trans. Joshua Fogel (Lanham, MD: University Press of America, 1990), pp. 59–60.
6. Weinreich, *History*, pp. 260–6.
7. Joshua Fishman, "Attracting a Following to High-Culture Functions for a Language of Everyday Life: The Role of the Czernowitz Language Conference in the Rise of Yiddish," in Joshua Fishman, ed., *Never Say Die: A Thousand Years of Yiddish in Jewish Life and Letters* (The Hague, New York: Mouton Press, 1981), pp. 369–70.
8. Chava Weissler, "For Women and For Men Who are Like Women: The Construction of Gender in Yiddish Devotional Literature," *Journal of Feminist Studies in Religion*, Fall 1989 5(2): 7–24.
9. The actual text of the *Tsenah u-re'enah* is a collage of text, midrash, and other interpretive texts with very little actual translation of the original.
10. Shmuel Niger, *Di yidishe literatur un di lezerin* (Vilna: Vilner farlag, 1919).
11. *Halachah*, literally "the way," refers to the structured Jewish way of life based on Jewish texts and laws, primarily found in the Talmud and other Rabbinic literature. Since girls/women could not, in theory, read Hebrew, they had to be taught those aspects of *halachah* that applied to them orally or through Yiddish-language texts.
12. Rogers Brubaker, *Citizenship and Nationhood in France and Germany* (Cambridge, MA: Harvard University Press, 1992), chapters one to three; and Pierre Birnbaum and Ira Katznelson, eds., *Paths of Emancipation: Jews, States, and Citizenship* (Princeton: Princeton University Press, 1995).
13. Osip Rabinowitch, "Russia – Our Native Land: Just as We Breathe Its Air We Must Speak Its Language," as cited in Paul Mendes-Flohr and Jehuda Reinharz, eds., *The Jew in the Modern World* (Oxford, New York: Oxford University Press, 1995), p. 400.
14. Israel Bartal, "From Traditional Bilingualism to National Monolingualism," in Lewis Glinert, ed., *Hebrew in Ashkenaz* (New York: Oxford University Press, 1993), p. 145.
15. A.B. Gottlober, *Ha-magid*, no. 40, 1873, p. 363 as cited in Nancy Beth Sinkoff, "Tradition and Transition: Mendel Lefin of Satanow and the Beginning of the Jewish Enlightenment in Eastern Europe, 1749–1826," (Ph.D. diss., Columbia University, 1996) p. 219.
16. Israel Zinberg, *The Haskalah Movement in Russia, vol.11* in Zinberg, *The History of Jewish Literature* (Cleveland: Case Western Reserve University Press, 1972–1978), pp. 22–3.

17. On Abramovich's role as father of both modern Jewish literatures, see Naomi Seidman, *A Marriage Made in Heaven: The Sexual Politics of Hebrew and Yiddish* (Berkeley, 1998), pp. 42–64, and Robert Alter, *The Invention of Hebrew Prose: Modern Fiction and the Language of Realism* (Seattle: University of Washington Press, 1988).
18. Weinreich, *History*, p. 286.
19. Dan Miron, *A Traveler Disguised: A Study in the Rise of Modern Yiddish Fiction in the Nineteenth Century* (Syracuse: Syracuse University Press, 1996).
20. Sinkoff, "Tradition," p. 218.
21. Zinberg, *History, vol. 11*, pp. 149–87.
22. For the emergence of a Russian-language Jewish press, see John Klier, *Imperial Russia's Jewish Question: 1855–1881* (New York, Cambridge: Cambridge University Press, 1995); Zinberg, *History, vol. 12*, pp. 31–68.
23. Zinberg, *History, vol. 12*, p. 104.
24. A. R. Mlachi, "Der 'Kol mevaser' un zayn redaktor," in Shloyme Bikel, ed., *Pinkes far der forshung fun der yidisher literatur un prese, vol. 1* (New York: Alveltlekher Yidisher Kultur-Kongres, 1965), pp. 70–1.
25. Michael Hrushevsky, *A History of Ukraine* (New Haven: Yale University Press, 1941), p. 484.
26. Volodymyr Kubijovych, *Ukraine: A Concise Encyclopedia* (Toronto: University of Toronto Press, 1963), vol. 1, p. 502.
27. Sh. Chkhetiia, *Tbilisi v XIX stoletii (1865–1869)* as cited in Ronald Suny, *The Making of the Georgian Nation* (Bloomington: Indiana University Press, 1988), p. 128.
28. Mlachi, "Der Kol mevaser," p. 73.
29. Weinreich, *History*, p. 287; Goldsmith, *Modern Yiddish*, p. 47. See chapter three for more on the development of Yiddish philology and linguistics.
30. For more on Yehoshua Lifshits, see David Fishman, "Di dray penemer fun Yehoshua Mordkhe Lifshits," *Yidishe Shprakh* no. 38, 1981.
31. Elias Schulman, *A History of Jewish Education in the Soviet Union* (New York: Ktav, 1971), p. 18.
32. See Jonathon Frankel, *Prophecy and Politics: Socialism, Nationalism, and the Russian Jews, 1862–1917* (New York, Cambridge: Cambridge University Press, 1981), p. 188–90.
33. Ibid., pp. 200–19.
34. Although Yiddish's "territory" was Eastern Europe and the ideological movement that made Yiddish as an end itself was in Eastern Europe, many of the developments these Eastern European Yiddishists lauded took place in the United States, specifically in New York. It was in New York that the theater, periodical and book publication, and other signs of "cultural status" first took flight.
35. *Di ershte yidishe shprakh-konferents* (Vilna: YIVO Farlag, 1931), p. 2, as translated in Goldsmith, *Modern Yiddish*, p. 183.
36. Fishman, *Never*, pp. 388–90.
37. Goldsmith, *Modern Yiddish*, p. 214.
38. See Theodore Weeks, *Nation and State in Late Imperial Russia: Nationalism and Russification on the Western Frontier, 1863–1914* (DeKalb, IL: Northern Illinois University Press, 1996).
39. Schulman, *A History of Jewish Education*, p. 36.
40. Schulman, *A History of Jewish Education*, p. 37.
41. Henry Tobias and Mordechai Altshuler agree that the roots of Soviet Jewish cultural policy can be found in the prerevolutionary Bund. See Tobias, *The Jewish Bund*,

and Mordechai Altshuler, *Ha-yevsektsiia bi-vrit ha-mo'atsot: beyn komunizm ve-leumiyut* (Jerusalem: Center for Contemporary Jewry of the Hebrew University, 1980).

42. This radical destruction of internal Jewish bilingualism had its equivalent in Palestine, where Hebraists, who reigned triumphant over Yiddish, shamed those who spoke Yiddish, denounced "unfaithful" Hebraists who showed any support for Yiddish culture, and made a concerted attack on any manifestations of Yiddish culture in the *Yishuv*. See Seidman, *A Marriage Made in Heaven*, p. 115–25.

43. Eugen Weber, *Peasants into Frenchmen: The Modernization of Rural France, 1870–1914* (Stanford: Stanford University Press, 1976).

44. Native language instruction was just one aspect of the "new pedagogy." In the radicalism of the War Communism period, there were many experimental theories of education debated among those responsible for remaking Russia's educational system. For more on Soviet experiments in education, see James Bowen, *Soviet Education: Anton Makarenko and the Years of Experiment* (Madison: University of Wisconsin Press, 1962).

45. GARF, f.2306 (*Narkompros*), op. 2,d. 306,l. 31. The petition is dated August 3, 1918.

46. Schulman, *Jewish Education,* p. 57.

47. GARF, f. 2306, op. 2, d. 306, l.33.

48. GARF, f.1318, op. 1, d. 22, l. 59. This petition is dated August 14, 1918.

49. It is important to remember that these discussions were focused on the Russian Republic alone. Ukraine and Belorussia were still not definitively within the borders of the new Soviet republic, so official decrees from Moscow did not have the power to mandate change in Jewish schools in the borderlands.

50. Hersh Smolar, *Fun inevenynik* (Tel Aviv: Perets farlag, 1978), p. 238.

51. Eli Lederhendler, *The Road to Modern Jewish Politics: Political Tradition and Political Reconstruction in the Jewish Community of Tsarist Russia* (New York, Oxford: Oxford University Press, 1989), pp. 45–55.

52. GARF, f. 2306, op. 1, d. 291, l. 45.

53. Ibid, l. 21. The "scholarly source" on which the Collegium based its claim was a report drafted by Itsik Zaretsky, the temporary head of the Jewish Subdivision's cultural section, and a Yiddish linguist. See chapter three for more on Zaretsky.

54. Ibid, l. 42.

55. See either RGASPI, f. 445, op. 1, d. 28, l. 87 or TsDAHOU, f. 1, op. 20, d. 91, l. 31.

56. GARF, f. 2306, op. 4, d. 758, l. 1? (poorly numbered).

57. RGASPI, f. 445, op. 1, d. 72, l. 168.

58. RGASPI, f. 445, op. 1, d. 69, l.127, dated May 17, 1922

59. GARF, f.3316, op.10, d.190, l. 90–1. The petition read: "The main bureau calls on all of you to take active part in the Chanukkah campaign for Hebrew language and literature. Don't be afraid of *Evsektsiia* persecution. Remember how our ancestors weren't afraid to face death in the name of the people (*naroda*). Remember how in our time hundreds of our comrades face torture, hunger and cold in jails and in exile for this brave battle."

60. GARF, f. 3316, op. 19, d. 190, l. 92.

61. Ibid, l. 23.

62. This file contains dozens of petitions all dated in late 1925 and early 1926.

63. Ibid, p. 93.

64. The total separation of Hebrew from Yiddish did not take place until 1919–20. In its 1918 publication, *Kultur un Bildung*, the Jewish Commissariat published the date in both

the Christian dating system and the Jewish dating system. The first issue, from August 19, 1918, was dated yud" bet Elul, Taf Resh Ayin" Khet [12 Elul 5678].

65. GARF f. 1318, op. 1, d. 603, l. 5.
66. RGASPI, f. 17, op. 60, d. 16, l. 67. The letter is dated September 30, 1920.
67. GARF, f. 1318, op. 1, d. 603, l. 5.
68. See Arlen Blium, *Evreiskii vopros pod sovetskoi tsenzuroi, 1917–1991* (St. Petersburg: Peterburgskii evreiskii universitet 1996), pp. 31–6.
69. Blium, *Evreiskii vopros*, p. 52.
70. GARF, f. 1318, op. 24, d. 7, l. 10. The emphasis is mine.
71. *Bereshit* (Moscow/Leningrad, 1926).
72. RGASPI, f. 445, op. 1,d. 78, l. 9. In his exposé of the East German publishing system, Robert Darnton found that the printing house was also the last stage in the censorial process. See Robert Darnton, "The Good Old Days," *New York Review of Books,* May 16, 1991, pp. 44–9.
73. Despite the impression that Jewish activists tried to prevent these writers' departures, the *Evsektsiia* grudgingly acceded to their request for exit visas. See RGASPI, f. 445, op. 1, d. 69, l. 58. The resolution is dated April 15, 1921. For more on the departure of the Hebrew writers from Odessa, see Yehoshua Gilboa, *A Language Silenced: The Suppression of Hebrew Literature and Culture in the Soviet Union* (Rutherford, NJ: Fairleigh Dickenson Press, 1982), pp. 92–5 and Joseph Nedava, *Trotsky and the Jews* (Philadelphia: Jewish Publication Society, 1972), pp. 106–7.
74. RGASPI, f. 445,op. 1,d. 68,l. 101. The letter is dated April 9, 1921.
75. Gilboa, p. 93.
76. RGASPI, f. 445, op. 1, d. 143, l. 177–8.
77. Ibid. Emphasis in the original.
78. Gnessin's support of Hebrew-language culture in the 1920s came back to haunt him during the 1940s purges of the Jewish cultural establishment. In 1948, his adversaries accused him of Zionist nationalism and cited his support of the Hebrew-language theater, *Habimah*, and his signature on this petition as proof of his undying support of Jewish nationalism. I thank Kiril Tomoff for the information on Gnessin's later persecution.
79. For more on Nikolai Marr, Soviet linguistics, and nationality politics, see Yuri Slezkine, "N.I. Marr and the National Origins of Soviet Ethnogenetics," *Slavic Review,* Winter 1996 55(4), pp. 826–62.
80. RGASPI, f. 445, op. 1, d. 172, ll. 59–60.
81. Ibid, l. 64.
82. RGASPI, f. 445, o.1, d. 172, ll. 3–6. The Moscow Writers' and Artists' Circle response is dated February 4, 1924.
83. Hofshteyn spent time in Europe and in Palestine before returning to the Soviet Union in 1926.
84. The Hebrew–Yiddish language battles appeared in all areas of culture. The other site of fierce battles was in the Soviet Jewish theaters. The state Yiddish theater (GOSET) and the Yiddish intelligentsia tried its best to cut off funding and state support of the Hebrew-language Jewish theater, *Habimah*. In the beginning, they were unsuccessful in their efforts, because the theater was quite popular among non-Jewish cultural and political elites. It took nearly eight years of pressure from the Soviet Yiddish intelligentsia before *Habimah* was forced to leave the country in 1926. For more on the Soviet Yiddish

theater, see Jeffrey Veidlinger, *The Moscow State Jewish Theater* (Bloomington: Indiana University Press, 2000).

85. The 1926 Soviet census counted 26,000 "Tat Jews," one of five categories of "Jewish ethnicities" counted in the census. Tat Jews was the colloquial name for Dagestani or Mountain Jews. See Gilboa, p. 62.

86. Francine Hirsch, "Soviet Union as a Work in Progress," *Slavic Review*, Summer 1997, p. 263. Karaite Jews, who lived primarily along the Black Sea in Russia, split off from traditional Rabbinic Jewish communities in the eighth century. Some Jews did not even consider Karaites Jews at all.

87. Judeo-Tat, spoken by Dagestani Jews, is one of two branches of Tat. According to the 1970 Soviet census, there were 17,109 Tat speakers in the USSR, of whom 72.6 percent considered Tat their native language. Others estimate the number of Tat speakers to be much higher. Tat has been a written language only since the 1920s, and it was primarily used for Jewish Tat speakers. See Bernard Comrie, *The Languages of the Soviet Union* (Cambridge: Cambridge University Press, 1981), p. 164.

88. By 1920 most of Central Asia and the Caucasus region was under Soviet control.

89. GARF, f. 1318, op. 1, d. 580, l. 9.

90. Ibid.

91. RGASPI, f. 445, op.1, d. 90, l. 69.

92. RGASPI, f. 445, op. 1, d. 133, l. 123.

93. GARF, f. 2307,op. 14, d. 9, l. 55.

94. The literary anthology also reflected the politics of nativization and nationalities policies in general. In addition to learning about Uzbek history, literary authorities thought it was important to include translations of Maxim Gorky, Lenin, and Ivan Goncharov in the Judeo-Tadzhik literary reader, showing how all nationalities needed to appreciate Russian culture as well as their own. There was little mention of non-Bukharan Jewish culture. See P. Abramov, and I. A. Yagudaev, *Literary Anthology for the Fourth Class* [in Judeo-Tadzhik] (Tashkent-Samarkand, Uzbek State Publishing House, 1933).

95. Nora Levin, *The Jews in the Soviet Union since 1917* (London: I.B. Tauris Publishing, 1988), p. 114. For more on Bukharan Jewish Culture, see Mikhail Zand, "Bukharan Jewish Culture under Soviet Rule," *Soviet Jewish Affairs*, 1979 (vol. 9, no. 2). Unlike Bukharan Jews, Georgian Jews' cultural development was always overseen by Georgian cultural leaders in Georgia, since Georgian Jews did not have their own language. See Mordechai Altshuler, "Georgian Jewish Culture under the Soviet Regime," *Soviet Jewish Affairs* 5(2): 21–39.

96. See the Judeo-Tadzhik card catalog at the Russian State Library. See also Solum Alekhem, *Nazili Xunafson*, Roman UGIZ, Tashkent, 1931.

97. See Weeks, *Nation and State*, for an analysis of the Russianization policies in the Western borderlands.

98. Yuri Slezkine, "The USSR as a Communal Apartment, or How a Socialist State Promoted Ethnic Particularism," *Slavic Review* Summer, 1994 53(2), pp. 414–52 and his book *Arctic Mirrors: Russia and the Small Peoples of the North* (Ithaca: Cornell University Press, 1994).

99. *Der Emes*, Oct. 25, 1918 (no.53), p. 2.

100. GARF, f. 1318, op.24, d. 7, l. 2.

101. GARF, f. 1318,op. 24,d. 8, l. 1, which contains excerpts from the published *Vestnik evreiskogo otdela narkomnatsa* (No. 1–2), August–September, 1920.

102. GARF, f.1318, op. 24, d. 7, l. 3.
103. YIVO, RG 205, folder 88, p. 7335. Letter from Agursky to Daniel Charny dated October 27, 1928.
104. GARF, f. 1318, op. 24, d. 7, l.3.
105. Elias Schulman visited the Soviet Union in 1936. He claims that it was instantly recognizable which Jews had gone to a Yiddish school and which ones to a Russian one. Those who went to the Jewish school knew about Yiddish literature and Jewish history, while those who went to a Russian school did not. See Schulman, *Jewish Education*, pp. 97–8.
106. RGASPI, f.445, op. 1, d. 90, l. 62.
107. This decision reflected the dominant tendency to send Russian-speaking Jews to Russian schools and Yiddish-speaking Jews to Yiddish ones. See RGASPI f. 445, op. 1, d. 68, l. 35 and f. 445, op. 1, d. 68, l. 96 for general statements on Russian-speaking Jewish children.
108. RGASPI, f. 445, op. 1, d. 20, l. 36.
109. Ibid.
110. Gennady Estraikh, *Soviet Yiddish: Language Planning and Linguistic Development* (Oxford: Clarendon Press, 1999), pp. 171–3.

Chapter Three

1. Mikhail Levitan, "Di grunt problemen fun der idisher kultur boyung: Di yidishe shprakh: a zelbsttsvek oder a mitl," *Royte Velt* May/June 1926 (no. 5–6), p. 84.
2. Terry Martin, *An Affirmative Action Empire* (Ithaca: Cornell University Press, 2001), p. 184.
3. Yuri Slezkine has shown that, especially in the 1920s, there was great interest in making high culture accessible to indigenous peoples of the empire, even if these peoples had to be encouraged to do so. See Yuri Slezkine, *Arctic Mirrors* (Ithaca: Cornell University Press, 1994), pp. 150–60.
4. Benedict Anderson, *Imagined Communities* (New York: Verso Press, 1991).
5. See, for example, Slezkine, *Arctic Mirrors* or Adrienne Edgar, "The Creation of Soviet Turkmenistan, 1924–1938," (Ph.D. diss., University of California, Berkeley, 1999).
6. In the Hebrew alphabet, there are five letters that have different forms if they fall at the end of the word (*khaf, mem, nun, fey,* and *tsadi*). These will be referred to as "final letters."
7. Joshua Fishman, *Never Say Die: A Thousand Years of Yiddish Life and Letters* (The Hague/New York: Mouton, 1981), p. 60. The Yiddish linguist Max Weinreich agrees with the assessment that "in the Soviet system there [wa]s no room for efforts of linguistic or communal circles or of interested individuals." See Weinreich, "Internal Jewish Bilingualism," *History of the Yiddish Language* (Chicago: University of Chicago Press, 1981), p. 304.
8. Gennady Estraikh, *Soviet Yiddish: Language Planning and Linguistic Development* (Oxford: Clarendon Press, 1999), p. 175.
9. RGASPI, f. 17, op. 33, d. 468, l. 159.
10. Among the mistakes outlined in the letter was the way the conference hall was decorated. It "had an exclusively national tone, without a portrait of Lenin, and no Soviet

flag at the opening." Also noted was the fact that speeches by Communist Party members had not properly represented the Party line. See ibid., l. 160. One other letter written to the secretariat pointed out that Lenin's statue was not at the center behind the speakers' podium, which suggested to the audience that he was not the center of attention. See l. 168.

11. For more on the emergence of modern Greek culture and role of language and literature in national cultures, see Gregory Jusdanis, *Belated Modernity and Aesthetic Culture: Inventing National Literature* (Minneapolis: University of Minnesota Press, 1991).

12. Jusdanis, *Belated Modernity*, pp. 44–5.

13. Shmuel Niger compares Jewish diglossia to Greek diglossia in his passionate defense of Jewish bilingualism in *Bilingualism in the History of Jewish Literature* (Lanham: University Press of America, 1990). He shows that, like Yiddish, only in the twentieth century did Greek *demotika* develop its own literature.

14. On Soviet Pontic Greek culture, see Apostolos Karpozilos, "Pontic Culture in the USSR between the Wars," *Journal of Refugee Studies* 4(4): 364–71.

15. See Weinreich, *History*, p.2.

16. Anderson, *Imagined Communities*, p. 71.

17. Abramovich was not an ideological Yiddishist and did not believe the language should be improved and developed for its own sake. Dan Miron, *A Traveller Disguised: A Study in the Rise of Modern Yiddish Fiction in the Nineteenth Century* (Syracuse: Syracuse University Press, 1996), p. 49.

18. Volodymyr Kubijovych, *Ukraine: A Concise Encyclopedia* (Toronto: University of Toronto Press, 1963), vol. 1, p. 442. Georgian, for example, got a Georgian-French-Russian dictionary in 1840. See George Suny, *The Making of the Georgian Nation* (Bloomington: Indiana University Press, 1988), p. 125.

19. Anderson, *Imagined Communities*, p. 74.

20. The dominance of a Germanized Yiddish became almost standard with the publication of the first Eastern European Yiddish-language daily newspaper, *Der Fraynd,* in St. Petersburg in 1903.

21. Moshe Shulman, "Razvitie evreiskoi orfografii i ee dal'neishie voprosy," April 8, 1938, unpublished article, RAN, f. 677, op. 6, d. 273, l. 39.

22. *Di ershte yidishe shprakh-konferents* (Vilna: YIVO, 1931), s pp. 2–3, as cited in Goldsmith, *Modern Yiddish*, p. 184.

23. Ibid., p. 43.

24. Ber Borochov, "Di ufgabn fun der yidisher filologie," *Der Pinkas: yorbukh far der geshikhte fun der yudisher literatur un shprakh, far folklor, kritik un bibliografie*, p. 1.

25. Ibid., p. 17.

26. See Estraikh, *Soviet Yiddish*, p. 172.

27. Borochov, "Di ufgabe," p. 18.

28. Ernest Gellner, *Nations and Nationalism* (Ithaca: Cornell University Press, 1993), p. 57.

29. Shulman, "Razvitie," l. 45.

30. Bernard Comrie and Gerald Stone, *The Russian Language Since the Revolution* (Oxford: Clarendon Press, 1978), pp. 200–1.

31. Ibid., pp. 208–9. The plans for reforming Russian had been developed before the revolution.

32. The first secular Yiddish language school was founded in 1898 in Minsk. But during the World War, many Yiddish language schools were founded in Moscow, Kiev, and

St. Petersburg where Jewish refugees had fled from the front. See Elias Schulman, *A History of Jewish Education in The Soviet Union* (New York: Ktav Press, 1971), pp. 18–28.

33. GARF, f. 2307, op. 2, d. 96, l. 37.

34. There are many differences between the two dialects. For example, Lithuanian Yiddish speakers pronounce the Yiddish letter *vav* "*oo*," while Polish Yiddish speakers pronounce it "*ee*"; the Lithuanian dialect has two grammatical genders, while the Polish one has three.

35. A. Kantor, "Vegn der yidisher orfografie,"*Kultur un Bildung*, March 10, 1919, no. 5–6 (21–22), pp. 9–11. *Naye Tsayt*, which was socialist but not state-sponsored, was edited by Moshe Kats (who later became a high ranking Yiddish cultural commissar in Ukraine), Moshe Litvakov, and a few others who became well-known Soviet Yiddish activists. According to Ber Slutsky, when *Naye Tsayt* phoneticized the Hebrew component their readership dropped by one half. See Estraikh, *Soviet Yiddish*, p. 138. Zalman Reyzen mentions *Letste Nayes* as technically having been the first periodical to use the reformed, phonetic orthography. See his *Yidishe Literatur un Yidishe Shprakh* (Buenos Aires: YIVO 1965), p. 155.

36. "Tsu undzere korespondentn," *Emes* Aug. 15, 1918 (no. 7), p. 2.

37. The journal was edited by Daniel Charny, and his brother, Shmuel Niger, was one of the main contributors. According to Shmuel Agursky, one of the leading Jewish Communists at the time, Niger and Charny were practically begged to edit and write for the journal due to the shortage of qualified writers. See Shmuel Agursky, *Der Yidisher Arbeter in der Komunistisher Bavegung, 1917–1921* (Minsk: Belorussian State Publishing House, 1925), p. 28. On Charny as editor-in-chief, see GARF, f. 1318, op. 1, d. 570, ll. 213, 215.

38. Y. Mitlinsky, "A revolutsie in der yidisher orfografie, *Kultur un Bildung*, October 1918, pp. 8–10.

39. He does not mention that the Bolsheviks' innovation was not the plan itself, which had been drafted in 1912, but was their insistent implementation of that plan.

40. Circular in *Kultur un Bildung*, November 26, 1918 (no. 11–12).

41. In 1919, the cultural division of the relatively independent Jewish Commissariat (*Evkom*) was brought under the bureaucracy of *Narkompros*, the general state commissariat for culture and education. This move meant that for important issues, final approval for project funding needed to come from the Executive Board of Narkompros. See the circular in *Kultur un Bildung,* December 10, 1918.

42. Ibid.

43. I. Zaretsky, "Di reforme-bavegung in yidisher oysleg," *Di Royte Velt,* Jan–Feb, 1926, no. 1(16), p. 117. The Soviet Union was not the first official body to recognize Yiddish as a language, but was the first to be involved in its modernization. According to Zalman Reyzen, that claim goes to South Africa, which recognized Yiddish as the language of the Jews at the turn of the century. See Reyzen, *Yidishe Shprakh*, p. 38.

44. Avrom Veviorke, "Vegn unzer oysleg," *Emes* Feb. 18, 1926 (no. 40), p. 2.

45. As we will see later in the discussion of Latinization, radical language reform was not isolated to the Soviet Union, but was part of a broader trend of making new (or remaking existing) national cultures in the wake of World War I and the collapse of European empires.

46. GARF, f. 2307, op. 2, d. 96, l. 38.

47. Soviet cultural activists took great pride that "their" orthography had been adopted by this branch of the avant-garde American Yiddish cultural élite. See *Komunistishe Velt*, March–April, 1920, no. 14–15, p. 33.
48. "Itsik Zaretsky," in *Leksikon fun der nayer yidisher literatur* (New York: World Jewish Culture Congress, 1960), vol. 3, col. 577.
49. GARF, f. 1318, op. 1, d. 570, l. 389, 396, 399.
50. Alfred Greenbaum, *Jewish Scholarship and Scholarly Institutions in Soviet Russia, 1918–1953* (Jerusalem: Hebrew University Press, 1978), p. 27.
51. Itsik Zaretsky, "Vegn der reform fun der yidisher orfografie," *Kultur un Bildung* (no. 1) 1920, p. 11.
52. Ibid., p. 13.
53. This parenthetical comment is in the original.
54. Ibid., p. 13.
55. Itsik Zaretsky, ed., *Klolim fun dem yidishn oysleg* (Odessa: Ukrainian State Publishing House, 1921).
56. *Yidish* (Kharkov: Ukrainian Commissariat of Enlightenment, 1921). On the establishment of this journal, see TsDAVODVU, f.166, op. 2, d. 616, l. 16. The Council for National Minorities (*Sovnatsmen*), a division of Narkompros Ukraine, pressed hard for *Yidish*'s speedy publication. See GARF, f. 296, op. 1, d. 27, l. 65.
57. On the history of the Jewish section of the Institute for Belorussian Culture (Inbelkult), see I. Gerasimova, "K istorii evreiskogo otdela instituta belorusskoi kul'tury (inbelkult) i evreiskogo sektora belorusskoi akademii nauk v 20-kh-30-kh godakh," *Vestnik evreiskogo universiteta v moskve* 1996 2(12): 144–167.
58. The complicated founding of the YIVO Institute, which eventually settled in Vilna, has been treated by Cecile Kuznitz in her dissertation, "The Origins of Yiddish Scholarship and the YIVO Institute for Jewish Research," (Ph.D. diss., Stanford University, 2000).
59. Other Jewish research centers in the Soviet Union, such as the Jewish Ethnographic Society, published in Russian.
60. "Byuletin fun der yidsektsie fun Inveyskult," *Shtern* (Minsk), January 1926, no. 1 (4), pp. 67–8.
61. GARF, f. 3316, op. 20, d. 211, l. 250? (The pages were not clearly numbered in this file.)
62. L. Rozenhoyz, "Tsaytshrift," *Shtern* Nov. 1926, no. 7–8, p. 68; N. Shtif, "Tsaytshrift," *Shtern* (Kharkov), Oct. 13 (no. 235), p. 3.
63. "Cultural Chronicle," *Shtern* (Minsk), Jan. 1926, no. 1(4), pp. 69–70.
64. Under Meir Viner's leadership, in the 1930s it became a major center of Yiddish literary studies. Thank you to Mikhail Krutikov for bringing this to my attention.
65. Henry Abramson, *A Prayer for the Government: Ukrainians and Jews in Revolutionary Times, 1917–1920* (Cambridge, MA: Harvard University Press, 1999), p. xv.
66. Kharkov became the capital of the Soviet Republic of Ukraine during the Civil War period when Kiev was considered too "nationalist" to make it the Soviet capital. Kharkov was the capital of Soviet Ukraine from 1920, when the Civil War ended, until 1934, when the capital was moved back to Kiev.
67. RGASPI, f. 445, op. 1, d. 179, l. 195.
68. David Shneer, "Making Yiddish Modern: The Creation of a Yiddish-Language Establishment in the Soviet Union," *East European Jewish Affairs* 30(2) 2000, p. 84.

69. The memorandum was signed illegibly by the director of the Central Jewish Bureau of Narkompros, presumably Mikhail Levitan, and was dated March 23, 1925. RGASPI, f. 445, op. 1, d. 172, l. 24–5.

70. TsDAVODV, f. 166, op. 6, d. 7229, l. 108.

71. For a detailed discussion of the negotiations by which *Di Yidishe Shprakh* came into being, see for example Shneer, "Making Yiddish Modern," pp. 77–98.

72. "Di Yidishe Shprakh," *Di Yidishe Shprakh: zhurnal far praktish yidish shprakhvisn*, March 1927 (no. 1), p.1.

73. The complicated relationship between vernacular and written, orality and textuality in Jewish bilingual culture is addressed in Sheila Jelen, "Oral and Written: Vernacular Literatures of the Hebrew Revival" (Ph.D. diss., University of California, Berkeley, 2000).

74. "Di Yidishe Shprakh," p. 2.

75. Ibid., p. 3.

76. Ibid., pp. 5–6.

77. YIVO Archives, RG 421, f. 54, Letter dated December 7, 1924. The three reforms were 1) writing a *vov* in place of *alef vov*, for the sound "oo"; 2) write *yud, khirik*, instead of *alef yud khirik* for the sound "ee"; and 3) do not double up the consonants when adding prefixes as in *onnemen* (to accept) or *farroykhern* (to finish smoking).

78. TsDAVODVU, f. 166, op. 6, d. 172, l. 87.

79. Ibid., l. 3. This brief statement also shows the intricate process though which ideas became printed Yiddish words.

80. A. Veviorke, "Vegn undzer oysleg," which was printed in three separate issues. See *Emes* Feb. 10, 1926 (33), p. 2; Feb. 18, 1926 (40), p. 2; Feb. 28, 1926 (49), p. 2.

81. "Tsu der kumendiker shprakhkonferents," *Oktyabr* Feb. 24 (45), p. 2.

82. Mordkhe Veynger, "Vegn dem yidishn alefbeys, oysleg, und shprakhgebrukh," *Shtern* (Minsk) Mar.1926, no. 2–3, p. 56.

83. Ibid.

84. Ibid., p. 56.

85. Ibid., p. 57. This emphasis on the practical reasons for standardization resembled the concerns of the *Emes* editors who, in 1918, called on their writers to use a standard Yiddish to make editing easier.

86. Itsik Zaretsky, "Vegn yidisher shrift un gramatik," *Shtern* [Minsk] May–June, 1926, no. 5–6 (8–9), pp. 66–7.

87. RGASPI, f.445, op.1, d. 171, p. 150.

88. Ibid., l. 152. See also RGASPI, f. 445, op. 1, d. 184, l.1.

89. B.S. [B. Slutsky, secretary of *Di Yidishe Shprakh*], "Alfarbandishe ortografishe tsugreyt konferents," *Oktyabr* (Minsk) Apr. 14, 1928, no. 89, p. 2. This article also appeared simultaneously in *Emes*.

90. For more on "left" and "right" in Soviet Jewish culture, see Mordechai Altshuler, *Ha-yevsektsiia bi-vrit ha-mo'atsot: beyn komunizm ve-leumiyut*.

91. Slutsky, "Alfarbandishe," p. 2.

92. Ibid.

93. Ibid.

94. Most Yiddish linguists date the establishment of an international standard Yiddish orthography to 1937, the year YIVO published its *Rules for Yiddish Spelling (Takones fun yidishn oysleg)* in Vilna. See Mordkhe Schaechter, "The 'Hidden Standard': A Study of Competing Influences in Standardization," in Fishman, *Never Say Die*, pp. 678–9.

95. M. Scripnik, *Di Naye Yidishe Ortografie* (Kiev, 1929), p. 10. This timetable had been worked out at the orthography conference itself. The original document is in Ts-DAVODVU, f. 3332, op. 1, d. 25, l. 15

96. What these edicts do not mention is handwritten Yiddish. One assumes that orthographic reform implemented through publications and schools would eventually permeate everyone's use of Yiddish. Most personal correspondence from the early 1930s had changed over to the new orthography. There are examples of people chastising their friends for using the old spellings of words, and occasionally materials that were moving toward publication would be edited to reflect the new reform well before these texts reached the printing press.

97. IMLI RAN, f. 346, op. 1, d. 83, l. 6. The contract is dated March 15, 1932.

98. On Latinization in the Soviet Union, see Terry Martin, "Language and Terror: Soviet Language Reform and Reaction, 1922–1940" (Ph.D. diss., University of Chicago, 1996).

99. There were also plans to Latinize Russian as early as 1919. See I.S. Ilinskaia, *Orfografiia i russkii iazyk* (Moscow: Nauka, 1966), p. 93.

100. P. Tedeev, "Novyi alfavit v Osetii," *Kultura i pis'mennost' vostoka*, 1928 no. 1, pp. 101–6 as cited in Martin, "Language and Terror," p. 793. See also Bernard Comrie, *The Languages of the Soviet Union* (Cambridge, New York: Cambridge University Press, 1981), p. 164. The original Cyrillic alphabets for Yakut and Ossetian were created in the mid-nineteenth century, undoubtedly as part of a larger cultural drive to Russify and convert native Russians to Orthodoxy.

101. GARF, f. 296, op. 1, d. 172, ll. 14, 25.

102. RGASPI, f. 17, op. 333, d. 468, l. 170.

103. GARF, f. 296, op. 1, d. 281, l. 5

104. GARF, f. 3316, op. 20, d. 218, ll. 43–44.

105. Yu. Nazirov, "Provedenie novogo tiurkskogo alfavita v SSSR i blizhaishie perspektivy," *Kultura i pis'mennost' vostoka*, 1928, no. 1, pp. 11–13, as cited in Martin, p. 797.

106. GARF, f. 3316, op. 20, d. 218, l. 70.

107. GARF, f. 3316, op. 22, d. 10, l. 35.

108. F.N. Nechaev, "Novyi persidskii alfavit," *Kultura i pis'mennost' vostoka*, 1932, no. 10, pp. 41–2, as cited in Martin, p. 820. Based on the card catalog of the Russian State Library, Judeo-Tadzhik was Latinized in 1929–30 as well.

109. *Revoliutsiia i pis'mennost'*, 1933, no. 1, pp. 140–1, as cited in Martin, p. 828.

110. Reyzen, *Yidishe Literatur*, p. 54.

111. Moshe Shulman, "Razvitie," p. 44. This unsigned article may very well have been written by Sotek or Nathan Birnbaum, one of his followers, who even proposed Latinizing Hebrew. See Reyzen, p. 54.

112. I. Zaretsky, "Latinizacie fun der jidisher shrift," *Ratnbildung* (Kiev) December, 1930 (no. 12), p. 44.

113. The journal *Der groyse kundes* caricatured Zhitlovsky's call for Latinization in a cartoon showing Zhitlovsky marching with a banner saying in Latinized Yiddish "Yiddish with Latin Letters." Below him are the Yiddish words, "Yiddishists of the World, Unite!"

and in the corner is a signature resembling that of Vladimir Lenin's. The cartoon shows that the idea of Latinizing Yiddish had a Communist connotation to it as early as 1926, well before Latinization was a serious proposition for Soviet Yiddish. Fishman, *Never Say Die*, p. 290.

114. At the 1924 Cultural Conference, Niepomniashchy mentioned to Charny that there was brief discussion about Latinizing Yiddish. See YIVO, RG 421, f. 54. Letter dated December 7, 1924.
115. Zaretsky, "Latinizacie," p. 45.
116. I. Zaretsky, "Di frage fun ortografie afn tsveytn alfarbandishn kultur tsuzamenfor," *Ratnbildung* March 1928 (no. 2), p. 34.
117. Moshe Kamenshteyn, "Vegn latinizirn dem idishn alefbeys," *Shtern* [Kharkov], Dec. 29, 1929 (no. 300), p. 3.
118. "Fun der tsentraler ortografisher komisie," *Di Yidishe Shprakh*, Mar–Apr, 1930 (no. 2–3), pp. 85–7.
119. Ibid.
120. See Nokhum Shtif and Elye Spivak "Vegn latinizatsie," *Afn Shprakhfront*, Feb.–Mar. 1932 (no. 2–3), cols. 93–100 for their more conservative viewpoint on Latinization.
121. Estraikh, however, points out that Dimanshteyn coauthored a report with Zaretsky on the Latinization of Yiddish in 1932, but does not make clear whether it was pro- or anti-Latinization. See Estraikh, *Soviet Yiddish*, p. 130.
122. See Shtif and Spivak, "Vegn Latinizatsie," and I. Zaretsky, "K probleme latinizatsii evreiskogo pis'ma," *Revoliutsiia i pis'mennost'*, Jan.–Feb., 1932 (no. 1–2), pp. 15–32.
123. Greenbaum, *Jewish Scholarship*, p. 111. In my research, I have found no other Latinized Yiddish book published in the Soviet Union.
124. Benjamin Harshav, *Language in Time of Revolution* (Berkeley, Los Angeles: University of California Press, 1993), p. 107.
125. M. Beregovsky, *Jidisher Muzik-Folklor: Band I* (Kiev: Institute for Proletarian Jewish Culture, 1934), p. 2.

Chapter Four

1. RGASPI, f. 445, op. 1, d. 78, l. 27. The document is a Workers' and Peasants' Inspectorate (*Rabkrin*) report on the paper theft dated May 19, 1921.
2. Brian Kassof, "The Knowledge Front: Politics, Ideology, and Economics in the Soviet Book Publishing Industry" (Ph.D. diss., University of California, Berkeley, 2000), Introduction, p. 2. I do not mean to suggest that film was not important – there were several Yiddish films produced in the 1920s, and one talkie in 1932 – but that film was not the primary domain Jewish cultural activists used in fostering a new Soviet Jewish culture.
3. On Soviet Yiddish publishing, see Chone Shmeruk, "Ha-pirsumim be-yidish bi-vrit ha-moatsot be-shanim 1917–1960," *Pirsumim yehudiim bi-vrit ha-moatsot: 1917–1960* (Jerusalem: Society for Research on Jewish Communities, 1960), pp. 55–131. On Yiddish literary cultural activity in the Soviet Union, see his *Mavo le-sifrut yidish bi-vrit ha-moatsot* (Jerusalem: Hebrew University Press, 1957). On the Soviet book publishing industry see Kassof, "The Knowledge Front." For more on print culture in the Soviet Union in general, see Jeffrey Brooks, *Discontinuity in the Spread of Popular Print Culture, 1917–1927* (Washington, DC: The Wilson Center, 1981).

4. Martin Luther published a German translation of the New Testament in 1522, and the complete Bible in 1534.

5. See Yisroel Zinberg, *A History of Jewish Literature,* trans. Bernard Martin (Cleveland: Case Western University Press, 1975), vol. 7, pp. 47–52. For a comprehensive history of Hebrew publishing in Italy, see David Amram, *The Makers of Hebrew Books in Italy* (Philadelphia: J.H. Greenstone, 1909) and Herman Frank, *Yidishe tipografie un bukhoysarbetung kunst* (New York: Hebrew American Typographical Union, 1938).

6. Ibid. See also Max Erik, *Di geshikhte fun der yidisher literatur fun di eltste tsaytn biz der haskole tekufe* (Minsk: Belorussian State Publishing House, 1928) for more on the ways various Yiddish literary genres developed.

7. J.S. da Silva Rosa, "Di Kurantin 1686–1687," in Yankev Shatsky, *Zamlbukh lekoved dem 250 yoyvl fun der yidisher prese, 1686–1936* (New York, 1937).

8. Chone Shmeruk, "Aspects of the History of Warsaw as a Yiddish Literary Centre," *Polin: A Journal of Polish-Jewish Studies, Volume 3* (Oxford: Basic Blackwell for the Institute of Polish-Jewish Studies, 1988), pp. 145–9.

9. Jeffrey Brooks, *When Russia Learned to Read* (Princeton: Princeton University Press, 1985), pp. 59–62, 92.

10. Yuri Shevelov, *The Ukrainian Language in the First Half of the Twentieth Century, 1900–1941* (Cambridge: Harvard University Press, 1989), p. 40.

11. Gennady Estraikh, "From Yehupets Jargonists to Kiev Modernists: The Rise of a Yiddish Literary Center, 1880–1914," *East European Jewish Affairs,* Summer 2000 30(1), p. 28.

12. Estraikh, "From Yehupets," pp. 19–21. See also Shmeruk, "Ha-pirsumim be-yidish," pp. 69–70.

13. Estraikh, "From Yehupets," pp. 30–2.

14. Dmitrii Eliashevitch, "Tsenzura izdanii na iazyke idish v rossiiskoi imperii v gody pervoi mirovoi voiny," paper presented at Yiddish Language and Culture in Eastern Europe, Indiana University, October 2001.

15. Sh. Genrich, "Periodishe oysgabes in rusland af yidish far di letste fuftsn yor," *Kultur un Bildung,* September 24, 1918 (no. 5), pp. 14–16.

16. On the history of Bundist newspaper publishing, see Susanne Marten-Finnis, "Instruction-Exclusion-Polemic. Bundist Journalism, 1897–1907," *East European Jewish Affairs,* Summer 2000, v. 30 (no. 1), pp. 39–59.

17. Susanne Marten-Finnis and Heather Valencia, *Sprachinseln: Jiddische Publizistik in London, Wilna, Berlin: 1880–1930* (Köln: Böhlau, 1999).

18. V.I. Lenin, "Partiinaia organizatsiia i partiinaia literatura," *Novaia zhizn',* November 13, 1905.

19. Kh. Pekler, "Tsu der teorie fun a lebedike tsaytung," *Veker* (Minsk), May 30, 1921 (no. 30), p. 2.

20. TsDAHOU, f. 1, op. 20, d. 776, l. 5.

21. "Di lebedike tsaytung," *Komunistishe Fon,* February 17, 1923 (no. 36), p. 3.

22. On the production of Yiddish oral newspapers, see RGASPI, f. 445, op. 1, d. 100, l. 10.

23. On Yiddish wall newspapers, see Anna Shternshis, "From the Eradication of Illiteracy to Workers' Correspondents: Yiddish–Language Mass Movements in the Soviet Union," *East European Jewish Affairs* 32 (1), Summer 2002: 130–2.

24. Zaynen,"Vi azoi ilustrirn a vanttsaytung on a moler," *Shtern*, Oct. 16, 1927 (no. 237), p. 3.

25. Marten-Finnis, "Instruction-Exclusion-Polemic," pp. 43–8.

26. Matthew Lenoe, *Agitation, Propaganda, and the 'Stalinization' of the Soviet Press, 1922–1930.* Carl Beck Papers in Russian and East European Studies, No. 1305 (Pittsburgh: University of Pittsburgh, 1998), p. 10.

27. *Veker/Oktyabr* was the only Yiddish newspaper to be published continuously throughout the 1920s and 1930s and only closed down in 1941. *Komfon/Shtern* began coming out consistently as a daily only in 1925 and was closed down in 1936. *Emes* was closed down in 1938 in a restructuring of the publishing industry.

28. On the distinctions between newspaper types, see Jeffrey Brooks, "The Press and Its Message: Images of America in the 1920s and 1930s," in Sheila Fitzpatrick et al., eds., *Russia in the Era of NEP: Explorations in Soviet Society and Culture* (Bloomington: Indiana University Press, 1991), p. 232.

29. S. Agursky, "Der veg fun der komunistisher prese in yidish," *Oktyabr*, March 7, 1928, (no. 57), p. 1.

30. "Unzer program" and "Greyt zikh tsu tsu milkhome," *Varhayt* (Petrograd), Mar. 1, 1918 (no. 1), p. 1.

31. Lenoe shows that *Pravda* and *Izvestiia* went from nuanced, complex coverage of news and Party policy in the 1920s to a presentation of Soviet society as an army at the command of the "generals" in the Politburo in the 1930s. See Lenoe, *Agitation*, pp. 1, 17.

32. *Varhayt* March 8, 1918 (no. 1), p. 3.

33. See Terry Martin, *The Affirmative Action Empire: Nations and Nationalism in the Soviet Union, 1923–1939* (Ithaca: Cornell University Press, 2000), pp. 10–13.

34. Mordechai Altshuler, *Ha-yevsektsiia bi-vrit ha-moatsot: beyn komunizm ve-leumiyut* (Jerusalem: Hebrew University Press, 1980), p. 36.

35. GARF, f. 1318, op. 1, d. 569, l. 9.

36. RGASPI, f. 445, op. 1, d. 4, l. 107. This document is dated July 22, 1919, and it officially granted *Komunistishe Velt* the status of "state publication."

37. RGASPI, f. 445, op. 1, d. 50, l. 77.

38. Ibid.

39. RGASPI, f. 445, op. 1, d. 46, l. 186.

40. See, for example, *Emes*, December 23, 1920 (32), p. 1.

41. Shmuel Agursky, "Der veg fun der komunistisher prese in yidish," *Oktyabr* March 7, 1928 (no. 57), p. 3.

42. Julie Kay Mueller, "A New Kind of Newspaper: The Origins and Development of a Soviet Institution, 1921–1928" (Ph.D. diss., University of California, Berkeley, 1992), pp. 15–25.

43. Ibid., p. 22.

44. RGASPI, f. 445, op. 1, d. 46, l. 189.

45. RGASPI, f. 445, op. 1, d. 37, l. 10; RGASPI, f. 445, op. 1, d. 29, l. 38.

46. GARF, f. 1318, op. 1, d. 570, ll. 213, 215.

47. RGASPI, f. 445, op. 1, d. 53, l. 4. In the end, the Jewish Division of the People's Commissariat for Nationalities (*Narkomnats*) ruled against the plan; in September 1920, shortly before *Emes'* reappearance in October, *Evsektsiia* named Shakhne Epshteyn

editor–in–chief. Litvakov had to wait one more year, until he left the *Fareynikte* and joined the Communist Party, to become editor–in–chief of *Emes*.

48. RGASPI, f. 445, op. 1, d. 29, l. 57.

49. The Soviet Russian/Yiddish writer and journalist Shlomo Niepomniashchy volunteered as a journalist on the front lines during the Polish campaigns of 1919–1920, and Nokhum Oyslender, a Soviet Yiddish literary critic and scholar served as a medic for a year. For more on Niepomniashchy's experience, see his correspondence with Daniel Charny, YIVO Archives, RG 421, Files 54–60. On Nokhum Oyslender's years in the Russian Army, see RGALI, f. 2536, op. 1, d. 7–13.

50. GARF f. 1318, op. 1, d. 571, l. 332.

51. Tony Michels, "Socialism with a Jewish Face: The Origins of the Yiddish-Speaking Communist Movement in the United States, 1907–1923," in Gennady Estraikh and Mikhail Krutikov, eds., *Yiddish and the Left* (Oxford: Legenda Press, 2001), pp. 24–55.

52. RGASPI, f. 445, op. 1, d. 46, l. 189. See also Ibid., d. 29, l. 40 for a list of the *Emes* staff with their positions and salaries. See also Ibid., d. 98, l. 24 for an employee list from late 1921.

53. On the economics of scarcity in publishing, see Kassof, "The Knowledge Front," chapter three, pp. 1–5. Charny includes several colorful stories about the lack of paper during the Civil War. Daniel Charny, *A yortsendlik aza*, pp. 200–300.

54. Maurice Friedberg, *Russian Classics in Soviet Jackets* (New York: Columbia University Press, 1962), pp. 30–4.

55. RGASPI, f. 17, op. 60, d. 886, l. 2. In his examination of the East German publishing system, Robert Darnton says that paper was in short supply and was a tool used to encourage or prevent publication of certain books. Robert Darnton, "The Good Old Days," *New York Review of Books*, May 16, 1991: 44–9.

56. Sh. Agursky, "Der veg fun der komunistisher prese in yidish," *Oktiabr* March 7, 1928 (no. 57), p. 2.

57. RGASPI, f. 17, op. 60, d. 886, l. 2.

58. "Vi makht men papir," *Shtern*, February 26, 1927 (no. 47), p. 2.

59. RGASPI, f. 445, op. 1, d. 46, l. 112.

60. RGASPI, f. 445, op. 1, d. 50, l. 77.

61. RGASPI, f. 445, op. 1, d. 69, l. 67.

62. RGASPI, f. 445, op. 1, d. 8, l. 137.

63. In 1921–1922, the cost of printing varied between 50 and 65 percent of publication costs. Between paper and printing, there was little money left to pay staff. See RGASPI, f. 445, op. 1, d. 127, l. 82.

64. RGASPI, f. 445, op. 1, d. 50, l. 77. These plans had been discussed as early as 1918. See "A tsentrale drukeray," *Emes*, Oct. 16, 1918 (no. 46), p. 3.

65. RGASPI, f. 445, op. 1, d. 73, l. 126.

66. GARF, f. 4033, op. 1, d. 6, ll. 220–3.

67. RGASPI, f. 445, op. 1, d. 54, l. 40.

68. RGASPI, f. 445, op. 1, d. 47, l. 23.

69. Shmeruk, "Pirsumim be-yidish," p. 72.

70. RGASPI, f. 445, op. 1, d. 97, l. 104.

71. RGASPI, f. 445, op. 1, d. 69, l. 76.

72. GARF, f. 2307, op. 5, d. 39, l. 37.

73. Ibid.

74. RGASPI, f. 445, op. 1, d. 133, l. 136.

75. RGASPI, f. 445, op. 1, d. 133, l. 131.

76. On Soviet German publishing, see Meir Buchsweiler, *Rußlanddeutsche im Sowjetsystem bis zum Zweiten Weltkrieg* (Essen: Klartext Verlag, 1997), pp. 24–38.

77. GARF, f. 1318, op. 1, d. 228, l. 1–10, 176. See also Shmeruk, "Pirsumim be-yidish," pp. 74–7.

78. RGASPI, f. 17, op. 60, d. 931, l. 78.

79. RGASPI, f. 17, op. 112, d. 575, protocol 10, point 7.

80. Boris Gorokhoff, *Publishing in the U.S.S.R.* (Bloomington: Indiana University Press, 1959), p. 199.

81. Shmeruk, "Pirsumim be-yidish," pp. 73–4.

82. Mueller, "A New Kind," pp. 77–8.

83. Ibid., p. 83.

84. Statistics on Soviet Yiddish periodicals between the Ninth Party Congress (April 1920) and the Tenth Party Congress (March 1921).

Newspaper	Location	Number of editions	Circulation (what happened as a result of self-sufficiency law)
Emes	Moscow	142	10,000
Veker	Minsk	257	5,000
Profbavegung	Minsk	37	2,000
Royter Shtern	Vitebsk	268	4,000 (transformed)
Komveg	Gomel	182	2,000 (transformed)
Komfon	Kiev	268	2,000 (transformed)
Komshtim	Odessa	31 (weekly)	800 (closed)
Kommunist	Ekaterinoslav	35 (weekly)	800 (closed)
Komvort	Kremenchug	33 (weekly)	700 (closed)
Komshtim	Zhitomir	36 (weekly)	500 (closed)
Komunist	Kharkov	12	2,000

See RGASPI, f. 445, op. 1, d. 102, ll. 146–7.

85. RGASPI, f. 445, op. 1, d. 114, l. 38 for *Emes*' loans. TsDAHOU, f. 1, op. 20, d. 1526, l. 41 for *Komfon*'s loans.

86. Ibid., l. 225.

87. Mueller, "A New Kind," p. 95.

88. RGASPI, f. 17, op. 60, d. 995, ll. 49–52.

89. Ibid., l. 84.

90. Gorokhoff, *Publishing in the U.S.S.R.*, p. 251.

91. RGASPI, f. 17, op. 60, d. 1004, l. 9.

92. RGASPI, f. 17, op. 60, d. 37, l. 28.

93. Mueller, "A New Kind," p. 182.

94. RGASPI, f. 445, op. 1, d. 133, l. 51.

95. The first ads began appearing late in 1921, just as the Press Crisis was beginning, and just before the *Sovnarkom* resolution forcing newspapers into financial self-sufficiency.

96. The Baltic America Company was the first regular advertiser in *Emes*. Its ads appealed to a Jewish community that had become fractured after the mass migrations related to World War I and the Russian Revolution. "Attention, people with relatives in the

United States of America or Canada. . . . If you have lost contact with your relatives in America, provide us with their most recent address and we will take all measures to find out their current place of residence."

97. Mueller, "A New Kind," p. 75.
98. Ibid., p. 76.
99. *Emes*, November 7, 1922.
100. GARF, f. 1318, op. 1, d. 588, l. 7. These statistics reflect the number of copies printed, not necessarily the number of copies read. During the Civil War, circulation numbers were generally high due to the low cost of printing and the lack of financial accountability.
101. To put the drop in circulation in perspective, of 231 newspapers mentioned in a questionnaire about the Party Press distributed at the Eleventh Party Congress, most had an average circulation between 3,500 and 4,000. Mueller, "A New Kind," pp. 80–2. For the Soviet Yiddish newspaper circulation statistics, see RGASPI, f. 445, op. 1, d. 102, l. 141.
102. Shmeruk, "Pirsumim be-yidish," p. 73.
103. This data comes from GARF, f. 4033, op. 1, d. 18, ll. 4–5.
104. Brooks, "Discontinuity," p. 11.
105. RGASPI, f. 445,op. 1, d. 161, l. 45
106. RGASPI, f. 445, op. 1, d. 118, l. 260.
107. On the problematic relationship of republican and all–Union nationalities politics and the awkward place of the Russian republic within those politics, see Yuri Slezkine, "The USSR as a Communal Apartment, or How a Socialist State Promoted Ethnic Particularism," *Slavic Review*, Summer 1994 53(2), pp. 414–52.
108. Avrom Merezhin, "Unzer prese-fragn," *Emes*, January 18, 1923 (no. 12), p. 2.
109. The Ukrainian-based *Komunistishe Fon* was transformed into a weekly publication until 1924 when it was moved from Kiev to Kharkov, the capital of Soviet Ukraine, and was relaunched as the daily newspaper *Shtern*.
110. RGASPI, f. 445, op. 1, d. 150, l. 176.
      Emes circulation statistics through the 1920s.

Date	Circulation
January 1922	10,000
July 1922	3,000
March 1923	3,000
November 1923	4,200
December 1923	4,400
March 1924	5,044
January 1925	7,200
May 1925	6,000
December 1927	12,000
January 1928	13,200
January 1929	22,000
January 1930	29,000

The 1925 drop is due to the reestablishment of a daily Ukrainian newspaper.

111. RGASPI, f. 445, op. 1, d. 40, l. 209.
112. Ibid.
113. RGASPI, f. 445, op. 1, d. 179, l. 58.
114. TsDAVODVU, f. 3298, op. 1, d. 4, l. 31.
115. Kassof, ch. 1, pp. 34–45.
116. TsDAVODVU, f. 166, op. 6, d. 7231, ll. 293–6.
117. GARF, f. 4033, op. 1, d. 36, l. 40; GARF, f. 4033, op. 1, d. 37, ll. 16–17. On the Ukrainian branch of the Central Publishing House of People's of the Soviet Union (*Tsentroizdat*), see TsDAVODVU, f. 413, op. 1, d. 352, ll. 34–5.
118. The 1924 catalogs list fifty-five authors of fiction published by School and Book (*Shul un Bukh*). *Katalog far der Farlag Aktsion-Gezelshaft "Shul un Bukh"* (Moscow: Shul un Bukh, 1924).
119. The publishing list did not include titles of publications, which is why it is not clear whether these were translations of these authors' Hebrew work into Yiddish or their original Yiddish work.
120. "*Vos mir viln*," *Der Yidisher Poyer*, February 3, 1926.
121. According to Marten-Finnis and Valencia, the didactic–propagandistic quality of Jewish journalism is its defining feature, stretching back to the first Yiddish newspaper, *Di Kurantin*, in Amsterdam (1686–1688). See Marten-Finnis and Valencia, *Sprachinseln*, pp. 15–16.
122. The circulation of *Emes* ranged from 5,000 to 10,000 – never as high as *Evsektsiia* hoped.
123. "Provints: Vitebsk and Berdichev," *Emes*, March 24, 1922, pp. 2–3. Also see "Provints: Vitebsk, Arbeter Lebn," *Emes*, March 25, 1922, p. 2.
124. Literary images of the Soviet shtetl portrayed a similarly bleak portrait of the Jewish heartland. See chapter six.
125. Izi Kharik, "Shtetl," 1924 as published in *Af der erd* (Moscow: Shul un Bukh, 1926).
126. On anti-religion campaigns, see Anna Shternshis, "Kosher and Soviet: Soviet Jewish Popular Culture, 1917–1941" (D. Phil. Diss., Oxford University, 2000), ch. 2.
127. See the article "Vegn yomim naroyim," *Emes*, August 24, 1923.
128. M. Altshuler, *Komsomolishe hagode* (Kharkov: Izdatelstvo Put' prosveshchneie, not listed). Altshuler published another haggadah called *Hagode far gloiber un apikorsim* (Moscow: Tsentroizdat, 1927).
129. "Antireligieze bavegung," Ibern land, *Emes*, March 24, 1923.
130. "A Trial Against Traditional Teachers," *Provints, Emes*, May 29, 1923.
131. *Emes*, February 2, 1922.
132. Terry Martin, "The Origins of Soviet Ethnic Cleansing," *Journal of Modern History* 1998 (70), pp. 813–61.
133. Maurice Friedberg, *Russian Classics in Soviet Jackets* (New York: Columbia University Press, 1962), pp. 22–3.
134. Lenoe, *Agitation*, p. 37.
135. Samuel Jordan, "El Lissitsky and the Optical Word: Visual Aspects to Soviet-Yiddish Language Planning and Construction," paper presented at *Beyond the Shtetl: Yiddish Language and Culture in 20th Century Eastern Europe*, Indiana University, October 2001. See also G. Kazovskii, "Shagal i evreiskaia khudozhestvennaia programma v Rossii," *Vestnik Evreiskogo universiteta v Moskve*, no. 1. Moscow–Jerusalem, 1992.

136. Camilla Gray, *The Russian Experiment in Art, 1863–1922,* new edition (New York, London: Thames and Hudson, 1986), p. 270.

137. M. L., "Arbkor: Organ far arbkorn, dorfkorn, kuskorn un yunkorn," a supplement of *Shtern* (Minsk), July 1925 (no. 2), pp. 66–7.

138. *Emes,* March 26, 1923. The letters have the appearance of being hand drawn and look three dimensional.

139. Gerald Janecek, *The Look of Russian Literature* (Princeton: Princeton University Press, 1984), pp. 149–203.

140. Gray, *The Russian Experiment,* pp. 253–69. Sans-serif type lacks the extra lines at the top and bottom of large letters, called serifs.

141. Mueller, "A New Kind," p. 39–41.

142. "Vi s'vert fartik a nomer *Oktyabr,*" *Oktyabr,* May 5, 1928 (no. 102), p. 2. All references to *Oktyabr's* editorial process come from this article.

143. For more on Yiddish workers' correspondents, see Shternshis, "On the Eradication of Illiteracy."

144. "Kunst-khronik," *Baginen,* June 1919 (no. 1), p. 85.

145. "Kiev 'Folks Farlag' in Berlin," *Moment,* April 22, 1921.

146. Noyekh Lurie served as both literary editor of Litvakov's All-Ukrainian Literary Committee and as the editor of the Jewish Section of *Vseizdat,* the Central Executive Committee's publishing house. The distinctions between the organizations were, thus, rather blurry.

147. Hersh Smolar, *Fun ineveynik* (Tel Aviv: Peretsfarlag, 1978), p. 153.

148. RGASPI, f. 445, op. 1, d. 152, l. 117.

149. TsDAVODVU, f. 413, op. 1, d. 2, l. 211.

150. RGASPI, f. 445, op. 1, d. 152, l. 25.

151. TsDAVODVU, f. 166, op. 6, d. 712, l. 14.

152. RGASPI, f. 445, op. 1, d. 186, l. 69.

153. Kh. Dunets, "Di dinamik," p. 42.

154. Dunets, "Di dinamik," p. 43.

155. GARF, f. 3316, op. 20, d. 211, l. 179.

156. GARF, f. 3316, op. 20, d. 211, l. 178.

157. "A yor *Oktyabr* in tsifirn," *Oktyabr,* Nov. 7, 1926 (no. 257), p. 5.

158. Herman Ermolaev, *Censorship in Soviet Literature, 1917–1991* (Lanham, MD: Rowman & Littlefield, 1997), p. 259.

159. Jan Plamper, "Abolishing Ambiguity: Soviet Censorship Practices in the 1930s," *Russian Review* 60(4) (Oct. 2001): 526–544; Darnton, "The Good Old Days."

160. RGASPI, f. 445, op. 1, d. 78, l. 126.

161. RGASPI, f. 445, op. 1, d. 97, l. 125; TsDAVODVU, f. 3298, op. 1, d. 2, l. 20.

162. RGASPI, f. 445, op. 1, d. 37, ll. 88–103. On the simultaneous chaos of the Russian-language publishing industry, see Kassof, "The Knowledge Front," chapter one.

163. *Partay materialn,* November 1920 (no. 2), p. 17.

164. Kassof, chp. 1, pp. 25–38.

165. RGASPI, f. 445, op. 1, d. 115, l. 3. The special commission for coordinating Yiddish publishing had its first meeting January 24–25, 1922, with Esther Frumkina (chair), Moshe Litvakov, Mikhail Levitan, M. Altshuler, E. Osherovich, M. Potash, and Yankev Rabichev in attendance. See RGASPI, f. 445, op. 1, d. 115, l. 5.

166. Blium, *Evreiskii vopros*, chapters two and three.
167. RGASPI, f. 445, op. 1, d. 117, l. 12. The Central Bureau permitted the circulation of Bialik's poetry in Russian translation and his original Yiddish works.
168. GARF, f. 3316, op. 21, d. 743, l. 1.
169. Alfred Greenbaum, *Jewish Scholarship and Scholarly Institutions in Soviet Russia, 1918–1953* (Jerusalem: Hebrew University Press, 1978), p. 80.
170. TsDAHOU, f. 1, op. 20, d. 1528, ll. 14, 162.
171. Ibid., l. 140.
172. Ibid., l. 174.
173. Ibid., ll. 71–2.
174. TsDAVODVU, f. 166, op. 6, d. 8209, l. 25.
175. TsDAVODVU, f. 166, op. 4, d. 979.
176. TsDAVODVU, f. 166, op. 6, d. 7229, ll. 1–20, 62–5.
177. TsDAVODVU, f. 166, op. 6, d. 7230, l. 31.
178. TsDAVODVU, f. 166, op. 6, d. 7231, ll. 346–50.
179. The charge of mysticism made B. Marshak even more concerned that this censor would reject the planned publication of a work by Der Nister, who was known specifically for his symbolist, mystical prose style.
180. TsDAVODVU, f. 166, op. 6, d. 7231, l. 333. Marshak's letter to the CJEB is dated November 30, 1928.
181. Jeffrey Veidlinger, *The Moscow State Jewish Theater* (Bloomington: Indiana University Press, 2000), pp. 68–71.
182. RGASPI, f. 445, op. 1, d. 46, l. 94.
183. RGASPI, f. 445, op. 1, d. 174, ll. 103–5.
184. GARF, f. 406, op. 25, d. 474, l. 2.
185. RGASPI, f. 445, op. 1, d. 174, l. 101.
186. GARF f. 406, op. 25, d. 474, l. 12. For an overview of Poaley Tsion in the Soviet Union, see Baruch Gurevitz, *National Communism in the Soviet Union: 1918–1928* (Pittsburgh: University of Pittsburgh Press, 1980), pp. 58–98. For its newspaper statistics, see RGASPI, f. 272, op. 1.
187. GARF, f. 406, op. 25, d. 474, l. 2.
188. RGASPI, f. 445, op. 1, d. 174, ll. 132–4.
189. RGASPI, f. 17, op. 113, d. 587, l. 111.
190. Ibid., ll. 109–10.
191. RGASPI, f. 445, op. 1, d. 177, l. 136. By 1926, the Russian currency was relatively stable after two different currency reforms between 1922–4.
192. RGASPI, f. 445, op. 1, d. 186, l. 10.
193. Ibid., l. 63.
194. Shmeruk shows that the establishment of Birobidzhan did not suddenly put Jews on equal footing with other ethnic minorities when it came to cultural production. See Shmeruk, "Pirsumim be-Yidish," pp. 86–7.
195. For comparison, the population of the Ukrainian Soviet Socialist Republic was Ukrainian 80 percent, Russian 9.2 percent, Jewish 5.4 percent, Polish 1.6 percent, and German 1.4 percent, according to 1932 statistics based on the 1926 Soviet census. Volodymyr Kubijovych, ed., *Ukraine: A Concise Encyclopedia* (Toronto: University of Toronto Press, 1963), p. 210.

196. GARF, f. 296, op. 1, d. 47, l. 112. Yiddish was allocated the most number of printer's pages in 1922 as well. See RGASPI, f. 445, op. 1, d. 37, l. 31.
197. Buchsweiler, *Rußlanddeutsche*, p. 31.
198. Lenoe, *Agitation*.
199. Shmeruk does an excellent job of describing the consolidation of the early 1930s. See Shmeruk, "Pirsumim be-yidish," pp. 80–3.

Chapter Five

1. On the relationship between literature, literary canons, and nationalism for "peripheral" European nations, see Gregory Jusdanis, *Belated Modernity and Aesthetic Culture: Inventing National Literature* (Minnesota: University of Minnesota Press, 1991).
2. Edward J. Brown, *Proletarian Episode in Russian Literature* (New York: Columbia University Press, 1953), p. 7.
3. Murphy, *Proletarian Moment*, pp. 24–5.
4. V.L. Lvov-Rogachevsky, *Ocherki proletarskoi literatury* (Moscow: Moscow Joint Stock Publishing Company, 1927), p. 178.
5. "Editorial Manifesto of the On Guard Group," translated in George Reavey and Marc Slonim, *Soviet Literature: An Anthology* (New York: Covici and Friede, 1934), p. 405.
6. The Serapion Brothers included Mikhail Zoshchenko and Viktor Shklovsky, among others. See Marc Slonim, *Soviet Russian Literature: Writers and Problems, 1917–1977* (New York: Oxford University Press, 1977), pp. 99–109.
7. "What Does LEF Fight For?" in Anna Lawton, ed., *Russian Futurism Through Its Manifestoes, 1912–1928* (Ithaca: Cornell University Press, 1988), p. 194.
8. George Luckyj, *Literary Politics in the Soviet Ukraine: 1917–1934* (Durham, NC: Duke University Press, 1990), pp. 36–7.
9. Oleh Ilnytzkyj, *Ukrainian Futurism, 1914–1930: A Historical and Critical Study* (Cambridge, MA: Harvard University Press, 1997), p. 43.
10. Seth Wolitz, "The Kiev Grupe (1918–1920) Debate: The Function of Literature" in *Studies in American Jewish Literature* 4(2), Winter 1978, pp. 97–106; Seth Wolitz, "*Di Khalyastre*: The Yiddish Modernist Movement in Poland: An Overview," in *Yiddish* 4(3), 1981, pp. 5–19; Seth Wolitz, "Between Folk and Freedom: The Failure of the Yiddish Modernist Movement in Poland," *Yiddish* 8(1), 1991.
11. See Wolitz, "The Kiev Grupe" and Chone Shmeruk, "Yiddish Literature in the Soviet Union," in Lionel Kochan, ed., *The Jews in Soviet Russia Since 1917* (Oxford, New York: Oxford University Press, 1978), pp. 242–80.
12. In creating the Penguin Anthology, Ruth Wisse explained, "There was not much point in including odes to Stalin of the 1930's, or other examples of Leftist fervor that the poets themselves subsequently excluded from their selected works. The forced quality of most of these poems argued as forcefully against them as their discredited political enthusiasms." See Ruth Wisse, "What Shall Live and What Shall Die: The Making of a Yiddish Anthology," Twelfth Annual Rabbi Louis Feinberg Memorial Lecture in Judaic Studies, University of Cincinnati, May 3, 1989, p. 17.
13. See Shmuel Rozhansky, "Dray yidishe madreyges in der sovetisher poezie," in Rozhansky, ed., *Oysgeklibene Shriftn: David Hofshteyn, Izi Kharik, Itsik Fefer* (Buenos Aires: Lifshits-Fond fun der literatur-gezelshaft baym YIVO in argentine, 1962).

14. Ilnytzkyj, *Ukrainian Futurism*, p. xv.
15. Mikhail Krutikov has shown that the move away from modernism toward realism was not particularly Soviet but was a trend within international Yiddish literature. See Mikhail Krutikov, "Between Mysticism and Marxism: Meir Wiener as Writer, Critic, and Literary Historian," *Jews in Eastern Europe* 25(3), Winter 1994, pp. 34–40 and Mikhail Krutikov, "Soviet Literary Theory in the Search for a Yiddish Canon: The Case of Moshe Litvakov," *Yiddish and the Left: Proceedings from the Third International Mendel Freedman Conference* (Oxford: Legenda Press, 2001), pp. 226–41.
16. The best study to date on pre-revolutionary modernist literary politics and its interaction with Soviet power is Katerina Clark, *Petersburg: Crucible of Revolution* (Cambridge: Harvard University Press, 1995).
17. David Hofshteyn, "Friling," *Eygns* no. 1 (Kiev, 1918), p. 60.
18. Nachman Mayzel, *Dos Yidishe Shafn un Der Yidisher Shrayber in Sovetfarband* (New York: IKUF, 1959), introduction.
19. Ilnytzkyj, *Ukrainian Futurism*, pp. 20–3.
20. Wolitz, "Kiev Grupe," p. 100.
21. G. A. Remenik, *Ocherki i portrety: stat'i o evreiskikh pistateleiakh* (Moscow: Sovetskii pisatel' 1975), pp. 23–4.
22. According to Hersh Smolar, Chaikov made a cubist sculpture of Karl Marx that adorned the entrance to the Kiev City Soviet. He mentions that it was later removed for its "formalist" appearance. See Hersh Smolar, *Fun ineveynik* (Tel Aviv: Perets Farlag, 1978), p. 246.
23. David Hofshteyn, "Shtot," *Baginen* no. 1 (Kiev, 1918–9), pp. 3–4.
24. Leyb Kvitko, "In Roytn Shturem," *Baginen* no. 1 (Kiev, 1918–9), pp. 5–10.
25. "A. Litvak," *Leksikon fun der nayer yidisher literatur*, vol. 5, col. 86.
26. A. Litvak, "Literatur un lebn," *Baginen*, July 1919, pp. 97–102.
27. Ibid., p. 98.
28. Vladimir Mayakovsky, "We, Too, Want Meat!" in Lawton, ed., *Russian Futurism*, p. 88.
29. A. Litvak, "Literatur un lebn."
30. RGASPI, f. 445, op. 1, d. 81, l. 12.
31. RGASPI, f. 445, op. 1, d. 1, l. 25. *Kamf* never appeared for the same material reasons that *Baginen* only appeared once.
32. *Khvalyes: Organ fun dem yidishn byuro bam Vitebsk gubkom fun Komsomol*, August–September 1920 (no. 1–2).
33. I define "Party-sponsored" as an initiative that originated within Party circles, rather than an initiative that began within non-Party circles that the Party eventually supported financially or materially, such as *Baginen*.
34. *Khvalyes*, pp. 1–3.
35. Ibid.
36. "Bibliografie," *Emes*, Nov. 25, 1920, (no. 15), p. 2.
37. Benjamin Harshav, *American Yiddish Poetry: A Bilingual Anthology* (Berkeley, Los Angeles: University of California Press, 1986).
38. Daniel Charny, *A yortsendlik aza* (New York, 1943), pp. 79, 165.
39. Wolitz, "*Di Khalyastre*," pp. 5–7.
40. *Emes*, Aug. 7, 1918 (no. 1), p. 4.
41. *Emes*, Nov. 28, 1920 (no. 18), p. 2.

42. For address lists of the Yiddish writers, see GARF, f. 2306, op. 22, d. 73, l. 1 and RGASPI, f. 445, op. 1, d. 29, l. 49.
43. RGASPI, f. 445, op. 1, d. 102, l. 7.
44. See *Emes,* January 12, 1922, for the announcement of the appearance of *Shtrom,* "which will appear at the end of the month"; *Emes,* April 2, 1922, advertises *Shtrom* as a journal that readers can now purchase.
45. Chagall served as a link between the Soviet Jewish community and those in other European centers, between Jewish and European modernism at large, and between art and literature. He published essays on art in Soviet Jewish journals as late as 1927, and in 1942, Chagall illustrated Itsik Fefer's collection, *Roytarmei'ish,* which was published in New York as part of the work of the Jewish Anti-Fascist Committee. See Benjamin Harshav, "The Role of Language In Modern Art: On Texts and Subtexts In Chagall's Paintings," *Modernism/Modernity* 1994 1(2): 51–87.
46. *Shtrom,* no. 1, p. 80.
47. Yehezkiel Dobrushin, "Unzer literatur," *Shtrom,* no. 1, pp. 47–53.
48. Ibid., p. 51.
49. Aaron Gurshteyn, "*Shtrom* no. 1," *Zhizn' natsional'nostei,* April 14, 1922 (no. 7), p. 24; see also RGALI, f. 2270, op. 1, d. 38, l. 16 for his original manuscript of the review.
50. "*Shtrom,* no. 3," *Zhizn' natsional'nostei,* 1923 (no. 5), p. 203.
51. On Markish's *Veyland* and on Yiddish images of Christianity, see Matthew Hoffman, "From Rebel to Rabbi: Reclaiming Jesus and the Making of Modern Secular Jewish Culture" (Ph.D. diss., Graduate Theological Union, 2000), chapter three.
52. Sholem Gordon, "In erdishn doyer: David Hofshteyn," *Shtrom* no. 3, pp. 76–7.
53. "Shtrom ovent in moskver klub, 3te internatsional," *Shtrom,* no. 2, p. 78.
54. *Shtrom,* no. 5–6, 1924.
55. "Yidishe kultur tuer kegn kemfendikn hebreizm," *Emes,* February 12, 1924 (no. 34), pp. 2–3.
56. "What Does LEF Fight for," in Lawton, ed., *Russian Futurism,* p. 194. Italics in the original.
57. RGASPI, f. 445, op. 1, d. 166, l. 7. The memo is dated April 4, 1924.
58. Gennady Estraikh, "Itsik Fefer: A Yiddish *Wunderkind* of the Bolshevik Revolution," *Shofar: An Interdisciplinary Journal of Jewish Studies* 20:3 (2002): 16.
59. Weinreich's modern English-Yiddish dictionary does not list the word, and Harkavy's Yiddish-English dictionary defines aftergrowth as "vidervaksung," but other native speakers claim that *vidervuks* is used in certain dialects. I thank Chana Kronfeld for pointing out the importance of the name *Vidervuks.*
60. David Hofshteyn, "Araynfir," to Itsik Fefer, *Shpener* (Kiev, 1922), pp. 3–4. The book was published by *Lirik,* a subsidiary of the *Kultur Lige* publishing house.
61. See especially the poem after which the journal was named, Esther Shumiacher's "Albatros." Melekh Ravitch, *Nakete reyd* (Vienna: Kval farlag, 1921).
62. See *Vidervuks'* advertisement in *Komunistishe Fon,* July 6, 1922 (no. 92), p. 4.
63. Y. Nusinov, "Vidervuks," *Komunistishe Fon,* July 16, 1922 (no. 101), p. 3.
64. "Literarishe Bletl," *Komunistishe Fon,* Jan. 13, 1923 (no. 8), p. 4. The expression *barg aroyf* (going uphill) was meant to counter one of the dominant tropes of the interwar modernism, the world in decline or *barg arop.* See for example Uri Tsvi Grinberg's *Velt Barg Arop,*" *Albatros* 1922: 12–14.

65. Nokhum Oyslender, "Literary Publishing House 'Vidervuks' Kiev," *Shtrom* (no. 4), pp. 89–90. Although Oyslender refers to the group as a "publishing house," *Vidervuks* described itself as a literary group.
66. On the lack of investment in *Proletkult* among Ukrainian writers, see Ilnytzkyj, *Ukrainian Futurism*, p. 40.
67. Harshav, *Meaning*, pp. 169–72.
68. See Bis, "Di ershte teg fun Komfon," *Komfon*, May 30, 1923 (no. 105), p. 3.
69. Kh. Dunets, "Di dinamik fun der yidisher farlag-arbet in Sovet Vaysrusland," *Shtern*, January 1929 (no. 1), p. 42. For the review of *Hamer klang*, see RGALI, f. 2270, op. 1, d. 38, l. 39. The review was published in *Zhizn' natsional'nostei*, September 11, 1922 (no. 18), p. 16.
70. Chaim Gildin, "Shpant," in David Utkes, Chaim Gildin, M. [Monye] Gurevitch, et al., *Lider* (Kiev-Kharkov: Melukhefarlag, 1921), pp. 31–3.
71. Chaim Gildin, "Afn veg tsu zikh," in Utkes, Gildin, Gurevitch, et al., *Lider*, p. 35.
72. RGASPI, f. 445, op. 1, d. 133, l. 65.
73. David Utkes, "Arum undzere literarishe grupirungen," *Emes*, October 3, 1923 (no. 222), p. 4.
74. RGASPI, f. 445, op. 1, d. 150, l. 19.
75. On the sites of Moscow Soviet Jewish culture in the 1920s, see Gabrielle Freitag, "Juden in Moskau, 1917–1932," Magisterarbeit, Johann Wolfgang Goethe Universität, Frankfurt, 2000.
76. "Literarishe Khronik," *Emes*, October 18, 1923 (no. 235), p. 4.
77. RGASPI, f. 445, op. 1, d. 150, l. 26.
78. Ibid.
79. Ibid., ll. 31–3.
80. RGASPI, f. 445, op. 1, d. 137, l. 131.
81. RGASPI, f. 445, op. 1, d. 172, l. 23. The petition is dated November 20, 1924.
82. Ber Orshansky, "Der birger krig in der literatur, *Oktyabr* un *Nayerd*," *Shtern*, January 1925 (no. 1), p. 59.
83. Ibid., p. 60.
84. Letter from Shlomo Niepomniashchy to Daniel Charny, December 24, 1924. YIVO, RG 421, file 54.
85. Ibid., p. 62.
86. "Finf yor Yidsektsiia MAPP," *Royte Velt*, No. 1–2, 1930 (no. 209).
87. Trotsky defined the thick journal in the most philosophical way possible. "We have in mind a journal as a spiritual focus of well-known social groups. The Russian journal will reach its end when the messianism of the Russian intelligentsia comes to an end." See Lev Trotsky, "*Sud'ba tolstogo zhurnala*," *Kievskaya Mysl'*, March 16, 19, 1914 (nos. 75–8).
88. RGASPI, f. 445, op. 1, d. 133, l. 116.
89. Ilnytzkyj shows that Ukrainian modernist literature also shifted from Kiev to Kharkov for material reasons. Ilnytzkyj, *Ukrainian Futurism*, pp. 49–58.
90. A fourth name appeared on the front of *Royte Velt* – M. Ravitch-Cherkassy, who directed the press division of the Ukrainian Communist Party's Central Committee, showing that despite *Royte Velt*'s independent aesthetic stance, its personnel was tied directly to the state and the Party.

91. RGASPI, f. 445, op. 1, d. 152, l. 84.

92. Smolar, *Fun ineveynik*, p. 251.

93. Moshe Kiper, "Nutst oys di *Royte Velt*," *Shtern* March 30, 1928 (no. 76), p. 2.

94. Moshe Tayf, "Vegn zhurnal *Shtern*," *Oktyabr*, December 18, 1925 (no. 36), p. 3.

95. Y.N., "Shtern, no. 2," *Royte Velt*, 1925 (no. 14), pp. 103–4.

96. Letter from Izi Kharik to H. Leyvik in Altshuler, *Briv*, p. 53.

97. K.I., "*Shtern, no. 1–4*," *Royte Velt*, Sept. 1926 (no. 9), p. 129.

98. B. Orshansky, "Vegn eyn vinkele in *Der Royte Velt*," *Shtern*, September–October 1926 (no. 9–10), p. 56.

99. Ibid., p. 58.

100. Trotsky, *Literature*, pp. 15–16, 218.

101. Murphy, *Proletarian Moment*, pp. 26–7.

102. Brown, *Proletarian Episode*, pp. 40–3.

103. Altshuler, *Briv*, pp. 48–52. *Frayhayt* became *Morgn Frayhayt* in 1929.

104. The letter was printed in *Emes*, April 20, 1926, and was reprinted in Altshuler, *Briv*, p. 106.

105. Letter from David Hofshteyn to Daniel Charny, August 10, 1928. YIVO RG 421, folder 23, p. 32. Hofshteyn's letter is written on *Prolit* stationery, a true sign that Hofshteyn was part of the Soviet Jewish literary establishment.

106. Altshuler, *Briv*, p. 27. Even though Markish became an honored member of the literary establishment, he did so without being a member of the Communist Party. He officially became a Party member in 1942. See David Shneer, "Perets Markish," in Sorrel Kerbel, ed., *Jewish Writers of the Twentieth Century* (London: Fitzroy Dearborn Publishers, 2003).

107. This description of the Markish celebration comes from a letter from Shlomo Niepomniashchy to Daniel Charny, February 7, 1927. YIVO, RG 209, File 57.

108. Letter from Niepomniashchy to Daniel Charny, February 16, 1927. YIVO RG 209, File 57. Despite the rhetorical distance these writers took from Bialik, all of them were interested in his work and thought of themselves as his legacy. In this particular letter, Niepomniashchy alludes to Markish's well-known *poema*, "Di Kupe," a modernist lament after the pogroms of 1921. For a close treatment of *Di Kupe*, and how it is tied and not tied to earlier forms of literary responses to catastrophe, see Seth Wolitz, "A Yiddish Modernist Dirge: *Di Kupe* of Perets Markish," *Yiddish* 6(4), 1987, pp. 56–67, and David Roskies, *Against the Apocalypse* (Cambridge: Harvard University Press, 1984), pp. 97–101.

109. Tilo Alt, "A Survey of Literary Contributions to the Post World War I Yiddish Journals of Berlin," *Yiddish*, Spring 1985 (vol. 6, no. 1), pp. 42–52.

110. D.B., "Dray tsentern," *In Shpan*, April 1926 (no. 1), pp. 84–96.

111. RGASPI, f. 445, op. 1, d. 174, l. 94. See *Shtern* (Kharkov), March 5, 1926, p. 2.

112. Ibid. The editors' response was printed just below Bergelson's letter.

113. Letter from Niepomniashchy to Charny, March 11, 1926. YIVO RG 206, File 26.

114. Altshuler, *Briv*, pp. 47–8.

115. IMLI RAN f. 346, op. 1, d. 105, l. 1. In the 1930s, Bergelson was the most widely published and highest paid Yiddish writer. The highest paid poet in the 1930s was Perets Markish.

116. RGASPI, f. 445, op. 1, d. 172, l. 26.

117. RGASPI, f. 445, op. 1, d. 172, ll. 28–9.

118. Ibid., ll. 30–2.

119. Ibid., l. 37.

120. Ibid., l. 34.

121. The Yiddish writer based in Minsk who was most known outside the Soviet Union was Moshe Kulbak, but he did not move to Minsk from Vilna until late 1928, at which point the Minsk literary group was well-established with Kharik as its leader.

122. "Literarishe nayes," *Oktyabr* December 15–16, 1928 (nos. 288–9), p. 3. See chapter six for more on Kharik.

123. Letter from Yehezkiel Dobrushin to H. Leyvik, in Altshuler, *Briv*, p. 68.

124. RGASPI, f. 445, op. 1, d. 172, ll. 38–40. The declaration was published in *Royte Velt* alongside the declaration of the Association of Jewish Revolutionary Writers in Ukraine, which shortly thereafter became the proletarian group of Ukraine. See "Deklaratsie fun der literarisher fareynikung *Boy*," *Royte Velt*, May–June, 1927 (no. 5–6), pp. 139–42.

125. Ibid.

126. "Afn literarishn front," *Royte Velt*, May-June 1927 (no. 5–6), pp. 139–42.

127. Ibid.

128. Clark, *Petersburg*, p. 195.

129. Brian Kassof, "The Knowledge Front: Politics, Ideology, and Economics in the Soviet Book Publishing Industry, 1925–1935," (Ph.D. diss., University of California, Berkeley, 2000) chapter six, p. 3.

130. Luckyj, *Literary Politics*, p. 138.

131. Kassof, "The Knowledge Front," chapter six, pp. 3–4.

132. Katerina Clark, "The Remaking of Literature," in Robert Daniels, ed., *The Stalin Revolution* (Toronto: University of Toronto Press, 1990), pp. 150–61.

133. Luckyj, *Literary Politics*, pp. 121–2.

134. Luckyj, *Literary Politics*, pp. 60–1.

135. A. Abchuk, "Af fremde vegn," *Prolit*, August–September, 1928 (no. 8–9), p. 78.

136. Shmeruk, "Yiddish Literature," pp. 242–80.

137. B. O., "Literarish-kinstlerisher, kritish-bibliografisher khoydesh zhurnal fun der al-ukrainisher asotsiatsie proletarishe shrayber. No. 1, April 1928," *Shtern*, March–April, 1928 (no. 3–4), pp. 55–8.

138. Ibid., p. 57.

139. M. Litvakov, "Der ideologisher tsushtand fun der yidisher literatur," *Oktyabr*, January 13, 1929 (no. 10), p. 3.

140. RGASPI, f. 445, op. 1, d. 172, l. 193. The two "Yashes" (Bronshteyn and Goldman) were the youngest ones attending, and both represented the Minsk group of proletarian writers. Goldman killed himself in 1929 at the age of 25 while suffering from a fatal illness.

141. Ibid.

142. TsDAODM, f. 3, op. 11, d. 855, l. 30.

143. Ibid., l. 30.

144. Ibid., l. 31.

145. "Literarishe nayes," *Prolit*, February–March, 1929 (no. 2–3), p. 91.

146. "Kritik fun *Di Royte Velt 1927*," *Prolit*, February 1928 (no. 2), pp. 38–45. For more criticism of *Royte Velt*, see M. Levitan, "Mer forzikhtikayt: vegn dem ideologishn inhalt fun der *Royter Velt*," *Shtern*, October 29, 1929 (no. 252), pp. 3–4.

147. Kassof, "The Knowledge Front," chapter six, pp. 10–12.

148. Levitan, "Mer forzikhtikayt," p. 4.

149. *Royte Velt* January 1933 (no. 1–3). Although the edition was sent to the printers in January, it did not actually appear until June.

150. "Mir boyen a proletarishe kultur," *Shtern*, February–March 1930 (no. 2–3), pp. 1–3.

151. Brown, *Proletarian Episode*, p. 150.

152. RGASPI, f. 445, op. 1, d. 186, l. 92.

153. RGASPI, f. 445, op. 1, d. 172, l. 194.

154. RGASPI, f. 445, op. 1, d. 186, ll. 88–9.

155. Tayf wasn't the only one purged from the group. The 1929 meeting of the Communist Group only involved five people – Chemerinsky, Litvakov, Strelits, Rabin, and Bronshteyn. Shoykhet, who was the secretary of the 1928 meeting, did not come, because "as a result of a purge, Shoykhet is no longer a member." See RGASPI, f. 445, op. 1, d. 172, l. 194.

156. Like other writers, Kvitko returned for material reasons as well as ideological ones. He wrote to H. Leyvik about his financial hardships living in Hamburg, where he was working as a longshoreman and living in a dangerous neighborhood. See Nora Levin, *The Jews of the Soviet Union* (New York: New York University Press, 1988), pp. 213–14.

157. Leyb Kvitko, "Der shtink foygl Moyli," in his collection *Gerangl* (Kharkov: Tsentrofarlag, 1929), pp. 290–1.

158. M. Litvakov, "Litkomande un litrekhiles," *Emes*, July 13, 1929, p.3.

159. RGASPI, f. 445, op. 1, d. 186, l. 114.

160. Ibid.

161. "Kegn antisovetish literarishe rekhiles," *Shtern* (Kharkov), September 12, 1929 (no. 210), p. 2.

162. Ibid.

163. "Literarishe nayes," *Shtern* (Kharkov), September 18, 1929 (no. 215), p. 3.

164. "Di yidsektsie VUSP vegn Kvitkos sharzhn," *Oktyabr*, September 22, 1929 (no. 217), p. 3.

165. "A vort funem redaktor," *Royte Velt*, December 1929 (no. 11–12), pp. 215–23.

166. TsDAODM, f. 3, op. 11, d. 855 l. 33.

167. *Shtern*, Oct. 3, 1929 (no. 228), p. 2. On Hofshteyn's and others' support for Kvitko, see Hersh Smolar, *Fun ineveynik*, p. 425.

168. Chone Shmeruk ed., *A shpigl af a shteyn* (Jerusalem: Magnes Publishing, Hebrew University, 1987), p. 761; M. Levitan, "A feler, vos muz farikht vern: vegn Kh' Litvakov's 'A Farshpilter zeks un zekhtsik," *Shtern* (Kharkov), December 17, 1929, p. 3.

169. Altshuler, *Briv*, p. 268.

170. Ibid., pp. 278–9.

171. TsDAODM, f. 386, op. 1, d. 1, l. 28. Feldman's "confession" or "self-criticism" was published in the Russian proletarian journal *Prolit*, no. 4–5, 1931, p. 120.

172. Ibid., l. 29. *Proletarishe Fon*, February 24, 1932.

173. Geoffrey Hosking, *The First Socialist Society* (Cambridge: Harvard University Press, 1985), p. 222.

174. Clark, "The Remaking of Literature," p. 159.

Chapter Six

1. For a more detailed theoretical discussion of the marginal as paragon, see Chana Kronfeld, *On the Margins of Modernism: Decentering Literary Dynamics* (Berkeley: University of California Press, 1996).

2. Chone Shmeruk suggests that the young writers, "outstanding among whom were Itsik Fefer in the Ukraine and Izi Kharik in Belorussia, represented a new stratum in Yiddish literature whose appearance was already tied directly to the Revolution. When they began, their poetry did not go beyond fiery and unreserved support for the Revolution." Chone Shmeruk, "Yiddish Literature in the U.S.S.R.," in Lionel Kochan, ed., *The Jews in Soviet Russia Since 1917* (London, New York: Oxford University Press, 1987), pp. 252–3. Irving Howe and Eliezer Greenberg argue that "younger Yiddish writers turned their backs upon the shtetl and the culture it had nourished.... Poets like Kharik launched sardonic attacks on clerical benightedness and shtetl idyllicism [sic]." See Irving Howe and Eliezer Greenberg, eds., *Ashes Out of Hope: Fiction by Soviet-Yiddish Writers* (New York: Schoken Books, 1977), pp. 4–6. Quite the opposite is true for Kharik in particular.

3. For a variety of biographical sources on Kharik, see Shmuel Rozhansky, ed., *Dovid Hofshteyn, Izi Kharik, Itsik Fefer: Oysgeklibene Shriftn* (Buenos Aires: YIVO, 1962), A. Roskin, "Izi Kharik: Introduction," *Mit Layb un Lebn* (Moscow, 1970), and Shmuel Agursky, *Izi Kharik* (Minsk, 1936); "Izi Kharik," *Bol'shaia Sovetskaya Entskiklopediya*, third ed., vol. 28, col. 587; See also Leonid Smilovitsky, *Evrei v Belarusi, 1905–1953* (Minsk: Arti-Fex, 1999).

4. During Kharik's short life, he published in the Soviet Union primarily in Yiddish, but also to a lesser extent in Russian. In addition, during the 1920s, he published abroad in journals in New York, Warsaw, Lodz, and Paris.

5. Izi Zembin, "Mir un zey" and "In Shturem," *Di Komunistishe Velt*, 1920, no. 14–15. The story about Agursky comes from Kh.L.F., "Izi Kharik," *Leksikon fun der nayer yidisher literature* (New York, 1961), vol. 4, col. 383.

6. See *Khvalyes: Organ fun yidish byuro bam vitebsk gubkom[guberniia komitet] fun ruslendishe komunisitishe yugnt farband*, no. 1–2 (August–September, 1920), p. 28. Only one issue of this Yiddish Komsomol (Communist youth) journal was ever published.

7. Kharik was a student there from 1923 until 1925. See RGALI, f. 596, op. 1, d. 780, l.1.

8. GARF, f. 1318, op. 1, d. 732, 733.

9. RGASPI, f. 445, op. 1, d. 166, l. 7. Kharik was one of six board members including Daniel Charny, Avrom Veviorke, Yekhezkel Dobrushin, Shmuel Godiner, and Aron Kushnirov.

10. *Emes*, November 1, 1923, no. 247, p.3. "In der fri" was Kharik's first publication in *Emes*.

11. *Emes*, December 7, 1924, no. 278, p. 3.

12. RGALI, f.596, op.1, d. 780, l. 4.

13. RGALI, f. 580, op. 1, d. 126, 1.2.

14. Letter from Niepomniashchy to Charny dated October 12, 1925, YIVO RG 421, file 55.

15. Izi Kharik, *Af der erd* (Moscow, 1926).

16. Yashe Bronshteyn, "Dos gezang fun beynerdikn vor," *Shtern*, Minsk; June, 1926, no. 6, p. 58.

17. Avrom Veviorke, "Izi Khariks *Af der erd*," *Der Emes*, May 16, 1926, no. 111, p. 3.

18. Yekhezkel Dobrushin, "*Af der erd*: Vegn Izi Khariks Lider-Bukh," *Di Royte Velt*, Kharkov, August 1926, no. 7, pp. 134–5.

19. For Sholem Aleichem's tenth *yortsayt* (anniversary of his death) the Belorussian Enlightenment Commissariat (*Narkompros*) set up this stipend of 100 rubles per month. It was given to an up-and-coming Jewish poet in Belorussia. See "Yidishe Nayes," *Shtern*, Kharkov, August 10, 1926 (no. 180), p.2.

20. See Katerina Clark, *The Soviet Novel: History as Ritual* (Chicago: University of Chicago Press, 1981), or Boris Groys, *The Total Art of Stalinism* (Princeton: Princeton University Press, 1992) for more on the emergence of socialist realism as a set of cultural norms.

21. "Literarishe Nayes: Izi Kharik – Mitglid fun BelAPP," *Oktyabr*, December 18, 1928, p. 3.

22. Interview with Semen Israelovitch Lipkin, October 25, 1999, Peredelkino, Russia.

23. See chapter five for a discussion of fellow travelers.

24. Although they became Yiddish writers, almost all *maskilim* started writing in Hebrew and only turned to Yiddish later in life, after reflecting on the problems expressed in these questions.

25. Shmuel Niger, "Proletkult un Haskalah: Vegn Max Eriks 'Di komedyes fun der Berliner oyfklerung,'" in his collection of essays, *Yidishe Shrayber in Sovet-Rusland* (New York: Alveltlekher yidisher kultur congress, 1958), pp. 174–5.

26. Even ideological-driven proletarian critics of Yiddish literature recognized the affinity between these writers and the *maskilim* of the nineteenth century. See Yashe Bronshteyn, "Layb un Lebn: Vegn Kharik's Poeme *Mit Layb un Lebn*," *Shtern*, Minsk, February 1929, no. 2, p. 51.

27. On Meir Viner, see Mikhail Krutikov, "Between Mysticism and Marxism: Meir Wiener as Writer, Critic, and Literary Historian," *Jews in Eastern Europe*, Winter 1994 (vol. 25, no. 3), pp. 34–41.

28. For more on contemporaneous Yiddish modernisms, see Kronfeld, *On the Margins of Modernism*, chapter eight.

29. Apocalyptic images, clearly apparent in Kharik's shtetl poems, were widespread in Yiddish expressionist poetry. See Avrom Nowersztern, "History, Messianism, and Apocalypse in Bashevis's Work," in Seth Wolitz, ed., *The Hidden Isaac Bashevis Singer* (Austin: University of Texas Press, 2001), pp. 28–61.

30. Y. Bronshteyn, "Dos gezang fun beynerdikn vor," *Shtern* [Minsk], May–June 1926, no. 5–6, pp. 54–5.

31. Y. Dobrushin, "Af der erd: vegn I. Kharik's lider bukh." *Royte Velt*, July–August, 1926, no. 7–8, pp. 130–1.

32. Khatskel Dunets, "Prelyudies fun sotsialistishn oyfboy: vegn Izi Kharik's poeme 'Mit Layb un Lebn,'" *Di Royte Velt*, May–June 1929, no. 5–6, p. 150.

33. On the dialogue between the shtetl, its Jews and the young, modern Jew, and on Mendele's persona, see Dan Miron, *A Traveller Disguised* (Syracuse: Syracuse University Press, 1996), especially chapter four. See also Leah Garrett, *Journeys Beyond the Pale* (Madison: University of Wisconsin Press, 2003).

34. In these shtetl poems, Kharik employs and reworks the first two of Miron's shtetl associations, and in other poems, notably *Broyt*, he represents the process of departure from the shtetls and subsequent resettlement on the land. See Dan Miron, "The Literary Image of the Shtetl," *Jewish Social Studies,* Spring 1995 (vol. 1, no. 3), pp. 1–43, as well as his book *Der Imazsh fun shtetl* (Tel Aviv: Peretsfarlag, 1981).

35. See appendix I for the original Yiddish of this poem.

36. Miron, "Literary Image of the Shtetl," pp. 27–8.

37. See Y. Bronshteyn, "Layb un Lebn: Vegn Kharik's Poeme *Mit Layb un Lebn*," *Shtern* [*Minsk*] February 1929, no. 2, p. 57.

38. Armin Zweite, *The Blue Rider* (New York, Munich: Prestel Publishers, 1989), plate 28.

39. Playing with time, of being neither past nor future, had become an expressionist trope in Yiddish poetry, most notably, in that of Perets Markish.

40. Izi Kharik, *Mit Layb un Lebn* (Moscow, 1970), p. 91. This is the introduction to a nineteen-part *poema*, and thus only gives a flavor of the full length poem. See appendix II for the original.

41. See appendix III for the original.

42. Micha Berdichevsky as cited in Lawrence Silberstein, *The Postzionism Debates: Knowledge and Power in Israeli Culture* (New York, London: Routledge Press, 1999), p. 39.

43. See appendix IV for the original.

44. Bronshteyn, "Dos gezang," pp. 56–7.

45. See appendix V.

46. Izi Kharik, *Mit Layb un Lebn* (Moscow, 1970). This anthology gives "In Your Little Houses" several dates. At the end of the four-section poem it gives the date August 1925, but after section three there is a date, 1926.

47. Thank you to Yael Chaver for this reading of the poem.

48. Bronshteyn agrees that "the mentioning of 'May' and 'Sivan' is a symbol of reconciliation between two opposed cultures." Bronshteyn, "Layb un Lebn," p. 48.

49. Esenin died in 1925, just when Kharik was writing this poem.

50. The concordance has many entries, mostly in Leviticus and Numbers, all connected with the burnt sacrifice and the pleasing odor it produces for God. Some references are: Lev.1:13, 17; 2:12; 3:16; 4:31; 6:8 Num. 15:3, 7, 10, 13, 14, and others. Yehoash's Yiddish translation of the Bible renders *reyach nichoyach* as *a geshmakn reyekh,* a fragrant smell.

51. Dobrushin, "Af der erd," p. 134.

52. Even ideologically driven Communist critics such as Moshe Litvakov, cultural commisar for the Jewish Section of the Communist Party (*Evsektsiia*), commented on the close relationship between Kharik's early work and the work of the Kiev group. In 1935, he wrote, "To be honest, in the first days of NEP Kharik had a moment of nationalistic weakness. He fell under the spell of the Kiev 'Yavne.'" Yavne was a center of Rabbinic thought during the Talmudic period of Jewish history. Moshe Litvakov, "Fuftsn Yor," in Shmuel Agursky, p. 37.

53. *Oktyabr,* 1928, February 7 (32), 4: "Mit Layb un Lebn: Afn Kharik ovent in minsker Lenin klub."

54. Ibid.

55. Dunets, "Preliudies," p. 157.

56. "Literarishe nayes," *Oktyabr,* November 25, 1928 (271), p. 3.

57. "Arbeter vegn literatur," *Oktyabr*, January 6, 1929 (4), p. 3.
58. Liberman, "Vos leyent der arbeter," *Shtern* [Minsk], October 1929, no. 10, p. 77.
59. In Russian, the *poema* has been translated as *Krov'iu i plotiu* (With Flesh and Blood), and as *Dushoi i telom* (With Body and Soul).
60. The play *200,000* is also known as *Groyse gevins* (The Great Victory).
61. On the literary image of the *talush* see Nurith Govrin, *Tlishut ve-hitkhadshut: ha-siporet ha-ivrit be-reshit ha-me'ah ha-20 ba-golah uve-erets yisrael* (Tel Aviv: Matkal, 1985), pp. 17–25. On the traveler in Yiddish literature, see Garrett, *Journeys*.
62. Bronshteyn, "Layb un Lebn," p. 56.
63. Traditional Russian homes reserve one corner of the room for Russian Orthodox icons. Soviet literature often played with the motif of icons by replacing traditional Orthodox saints with Communist heroes and the famous theoreticians of Marxism–Leninism.
64. Sheila Fitzpatrick has applied the phrase "Potemkin village" to describe the alternate reality that Soviet discourse created from the late 1920s through World War II and beyond. See Fitzpatrick, *Stalin's Peasants* (Cornell: Cornell University Press, 1995). See also Stephen Kotkin, *Magnetic Mountain* (Princeton: Princeton University Press, 1996) for an alternative view, which sees socialist realism and Soviet discourse of socialist building not as an alternate reality, but as the reality of living as a Soviet person. He calls the process by which people absorbed this discourse "learning to speak Bolshevik."
65. Dunets, "Preludies," p. 152.
66. See Appendix VI.
67. The proud "pioneer" was also a dominant trope in Palestinian Zionist discourse.
68. *Mit Layb un Lebn*, p. 195.
69. Ibid., pp. 198–9.
70. Ibid., pp. 196–7.
71. S. Zhukovsky, "Mit Layb un Lebn: Vegn Khariks letste verk," *Prolit*, May 1929, no. 5, p. 48 and Kh. Dunets, "Preliudies," pp. 157–8.
72. Kh. Dunets, "Preliudies," p. 158.
73. Letter from Shlomo Niepomniashchy to Daniel Charny, undated, YIVO Archives, RG 421, file 54.
74. Anna Shternshis, "Kosher and Soviet: Soviet Jewish Popular Culture, 1917–1941," D. Phil. diss., Oxford University, 2000.

Afterword

1. Rufus Mathewson, "The First Writers' Congress: A Second Look," in Max Hayward and Leopold Labedz, eds., *Literature and Revolution in Soviet Russia* (Oxford: Oxford University Press, 1963), p. 63.
2. Letter from David Hofshteyn in Altshuler, *Briv*, p. 120.
3. Nachman Mayzel, *Dos yidishe shafn un der yidisher shrayber in Sovetfarband* (New York: YKUF, 1959), p. 149. Mayzel notes that there were twelve Jewish writers who wrote in Russian (in addition to those who wrote in Yiddish), who sat on the board's management, meaning that Jews made up 14 percent of the union's leadership.
4. RGALI, f. 631, op. 6, d. 179, ll. 1–2.
5. Jeffrey Veidlinger, *The Moscow State Yiddish Theater* (Bloomington: Indiana University Press, 2001), p. 187.

6. RGALI, f. 631, op. 6, d. 77, ll. 11–13.
7. RGALI, f. 631, op. 6, d. 97, l. 78.
8. Veidlinger, *Moscow State Yiddish Theater,* pp. 186; see also Robert Weinberg, "Purge and Politics in the Periphery: Birobidzhan in 1937," *Slavic Review* 1993 52(1): 13–27.
9. Terry Martin, *The Affirmative Action Empire*, chapters eight and nine.
10. On how Soviet Jews identified with secular Yiddish culture, see Anna Shternshis, "Kosher and Soviet: Soviet Jewish Popular Culture, 1917–1941," D. Phil. diss., Oxford University, 2000.

Bibliography

Archival Materials

Ukraine

Tsentral'nyi derzhavnyi arkhiv hromads'kykh ob'iednan Ukraïny (TsDAHOU), Central State Archive of Social Organizations of Ukraine, Former Central Communist Party Archive of Ukraine, Kiev

Files Used:

f.1, op.20 (Central Committee of the Ukrainian Communist Party)

Tsentral'nyi derzhavnyi arkhiv vyshchykh orhaniv derzhavnoi vlady Ukraïny (TsDAVODVU), Central State Archive of Higher Organs of State Institutions in Ukraine, Former Ukrainian State Archives, Kiev

Files Used:

f. 1 (Presidium of the Central Executive Committee)

f. 413 (NKVD, People's Commissariat for Internal Affairs)

f. 166, op. 6 (*Narkompros*, Commissariat of Enlightenment)

f. 3298 (Central Jewish Enlightenment Bureau, Sovnatsmen Ukraine)

f. 3332 (Institute of Jewish Culture, Ukrainian Academy of Sciences)

Russia

Arkhiv rossiiskoi akademii nauk (ARAN), Russian Academy of Sciences, Moscow

Files Used:

f. 677, op. 1, 5, 6, 7 (Institute of Languages and Alphabets)

Tsentral'nyi gosudarsvennyi arkhiv obshchestvennykh dvizhenii Moskvy (TsDAODM), Moscow State Central Archives of Social Movements, Former Moscow City Party Archives, Moscow

Files Used:

f. 386 (Der Emes)

f. 3, op. 11 (Moscow City Communist Party Records)

Gosudarstvennyi arkhiv Rossiiskoi Federatsii (GARF), State Archives of the Russian Federation, Moscow
Files Used:
Embankment Branch
f. 296, op. 1 (*Sovnatsmen RSFSR*, Council for National Minorities)
f. 406, op. 25 (*Rabkrin*, Workers and Peasants Inspectorate)
f. 1575, op. 10 (*Glavsotsvos*, Main Administration for Social Upbringing)
f. 2306, op. 1, 2, 4, 19, 22, 69 (*Narkompros*, Commissariat of Enlightenment)
f. 2307, op. 2, 5, 14 (*Glavnauka*, Main Administration for Scholarship)
f. 2313, op. 1, 6 (*Glavpolitprosvet*, Main Administration of Political Enlightenment)
f. 2314, op.6 (*VChKLB*, All-Russian Special Commission to Eradicate Illiteracy)
Pirogovskaia (Main) Branch
f. 1318, op. 1, 24 (*Narkomnats*, People's Commissariat for National Minorities)
f. 3316, op. 13, 17, 18, 19, 20, 21, 22, 65 (*TsIK*, Central Executive Committee)
f. 4033 (*Tsentroizdat*, Central Publishing House of National Minorities)

Institut mirovoi literatur im. A.M.Gor'kogo (IMLI RAN), Gorky Institute of World Literatures, Moscow
Files Used:
f. 346 (Der Emes Publishing House)

Tsentral'nyi munitsipal'nyi arkhiv Moskvy (TsMAM), Moscow Central Municipal Archives, Moscow
Files Used:
f. 714, op. 2 (2nd Moscow State University)

Rossiiskii gosudarstvennyi arkhiv literatury i isskustva (RGALI), Russian State Archive of Literature and Art, Moscow
Files Used:
f. 596 (Bryusov Institute of Art and Literature)
f. 613 (Union of Soviet Writers)
f. 2270 (Personal Files of Aaron Gurshteyn)
f. 2536 (Personal Files of Mire Khenkina)

Rossiiskii gosudarstvennyi arkhiv sotsial'no-politicheskogo issledovaniia (RGASPI), Russian State Archive of Social and Political Research, Former Party Archives to 1945, Moscow
Files Used:
f. 17, op. 3, 33, 60, 85, 112, 113 (Central Committee of the Communist Party)
f. 445 (Jewish Section of the Communist Party, *Evsektsiia*)

United States

YIVO Institute of Jewish Research, New York
Files Used:
RG 205 (Files of Kalman Marmor)
RG 421 (Files of Daniel Charny)
RG 500 (Files of Alexander Pomerants)

Hoover Archives, Stanford, California
Axelbank Collection

Journals/Newspapers/Literary Collections

Title: City, Years Examined

Hebrew

Tsiltselei shama. Kharkov: 1923.
Bereshit. Berlin–Moscow–Leningrad: 1926.

Yiddish

Afn Sprakhfront. Kiev: 1930–1933.
Albatros. Warsaw: 1922–1924.
Baginen. Kiev: 1918.
Birobidzhaner Shtern. Birobidzhan: 1930.
Byulletin fun der katedre fun yidisher kultur ba di alukrainshe visnshaftlekhe institut. Kiev: 1926–1928.
Byulletin fun der yidishe opteilung fun Inveyskult. Minsk: 1925–1930.
Arbeter. Berdichev: 1929–1930.
Idisher Arbeter. Petrograd: 1920–1921.
Pinkas. Vilna: 1913.
Yidisher Poyer. Kharkov: 1928–1930.
Emes. Moscow: 1918–1931.
Emes Zhurnal. Moscow: 1926–1928.
Forpost. Birobidzhan: 1936.
Farmest. Kharkov: 1934.
Hamer. New York: 1926.
In Shpan. Vilna: 1926.
In Zikh. New York: 1920–1925.
Albatros. Warsaw-Berlin: 1922–1924.
Khvalyes. Vitebsk: 1920.
Komunistishe Velt. Moscow: 1919–1920.
Komunistishe Fon. Kiev: 1919–1924.
Kultur un Bildung. Moscow: 1918–1920.
Mayrevnik. Moscow: 1927–1930.
Milgroym. Berlin: 1922–1924.
Morgn Frayhayt. New York: 1929.
Naye Tsayt. Vilna-Kiev: 1918.
Nayerd. Moscow: 1925.
Oktyabr. Minsk: 1925–1930.
Oktyabr. Moscow: 1925.
Oyfgang. Kiev: 1918–1919.
Partay materialn. Moscow: 1920.
Proletarishe Fon. Kiev: 1928–1930.
Prolit. Kharkov: 1928–1930.
Ratnbildung. Kharkov: 1928–1930.
Royte Velt. Kharkov: 1924–1933.

Shtern. Kharkov: 1925–1932.
Shtern. Minsk: 1925–1930.
Shtrom. Moscow: 1922–1924.
Sovetish. Moscow: 1934.
Sovetish Heymland/Di yidishe gas. Moscow: (1961–).
Undzer Veg. Kiev: 1917–1918.
Varhayt. Petrograd: 1918.
Veker. Minsk: 1918–1925.
Visnshaft un Revolutsye. Kiev: 1934–1935.
Yidishe Shprakh. Kiev: 1927–1930.
Yidisher Poyer. Moscow: 1926–1930.

Russian

Izvestiia. Moscow: 1918–1925.
Kultura i pis'mennost' vostoka. Baku-Moscow: 1928–1931.
Oktiabr'. Moscow: 1924–1926.
Pravda. Moscow: 1918–1930.
Revoliutsiia i pis'mennost'. Moscow: 1932–1933.
Vestnik evreiskogo narodnogo komissariata po delam natsional'nostei. Moscow: 1920.
Zhizn' natsional'nostei. Moscow: 1918–1924.

Interviews

Lipkin, Semen Israelovich, October 30, 1999.
Khenkina, Elizaveta Isaakovna, June 14, 1999.

Published Primary Materials

——, "Di ershte fabrik-tsaytung," *Shtern*, May 12, 1928 (no. 109), p. 3.
——, "Di Yidishe Shprakh," *Di Yidishe Shprakh: zhurnal far praktish yidish shprakhvisn*, March 1927 (no. 1).
——, "Evreiskaia filologicheskaia komisiia," *Zhizn' natsional'nostei*, April 1, 1922 (no. 5).
——, "Fun der tsentraler ortografisher komisie," *Di Yidishe Shprakh*, March–April, 1930 (no. 2–3).
——, "Kultur khronik," *Shtern* (Minsk), January 1926, no. 1(4).
——, "Unzer program" and "Greyt zikh tsu tsu milkhome," *Varhayt* (Petrograd), March 1, 1918 (no. 1), p. 1.
——, "Vegn der tirazh fun *Shtern*," *Shtern*, November 1, 1926 (no. 142), p. 2.
——, "Vi s'vert fartik a nomer *Oktyabr*," *Oktyabr*, May 5, 1928 (no. 102), p. 2.
——, "A tsentrale drukeray," *Emes*, October 16, 1918 (no. 46), p. 3.
——, "A vort funem redaktor," *Royte Velt*, December 1929 (no. 11–12).
——, "A yor *Oktyabr* in tsifirn," *Oktyabr*, November 7, 1926 (no. 257), p. 5.
——, "Afn literarishn front," *Royte Velt*, May–June, 1927 (no. 5–6).
——, "Antireligieze bavegung," *Emes*, March 24, 1923, p. 3.
——, "Deklaratsie fun der literarisher fareynikung *Boy*," *Royte Velt*, May–June, 1927 (no. 5–6).

——, "Di lebedike tsaytung," *Komunistishe Fon*, February 17, 1923 (no. 36), p. 3.

——, "Di vanttsaytung in fabrik un klub," *Shtern* (Kharkov), May 5, 1926 (no. 100), p. 4.

——, "Di yidsektsie VUSP vegn Kvitkos sharzhn," *Oktyabr*, September 22, 1929 (no. 217), p. 3.

——, "Emigratsione plonter," *Emes*, April 11, 1923, p. 2.

——, "Finf yor Yidsektsiia MAPP," *Royte Velt*, no. 1–2, 1930 (no. 209).

——, "Fun der redaktsie," *Royte Velt*, Oct. 1929 (no. 10).

——, "Gomel: Emigratsie" *Emes*, March 25, 1923, p. 2.

——, "Idishe kultur tuer kegn kemfendikn hebreizm," *Emes*, February 12, 1924 (no. 34), pp. 2–3.

——, "Izdatel'stvo 'Evotdel-Evobshchestkom,'" *Zhizn' natsional'nostei*, July 26, 1922 (no. 15).

——, "Kegn antisovetish literarishe rekhiles," *Shtern* (Kharkov), September 12, 1929 (no. 210), p. 2.

——, "Kiev 'Folks Farlag' in Berlin," *Der Moment*, April 22, 1921.

——, "Kritik fun *Di Royte Velt 1927*," *Prolit*, February 1928 (no. 2).

——, "Kunst-khronik," *Baginen*, July 1919, p. 85.

——, "Literarishe Bletl," *Komunistishe Fon*, January 13, 1923 (no. 8), p. 4.

——, "Literarishe nayes," *Oktyabr*, December 15–16, 1928 (nos. 288–9), p. 3.

——, "Literarishe nayes," *Shtern* (Kharkov), September 18, 1929 (no. 215), p. 3.

——, "Mir boyen a proletarishe kultur," *Shtern*, February–March 1930 (no. 2–3).

——, "Shtrom oventn inem moskver klub, dritte internatsional," *Shtrom*, no. 2, p. 78.

——, "Shtrom, no. 3," *Zhizn' natsional'nostei*, 1923 (no. 5), p. 203.

——, "Tsu der kumendiker shprakhkonferents," *Oktyabr*, February 24 (45), p. 2.

——, "Tsu undzere korespondentn," *Der Emes*, August 15, 1918 (no. 7), p. 2.

——, "Vegn yomim naroyim," *Emes*, August 24, 1923, p. 3.

——, "Vi makht men papir," *Shtern*, February 26, 1927 (no. 47), p. 2.

——, *Af di shlakht pozitsies: Barikht fun der tsveyter alukrainisher konferents fun di yidishe proletarishe shrayber*, April 27–30, 1931. Kharkov: Tsentroizdat, 1932.

——, *Alfarbandishe baratung fun di yidishe sektsies fun der Al.K.P.* Moscow: Shul un Bukh, 1927.

——, *Di ershte alukrainshe baratung fun yidishe arbdorfkustkorn*. Kharkov: Tsentroizdat, 1927.

——, *Di ershte yidishe shprakh-konferents*. Vilna: YIVO, 1931.

——, *Di natsionale frage in der RKP zamlbukh: mit a forrede fun A. Merezhin*. Moscow: RKP, 1922.

——, *Di naye yidishe ortografie*. Kiev: Kultur Lige, 1929.

——, *Di sovetishe yidishe ortografie, klolim funem nayem yidishn oysleg*. Kharkov: Gosizdat natsmenshinstv, 1932.

——, *Rezolutsies fun der ershter alukrainer kongres fun yidishe kultur un bildung tuers*. Kharkov: Narkompros, June 1922.

——, "Rezolutsies fun der TsK KPB," *Oktyabr*, June 6, 1926 (no. 128), p. 2.

——, *Rezolutsies fun dem ershtn alukrainishn tsuzamenfor fun yidishe kultur un bildungs tuer*. Kiev: n.p., 1922.

——, *Rezolutsies: ongenumene af der alukrainsher baratung fun di Idsektsies fun K.P.* Kiev: Kultur Lige, 1926.

——, *RSFSR Narodnyi kommissariat prosveshcheniia, Sbornik prikazov i instruktsii po Narkomprosu*. Moscow: Narkompros.

——, *Shriftn*. Kiev: Kultur Lige, 1928.

——, *Shul un Bukh. Katalog far der Farlag Aktsion-Gezelshaft "Shul un Bukh."* Moscow: Shul un Bukh, 1924.

——, *Takones fun yidishn oysleg*. Vilna: YIVO, 1937; New York: 1941, 1947.

——, *Tsaytshrift*. Minsk: Inbelkult, 1932.

——, *Vegn der masn-arbet af yidish: fortrogn fun di Khs Dunets un Galbraykh afn plenum fun Yidbyuro bam TsKKPU*. Minsk: Gosizdat Belorussia, 1929.

Abchuk, A., "Af fremde vegn," *Prolit*, August–September, 1928 (no. 8–9).

Agursky, Shmuel, "Der veg fun der komunistisher prese in yidish," *Oktyabr*, March 7, 1928, (no. 57).

Agursky, Shmuel, "Tsen yor *Emes*," *Oktyabr*, August 8, 1928.

Agursky, Shmuel, "Tvishn fargesene," *Emes*, November 16, 1921.

Agursky, Shmuel, *Di yidishe komisariatn un di yidishe sektsies*. Minsk: Gosizdat Belorussia, 1928.

Agursky, Shmuel, ed., *Di sotsialistishe literatur af yidish in 1875–1897*. Minsk: Inbelkult, 1935.

Altshuler, Mordechai, ed., *Briv fun yidishe sovetishe shraybers*. Jerusalem: Hebrew University, 1979.

Beregovsky, M., *Jidisher Muzik-Folklor: Band I*. Moscow: Gosmuzikizdat, 1934.

Bergelson, Dovid, "Briv fun Dovid Bergelson," *Shtern* (Kharkov), March 5, 1926.

Bergelson, Dovid, "Dray tsentren," *In Shpan*, April 1926 (no. 1).

Bezymensky, A., "Prolog," *Oktyabr'*, June–July 1924.

Bis, "Di ershte teg fun Komfon," *Komfon*, May 30, 1923 (no. 105).

Borokhov, Ber, "Di ufgabn fun der yidisher filologie," *Der Pinkas: yorbukh far der geshikhte fun der yudisher literatur un shprakh, far folklor, kritik un bibliografie*. Vilna: 1913.

Borokhov, Ber, *Di klasn-interesn un di natsionale frage*. Vilna: Rom, 1906.

Brakhman, A., and Zhiv, Y., eds., *Yidn in FSSR*. Moscow-Kharkov-Minsk: Tsentronats-menshinstv, 1930.

Charny, Daniel, *A yortsendlik aza*. New York: CYCO, 1943.

Chemerinsky, Alexander, *Di alfarbandishe komunistishe partay un di yidishe masn*. Moscow: Shul un Bukh, 1926.

Dimanshteyn, S., "10 yor komprese in yidish," *Oktyabr*, March 7, 1928 (no. 57).

Dimanshteyn, Semen, *Di natsionale frage afn tsveitn tsuzamenfor fun der partei*. Moscow: Emes, 1934.

Dimanshteyn, Semen, *Itogi razresheniia natsional'nogo voprosa v SSSR*. Moscow: 1935.

Dinershteyn, E.A., *Izdatel'skoe delo v pervye gody sovetskoi vlasti (1917–1922)*. Moscow: Kniga, 1972.

Dobrushin, Yekhezkel, "Unzer literatur," *Shtrom*, no. 1.

Dunets, Kh., "Di dinamik fun der yidisher farlag-arbet in Sovet Vaysrusland," *Shtern*, January 1929 (no. 1).

Epshteyn, Sh., "Vi Khaver Levitan kritikirt," *Shtern*, November 12, 1929 (no. 260).

Epshteyn, Shakhne, ed., *Di yidishe kinstlerishe literatur un di partay onfirung*. Kharkov: Gosizdat, 1929.

Ester (Maria Frumkina), *An entfer af di gegners fun yidish*. Czernowitz: Orient, 1922.

Ester, "Eynike bamerkungen vegn natsionaler dertsiung," *Tsayt fragn*, vol. 1. Vilna: 1909.

Ester, "Glaykhbarekhtigung fun shprakhn," *Tsayt fragn*, Vilna: 1911.

Ester, *Tsu der frage vegn der idisher folkshule*, third ed. Petrograd: Di Velt, 1917.

Fefer, Itsik, *Shpener.* Kiev: Vidervuks, 1922.

Goldberg, H., "Zhurnal *Shtern* Nov.-Dec. 1928," *Oktyabr,* January 13, 1929 (no. 10).

Gordon, Sholem, "In erdishn doyer: Dovid Hofshteyn," *Shtrom* no. 3.

Gurshteyn, Aron, "Shtrom no. 1," *Zhizn' Natsional'nostei,* April 14, 1922 (no. 7).

Hofshteyn, Dovid, "Araynfir," to Itsik Fefer, *Shpener* (Kiev, 1922).

Hurvich, Sh., "Vos vil der *Oktyabr,*" *Oktyabr,* November 8, 1925 (no. 2).

I.,K., "*Shtern, no.* 1–4," *Royte Velt,* September 1926 (no. 9).

Kalinin, Mikhail, "Evreiskii vopros i pereselenie evreev v Krym," *Izvestiia,* July 11, 1926.

Kalmanovich, Zelig, *Yidishe gramatik.* Minsk: Gosizdat Belorussia, 1921.

Kamenshteyn, Moshe, "Vegn latinizirn dem idishn alefbeys," *Shtern* [Kharkov], December 29, 1929 (no. 300).

Kantor, A., "Vegn der yidisher orfografie," *Kultur un Bildung,* March 10, 1919, no. 5–6 (21–22).

Kantor, Ya., *Natsional'noe stroitel'stvo sredi evreev v SSSR.* Moscow: 1935.

———, *Katalogn far di Farlag Aktsien-Gezelshaft "Shul un Bukh."* Moscow: Shul un bukh, 1924–1928.

Katz, Moshe, "Di kultur lebn in Ukraine," *Di Tsukunft,* March, 1921 (vol. 23, no. 3).

Kazakevitch, Henekh, et al., "Ufruf fun der filologisher komisie bam folkombild fun UkSRR," *Di Royte Velt,* December 1924, no. 12.

Kiper, Moshe, "Nutst oys di *Royte Velt,*" *Shtern,* March 30, 1928 (no. 76).

Kirzhnits, A., *Di yidishe prese in der gevezener rusisher imperie, 1823–1916.* Moscow: Tsentroizdat, 1930.

Kirzhnits, A., *Di yidishe prese in ratnfarband, 1917–1927.* Minsk: Gosizdat Belorussia, 1928.

Kolychev, O., *Evreiskie poety: D. Gofshtein, A. Kushnirov, P. Markish, I. Fefer, I. Kharik, O. Shvartsman.* Moscow: Ogonyek, 1932.

Kolychev, Osip, *Iz evreiskikh poetov: sbornik stikhov.* Moscow: Khodozhestvennaya literatura, 1935.

Korman, Ezra, ed., *Brenendike brikn: antologye fun revolutsionerer lirik in der nayer yidisher dikhtung fun ukraine.* Berlin: Yidisher literarisher farlag, 1923.

Korman, Ezra, ed., *In fayerdikn doyer: zamlung fun revolutsionerer lirik in di nayer yidisher dikhtung.* Kiev: Gosizdat, 1921.

Kvitko, L., "Derklerung," *Royte Velt,* September 1929 (no. 9).

L., M., "Arbkor: Organ far arbkorn, dorfkorn, kuskorn un yunkorn," *Shtern* (Minsk), July 1925 (no. 2).

Lelevich, L.G., "Puti proletarskoi literatury," *Oktiabr',* June–July 1924

Lelevich, L.G., *Tvorcheskie puti proletarskoi literatury.* Leningrad: Priboi, 1925.

Lenin, V.I., "Partiinaia organizatsiia i partiinaia literatura," *Novaia zhizn',* November 13, 1905. Petersburg.

Lenin, Vladimir I., "Kriticheskie voprosy po natsional'nomy voprosu," *Prosveshcheniie* nos. 10, 11, 12, 1913.

Levitan, M., "A feler, vos muz farikht vern: vegn Kh' Litvakov's 'A Farshpilter zeks un zekhtsik,'" *Shtern* (Kharkov), December 17, 1929.

Levitan, M., "Tsu der efenung fun der alfarbandisher yidisher ortografisher konferents," *Shtern* [Kharkov], April 7, 1928 (no. 83).

Levitan, M., "Mer forzikhtikayt: vegn dem ideologishn inhalt fun der *Royter Velt,*" *Shtern,* October 29, 1929 (no. 252).

Levitan, Mikhail, "Di grunt problemen fun der idisher kultur boyung: 'Di yidishe shprakh: a zelbsttsvek oder a mitl,'" *Royte Velt*, May–June 1926 (no. 5–6).

Litvak, A., "Literatur un lebn," *Baginen*, July 1919, pp. 97–102.

Litvakov, M., "Litkomande un litrekhiles," *Emes*, July 13, 1929.

Litvakov, Moshe, *Finf yor melukhisher idisher kamer-teatr, 1919–1924*. Moscow: Shul un bukh, 1924.

Litvakov, Moshe, *In Umru*. Moscow: Shul un bukh, 1926. (originally published in Kiev: 1917.)

Litvakov, Moshe, *Af tsvey frontn*. Moscow-Kharkov-Minsk: Tsentorizdat, 1931.

Makagon, A., "Yidishe farlagarbet af Ukraine (1924–1925)," *Di Royte Velt*, October 1925 (no. 15).

Merezhin, Avrom, "Unzer prese-fragn," *Emes*, January 18, 1923 (no. 12).

Merezhin, Avrom, "A tsaytmesige frage," *Emes*, November 21, 1921.

Mitlinsky, Y., "A revolutsie in der yidisher orfografie," *Kultur un Bildung*, October 1918.

N.Y. [Y. Nusinov], "Shtern, no. 2," *Royte Velt*, 1925 (no. 14).

Nusinov, Y., "Briv in redaktsie," *Royte Velt*, September 1929 (no. 9).

Nusinov, Y., "Oykh dikhter darfn mithelfn der partay-reinikung," *Royte Velt*, August 1929 (no. 8).

Nusinov, Y., "Vidervuks," *Komunistishe Fon*, July 16, 1922 (no. 101).

Orshansky, Ber, "Der birger krig in der literatur, *Oktyabr un Nayerd*," *Shtern*, January 1925 (no. 1).

Orshansky, Ber, "Der literarisher dor: Shtern-Oktyabr," *Oktyabr*, December 27, 1928 (no. 298).

Orshansky, Ber, "Vegn eyn vinkele in *Der Royte Velt*," *Shtern*, September–October 1926 (no. 9–10).

Oyslender, Nokhum, "Literary Publishing House 'Vidervuks' Kiev," *Shtrom* (no. 4).

Pekler, Kh., "Tsu der teorie fun a lebedike tsaytung," *Veker* (Minsk), May 30, 1921 (no. 30).

Radbil' E. V., *Iz novykh evreiskikh poetov: David Gofshtein, Perets Markish, Moshe-Leib Gal'perin, L. Kvitko*. Kiev: Assotsiatsiia revoliutionnykh russkikh pisatelei v kieve, 1928.

Ravitch, Melekh, *Nakete Reyd*. Vienna: Kval Farlag, 1921.

Reyzen, Zalmen, *Yudishe gramatik*. Warsaw: Progres, 1908.

Rozenhoyz, L., "Tsaytshrift," *Shtern*, Nov. 1926, no. 7–8.

S. B., [Ber Slutsky], "Alfarbandishe ortografishe tsugreyt konferents," *Oktyabr*, April 14, 1928, no. 89.

Shtif, Nokhum, "Frages fun yidish oysleg," *Di Yidishe Shprakh*, January–April, 1928, no. 1–2 (8–9).

Shtif, Nokhum, "Tsaytshrift," *Shtern* (Kharkov), October 13 (no. 235).

Shtif, Nokhum, and Spivak, Elye, "Vegn latinizatsie," *Afn Shprakhfront*, February–March 1932 (no. 2–3).

Slutsky, B., "A nomer *Shtern*," *Di Yidishe Shprakh*, September–October 1927, no. 5–6.

Smolar, Hersh, *Fun ineveynik*. Tel Aviv: Perets Farlag, 1978.

Soliterman, M., and Zarudny, M., *Handbikhl far yidisher ortografie*. Kamenets: Bildinspektor, 1929.

Stalin, Joseph, *Natsional'nyi vopros i marksizm*. St. Petersburg, Priboi, 1914.

Tayf, Moshe, "Vegn zhurnal *Shtern*," *Oktyabr*, December 18, 1925 (no. 36).

Trotsky, Lev, "Sud'ba tolstogo zhurnala," *Kievskaya Mysl*, March 16, 19, 1914 (nos. 75–78).

Trotsky, Lev, *Literatura i revoliutsiia*. Moscow: Gosizdat, 1924.

Tsvayg, A., "Dos naye gezang af likhtike ruinen," *Oktyabr*, August 27, 1927 (no. 194).

Utkes, Dovid, "Arum unzere literarishe grupirungen," *Emes*, October 3, 1923 (no. 222).

Veviorke, A., "Iberzikht fun di yidishe zhurnaln in ratnfarband un oysland," *Royte Velt*, April 1929 (no. 4).

Veviorke, Avrom, "Vegn undzer oysleg," which was printed in three separate issues. See *Emes*, February 10, 1926 (33), p. 2; February 18, 1926 (40), p. 2; February 28, 1926 (49).

Zaretsky, I., "Di frage fun ortografie afn tsveytn alfarbandishn kultur tsuzamenfor," *Ratnbildung*, March 1928 (no. 2).

Zaretsky, I., "Di reforme-bavegung in yidisher oysleg," *Di Royte Velt*, January–February, 1926, no. 1(16).

Zaretsky, I., "K probleme latinizatsii evreiskogo pis'ma," *Revoliutsiia i pismennost'*, January–February, 1932 (no. 1–2).

Zaretsky, I., "Latinizacie fun der jidisher shrift," *Ratnbildung* (Kiev), December, 1930 (no. 12).

Zaretsky, I., "Vegn der reform fun der yidisher orfografie," *Kultur un Bildung* (no. 1) 1920.

Zaretsky, I., *Yidishe gramatik*. Vilna: Kletskin, 1929.

Zaretsky, Itsik, "Vegn yidisher shrift un gramatik," *Shtern* [Minsk] May–June, 1926, no. 5–6 (8–9).

Zaretsky, Itsik, ed., *Klolim fun dem yidishn oysleg*. Odessa: Gosizdat Ukraine, 1921.

Zaretsky, Itsik, *Yidishe ortografye: klolim fun nayem yidish oysleg*. Moscow: Tsentrizdat, 1931.

Zaynen, "Vi azoi ilustrirn a vanttsaytung on a moler," *Shtern*, October 16, 1927 (no. 237).

Zinger, L. G., *Evreiskoie naselenie v SSSR*. Moscow: Gossotsekonizdat, 1932.

Secondary Literature

——, *Bolshaia Sovetskaia Entsiklopediia*, first ed., Moscow: Ogiz, 1932; third edition, Moscow, 1972.

——, *Pechat' SSSR 1917–1954*. Moscow: Izdatelstvo vsesoiuznoi knizhnoi palaty, 1955.

——, *Leksikon fun der nayer yidisher literatur*. New York: CYCO,1956–1981.

——, *Pechat' SSSR za 50 let*. Moscow: Kniga, 1967.

Abramson, Henry, *A Prayer for the Government: Ukrainians and Jews in Revolutionary Times, 1917–1920*. Cambridge, MA: Harvard, 1999.

Agranovsky, G., *Stanovlenie evreiskogo knigopechataniia v litve*. Moscow: Jewish University of Moscow; Jerusalem; State Jewish Museum of Lithuania, 1993.

Alt, Tilo, "A Survey of Literary Contributions to the Post World War I Yiddish Journals of Berlin," *Yiddish*, Spring 1985 (vol. 6, no. 1), pp. 42–52.

Altshuler, Mordechai, ed., *Ha-teatron ha-yehudi bi-vrit ha-moatsot*. Jerusalem: Hebrew University, 1996.

Altshuler, Mordechai, *Ha-yevsektsiya bi-vrit ha-mo'atsot: beyn komunizm ve-leumiyut*. Tel Aviv: Sifriyat po'alim, 1981.

Altshuler, Mordechai, *Reshet ha-yevsektsiia, 1918–1921*. Jerusalem: Hebrew University, 1966.

Altshuler, Mordechai, *Soviet Jewry on the Eve of the Holocaust; A Social and Demographic Profile*. Jerusalem: Hebrew University, 1998.

Altshuler, Mordechai, "Georgian Jewish Culture under the Soviet Regime," *Soviet Jewish Affairs* 5(2): 21–39.

Altshuler, Mordechai, Ara, Yitzhak, and Krakovsky, Shmuel, eds., *Sovetskie evrei pishut Ilye Erenburgu*. Jerusalem: Prisma, 1993.

Amram, David, *The Makers of Hebrew Books in Italy*. Philadelphia: J.H. Greenstone, 1909.

Anderson, Benedict, *Imagined Communities*. New York: Verso, 1991.

Baron, Salo, *The Russian Jew Under Tsars and Soviets*. New York: Schoken, 1976.

Barone, Charles, *Marxist Thought on Imperialism: Survey and Critique*. New York, M.E. Sharpe, 1985.

Bartal, Israel, "From Traditional Bilingualism to National Monolingualism," in Lewis Glinert, ed., *Hebrew in Ashkenaz*. New York and Oxford: Oxford University Press, 1993.

Bar-Yosef, Hamutal, "Reflections on Hebrew Literature in the Russian Context," *Prooftexts*, May 1996 (vol. 16, no. 2), pp. 127–49.

Bernstein, Michael André, *Foregone Conclusions: Against Apocalyptic History*. Berkeley: University of California Press, 1994.

Bikel, Shloyme, ed., *Pinkas far der forshung fun der yidisher literatur un prese*, vol. 1. New York: Congress for Jewish Culture, 1965.

Birnbaum, Pierre and Katznelson, Ira, eds., *Paths of Emancipation*. Princeton: Princeton University Press, 1995.

Blank, Stephen, *The Sorcerer as Apprentice: Stalin as Commissar of Nationalities, 1917–1924*. Westport: Greenwood, 1994.

Blattberg, Wolf, *The Story of the Hebrew and Yiddish Writers in the Soviet Union*. New York: Institute of Jewish Affairs, 1953.

Blitstein, Peter, "Stalin's Nations: Soviet Nationality Policy between Planning and Primordialism, 1936–1953," Ph.D. diss., University of California, Berkeley, 1999.

Blium, Arlen, *Za kulisami "Ministersta pravdy": tainaia istoriia sovetskoi tsenzury, 1917–1929*. St. Petersburg: Akademicheskii proekt, 1994.

Blium, Arlen, *Evreiskii vopros pod sovetskoi tsenzuroi, 1917–1991*. St. Petersburg: St. Petersburg University Press, 1996.

Brenner, Michael, *Renaissance of Jewish Culture in Weimar Germany*. New Haven: Yale University Press, 1996.

Brooks, Jeffrey, "The Press and Its Message: Images of America in the 1920s and 1930s," in Sheila Fitzpatrick et al., eds., *Russia in the Era of NEP*. Bloomington: Indiana University Press, 1991.

Brooks, Jeffrey, "Discontinuity in the Spread of Popular Print Culture, 1917–1927," Conference on the Origins of Soviet Culture, May 1981.

Brooks, Jeffrey, *When Russia Learned to Read*. Princeton: Princeton University Press, 1985.

Brower, Daniel and Lazzerini, Edward, eds., *Russia's Orient: Imperial Borderlands and Peoples, 1700–1917*. Bloomington: Indiana University Press, 1997.

Brown, Edward, *The Proletarian Episode in Russian Literature*. New York: Columbia University Press, 1953.

Brubaker, Rogeres, *Citizenship and Nationhood in France and Germany*. Cambridge, MA: Harvard University Press, 1992.

Buchsweiler, Meir, *Rußlanddeutsche im Sowjetsystem bis zum Zweiten Weltkrieg: Minderheitenpolitik, Nationale Identität, Publizistik*. Essen: Klartext, 1995.

Chatterjee, Partha, *The Nation and Its Fragments: Colonial and Postcolonial Histories*. Princeton: Princeton University Press, 1993.

Clark, Katerina, "The Remaking of Literature," in Robert Daniels, ed., *The Stalin Revolution.* Toronto: Heath, 1990.

Clark, Katerina, *Petersburg: Crucible of Revolution.* Cambridge, MA: Harvard University Press, 1995.

Clark, Katerina, *The Soviet Novel: History as Ritual.* Chicago: University of Chicago Press, 1981.

Comrie, Bernard and Stone, Gerald, *The Russian Language Since the Revolution.* Oxford: Clarendon, 1978.

Comrie, Bernard, *The Languages of the Soviet Union.* New York: Cambridge University Press, 1981.

da Silva Rosa, J.S., "Di Kurantin 1686–1687," in Yankev Shatsky, *Zamlbukh lekoved dem 250 yoyvl fun der yidisher prese, 1686–1936.* New York: YIVO, 1937.

Darnton, Robert, *Literary Underground of the Old Regime.* Cambridge: Harvard, 1982.

Darnton, Robert, "The Good Old Days," *New York Review of Books,* May 16, 1991.

Dinershtein, E.A., *Izdatel'skoe delo v pervye gody sovetskoi vlasti, 1917–1922.* Moscow: Kniga, 1972.

Dubnov, Shimon, *History of the Jews in Russia and Poland From the Earliest Times Until the Present Day,* trans. I. Friedländer. Philadelphia: Jewish Publication Society, 1916.

Edgar, Adrienne, "The Creation of Soviet Turkmenistan, 1924–1938," Ph.D. diss., University of California, Berkeley, 1999.

Englander, Nathan, *For the Relief of Unbearable Urges.* New York: Knopf, 1999.

Erik, Max, *Di geshikhte fun der yidisher literatur fun di eltste tsaytn biz der haskole tekufe.* Minsk: Inbelkult, 1928.

Estraikh, Gennady, "Pyrrhic Victories of Soviet Yiddish Language Planners," *East European Jewish Affairs,* 1993 (vol. 23, no. 2).

Estraikh, Gennady, "From Yehupets Jargonists to Kiev Modernists: The Rise of a Yiddish Literary Center, 1880–1914," *East European Jewish Affairs,* Summer 2000 (vol. 30, no. 1).

Estraikh, Gennady, *Soviet Yiddish: Language Planning and Linguistic Development.* Oxford: Clarendon, 1999.

Estraikh, Gennady, "Itsik Fefer: A Yiddish *Wunderkind* of the Bolshevik Revolution," *Shofar: An Interdisciplinary Journal of Jewish Studies* 20:3 (2002).

Even-Zohar, Itamar, "Polysystem Studies," *Poetics Today,* Spring 1990 (vol. 1, no. 1).

Fishman, David, *Russia's First Modern Jews: The Jews of Shklov.* New York: New York University Press, 1995.

Fishman, David, "Di dray penemer fun Yehoshua Mordkhe Lifshits," *Yidishe Shprakh* 38, 1981.

Fishman, Joshua, ed., *Never Say Die: A Thousand Years of Yiddish in Jewish Life and Letters.* The Hague, New York: Mouton, 1981.

Fitzpatrick, Sheila, *Commissariat of Enlightenment, Soviet Organization of Education and the Arts under Lunacharsky, October 1917–1921.* Cambridge: Cambridge University Press, 1970.

Fitzpatrick, Sheila, *Stalin's Peasants.* Ithaca: Cornell University Press, 1995.

Frank, Herman, *Yidishe tipografie un bukh-oysarbetung kunst.* New York: Hebrew American Typographical Union, 1938.

Frankel, Jonathon, *Prophecy and Politics: Socialism, Nationalism, and the Russian Jews, 1862–1917.* New York: Cambridge University Press, 1981.

Freitag, Gabrielle, "Juden in Moskau, 1917–1932," Magisterarbeit, Johann Wolfgang Goethe Universität, Frankfurt, 2000.

Friedberg, Maurice, *Russian Classics in Soviet Jackets*. New York: Columbia University, 1962.

Funkenstein, Amos, *Perceptions of Jewish History*. Berkeley: University of California Press, 1993.

Garrett, Leah, *Journeys Beyond the Pale*. Madison: University of Wisconsin Press, 2003.

Gay, Peter, *Weimar Culture: The Outsider and Insider*. New York, Harper and Row: 1968.

Gellner, Ernest, *Nations and Nationalism*. Ithaca: Cornell University Press, 1993.

Genrich, Sh., "Periodishe oysgabes in rusland af yidish far di letste fuftsn yor," *Kultur un Bildung*, Sept. 24, 1918 (no. 5).

Gerasimova, I. "K istorii evreiskogo otdela instituta belorusskoi kul'tury (inbelkult) i evreiskogo sektora beloruskkoi akademii nauk v 20-kh-30-kh godakh," *Vestnik evreiskogo universiteta v moskve* 1996 2(12): 144–67.

Gershuni, A., *Yahadut be-rusiya ha-sovietit*. Jerusalem: Mosad ha-rav Kook, 1961.

Gilboa, Y., *The Black Years of Soviet Jewry*. Boston: Little, Brown, 1971.

Gilboa, Yehoshua, *A Language Silenced: The Suppression of Hebrew Literature and Culture in the Soviet Union*. Rutherford, N.J.: Fairleigh Dickinson, 1982.

Gitelman, Zvi, *Jewish Nationality and Soviet Politics: The Jewish Sections of the CPSU, 1917–1930*. Princeton: Princeton University Press, 1972.

Gitelman, Zvi, *Century of Ambivalence*. New York: Schocken, 1988.

Goldsmith, Emanuel, *Modern Yiddish Culture*. New York: Fordham, 1997.

Gorokhoff, Boris, *Publishing in the U.S.S.R.* Bloomington: Indiana University Press, 1959.

Govrin, Nurith, *Tlishut ve-hitkhadshut: ha-siporet ha-ivrit be-reshit ha-me'ah ha-20 ba-golah uve-erets yisrael*. Tel Aviv: Matkal, 1985.

Gray, Camilla, *The Russian Experiment in Art, 1863–1922*, new ed. New York: Thames and Hudson, 1986.

Greenbaum, Alfred, *Jewish Scholarship and Scholarly Institutions in Soviet Russia, 1918–1953*. Jerusalem: Hebrew University Press, 1978.

Groys, Boris, *The Total Art of Stalinism*. Princeton: Princeton University Press, 1992.

Gurevitz, Baruch, *National Communism in the Soviet Union: 1918–1928*. Pittsburgh: University of Pittsburgh Press, 1980.

Halfin, Igor, "From Darkness to Light; Student Communist Autobiography," *Jahrbücher für Geschichte Osteuropas*, 1997 (vol. 45, no. 2).

Harshav, Benjamin, *Language in Time of Revolution*. Berkeley: University of California Press, 1993.

Harshav, Benjamin, *The Meaning of Yiddish*. Berkeley: University of California Press, 1990.

Harshav, Benjamin "The Role of Language in Modern Art: On Texts and Subtexts in Chagall's Paintings," *Modernism/Modernity* 1994 1(2): 51–87.

Hayward, Max and Labedz, Leopold, eds., *Literature and Revolution in Soviet Russia*. London-New York: Oxford University Press, 1963.

Hirsch, Francine, "Soviet Union as a Work in Progress," *Slavic Review*, Summer 1997 (vol. 56, no. 2).

Hirsch, Francine, "Toward an Empire of Nations: Border-Making and the Formation of Soviet National Identities," *Russian Review*, April 2000 (vol. 50, no. 2).

Hobsbawm, Eric and Ranger, Terence, *The Invention of Tradition*. Cambridge: Canto, 1992.

Hobson, J.A., *Imperialism: A Study*. London: K. Nisbet and Co., 1902.

Hoffman, Matthew, "From Rebel to Rabbi: Images of Jesus and the Making of Modern Jewish Culture," Ph.D. diss., Graduate Theological Union/University of California, Berkeley, 2000.

Hokanson, Katya, "Literary Imperialism, Narodnost' and Pushkin's Invention of the Caucasus," *Russian Review,* July 1994 (vol. 53, no. 3).

Hosking, Geoffrey, *The First Socialist Society.* Cambridge: Cambridge University Press, 1985.

Howe, Irving and Greenberg, Eliezer, eds., *Ashes Out of Hope: Fiction by Soviet-Yiddish Writers.* New York: Schocken, 1977.

Hrushevsky, Michael, *A History of Ukraine.* New Haven: Yale University Press, 1941.

Hunt, Lynn, ed., *The New Cultural History.* Berkeley: University of California Press, 1989.

Ilinskaia, I.S., *Orfografiia i russkii iazyk.* Moscow: Nauka, 1966.

Ilnytzkyj, Oleh, *Ukrainian Futurism, 1914–1930: A Historical and Critical Study.* Cambridge: Harvard, 1997.

Janecek, Gerald, *The Look of Russian Literature.* Princeton: Princeton University Press, 1984.

Jelen, Sheila, "Oral and Written: Vernacular Literatures of the Hebrew Revival," Ph.D. diss., University of California, Berkeley, 2000.

Jusdanis, Gregory, *Belated Modernity and Aesthetic Culture: Inventing National Literature.* Minnesota: University of Minnesota, 1991.

Jusdanis, Gregory, *The Necessary Nation.* Princeton: Princeton University Press, 2000.

Kagedan, Allan, *Soviet Zion: The Quest for a Russian Jewish Homeland.* New York: St. Martin's, 1994.

Karpozilos, Apostolos, "Pontic Culture in the USSR between the Wars," *Journal of Refugee Studies* 4(4): 364–71.

Kassof, Brian, "The Knowledge Front: Politics, Ideology, and Economics in the Soviet Book Publishing Industry," Ph.D. diss., University of California, Berkeley, 2000.

Kenez, Peter, *Cinema and Soviet Society, 1917–1953.* Cambridge, New York: Cambridge University Press, 1992.

Kirkwood, Michael, ed., *Language Planning in the Soviet Union.* Hampshire: Macmillan, 1989.

Klier, John, *Imperial Russia's Jewish Question: 1855–1881.* New York: Cambridge University Press, 1995.

Kochan, Lionel, ed., *The Jews in Soviet Russia Since 1917.* New York, Oxford: Oxford University Press, 1987.

Kotkin, Stephen, *Magnetic Mountain.* Princeton: Princeton University Press, 1996.

Kronfeld, Chana, *On the Margins of Modernism: Decentering Literary Dynamics.* Berkeley: University of California Press, 1996.

Krutikov, Mikhail, "Between Mysticism and Marxism: Meir Wiener as Writer, Critic, and Literary Historian," *Jews in Eastern Europe,* Winter 1994 (vol. 25, no. 3).

Krylova, Anna, "The Tenacious Liberal Subject in Soviet Studies," *Kritika,* Winter 2000 (vol. 1, no. 1).

Kubijovych, Volodymyr, *Ukraine: A Concise Encyclopedia* vol. 1. Toronto: University of Toronto Press, 1963.

Kuznitz, Cecile, "The Origins of Yiddish Scholarship and the YIVO Institute for Jewish Research," Ph.D. diss., Stanford University, 2000.

Lahusen, Thomas, *How Life Writes the Book.* Ithaca: Cornell University Press, 1997.

Layton, Susan, *Russian Literature and Empire: Conquest of the Caucasus from Pushkin to Tolstoy.* Cambridge: Cambridge University Press, 1994.

Lederhendler, Eli, *The Road to Modern Jewish Politics: Political Tradition and Political Recon-struction in the Jewish Community of Tsarist Russia*. New York: Oxford University Press, 1989.

Lenin, Vladimir, *Imperialism: The Highest Stage of Capitalism*. New York: International Pub-lishers, 1970.

Lenoe, Matthew, *Agitation, Propaganda, and the 'Stalinization' of the Soviet Press, 1922–1930*. Carl Beck Papers in Russian and East European Studies, No. 1305. Pittsburgh: University of Pittsburgh Press, 1998.

Leshtsinsky, Y., *Dos Sovetishe Yidntum*. New York: Poalei Zion, 1941.

Levin, Nora, *The Jews of the Soviet Union Since 1917: Paradox of Survival*. New York: New York University Press, 1987.

Luckyj, George, *Literary Politics in the Soviet Ukraine: 1917–1934*. Durham: Duke University Press, 1990.

Lvov-Rogachevsky, V.L., *Ocherki proletarskoi literatury*. Moscow: Moskovskoe akts. izdat. ob-shchestvo, 1927.

Mally, Lynn, *Culture of the Future: The Proletkult Movement in Revolutionary Russia*. Berkeley: University of California Press, 1990.

Marten-Finnis, Susanne and Valencia, Heather, *Sprachinseln: Jiddische Publizistik in London, Wilna, Berlin: 1880–1930*. Köln: Böhlau, 1999.

Marten-Finnis, Susanne, "Instruction-Exclusion-Polemic. Bundist Journalism, 1897–1907," *East European Jewish Affairs*, Summer 2000, (vol. 30, no. 1).

Martin, Terry, *An Affirmative Action Empire*. Ithaca: Cornell University Press, 2001.

Martin, Terry, "The Origins of Soviet Ethnic Cleansing," *Journal of Modern History* 1998 (vol. 70), pp. 813–61.

Martov, Vladimir, *Russian Futurism*. Berkeley: University of California Press, 1968.

Matejka, Ladislav and Pomorska, Krystyna, eds., *Readings in Russian Poetics: Formalist and Structuralist Views*. Ann Arbor: University of Michigan Press, 1978.

Mayzel, Nachman, *Dos yidishe shafn un der yidisher shrayber in Sovetfarband*. New York: YKUF, 1959.

Mendelssohn, Ezra, *The Jews of East Central Europe Between the Wars*. Bloomington: Indiana University Press, 1989.

Michels, Tony, "Socialism with a Jewish Face: The Origins of the Yiddish-Speaking Com-munist Movement in the United States, 1907–1923," in Gennady Estraikh and Mikhail Krutkov, eds., *Yiddish and the Left* (Oxford: Legenda, 2001).

Miron, Dan, *A Traveler Disguised: A Study in the Rise of Modern Yiddish Fiction in the Nineteenth Century*. Syracuse: Syracuse University Press, 1996.

Miron, Dan, "Editor's Introduction," to Dan Miron and Ken Frieden, eds., *Tales of Mendele the Book Peddler*. New York: Schocken, 1996.

Miron, Dan, *Der imazsh fun shtetl*. Tel Aviv: Perets Farlag, 1981.

Mueller, Julie Kay, "A New Kind of Newspaper: The Origins and Development of a Soviet Institution, 1921–1928," Ph.D. diss., University of California, Berkeley, 1992.

Murphy, James, *The Proletarian Moment: The Controversy over Leftism in Literature*. Urbana-Champaign: University of Illinois Press, 1991.

Nathans, Benjamin, *Beyond the Pale: The Jewish Encounter with Late-Imperial Russia*. Berkeley, Los Angeles: University of California Press, 2002.

Nazarov, A., *Ocherki istorii sovetskogo knigoizdatel'stva*. Moscow: Iskusstvo, 1952.

Nedava, Joseph, *Trotsky and the Jews*. Philadelphia: Jewish Publication Society, 1972.

Niger, Shmuel, *Bilingualism in the History of Jewish Literature*. Lanham, MD: University Press of America, 1990.

Niger, Shmuel, "Proletkult un Haskalah: vegn Max Eriks 'Di komedyes fun der Berliner oyfklerung,'" in Niger, Shmuel, *Yidishe Shrayber in Sovet-Rusland*. New York: Alveltlekher yidisher kultur-kongress, 1958.

Niger, Shmuel, *Di yidishe literatur un di lezerin*. Vilna: Vilner Farlag, 1919.

Nilsson, Nils Åke, *The Russian Imaginists*. Uppsala: Almqvist and Wissells, 1970.

Pinkus, Benjamin, *The Jews of the Soviet Union*. New York: Cambridge University Press, 1988.

Pipes, Richard, *The Formation of the Soviet Union*. Harvard: Harvard University Press, 1964.

Pomerants, Alexander, *Di sovetishe haruge-malkhus: tsu zayer 10tn yortsayt: vegn dem tragishn goyrl fun di yidishe shraybers un der yidisher literatur in Sovetnland*. Buenos Aires: YIVO, 1962.

Prokushev, Yuri, *Sergey Esenin: The Man, the Verse, the Age*. Moscow: Progress Publishers, 1979.

Reavey, George and Slonim, Marc, *Soviet Literature: An Anthology*. New York: Covici, Friede, 1934.

Remenik, G.A., *Ocherki i portrety: stat'i o evreiskikh pistateleiakh*. Moscow: 1975.

Reyzen, Zalman, *Yidishe Literatur un Yidishe Shprakh*. Buenos Aires: YIVO, 1965.

Rosenberg, William, ed., *Bolshevik Visions*, 2 vols. Ann Arbor: University of Michigan Press, 1990.

Roskies, David, *Against the Apocalypse: Responses to Catastrophe in Modern Jewish Culture*. Cambridge, MA: Harvard University Press, 1984.

Rozhansky, Shmuel, ed., *Dovid Hofshteyn, Izi Kharik, Itsik Fefer: Oysgeklibene Shriftn*. Buenos Aires: YIVO, 1962.

Russell, John and Brown, Ashley, eds., *Satire: A Critical Anthology*. Cleveland: World Publishing, 1967.

Said, Edward, *Culture and Imperialism*. New York: Vintage, 1994.

Said, Edward, *Orientalism*. New York: Vintage, 1979.

Schulman, Elias, *A History of Jewish Education in the Soviet Union*. New York: Ktav, 1971.

Seidman, Naomi, *A Marriage Made in Heaven: The Sexual Politics of Hebrew and Yiddish*. Berkeley: University of California, 1998.

Shapiro, Leon, *A History of ORT: A Jewish Movement for Social Change*. New York: Schocken, 1980.

Shatsky, Yankev, *Di geshikhte fun yidn in Varshe*, 3 vols. New York: YIVO, 1947–1953.

Shepherd, Naomi, *A Price Below Rubies*. Cambridge: Harvard University Press, 1993.

Shevelov, George, *The Ukrainian Language in the First Half of the Twentieth Century, 1900–1941*. Cambridge, MA: Harvard University Press, 1989.

Shmeruk, Chone, "Aspects of the History of Warsaw as a Yiddish Literary Centre," *Polin: A Journal of Polish-Jewish Studies, Volume 3*. Oxford: Basic Blackwell for the Institute of Polish-Jewish Studies, 1988.

Shmeruk, Chone, *Pirsumim yehudiim bi-vrit ha-moatsot: 1917–1960*. Jerusalem: Society for Research on Jewish Communities, 1960.

Shneer, David, "Making Yiddish Modern: The Making of a Yiddish Language Establishment in the Soviet Union," *East European Jewish Affairs*, Winter 2000 (vol. 30, no. 2).

Shternshis, Anna "Kosher and Soviet: Soviet Jewish Popular Culture, 1917–1941," D. Phil. diss., Oxford University, 2000.

Shternshis, Anna, "From the Eradication of Illiteracy to Workers' Correspondents: Yiddish-Language Mass Movements in the Soviet Union," *East European Jewish Affairs* 32 (1), Summer 2002.

Silberstein, Lawrence, *The Postzionism Debates: Knowledge and Power in Israeli Culture*. New York, London: Routledge, 1999.

Sinkoff, Nancy Beth, "Tradition and Transition: Mendel Lefin of Satanow and the Beginnings of the Jewish Enlightenment in Eastern Europe, 1749–1826," Ph.D. diss., Columbia University, 1996.

Slezkine, Yuri, "N.I. Marr and the National Origins of Soviet Ethnogenetics," *Slavic Review*, Winter 1996 (vol. 55, no. 4).

Slezkine, Yuri, "Imperialism as the Highest Stage of Socialism," *Russian Review*, April 2000 (vol. 50, no. 2).

Slezkine, Yuri, "The USSR as a Communal Apartment, or How a Socialist State Promoted Ethnic Particularism," *Slavic Review*, Summer 1994 (vol. 53, no. 2).

Slezkine, Yuri, *Arctic Mirrors: Russia and the Small Peoples of the North*. Ithaca: Cornell University Press, 1994.

Slonim, Marc, *Soviet Russian Literature: Writers and Problems, 1917–1977*. New York: Oxford University Press, 1977.

Smith, Michael, *Language and Power in the Creation of the USSR, 1917–1953*. New York: Mouton de Gruyter, 1998.

Sorkin, David, *Moses Mendelssohn and the Religious Enlightenment*. Berkeley: University of California Press, 1996.

Stanislawski, Michael, *For Whom Do I Toil?: Judah Leib Gordon and the Crisis of Russian Jewry*. New York: Oxford University Press, 1988.

Stanislawsky, Michael, *Tsar Nicholas I and the Jews*. Philadelphia: Jewish Publication Society, 1983.

Stites, Richard, *Revolutionary Dreams: Utopian Vision and Experimental Life in the Russian Revolution*. New York: Oxford University Press, 1989.

Suny, Ronald, *The Making of the Georgian Nation*. Bloomington: Indiana University Press, 1988.

Suny, Ronald, *The Revenge of the Past: Nationalism, Revolution, and the Collapse of the Soviet Union*. Stanford: Stanford University, 1993.

Tobias, Henry, *The Jewish Bund in Russia*. Stanford: Stanford, 1972.

Vardi, David, *Be-derech hilukhi*. Tel Aviv: Eked, 1982.

Veidlinger, Jeffrey, "Klezmer and the Kremlin: Soviet Yiddish Folk Songs of the 1930s," *Jews in Eastern Europe*, Spring 2000.

Veidlinger, Jeffrey, *The Moscow State Jewish Theater*. Bloomington: Indiana University Press, 2000.

von Geldern, James, *Bolshevik Festivals, 1917–1920*. Berkeley: University of California Press, 1993.

Weeks, Theodore, *Nation and State in Late Imperial Russia: Nationalism and Russification on the Western Frontier, 1863–1914*. DeKalb: Northern Illinois University Press, 1996.

Weinberg, Robert, *Stalin's Forgotten Zion: Birobidzhan and the Making of a Soviet Jewish Homeland*. Berkeley: University of California, Judah Magnes, 1998.

Weinreich, Max, *History of the Yiddish Language*. Chicago: University of Chicago Press, 1981.

Weissler, Chava, "For Women and For Men Who are Like Women: The Construction of Gender in Yiddish Devotional Literature," *Journal of Feminist Studies in Religion*, Fall 1989 (vol. 5, no. 2).

Wiesel, Elie, *The Jews of Silence*. New York: Holt, Rinehart, and Winston, 1966.

Wisse, Ruth, "What Shall Live and What Shall Die: The Making of a Yiddish Anthology," Twelfth Annual Rabbi Louis Feinberg Memorial Lecture in Judaic Studies, University of Cincinnati, May 3, 1989.

Wisse, Ruth, Howe, Irving, Shmeruk, Chone, eds., "Introduction," *Penguin Anthology of Yiddish Verse*. New York: Penguin, 1989.

Wolitz, Seth, "A Yiddish Modernist Dirge: *Di Kupe* of Perets Markish," *Yiddish* 1987 (vol. 6, no. 4).

Wolitz, Seth, "Between Folk and Freedom: The Failure of the Yiddish Modernist Movement in Poland," *Yiddish* 1991 (vol. 8, no. 1).

Wolitz, Seth, "Di *Khalyastre*: The Yiddish Modernist Movement in Poland: An Overview," in *Yiddish* 1981 (vol. 4, no. 3).

Wolitz, Seth, "The Kiev Grupe (1918–1920) Debate: The Function of Literature," in *Studies in American Jewish Literature*, Winter 1978 (vol. 4, no. 2).

Yarmolisnky, Avrom, *Literature Under Communism: The Literary Policy of the Communist Party of the Soviet Union from the End of World War II to the Death of Stalin*. Bloomington: Indiana University Press, 1960.

Yeshurin, Ephim, *Dovid Hofshteyn, Izi Kharik, Itsik Fefer, Bibliografie*. Buenos Aires: YIVO, 1962.

Youngblood, Denise, *Soviet Cinema in the Silent Era*. Austin: University of Texas Press, 1991.

Zand, Mikhail, "Bukharan Jewish Culture under Soviet Rule," *Soviet Jewish Affairs*, Summer 1979 (vol. 9, no. 2).

Zeltser, Arkadii, "The Liquidation of Yiddish Schools in Belorussia and Jewish Reaction," *Jews in Eastern Europe*, Spring 2000.

Zimarina, N.P., ed., *Russkii rubl': dva veka*. Moscow: Progres-Akademiia, 1994.

Zinberg, Israel, *The History of Yiddish Literature*. Cincinnati, New York: Ktav, Hebrew Union College, 1972–1978.

Zipperstein, Steven, *Imagining Russian Jewry: Memory, History, Identity*. Seattle: University of Washington Press, 1999.

Zipperstein, Steven, *The Jews of Odessa: A Cultural History, 1794–1881*. Stanford: Stanford, 1985.

Zweite, Armin, *The Blue Rider*. Munich, New York: Prestel, 1989.

Index

Moscow, Russia *(cont.)*
  center of modernism, 136
  center of Soviet Yiddish culture, 88, 97,
      111, 122
  during the Civil War, 145
Mystetstvo. See Ukrainian-language journals,
      Art

Na postu. See Russian-language journals, On
      Guard
"Naked speech," 152
Narkompros, See Commissariat
nation, 1–8, 10, 12, 16, 23, 32, 96
  liberation movements, 9
  nation-building, 13, 16, 19, 149,
      229
  Russian, 7
  Soviet Jewish, 5, 8, 10, 18, 41, 53, 87
"National deviations," 22–3
  rise of, 32–9
nationalism, 5, 6, 7, 8, 9, 16, 36, 46, 61,
      66, 79
  anti-colonial, 9
  bourgeois, 17, 216
  and Communism, 137
  fear of, 19–20, 22–3, 63, 132,
      168
  Jewish, 10, 15, 26–9, 50, 91, 92, 96,
      164, 183
  linguistic, 64
  Romantic, 71
  scholarship on, 7
  Ukrainian, 137
Nationalities Institute, Central Executive
      Committee, 29
nationality, 5, 12, 18, 21. *See also Soviet*
      policies
nationhood, 5, 16, 66
nativization (*korenizatsiia*), 22–3, 25–6, 27,
      55, 59, 72–3, 114, 238
Nazis, 11
New Economic Policy (NEP), 21–2, 78,
      104–6, 110, 123, 131, 161, 185,
      208
New Turkic Alphabet Commission, 82
New York, United States, 18, 136

news, 121
newspapers, 5, 7, 38, 40, 77, 79, 80, 92,
      93–5, 98, 121, 123
  Advocate (Ha-melits), 35
  Alarm (Der Veker), 92, 180, 247
  Bolshevik Yiddish, 92
  Communist Banner (Komunistishe Fon),
      93, 94, 152, 153–4
  Dawn (Rassvet), 33
  Forward (Forverts), 117, 165
  Fraynd, 240
  Freedom (Frayhayt), 100, 162
  Herald (Kol Mevaser), 35–6
  The Jewish Peasant (Der yidisher poyer),
      111–12
  Kavkaz Rosta, 54
  Kiev Voice (Kievskaia Mysl'), 27
  Kurantin, Kol Mevaser, 90
  Latest News (Letste Nayes), 68, 241
  Moment, 90, 91
  New Times (Naye Tsayt), 27, 68, 92, 151,
      241
  News (Yedies), 129
  Party, 24
  Pravda, 57
  Revolution and Nationalities (Revoliustiia I
      natsional'nost'), 29
  subscriptions, 105
  Today (Haynt), 91
  The Truth (Ha-emes), 95
  Truth (Varhayt), 95–6, 97
  The Week (Di vokh), 97
  Workers' Voice (Arbeter Shtime), 8
  See also Emes, Star, October
Nicholas I, Tsar, 34–5
Niepomniashchy, Shlomo, 158, 164, 181,
      213, 248
Niger, Shmuel, 24, 65, 70, 97, 100, 184,
      241
Nikolaev, Ukraine, 18
Nizhnii Novgorod, Russia, 41
nostalgia in the creation of Soviet Yiddish
      culture, 179, 186, 196, 198,
      200
Nuremberg Laws, 10, 231
Nusinov, Yitzhak, 150–1, 152, 159